THE VALUE GAP

TEXAS FILM AND MEDIA STUDIES SERIES
Thomas Schatz, Editor

Also in the series

Joshua Gleich, *Hollywood in San Francisco: Location Shooting and the Aesthetics of Urban Decline*

Stanley Corkin, *Connecting* The Wire: *Race, Space, and Post-Industrial Baltimore*

Emily Carman, *Independent Stardom: Freelance Women in the Hollywood Studio System*

Charles Ramírez Berg, *The Classical Mexican Cinema: The Poetics of the Exceptional Golden Age Films*

Barry Keith Grant, ed., *The Dread of Difference: Gender and the Horror Film*, 2nd ed.

Avi Santo, *Selling the Silver Bullet: The Lone Ranger and Transmedia Brand Licensing*

Alisa Perren, *Indie, Inc.: Miramax and the Transformation of Hollywood in the 1990s*

J. E. Smyth, *Edna Ferber's Hollywood: American Fictions of Gender, Race, and History*

Lisa Kernan, *Coming Attractions: Reading American Movie Trailers*

Jonathan Buchsbaum, *Cinema and the Sandinistas: Filmmaking in Revolutionary Nicaragua*

Megan Mullen, *The Rise of Cable Programming in the United States: Revolution or Evolution?*

Charles Ramírez Berg, *Latino Images in Film: Stereotypes, Subversion, and Resistance*

THE VALUE GAP

Female-Driven Films from Pitch to Premiere

Courtney Brannon Donoghue

University of Texas Press   *Austin*

This book has been made possible in part by a grant from the National Endowment for the Humanities. Any views, findings, conclusions, or recommendations expressed in this book do not necessarily represent those of the National Endowment for the Humanities.

Excerpts from the following were reprinted with permission:
Courtney Brannon Donoghue, "Gendered Expectations for Female-Driven Films: Risk and Rescue Narratives around Warner Bros.' *Wonder Woman*," *Feminist Media Studies* (Taylor & Francis, 2019), DOI: 10.1080/14680777.2019.1636111.
　　Courtney Brannon Donoghue, "Hollywood and Gender Equity Debates in the #MeToo Time's Up Era," *Women in the International Film Industry: Policy, Practice and Power*, ed. Susan Liddy (Palgrave Macmillan, 2020), 235–252.

Requests for permission to reproduce material from this work should be sent to:
　　Permissions
　　University of Texas Press
　　P.O. Box 7819
　　Austin, TX 78713-7819
　　utpress.utexas.edu/rp-form

♾ The paper used in this book meets the minimum requirements of ANSI/NISO Z39.48-1992 (R1997) (Permanence of Paper).

Library of Congress Cataloging-in-Publication Data

Names: Brannon Donoghue, Courtney, author.
Title: The value gap : female-driven films from pitch to premiere / Courtney Brannon Donoghue.
Other titles: Texas film and media studies series.
Description: First edition. | Austin : University of Texas Press, 2023. | Series: Texas film and media studies series | Includes index.
Identifiers: LCCN 2022034829
　　ISBN 978-1-4773-2729-6 (hardcover)
　　ISBN 978-1-4773-2730-2 (paperback)
　　ISBN 978-1-4773-2731-9 (PDF)
　　ISBN 978-1-4773-2732-6 (ePub)
Subjects: LCSH: Women motion picture producers and directors—Social conditions. | Women screenwriters—Social conditions. | Women in the motion picture industry—Social conditions. | Motion pictures—Production and direction—Social aspects. | Motion picture authorship—Social aspects. | Motion pictures—Distribution—Social aspects. | Motion picture industry—Social aspects.
Classification: LCC PN1995.9.W6 B728 2023 | DDC 791.4302/33082—dc23/eng/20220825
LC record available at https://lccn.loc.gov/2022034829

doi:10.7560/327296

The publication of this book was made possible by the generous support of the Louann Atkins Temple Women & Culture Endowment.

For Mom and Dad
and
for my Brian

Contents

THE VALUE GAP

Mind the Gaps

The Value Gap grew out of a series of conversations with a white independent producer named Emma.[1] Conversations over countless dinners and coffees, during which we discussed the challenges faced in producing female-led films, inspired this book project. After two critically and financially successful independent films with back-to-back premieres at Cannes and Sundance, she did not see the career boost from film festival premieres that her male peers were experiencing. Strong festival buzz can serve as a launchpad for an up-and-coming filmmaker in finding the financing or resources they need for the next project. But Emma hit what many above-the-line female creatives experience—the so-called postfilm festival chasm.[2] The producer frustratedly recounted watching her male director peers from these projects move on to bigger-budgeted, higher-profile projects while she struggled to finance her next film.

Producer credits and a robust professional network signaled Emma's rising career. She was getting into the right rooms for pitch meetings at major studios and production companies for feature film and television projects. Emma described pitching a new project to studios, a story about two middle-aged female leads finding love on the West Coast. She presented solid comparisons to commercially successful films, including Nancy Meyers's *Something's Gotta Give* (2003). With a modest budget, the film had the market potential to recoup costs during its theatrical release and perform well in the VOD (video-on-demand) distribution window.

In meeting after meeting, male executives consistently described the story as "too small" and potential actresses as having "no value." Recommendations ranged from lowering the female leads' age by decades and casting a young Reese Witherspoon type to changing the story's location and cutting her budget in half. One executive suggested abandoning the project completely because "there is no audience for this story." The producer later recalled: "If I wanted to make a movie about two white men, I would already have financing. . . . Problem is that most executives and financiers are middle-aged white men. They don't value female-driven movies or female audiences. They tell you in so many ways."[3] As a result, the script was shelved, indefinitely waiting to be made.

Emma's experience is not exceptional. Industry logic that female-driven projects—those starring a multidimensional female protagonist and led by a female director, writer, and/or producer—have no commercial value has long circulated not only within Hollywood but also in the global film industry at large. Of the dozens of women I interviewed for this book, nearly every one working above the line and across different stages of filmmaking shared similar experiences in which studio executives, financiers, festival leaders, distributors, and other industry gatekeepers too often dismissed, discounted, or derailed female-driven films. This gendered logic, deeply rooted in Hollywood industry cultures and business practices, has long masked the historical and systemic devaluation of women's stories and labor. Intrinsic in the valuation of individual film projects is the questioning of the worth and contributions of female creative workers in the film industry.

The Value Gap explores gender inequity, the pervasive industry myths about female-driven films, and the challenges female filmmakers face in bringing their stories to the big screen. From 2016 to 2021, I conducted a series of primary interviews with eight women working above the line as directors, writers, and/or producers. I also conducted secondary interviews with a bigger pool of above-the-line creatives as well as with key industry professionals, including development executives, below-the-line workers like editors and line producers, film festival staff and programmers, international sales agents, and distributors. Based on these extensive interviews, trade and popular press coverage, industry events and film festivals, and additional economic and industry data, *The Value Gap* examines the barriers and challenges female-driven projects and their filmmakers faced during this period at each stage of the filmmaking pipeline—development, financing, production, film festivals and markets, and distribution and marketing.

The Hollywood film industry underwent a series of seismic shifts over the course of researching and writing this book. In general, the film industry sits at a crossroads where many of the economic, political, technological, and cultural distinctions that shaped and informed the twentieth-century Hollywood studio system are being questioned, challenged, and transformed in the twenty-first century. By the late 2010s and early 2020s, a new wave of gender equity and racial justice movements arguably pushed conversations around systemic inequities, inclusion, representation, and parity to the public forefront. Continuing revelations surrounding industry-wide cultures that ignored or enabled sexual harassment and misconduct across a variety of media workplaces culminated in movements like #MeToo and Time's Up. Furthermore, digitization of the media industries has remade the processes of commercial production, distribution, and exhibition for feature filmmaking and further blurred the lines and mobility of specialized media work, development, financing, and distribution windows. Dominant Big Tech platforms Netflix, Amazon Prime Video, and Hulu launched streaming services from 2006 to 2008, driving conglomerate owners of the Hollywood studios into the so-called streaming wars. Between 2019 and 2021, the legacy studios launched their own subscription services: Disney's Disney+, formerly AT&T's HBO Max; then Viacom's Paramount+; and Comcast's Peacock. With these new digital outlets came new opportunities for established players in front of and behind the camera to secure development deals and support for film and television projects.

Many of these factors impacted female-driven projects across media sectors including an accelerated output of new broadcast and cable television series as well as the expansion of major platforms into producing original direct-to-streaming film and television content. However, the scope of the book focuses on feature-length narrative filmmaking, both studio and independent, intended for theatrical release. Furthermore, the rapid emergence of the global coronavirus pandemic in early 2020 had an immeasurable impact on the Hollywood studios, filmmaking pipeline, film workers, and movie theaters as traditional physical production and theatrical distribution seemingly shut down overnight. The impact of COVID will be addressed at key points. However, for the purposes of crafting a manageable and focused project in an unwieldy industrial moment, *The Value Gap* primarily focuses on the contemporary Hollywood industrial period and traditional theatrical filmmaking pipeline ending in early 2020.

2015–2017: An Industrial Sea Change?

During the mid-2010s, a series of significant events began to unfold, representing a transformative moment with wide-reaching repercussions for the media industries worldwide. A hack into Sony Pictures Entertainment's network resulted in leaked internal documents, revealing salaries for the top-earning studio employees in 2014. Of the seventeen executives making a million dollars or more, only one was a woman—Amy Pascal, cochair of SPE and president of the Sony Pictures Entertainment Motion Picture Group.[4] These leaked documents also shed light on discrepancies in on-screen talent's compensation. In one widely reported example from the David O. Russell–directed *American Hustle* (2013), Jennifer Lawrence and Amy Adams made significantly less than their male costars, Christian Bale, Bradley Cooper, and Jeremy Renner. In response, Lawrence released an essay for *Lenny Letter*, Lena Dunham and Jennifer Konner's online feminist newsletter, "Why Do I Make Less Than My Male Co-Stars?"[5] On the one hand, it is a significant move for one of the industry's most bankable A-list actresses to call attention to the gender wage gap; on the other hand, as one white LA-based publicist told me, "[The real issue] is why does it take a 25-year-old white woman, one of the highest paid actresses, to start this conversation [at this moment]? We are asking the wrong questions."[6] As an unprecedented PR disaster, the hack revealed embarrassing Sony communications and sensitive documents that exposed many of the industry's open secrets—foremost among them that women working in front of and behind the camera are not hired or compensated at the same rates as their male peers. Ultimately, Pascal, one of the most powerful women in Hollywood at the time, was the only executive fired after the hack's fallout.[7] Her forced exit was seen by many as Sony's way of making its top female executive a scapegoat for its own mismanagement.

At the same time, journalists, filmmakers, activists, and scholars issued growing calls to address the shockingly low rates of women in key above-the-line production jobs and studio executive levels.[8] Maureen Dowd's 2015 *New York Times Magazine* cover story, "The Women of Hollywood Speak Out," trains a critical lens on "Hollywood's toxic brew of fear and sexism." Through interviews with dozens of industry professionals, many portrayed in striking profiles arranged as a grid on the magazine's cover, the article unveils "an avalanche of previously pent-up fears, regrets, recriminations and recommendations."[9] Widely circulated quantitative studies that highlight the staggering lack of women directing, producing, and writing feature films became a lightning rod for growing attention in trade publications and at industry events. The most cited statistics early on emerged from data studies coming from academic research centers at the University of Southern California, University of California San Diego, and University of California, Los Angeles. These studies highlight employment numbers indicating that women hold only a small percentage of leadership and management positions of power on commercial film projects, whether studio or independently financed.[10] For example, Martha M. Lauzen's annual "The Celluloid Ceiling Report," a routinely cited study, highlights the gender inequity across above-the-line and department heads rankings for the 250 top-grossing domestic films. For example, in 2019, women made up 27 percent of producers in contrast to directors (13 percent), writers (19 percent), editors (23 percent), and cinematographers (5 percent).[11] Despite a glaring lack of industrial context in gathering and interpreting these statistics, as discussed in more detail in the following chapter, big-picture data-driven studies would continue to shape critical industry discourse and press coverage for years to follow.

The push toward equitable employment is only one part of this seismic shift. The film industry's rampant culture of sexism, misconduct, abuse, and harassment is another significant part. From expectations about actresses and the casting couch to the verbal abuse experienced by too many young assistants, Hollywood's mistreatment of women has long been known though rarely openly discussed.[12] In October 2017, two investigative reports in the *New York Times* by Jodi Kantor and Megan Twohey and the *New Yorker* by Ronan Farrow exposed the truth behind the long-standing rumors about former Miramax and Weinstein Company executive Harvey Weinstein's decades of sexual intimidation and abuse.[13] A week later, the head of Amazon Studios, Roy Price, resigned after sexual harassment accusations emerged in an article by Kim Masters in the *Hollywood Reporter*.[14] A tweet by actress Alyssa Milano went viral a few days later: "If you've been sexually harassed or assaulted write 'me too' as a reply to this tweet." Women across Hollywood and the entertainment industries—from A-list actresses to office interns—began speaking up and recounting devastating stories of predatory behavior and workplace misconduct by bosses and coworkers, reinvigorating and expanding the #MeToo movement founded in 2006 by Tarana Burke for women and girls of color who are survivors of sexual violence. A snowball effect ensued in the following days, months, and years, as mounting accusations against men in powerful positions—from technology and entertainment companies to newsrooms and studio boardrooms—exposed larger systemic patterns at the core of the media and entertainment industries.[15]

One of the most publicly visible responses came on New Year's Day in 2018 when a group of Hollywood A-list talent, including Oprah Winfrey, Salma Hayek, Reese Witherspoon, Shonda Rhimes, and America Ferrera, introduced Time's Up. In response to public support from the female farmworkers of Alianza Nacional de Campesinas, hundreds of women working in the entertainment industries signed an open letter appearing as full-page ads in the English-language *New York Times* and Spanish-language *La Opinión*. According to the official website, Time's Up works for "safe, fair and dignified work for women of all kinds." The statement goes on to say:

> We want women from the factory floor to the floor of the Stock Exchange, from childcare centers to C-suites, from farm fields to the tech field, to be united by a shared sense of safety, fairness and dignity as they work and as we all shift the paradigm of workplace culture. Powered by women, our TIME'S UP™ programming addresses the systemic inequality and injustice in the workplace that have kept underrepresented groups from reaching their full potential.[16]

One of the organization's initiatives, Time's Up Legal Defense Fund, raised donations of more than $22 million in its first year. The defense fund supports cases of workplace sexual harassment as well as survivor support, mentorship initiatives, and policy activism for industries beyond the Hollywood studios.[17]

Battles for equity and access are taking place not in isolation, but as a dialogue. In trying to map this so-called consciousness-raising moment, the acknowledgment of the transnational context of this twenty-first-century movement for gender equity is vital.[18] The fight for gender equity is not Hollywood's battle alone. As audiovisual industries worldwide report a consistent lack of women holding creative and financial positions of power, individuals and movements are working together to push back. After her appointment as head of Sweden's state-financed film company, Svenska Filminstitutet (Swedish Film Institute), Anna Serner made supporting female filmmakers a priority and became a leading global voice for gender parity in the film industry. Serner and her team inspired broader debates about the potential of quotas and policy measures as a corrective. In France, the 5050×2020 campaign launched in 2016 to push state-supported film industries and film festivals toward 50 percent gender parity by 2020. Efforts included releasing employment statistics, participating in the 2018 Cannes Film Festival's women's march, and committing international film festivals to sign gender parity pledges.[19] In 2016, after tone-deaf comments about Dublin's Abbey Theatre male-dominated program by its artistic director, Irish women in the creative community organized around #wakingthefeminist on Twitter. What evolved was a collective feminist movement mobilizing "women in the arts, the media and beyond to publicly question and expose the mechanisms by which they have been excluded and marginalized."[20] In contrast, prior to the reemergence of #MeToo, Brazilian women began to speak out in 2015 on social media against widespread abuse extending beyond the media industries. With the emergence of #MeuPrimeiroAssédio, women began sharing their experiences across social media in order to call public attention and media coverage to the sexual abuse and harassment experienced in their daily lives.[21]

As each of these evolving moments and movements illustrates, localized pressure points coexist and represent growing industry, scholarly, and popular conversations that increasingly transcend borders, languages, and film cultures.[22] Keeping in mind the historically powerful and complicated position of the American film industry, as I have argued elsewhere, the Hollywood studio system should always be seen as an exception even while serving as a productive industrial cultural space for viewing the complexities and contradictions of the gendered work and experience of film professionals.[23] Because of the limited scope of this project, further work is needed to understand how the current US climate operates in dialogue with local industries and broader global initiatives as sites of negotiation, struggle, and exchange.

Over the course of my research, I encountered a community of resilient, determined creative workers navigating the gaps between macrolevel structural barriers and industry practices and microlevel project-by-project conditions and individual tactics. A founding member of the Los Angeles–based Alliance for Women Directors, an organization formed in 1997, pointed to the 2010s as a pivotal moment for the changing tide around gender equity. She emphasized, "We've been pushing this rock up a hill for over twenty years. The difference is the talk is being taken more seriously."[24] Systemic gender disparities, discrimination, sexual harassment, and misconduct that long operated as an open secret in Hollywood were pushed to the forefront of public discourse with the #MeToo and Time's Up movements.

Due to this industrial landscape, my project transformed at various points, some of which I addressed extensively when conducting interviews and gathering research while others unfolding at the end of the writing process raised more complicated questions than definitive answers for the book's conclusion. Set against this larger, and rapidly evolving, industrial moment, *The Value Gap* highlights studio business models and industry cultures that preceded and then faced criticism with the growing awareness around equity, inclusion, and access—namely, gendered barriers, or "gaps" as the title denotes, to sustainable employment, filmmaking opportunities, and career advancement. In turn, an examination of female-driven films serves as a site of struggle inside the Hollywood film industry that continues to grapple with complex, ongoing conversations around power, privilege, and pervasive inequity.

Layers of Value

With a focus on contemporary Hollywood, my objective is to build upon a body of robust film studies and media industry studies scholarship, highlighting and complicating the histories of women in the film industry. Scholarly approaches to examining women's film work and contributions cover a wide array of historical periods, specific industry roles, and extensive archival sources: silent era (Jane Gaines, Hilary A. Hallett, Shelley Stamp), classical studio era (Emily Carman, Erin Hill, J. E. Smyth), and the post-classical and contemporary eras (Hill, Christina N. Baker, Miranda J. Banks, Shelley Cobb, Christina Lane, Maya Montañez Smukler).[25] *The Value Gap* is the first book-length academic study with a Conglomerate Hollywood focus, incorporating extensive industry interviews and first-person accounts to examine the experiences of female filmmakers and their female-driven projects in the 2010s. The book uniquely examines the slippery construction of gendered value and risk within the contemporary film business and how this materializes across structural, institutional, interpersonal, and individual levels. In other words, how are women, their work, and their film projects valued within current industry practices and cultures and what gaps exist at each phase of the filmmaking process?

From pitch to premiere, a film project is constantly evaluated and reevaluated, specifically for whether the estimated financial investment and potential return can outweigh the resources expended and risked in making it. The practice of economic valuation involves assessing a film's bankability at the theatrical box office and profit streams from additional distribution windows. Yet, the commercial profit-driven logic that has come to epitomize Hollywood's powerful players—and increasingly shape commercial filmmaking worldwide—is often bound up with larger markers of economic, cultural, and industrial value. An array of stakeholders and marketplaces, film professionals and gatekeepers, audiences and communities factor into the complex hierarchies of value and taste beyond economic worth. Value also operates discursively, reflecting broader institutional priorities, industrial trends, societal expectations, and cultural biases. And these layers of value, as I argue throughout *The Value Gap*, reflect narratives impacting entire groups of above-the-line workers and their voices, modes and genres of filmmaking, and audience segments.

Economic Value: The Product

In the contemporary industrial moment, technological, structural, and economic convergence has transformed and continues to transform Hollywood studio structures and practices. Specifically, a concentration of ownership through waves of conglomeration produced an exceedingly risk-averse mentality grounded in licensing intellectual property and cross-media franchises.[26] By the time Disney closed the deal to buy 21st Century Fox in 2019, the major studios had become even more dependent on big-budget media franchises that had to justify themselves by extending across multiple conglomerate divisions (for example, film, television, gaming, streaming, and music) and supplying content for an ever-growing and longer tail of global distribution (for example, theatrical, subscription VOD, transactional VOD, DVD, and television). With financial and creative stakes this high, entertainment divisions, nestled inside their global parent companies, actively worked to mitigate risk against failed property releases in a streamlined production slate.[27] The demand to expand tested franchises largely drove studio production cultures. The fourteen top-grossing films of the 2018 domestic box office were remakes, reboots, or part of a larger male-driven franchise, like Disney/Marvel's *The Avengers*, Disney/Lucas-film's *Star Wars*, and Paramount's *Mission: Impossible* series.

In a keynote address at the 2019 Sundance Producer's Brunch, former Disney executive Nina Jacobson spoke about major industrial shifts since the 2000s:

> The ground started to shift in my last few years as an executive [in the early to mid-2000s]. We went from making 22 movies a year to 12. The emphasis moved from eclecticism, something for everyone, to more branded content. . . . [Today] most traditional studio executives manage a slate that is dominated by franchises and sequels, with only a few slots a year for free balls. And those are scrutinized within an inch of their lives.[28]

Jacobson spoke from both her previous experience as a studio gatekeeper and her current role as an independent producer competing for that handful of slots on the major studios' theatrical film slates each year.

Filmmaking has always been a high-cost, high-risk business often compared to high-stakes gambling or the stock market. Before financially investing in a project, production companies and film studios assess the project's viability—that is, potential profit value—using data-driven market comparison beginning in the development phase. This highly speculative process involves various departments from accounting to marketing that track expenditures (development, production, distribution costs) and revenue (distribution returns). This assessment includes comparing past financial data of films that may have a similar star, genre, or budget—known as "comps" or comparables—to estimate the potential box office success or failure and inform decision making. As a standard method used by both small-budget indies and big-budget studio blockbusters, comps help to calculate the potential risks and rewards of a film project, ultimately to mitigate losses and maximize profits for investors.[29] In other words, if the numbers add up, the film's risk must be worth its rewards.

Risk aversion and the increasingly precarious nature of film work impacts decision making at all levels—to protect an individual's job security or the studio's bottom line. One established white female screenwriter I followed for five years talked at length about working in a studio climate in which top-level male talent steers many tested male-driven media properties as the dominant commercial model. She described both larger structural shifts like industry-wide conglomeration that were producing an increasingly risk-averse corporate environment and the impact of long-held perceptions around the viability and universal appeal of female-targeted stories. "Basically, every executive is afraid they're going to get fired for whatever their next choice is. They want to be able to defend it. And when you can say 'Ok, we're doing something that has a proven track record [or] we're remaking this property, using this existing brand' . . . that [project] now has proven value and it's less their fault if something goes wrong with it."[30]

When factoring in the political, economic, industrial, and sociocultural freight that female-driven projects carry, the burden of proof necessary to justify new concepts and storytelling is often astronomical. With largely male-driven franchises like Disney/Marvel's Marvel Cinematic Universe, Universal's Fast and Furious, or Warner Bros.' multiple iterations of Batman as the blockbuster gold standard, few studios during the 2010s risked investing in female-driven stories and creative talent. The potential for new, untested story ideas and original scripts not anchored by a known media property are harder to predict, and in turn, harder to finance. Undoubtedly, this model of economic justification will increase exponentially beyond the global pandemic.

Industrial and Cultural Value: Female-Driven Films

From midcentury Technicolor melodramas to long-running daytime soap operas, popular culture produced for and consumed by women has a history of being culturally discounted, dismissed, and denigrated as superficial or frivolous feminine escapist fantasy. Contemporary women's relationships, ambitions, desires, and romantic fantasies are rarely afforded the same cultural seriousness as male-driven genres like superheroes, spy thrillers, and war epics.

No genre exemplifies the film industry's long and complicated relationship with female audiences as well as the oft-derided romantic comedy. A conventional studio genre dating back to Classical Hollywood's heyday, the "rom-com" has undergone numerous iterations since the fast-talking screwball comedies of Katharine Hepburn and Rosalind Russell, like *Bringing Up Baby* (1938) and *His Girl Friday* (1940). With stars from Doris Day to Julia Roberts, the genre's long legacy of a plucky female protagonist's evolution from meet-cute to coupling has seen its share of commercial and cultural ebbs and flows.[31]

Later deemed "chick flicks," or what Hilary Radner categorizes as "girly films," rom-coms saw a successful cycle in the 1990s and 2000s with films that followed (almost exclusively white) single career women: Meg Ryan in *Sleepless in Seattle* (1993) and *You've Got Mail* (1998), Roberts in *Notting Hill* and *Runaway Bride* (1999), Renée Zellweger in *Bridget Jones's Diary* (2001), Jennifer Lopez in *The Wedding Planner* (2001) and *Maid in Manhattan* (2002), Reese Witherspoon in *Sweet Home Alabama* (2002), Kate Hudson in *How to Lose a Guy in 10 Days* (2003), Julia Stiles in *The Prince and Me* (2004), and Sandra Bullock in *Two Weeks Notice* (2002) and *The Proposal* (2009). These star vehicles for a new generation of leading ladies feature ambitious artists, journalists, and entrepreneurs in quirky heterosexual romantic adventures. Familiar conventions extended to television shows like HBO's *Sex and the City* (1998–2004), which followed a group of thirty-something singles—Carrie, Samantha, Charlotte, and Miranda—looking for love, friendship, and successful careers in New York City.[32] As Radner argues, female-targeted studio films released from 1990's *Pretty Woman* to 2008's *Sex and the City: The Movie* operate as "a lynchpin element in a system of media synergies." She notes that "films often include highly schematic representations of contemporary discourses in which the tensions and controversies of the era are writ large."[33]

In tracing the genre's evolution since the 1980s, Owen Gleiberman describes the 2000s cycle as:

> the moment when the rom-com entered its Guilty Pleasure Phase, or maybe we should call it the "I'm Watching This at Home With a Pint of Designer Ice Cream Phase," as it now became acceptable, by women, to refer to these movies as "chick flicks," a term of ownership that reclaimed a certain knowing girlishness as a stance of post-feminist attitude. That said, the chick-flick-ization of the romantic comedy was an acknowledgement that these movies had now achieved a certain low-camp, low-expectation cookie-cutter utilitarian cheesiness.[34]

Despite a new cultural zeitgeist, self-aware audiences, and mixed profitability for their parent companies, this cycle of rom-coms was critically and popularly framed as the studio system's worst reliance on a predictable genre formula and uninspired commercial conventions. Karen Hollinger points to the genre's commonly devalued and derided status, which "has been defined variously as escapist entertainment for women, any film that men don't like, examinations of the empowerment of capable independent female characters, emotional 'tearjerkers,' tales of female bonding, and the antithesis to male-oriented action films."[35] Often compared to sugary cotton candy, romantic comedies are collectively dismissed by critics and audiences as cloying, substanceless, and quickly consumed to be quickly forgotten.

Indeed, the rom-coms of this era were largely limited to the experiences of straight, cisgender, upper-middle-class white women. Stars like Roberts, Ryan, Bullock, Witherspoon, Hudson, and others saw lucrative periods in their careers as they looked for love in the city (or, occasionally, a small town) in a succession of commercially successful projects. In a cinematic fantasy space where white women's entire narrative trajectory is driven by finding love, where are the Black or Asian or Latinx or Native American and Indigenous rom-coms? If a woman of color was successfully attached to a star-driven studio rom-com, her character was often racially ambiguous or lacked cultural specificity. The most obvious example is Jennifer Lopez in a string of commercial hits in the early 2000s. In the case of *The Wedding Planner* (2001), the Latinx star plays a single Italian American woman with a successful career, an overly protective father, and an unfulfilled love life. In the case of a handful of successful Black romantic comedies and dramas during this industrial period like *Love Jones* (1997), *How Stella Got Her Groove Back* (1998), *The Best Man* (1999), *Brown Sugar* (2002), and *Something New* (2006), most were typically one-offs, marginalized even further as they were categorized as "Black films" and marketed primarily to Black audiences, a group historically underserved and undervalued by Hollywood studios.[36] Even within a discounted industrial space, as I will explore throughout this book, risk does not operate evenly within female-driven genres.

As the commercial cycle waned due to shifting economic, industrial, and cultural conditions, critics alternately bemoaned or celebrated the "death of the rom-com."[37] Yet, female-targeted filmmaking did not disappear; instead, studios rebranded the so-called chick flick as a new production model for women audiences. Hollywood shifted its focus to a broader category of "female-driven films," a descriptor *Variety* and other industry publications soon adopted. Media journalists and creatives began using the label in larger numbers after a 2008 cycle of commercial female-driven properties: Summit's *Twilight*, Warner Bros./New Line Cinema's *Sex and the City: The Movie*, and Universal's *Mamma Mia!* In effect, an industrial value shift reframed women-targeted films, pivoting away from formulaic, guilty pleasures to a more commercially viable product emulating IP-driven tentpole production and distribution strategies.[38]

What Ashley Elaine York identifies as high concept, the franchise-focused wave of "new women's blockbusters" earned number one spots at the opening-weekend box office that year. Trade headlines like *Variety*'s "2008: The Year That Broke the Rules" and "Women Take Center Stage at Summer B.O." reflect the similar celebratory press attention routinely granted to better-marketed male-driven properties. The level of surprise following these midbudget romance and friendship films, garnering as they did more than $140 million domestically, embodies the long-held skepticism and undervaluing of women's stories and audiences that has plagued the rom-com and the female-driven film in general. The first *Twilight* installment outgrossed a new James Bond movie in 2008. In 2011, Disney's *The Help* and Universal's *Bridesmaids* each earned $169 million, closely approaching Disney/Marvel's *Captain America* domestic box office gross of $176 million. Women's stories are too often culturally discounted in ways that male-driven fantasies, from superheroes to spy thrillers, are not. Even as this cycle of female-driven films increasingly extended into lucrative franchises—encompassing multiple films, soundtracks, merchandise, and other product tie-ins by the late 2000s—industrial and cultural value–equated commercial success is still often regarded as a gendered exception, as explored throughout this book.

Despite the formal appearance of the term "female-driven" in trade press and informal mentions in my conversations with film professionals, the term has no single, industry-wide definition. In one interview I conducted, an established Los Angeles–based independent producer suggested that "female-driven" could be broadly defined as involving a woman in a key above-the-line leadership role and, as she explained, generally signals media made for and by women.[39] She pointed to female-driven films with women credited as a producer and/or screenwriter—*Girls Trip* (2017), *Ocean's 8* (2018), *Tully* (2018)—adding that all these examples had also been led by established male directors and/or producers. As such, she asked, "Where do we draw the line?" Is a film female-driven if it is directed by a man when women hold other key above-the-line roles? Based on how the majority of film professionals used the category during interviews, for the purposes of this book, I define "female-driven" as a broad category to describe both a film property aimed at female audiences and a project led by a woman, or women, in at least one central above-the-line role with creative and financial decision-making control.[40]

The Value Gap calls into question long-held industry logic that determines who is granted access to resources, networks, and other opportunities as well as who is marginalized, overlooked, or denied entry to tell their story or have their story told. As this book explores, as in so many other male-dominated industries—from the STEM fields to the Fortune 500—value in the global film industry is historically gendered. One of the most complicated examples of gendering value, the female-driven film exists as a studio business model fraught with contradictory appraisals around its critical, financial, and cultural worth. Like many female-targeted forms, the rom-com has been systematically discounted in the industrial marketplace as not commercial enough, not widely marketable, or too niche for universal appeal to conventional "mainstream" (i.e., white male) audiences. Even as the major studios shifted from a production cycle of rom-coms to developing female-driven films using a commercial blockbuster model, the layers of gendered value—economic, industrial, cultural—were perpetuated throughout the 2000s and 2010s.

Research Methods and Approaches

One of the central aims of this book is to examine how women's creative labor and stories are valued—or, more accurately, devalued in twenty-first-century Hollywood. I am interested in complicating how value is understood and wielded in the film industry, explicating such calculation as a layered process, neither neutral nor universally defined or static. *The Value Gap* offers an interdisciplinary and multilayered analysis, identifying how complex gendered dynamics play out within Hollywood industry cultures and institutional practices. My research pulls from media industry studies, film history, production studies, feminist media studies, political economy, sociology, business and management studies, and cultural studies to explore how industrial complexities of gendered labor unfold across industry sectors and spaces. This project contributes a feminist critique to media industry studies work on production and distribution cultures by tracing how industry-specific structures, strategies, and cultures too often limit the trajectory—access, opportunities, advancement—of female-driven films and their filmmakers.

Borrowing from John Caldwell's integrated cultural-industrial methodology and Timothy Havens, Amanda Lotz, and Serra Tinic's "critical media industry studies" framework, my midlevel approach offers a "helicopter view," considering macrolevel shifting industry practices alongside microlevel individual experiences in a particularly transformative period.[41] I incorporate a variety of sources: (1) in-depth industry interviews and participant observation at industry events such as film festivals, markets, and panels; (2) trade and popular press coverage; and (3) economic data such as box office numbers, employment studies, and industry texts such as marketing and other studio-produced materials. This multilayered perspective employs discourse analysis to examine Hollywood business cultures and phases of female-driven filmmaking alongside women's work and experiences in above-the-line roles.

While this project builds upon international fieldwork conducted from 2010 to 2015 for previous publications, I conducted a series of primary and secondary interviews for *The Value Gap* with film professionals working across development, financing, production, film festivals, and distribution between 2016 and 2021. Overall, I interviewed more than fifty film professionals working at various phases of filmmaking and across industry sectors. For the primary interviews, I conducted ongoing individual conversations with eight women who have worked above the line for at least ten years as producers, directors, and screenwriters. For secondary interviews, I spoke with an additional set of above-the-line workers as well as key professionals at each phase of filmmaking, including development executives, editors, line producers, festival programmers and staff, international sales agents, and distributors. I conducted primary interviews in person mainly in the Los Angeles area but also via phone and Zoom calls with women in California, New York, Texas, and parts of the Midwest. Additionally, international fieldwork in Canada, France, Germany, and Sweden allowed a more expansive view of industry operations and rituals connected to Hollywood's international business and global footprint. I conducted secondary interviews and participant observations at international film festivals, production offices, and industry events.

A unique contribution of this project to media industry studies is twofold: first, it offers a longitudinal and latitudinal methodological approach, while second, it presents a layered conceptual framework, examining gendered value through multiple industrial lenses and levels. Much of my early research began with listening to professional experiences—stories of career timing, life-changing jobs, frustrations, missed opportunities, long hours, abusive bosses, microaggressions, and blatant sexism and racism. Using an *intersectional lens*, I aimed to build a network of female industry contacts diverse in age, race, role, experience, and position in the industry. Women of color (primarily Black and Asian American) make up around one-third of primary and secondary interviews, whereas white women compose the remaining two-thirds. It is also important to highlight that both interview groups consisted of cisgender women. Because transgender women and nonbinary creatives face even steeper barriers to entering and remaining in the pipeline, the women working in creative and economic positions of power in the film industry are still largely cisgender. Ages and experiences range from emerging creative workers in their twenties and thirties with two to ten years in the industry to more established women in their forties to sixties who have been working in independent and/or studio filmmaking for ten to thirty years. Furthermore, this project aims for depth beyond what a one-time conversation can reveal. By conducting follow-up interviews every six to twelve months with the smaller, more focused group featured in this book, I gained significant insights into the successes and failures of specific creative projects from development to distribution as well as into how individuals understand and manage their broader career trajectories. A longitudinal approach afforded unprecedented insights into the evolving careers—both setbacks and triumphs—of women working in the film industry over an extended five-year period.

There is so much to be learned from struggle as an experience and process in the creative industries. My aim is to elucidate failures and successes, independent production culture and studio culture, and notions of access and privilege in a system of gatekeepers and powerful players. Conducting a series of follow-up interviews and mapping these conversations in terms of their production credits, professional networks, trade coverage, and social media presence offers unique insight into how women navigate their careers in public and private spaces.

Production studies as a subfield calls attention not only to questions of power, hierarchies, routines, and rituals ingrained in media work but also to the stories these creative professionals tell about their contributions, identities, and experiences. On an *individual level*, my approach is grounded in John Caldwell's conceptualization of industry workers, which is "less about finding an 'authentic' reality 'behind the scenes'—an empirical notion that tends to be naïve about the ways that media industry realities are *always* constructed—than it is about studying the industry's own self-representation, self-critique, and self-reflection."[42] What film industry workers disclose, or many times do not disclose, in a private conversation as compared to a major publication can be quite revealing. Throughout *The Value Gap*, I incorporate a variety of first-person accounts from anonymized interviews, on-the-record interviews, and public-facing interviews in the trades. I am interested not just in the stories that Hollywood tells with its media products but also in the stories these institutions and industry workers tell about themselves.

A production cultures approach demonstrates an "anthropological interest in workers' meaning-making activities" and takes a closer look at "the cultural values and logics that orient these people as industrial workers."[43] How women's work and creative labor are valued across industry spaces varies, revealing the complexities and contradictions of the contemporary film business. In seeking to shed light on these intricacies, this book operates as a reflective space for women navigating these dynamics across a range of sites and circumstances. According to Vicki Mayer, on-the-ground production studies elucidate "the ways that power operates locally through media production to reproduce social hierarchies and inequalities at the level of daily interactions. Production studies, in other words, 'ground' social theories by showing us how specific production sites, actors, or activities tell us larger lessons about workers, their practices, and the role of their labors in relation to politics, economics, and culture."[44] Examining personal self-reflections by female creatives alongside larger shifting industrial discourses and dynamics, I track how the struggle to make female-driven films reveals the hierarchies, boundaries, and power dynamics of an increasingly commercialized and deterritorialized industrial period. Over the course of our conversations, from casual to in-depth, film professionals describe the intense work of negotiation and emotional labor—so often invisible—that women must do to exist and thrive in an industry still largely dominated by men.

On the *industrial level*, my approach is to explicate how gender inequity impacts all phases of filmmaking. Gatekeepers oversee each sector of the pipeline—development and financing, production, film festivals and markets, and theatrical distribution and marketing. I spoke with important stakeholders at each stage, which informed my understanding of the myriad barriers, both structural and discursive, hindering women filmmakers. In contrast to widely circulated quantitative data studies from research centers at UCLA, USC, and UCSD tracking macrolevel gendered employment and filmmaking gaps, *The Value Gap* incorporates a multimodal approach for locating and mapping patterns of industry discourse impacting female-driven filmmaking across different industrial periods. Pairing interviews and fieldwork with public- and industry-facing sources like popular and trade publications, published interviews, and professional memoirs allows for richer discursive mapping. This provides a more nuanced look into how complex and slippery gendered lore or myths permeate and inform all levels and areas of the film industry. Drawing upon these rich first-person insights, my project complicates broader contemporary neoliberal and postfeminist conversations about gender in the twenty-first-century workplace that place the onus on women to change their individual behavior (i.e., "lean in, ladies!").

Timothy Havens describes how industry narratives—what he calls "industry lore"—often reflect "organizational priorities that find their way into representational practices, specifically through organizational common sense."[45] Lore, a productive concept for this book, allows me to examine how commonsense ideas about experience, qualifications, risk, and failure circulate and rationalize disparities that play out differently across gendered and racialized lines.[46] Widely circulated "truths" about the film business—"Women don't go to the movies!," "Female-led movies don't make money!," and "Female directors don't have the experience (or desire) to direct big-budget action blockbusters!"—historically served to explain away structural gender inequities and reinforce and normalize studios prioritizing the male-driven status quo. Commonly circulated gendered myths devalue women's contributions as well as impede access to jobs, resources, and career advancement. As many female-driven films struggled to be made and women lost out on leadership roles, a self-fulfilling cycle emerged in the 2000s and 2010s. Because women's voices and creative contributions have historically been marginalized, many women lack the opportunity to even contradict these deeply ingrained gender biases.

Often, a handful of very successful executives, actresses, and producers are given a platform with interviews, award show speeches, and social media movements. Hollywood A-listers like Ava DuVernay, Salma Hayek, Reese Witherspoon, Oprah Winfrey, Cate Blanchett, Jessica Chastain, and others have played an important role in foregrounding the critical debates and mobilizing their peers. However, a methodological objective of this book is to shine a light on the often invisible and undervalued labor of creative workers who work relentlessly for gender parity as they simultaneously seek to build their careers. I focus on gathering the stories of women who are early in their careers as well as those with established careers, many whose livelihoods remain precarious due to the largely freelance and project-by-project nature of the film industry. As Natalie Wreyford and Shelley Cobb argue: "In labor markets where there is a gender imbalance, hearing from members of an underrepresented group still only involves the voices and experiences of those who have had some degree of success. It does not tell us about the women who are unable to be part of that profession, or the scale or reasons for their exclusion."[47]

While the majority of women interviewed for this book have built sustainable careers, some continue to struggle with steady employment and creative opportunities, while a smaller number have left the film industry completely. This research does not speak for the many women who hope to enter the film industry and build long-term careers but who leave after facing insurmountable barriers. One may not have the luxury of taking an unpaid internship or underpaid assistantship, have no family or partner to subsidize the cost of living, be unable to secure an agent necessary to book interviews and jobs, and so on. The unstable and exclusionary nature of the film industry is a persistent concern raised in most of the interviews I conducted, even as focusing on working film professionals presents a limitation of the project's scope.

Most media workers I spoke to did not have the status or industry weight to leverage big, sweeping actions or attention-grabbing headlines. Yet, they were still fighting for better financing, gender-balanced crews, more female-driven films in festivals, and so on, without the privilege or protection that come with A-list status. Due to the uncertain and sensitive nature of film work, I am careful to protect the identities of the women interviewed and, upon request, anonymize or change their names. During the course of the research for the project, I was committed to building genuine relationships with female creatives who shared their professional, and often personal, lives in detail. Many of these women offered introductions to filmmaker friends, mentors, and peers, growing my access and enriching this book's insights and conclusions. This project would not be possible without the trust and openness of these conversations and the generous introductions and sharing of networks that often followed.

Organization of the Book

Key industrial developments of the Hollywood studio system from the 1910s to 1980s resulted in the increasingly marginalized and gendered nature of women's film work. Chapter 1, "The Gendered Workplace (Employment Gap)," begins by tracing the ways in which the studios' industrialization—developing in the early 1900s and maturing by the 1920s, with power consolidating by the 1930s—had lasting repercussions for women filmmakers' ability to secure employment as directors, writers, and producers. Grounded in a recent body of robust historical film industries work, the evolving Hollywood studio system provides the foundational context necessary to understanding how the shifting nature of gendered work over the twentieth century reveals deeply rooted structural disparities that directly affect women in the film industry today.

The remainder of the chapter examines the gendered employment gap characterizing the twenty-first-century film industry across different sectors and levels of filmmaking—from above-the-line jobs to the top-level "chief" executives who occupy what's known as the "C-suite." Recent quantitative studies aim to shed light on this gap by mapping Hollywood's pervasive employment disparities. Despite how widely data studies circulate through trade publications and social media campaigns, quantitative methods often lack vital industrial and institutional context for understanding how gender disparities affect the filmmaking pipeline beyond employment as an entry point. In exploring employment experiences and film work cultures, female creatives report facing in-group biases and prescriptive gender stereotypes as they try to navigate the female likability trap and "cool girl" persona inside many male-driven workplaces. Whether instructing women on how to break the "glass ceiling" of male-dominated industries or how to navigate mansplaining coworkers by "leaning in," advice for women in the workplace traditionally encourages them to change individual behavior or demeanor as a way to combat larger structural issues holding back their careers. According to a series of interviews conducted with independent producers, directors, and writers, much of the "how-to-succeed in the workplace" advice did little to change or merely reinforced the Hollywood boys' club.

After a new wave of mergers and acquisitions, and with major studio divisions releasing a dozen or fewer films each year, the development focus in Hollywood from 2009 to 2019 was increasingly invested in known franchises and intellectual properties, the lion's share of which were big-budget, male-driven blockbusters. As a result, many of the major studios largely abandoned the midbudget, adult-targeted project, which, since the 1980s, has served as a vital space for female filmmakers and their audiences. Chapter 2, "Script Market to Pitch Meetings (Development Gap)," examines the changing Hollywood development process and how it has affected female-driven projects. As studio investment in the "spec" (speculative) script market and first-look deals has dramatically decreased since the 2000s, female-driven projects have suffered as women creatives struggle to get into the filmmaking pipeline. This chapter examines the development process in this period for what stories women can and cannot tell and how they pitch these stories through the lens of individual experiences and industry lore. Masculine expectations as well as the invisible and gendered labor dynamic of physical production directly impacts women's access and advancement in two key above-the-line positions, director and producer.

Chapter 3, "Production Work and Gendered Cultures (Leadership Gap)," first considers the long-held romantic image of the film director as creative auteur or "boy genius." Sociocultural and industry-specific gendered leadership expectations force many female directors to prove their own competence and qualifications on a film production. The chapter then highlights the misunderstood role of the creative producer, often described as the control system center for the production phase, who follows a film project from initial development to distribution. Based on interviews with independent creative producers, I identify relational and management patterns involving everyday challenges for an all-encompassing role expending various types of emotional labor.

Major international film festivals play a pivotal role as both an exclusive marketplace for programming decisions and a space for distribution deal-making and networking. Chapter 4, "Film Festivals and Markets (Programming Gap)," highlights how annual industry events, such as the Toronto International Film Festival (TIFF), Cannes Film Festival, Berlin International Film Festival (Berlinale), and Sundance Film Festival, operate as powerful gatekeepers. With historically low acceptance rates for female-driven films, the international festival circuit faced mounting pressure to increase rates of inclusive programming in the mid-2010s. While securing a programming spot at an international film festival often comes with a potential career boost from press coverage and on-site networking, many female creatives reported not seeing the same career advancement as their male peers. Based on fieldwork conducted at TIFF, Cannes, Berlinale, and Sundance, this chapter examines the gender gap from two perspectives: how festival organizations have responded to the criticism of inequitable programming and support for female filmmakers as well as the experiences of female-driven films and their filmmaking teams navigating festival spaces and cultures.

Female-driven films have long faced challenges at the marketing and distribution phase. Trade press headlines during the 2000s and 2010s were quick to hail the box office success of female-driven films as reflecting the "year of the woman" only to dismiss their economic viability as an exception or anomaly, what I call an "amnesia loop." Chapter 5, "Distribution and Marketing (Bankability Gap)," identifies industry myths around bankability, specifically exploring gendered ideas of risk and uncertainty during theatrical distribution. Disparities emerge in how box office failure was measured around long-held lore that women "don't go to the movies" and ways in which female directors were disproportionately punished in "movie jail."

The conclusion serves less as a definitive wrap-up and more as a springboard to consider evolving initiatives or sites of inquiry emerging at the start of a new decade in Hollywood. First, the emergence of the COVID-19 pandemic and new momentum in the racial justice movement in 2020 resulted in unparalleled impacts and pressures on the film industry in every sector. I briefly discuss not only film productions shutting down and theaters closing but also wide-scale racial justice protests and organizing that heightened the scrutiny of Hollywood's structural failure to address intersectional inclusion and equity in front of and behind the camera. Second, new directions for interrogating gender equity initiatives moving forward, specifically the streaming wars and emerging legacy studio streaming platforms, increasingly have blurred boundaries between film and television creation and opportunities for female filmmakers in the new streaming landscape. Finally, the revelations surrounding the Time's Up organization by 2021 offer a cautionary tale of the problematic power structures, poor leadership, and toxic work cultures the organization set out to disrupt.

Conclusion

While I attended the 2017 Toronto International Film Festival, the topic of this book came up during a lunch with two former studio executives—both middle-aged, white professional men who had worked in Hollywood for more than three decades. I had a good rapport with the executives, whom I interviewed for my book about Hollywood's shifting international operations from the 1990s to 2010s. When asked about my new project, I offered my elevator pitch, outlining Hollywood's historical glass ceiling and the driving question behind my research: Where are all the women working in position of powers in the studio system? As they exchanged amused glances, one scoffed in response: "Too bad that is your next book! You're not going to find much of an audience for such a small topic." They proceeded to pitch me other ideas they considered more "marketable," a more compelling "untold story" than the barriers women face from development to distribution. They declared my efforts examining global business practices as a more valuable contribution to media industry studies.

For a conversation happening in September 2017, their reaction was symptomatic of numerous film executives I had interviewed in the preceding years and in many ways reflected larger studio priorities in addressing the international market during the mid-2010s. However, something struck me in that moment. I found myself in a situation similar to that experienced by Emma (with whom I open this chapter) and other female creatives I interviewed. *My female-driven story* was deemed unrelatable, irrelevant, and not captivating enough to a garner a large readership. What could be more globally relevant than the gender inequity female filmmakers experience in industries worldwide? This exchange reinforced for me, as a woman writer and academic, how ingrained gendered beliefs are, and how men controlling the global film industry for more than a hundred years continue, so self-assuredly, to wield their power and privilege in determining whose stories have value.

The following month, in October 2017, this "small story" blew up in a big way. Accounts of misconduct and abuse led to larger questions about a male-driven industry in which women lack equal access to jobs, higher wages, career advancement, and so on. A Los Angeles–based white female producer characterized the events unfolding by fall 2017 in the following way: "Like a dead canary laying in front of us all is what's going on with bro culture within the film culture. What's happening all of a sudden, [a realization of] this gross underbelly that there's not a safe space for women in a lot of circles."[48] In turn, the emergence of the #MeToo and Time's Up movements led my research into unexpected and heartbreaking directions as the women I interviewed grappled with the fallout.

This broader dynamic created a unique research space for me as an industry scholar. Both I and many of the women I encountered were still in the middle of processing what was happening, and the accounts interweaved into this book serve as snapshots. In this watershed moment, I approached the study of women's film work as chasing an open-ended story, one with an unpredictable momentum of change and uncertainty for long-term outcomes. The rapidly changing news cycle that followed over the next few years lent these interviews a heightened sense of immediacy and relevance and in turn raised the stakes of this project significantly. What started as a scholarly project hoping to amplify the voices of women working above the line became an experiential account of the film community at a pivotal juncture in an escalating industry-wide fight for women's equity and inclusion. The stories I gathered and conclusions I have drawn are but a modest window into a much longer, multifaceted generational view of women's stories that will continue to unfold long after this book's publication.

CHAPTER 1

The Gendered Workplace (Employment Gap)

The Hollywood Reporter (*THR*) decided to end rankings for its "Women of Entertainment Power 100" list in 2015. The highly anticipated annual list of executives, management, and above-the-line creatives began in 1992 to "celebrate how far women in the industry have come" in a historically male-dominated system.[1] In a rather bold farewell from *THR*'s president and COO at the time, Janice Min criticized both the denigrated, and often invisible, role of women in Hollywood: "The acceptance of women as 'lesser' in Hollywood is so commonplace, it's as if we've grown comfortable living with our own ugly furniture. We don't even know it looks bad." Min also called out *THR* for creating an annual ranking that transformed into what she describes as a "female cage match" for those angling to appear in it. She concluded by speaking directly to women in positions of power to work together to make change: "As part of this decision, I challenge the groups of women we cover, who create content, who move billions of dollars of business, to work together. To hunt as a pack. And for those who can, to take a leadership role in addressing the gender issues that we both unconsciously and willfully ignore. After all, there is no greater sense of power than being able to use it." A "work together" and "hunt as a pack" network strategy places the responsibility again on individual women to provide the structural fix to address the complexities of gender equity and employment disparities. While Min recommended a new equal opportunity list featuring the most powerful women *and* men in the entertainment industries, the following year *THR* reversed course and continued publishing the power list of women.[2]

Min's hope for reimagining *THR*'s power list reflects a desire in that industrial moment to move beyond identifying the marginalization of women across all sectors of filmmaking without any of the industry-wide structural or institutional work to get there. By the early 2020s, employment disparities still existed at all levels of the film industry and continue to be a major issue holding women back from entering the filmmaking pipeline and developing a professional path. In turn, this chapter looks at occupational sex segregation and the gendered employment gap in the early twenty-first century—from broader film industry histories and contemporary employment data studies to more specific individual pressures and the burden of likability in the workplace. The first section offers a historical overview of women's work in twentieth-century Hollywood based on a recent body of archival research by film and media industry scholars—specifically, Emily Carman, Jane Gaines, Erin Hill, Maya Montañez Smukler, J. E. Smyth, and Shelley Stamp—that complicates entrenched narratives in popular and academic accounts of Hollywood's gender inequity.[3] Instead of a story of complete erasure, a deeper examination both implicates and explicates the industry's systemic marginalization of women and their rich contributions.

The next section considers a number of quantitative data studies by highlighting inequitable employment across different sectors and levels of contemporary Hollywood filmmaking—from above-the-line jobs to the C-suite. These studies began to circulate widely in the 2010s. On the one hand, employment statistics have been instrumental in calling attention to the shocking disparities through trade publications, popular press, and social media campaigns. Championed by research initiatives like Geena Davis's Institute on Gender in Media and a handful of academic centers, this macrolevel approach assumes that pressuring industry gatekeepers with the dismal realities of employment numbers for women will result in structural changes in the filmmaking pipeline. A quantitative-driven approach, on the other hand, offers a limited perspective of macrolevel industry dynamics and works best when contextualized and used in conversation with qualitative research methods. In turn, the remainder of the chapter offers a qualitative approach for examining how female executives and creative workers experience and seek to navigate deeply ingrained gendered workplace cultures about "fit" that have historically hindered career advancement. Women interviewed report facing in-group biases and prescriptive gender stereotypes as they try to negotiate the female likability trap and "cool girl" persona prevalent inside male-driven work-places. What results is an industrial climate in which women are expected to individually *and* collectively tackle structural and cultural barriers.

How Twentieth-Century Hollywood Shut Women Out

By 1909, women filmmakers actively worked in almost all sectors of the American film business and contributed significantly to building a developing industry. During this early period of cinema, films were cheap to make and production roles were not clearly defined. Women ascended from crew positions or acting into directing, writing, and producing. The number of female filmmakers peaked between 1918 and 1922—directing forty-four feature films, heading more than twenty production companies, and writing hundreds of produced scripts.[4] From her star status as a comedic actress, Mabel Normand began directing films for Mack Sennett's Keystone Pictures and some of Charlie Chaplin's earliest roles.[5] Lois Weber emerged as one of Universal Pictures' most commercially successful and prolific writer-directors of this period before starting her own short-lived production company. According to Shelley Stamp, Weber's influential career "maps the arc of American cinema's evolution from a series of companies scattered throughout the country churning out thousands of one- and two-reel shorts each week, to a massive, capitalized industry based in Hollywood and controlled by a few names that still dominate in today's media landscape."[6]

Even as early Hollywood appealed directly to the sensibilities and aspirations of a generation of modern "woman-made women" flocking to the West Coast, they arrived to find increasingly limited access and opportunities for employment by the 1920s.[7] As the late-1920s industry transitioned from silent to sound technology, nascent major studios strategically sought what Karen Ward Mahar describes as "financial legitimacy" through consolidation and concentration of ownership. Vertically integrated studios came to control the entire filmmaking process—from the means of production to exhibition—and strong-armed competing independent theaters to program their films.[8] Opportunities for female filmmakers declined dramatically when the industry consolidated into a powerful studio system. Jane Gaines notes that "as women were phased out it was not so much that they were unnecessary as that they could easily be replaced by men, especially as producers, directors, and writers. . . .

Women as creative workers *would be made redundant*."[9] It is important to acknowledge that the women who had been working in early studio film production and were affected by this major transitional period in Hollywood were white. Kyna Morgan and Aimee Dixon highlight a small group of pioneering Black women who "have not come to the attention of historians." Black female filmmakers like Tressie Souders, Madame E. Touissant Welcome, Maria P. Williams, and Zora Neale Hurston "helped to establish the US cinema industry and to better the representation of African-Americans on film" by working independently during this period.[10]

By the following decade, the Big Five (Twentieth Century-Fox, RKO Pictures, Paramount Pictures, Warner Bros., and Metro-Goldwyn-Mayer) and the Little Three (Universal Pictures, Columbia Pictures, and United Artists) had transformed the American film industry into a global business in which financial stakes grew with ever-expanding budgets and proliferating audiences. Men dominated filmmaker ranks and controlled executive suites during the classical studio era. Women largely lost access to technical and creative positions—camera work, editing, and directing—in large numbers. Many shifted to behind-the-scenes creative contributions to production work, what Erin Hill describes as "underpaid, underestimated, and undercredited in comparison to men's."[11] A handful of extraordinary exceptions—for example, director Dorothy Arzner, producer and writer Virginia Van Upp, writers Anita Loos and Frances Marion, actress-director-producer Ida Lupino, actress-turned-producer-executive Mary Pickford—actively worked behind the camera in above-the-line roles.[12] Arzner, who rose from clerical work to become a chief editor for Paramount, leveraged production experience in the 1920s into directing her first feature for Columbia in 1927 and continuing into the 1940s.[13]

In contrast, J. E. Smyth, in her book *Nobody's Girl Friday: The Women Who Ran Hollywood* challenges the scarcity of narratives around women's work in the studio era: "Although the overall numbers of female directors declined from the silent era, women remained active in the industry as producers, writers, script readers, researchers, actors, costume and makeup designers, set dressers, secretaries, publicists, agents, and editors. Yet, given the dominance of auteurist ideologies in the writing of Hollywood history, these other branches of filmmaking, more heavily represented by women, have been marginalized or ignored."[14] For example, early film cutters who assembled rough cuts and at times the final cut for the director were primarily women. Early continuity work was a low-paid and

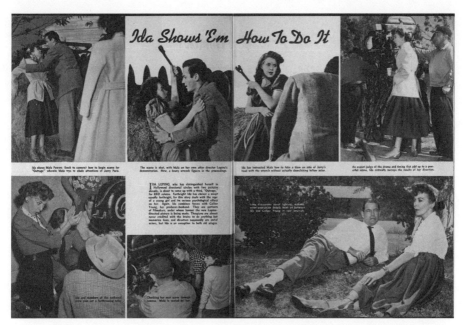

1.1. A feature about actress-director-writer Ida Lupino on the set of her film *Outrage*, in the September 1950 issue of the fan magazine *Screenland*. (Screenshot from Lantern, an open access production of the Wisconsin Center for Film and Theater Research at the University of Wisconsin-Madison.)

undercredited role requiring attention to detail and organizational skills for which women were seen as "naturally" inclined. After "cutting rose in desirability and prestige" due to the creative importance of the position as well as the structural and technological shifts to sound inside the studios, the position moved away from its feminized categorization of the early years.[15] Yet, as Smyth contends, film editing remained a professional space for some women in the studio era. Two of the most famous editors of Classical Hollywood, Margaret Booth at MGM and Barbara McLean at Twentieth Century-Fox, were not alone, as other notable female counterparts included Blanche Sewell, Anne Bauchens, and Viola Lawrence.[16]

In a stark contrast to the contemporary studio system, the women's picture—focusing on female protagonists and targeting female audiences—emerged as one of the most valuable and bankable genres in its heyday in the 1930s and 1940s. As Emily Carman contends, women "were a mainstay *in front* of the camera in the following decade of sound cinema, when female stars truly rule the Hollywood screen as top box-office attractions."[17] As a result, a small group of A-list female stars pushed back against the constraining studio contracts of their era for greater control over their careers and greater financial gains. By employing what Carman calls "professional agency," Olivia de Havilland, Carole Lombard, Constance Bennett, Dolores del Río, Barbara Stanwyck, and Katharine Hepburn operated as "business-savvy women who challenged the hierarchical and paternalistic structures of the film industry" and gained employment independently, outside standard, long-term studio contract agreements typical of the era.[18] She argues that "box-office power and off-screen agency" allowed these women to negotiate unprecedented freelance labor practices, production deals, and profit-earning percentages.[19] In the case of de Havilland, her 1943 lawsuit against Warner Bros. resulted in a momentous ruling giving actors the right to freelance work after completing a studio contract. Furthermore, after establishing her star status as "America's Sweetheart" during the silent era, Mary Pickford went on to approve materials she starred in, wrote scripts, and at times directed without receiving credit. As a founding member of United Artists along with D. W. Griffith, Charlie Chaplin, and Douglas Fairbanks, Pickford created a production unit inside the studio in the 1930s and remained the only female UA executive for decades.[20]

But focusing on a limited number of women occupying above-the-line positions bypasses other roles and departments in which women sustained large numbers. Archival accounts trace female employees working in various studio sectors and roles throughout the mid-twentieth century. Hill's pivotal contribution to the history of women's film work challenges what she calls myths about Hollywood. It is worth citing her intervention in detail as she contends:

> Women were never absent from film history; they often simply weren't documented as part of it because they did "women's work," which was—by definition—insignificant, tedious, low status, and noncreative. In the golden age of Hollywood, women could be found in nearly every department of every studio, minding the details that might otherwise get in the way of more important, prestigious, or creative work (a.k.a. men's work). If film historians consider the classical Hollywood era's mode of production a system, we ought to consider women this system's mainstay, because studios were built on their low-cost backs and scaled through their brush and keystrokes.[21]

In the 1930s and 1940s studio system, women held a variety of roles in food and janitorial services, teaching, nursing, and clerical and administrative positions. Specifically, feminized clerical work in studio libraries, story departments, casting departments, and publicity departments involved "paper planning" that contributed to the essential "flow" of scripts, communications, and other key production documentation.[22]

The 1950s and 1960s proved a transitional period for the studio economic model, and production practices with women saw few employment gains. The Paramount Decree, issued after a 1948 anti-trust ruling, resulted in the majors losing theater holdings and the previously tight grip they held over exhibition practices. The number of films each studio produced decreased dramatically after the post–World War II peak. Janet Staiger identifies the 1950s as a transformative moment for Hollywood's mode of production, which still shapes contemporary studio operations. The producer-unit system of the 1930s and 1940s, in which a central producer exclusively oversaw six to eight films per year for a major studio, evolved into a decentralized package-unit system. Under this new model, the producer assembled financing, hired above-the-line and below-the-line workers, and oversaw the production from beginning to end. Mass manufacturing of a variety of studio films meant producing fewer, more specialized films that carried increasing financial and creative risk.[23]

Organizational ownership began to change significantly. The Gulf and Western purchase of Paramount Pictures in 1966 marked the first big wave of conglomeration in the late 1960s as manufacturing and financing companies began acquiring the major studios. Alongside the introduction of the rating system, which replaced the Production Code and loosened on-screen restrictions, institutional restructuring ushered in a period of significant transformation for Hollywood.[24] Yet, in the midst of this upheaval, the number of working women filmmakers for the major studios did not change. Some female talent found a creative pathway in the developing television industry. Ida Lupino steadily directed television shows including episodes of *Have Gun—Will Travel* (1957–1963), *The Fugitive* (1963–1967), and *Gilligan's Island* (1964–1967).[25] Lucille Ball's Desilu Productions, formed with her *I Love Lucy* costar and husband, Desi Arnaz, became a major production house during this period. Desilu built the creative and financial autonomy that Ball had never experienced as a contract player for RKO Pictures from the 1930s to 1940s.[26]

The struggling studios were slow to respond to changing youth demographics and the contemporary cultural climate.[27] Coming-of-age Baby Boomers contributed to declining theatrical audiences as sweeping political and social movements began to reshape the American landscape and with it an entire generation's relationship to popular culture. Now competing with television, the majors increasingly invested in expensive international coproductions, Biblical epics, and bloated big-budget family musicals. As the studios struggled to adapt to a new economic and cultural landscape, a new generation of male filmmakers and executives took over from the old Hollywood moguls. Beginning in the late 1960s, the studios produced darker, more introspective, and politically engaged films in an effort to speak to a changing American political and cultural climate.[28] But films like *Bonnie and Clyde* (1967), *The Graduate* (1967), and *Easy Rider* (1969)—reflecting the mind-set of their historical moment—continued to privilege stories about the straight white male experience. A number of commercially and critically successful female-led films premiered during this period, including Jane Fonda in *Klute* (1971), Liza Minnelli in *Cabaret* (1972), Ellen Burstyn in *Alice Doesn't Live Here Anymore* (1974), Barbra Streisand in *A Star Is Born* (1976), Diane Keaton in *Annie Hall* (1977), Anne Bancroft and Shirley MacLaine in *Turning Point* (1977), and Sally Field in *Norma Rae* (1979). Male directors still largely helmed this small wave of films featuring complex white female characters.

By 1965, women began entering the US workforce in larger numbers, making up 40 percent of workers over sixteen years old and, by 1975, more than 46 percent.[29] Even as industry-wide employment numbers increased at a glacial rate, women began to slowly move into roles as junior story executives, production coordinators, casting directors, and publicists. In her book *Hello, He Lied and Other Truths from the Hollywood Trenches*, veteran producer Lynda Obst describes her first job in the 1970s after moving from New York–based journalism to the Los Angeles film business: "Unbeknownst to me, the era had just dawned in Hollywood when there was one 'girl' at every meeting to read scripts, write notes, and dispense mineral water. The people doing this job, the nonclerical one widely open to women, have come to be known as 'd' girls, short for development girls. . . . We worked with the writers, fashioning the stories, structuring the scripts-to-be."[30] Obst's recollection speaks to a new generation of female workers sitting in creative meetings and contributing feedback during the development phase. However, despite her labeling the role as "nonclerical," the entry-level development position was firmly rooted in traditionally femininized administrative work. The devaluation of women's work is illustrated clearly by the industry-wide use of sobriquets ranging from pejorative ("development girls") to outright misogynistic ("d girl").

Maya Montañez Smukler identifies the 1970s as a "crucial decade" for women directors in Hollywood. She argues, "For the first time in almost forty years, the number of women directors began to increase beginning in 1967: between then and 1980, sixteen women made at least one feature film within the commercial US-based film industry, either as part of the studio system or as independent filmmakers."[31] This cycle of female-directed films ranged from Barbara Loden's independent drama *Wanda* (1970) to Elaine May's studio comedy *A New Leaf* (1971). Comedian, actress, and screenwriter May became the first woman to direct a film for Paramount since Dorothy Arzner in 1932. Smukler argues this strategic hiring was largely a public relations move allowing Paramount "to economize on paying for talent but also to exploit her skills and position in the industry because she was a first-time director and a woman."[32] After *A New Leaf*, May helmed three more features until the disastrous release of *Ishtar* (1987) for Columbia Pictures, discussed in a later chapter, ended her directing career. Studio leadership slowly began to trickle down to a younger generation of women the following decade. Even as Twentieth Century-Fox appointed Sherry Lansing as the first female president of production in 1980, followed by the 1987 hiring of Dawn Steel as the first female studio president at Columbia, the number of women moving into powerful financial and creative decision-making roles remained minimal.[33]

The 1970s proved to be a pivotal moment for women to collectively push back against Hollywood's enduring and long-lasting sex segregation. With the rise of Second Wave feminism and the women's liberation movement, demands for equal pay, fair employment, and accessible childcare resulted in major legislation such as the 1972 Title IX statute protecting women against sex discrimination in federally funded education programs or activities.[34] The widespread feminist movement had a growing impact on women organizing to effect change.

Established between 1972 and 1973, Women in Film and the American Film Institute's Directing Workshop for Women have become significant mentorship and training programs for emerging filmmakers. Additionally, members of major professional guilds—Directors Guild of America (DGA), Writers Guild of American (WGA), Screen Actors Guild (SAG)—worked together to create women's committees inside their organizations and pushed to address employment discrimination during this period.[35] Both the WGA and SAG conducted surveys tracking how discriminatory hiring practices disenfranchised women members, and for the first time, industry press widely reported the survey results.

In an unprecedented series of events, the DGA women's committee met with the major studios to push for the inclusive hiring of women and directors of color in 1980. As the talks fell apart, Guild representatives filed a lawsuit in 1983 against Columbia Pictures and Warner Bros. for employment discrimination.[36] The major studios won the court case in 1985 proving "no reliable legal recourse against discrimination based on sex and race, specifically with regard to the position of director."[37] Despite the loss, Smukler explains that "the suit was a landmark case" as a historic effort taken by the DGA acting as a whole organization and not just coming from the women's committee. The action may have been unprecedented for the industry organization, and it drew widespread industry attention to women and minority directors for the first time.[38] However, the Hollywood studios returned to business as usual. The film industry would not experience such a highly publicized and sweeping women's movement again for decades.

The first notable group of (almost exclusively white) women directing studio films in the 1980s coincided with growing university film programs including NYU (Martha Coolidge, Amy Heckerling, and Susan Seidelman), UCLA (Penelope Spheeris), and Columbia (Kathryn Bigelow). Other paths to the studio director's chair included on-screen star power (Barbra Streisand, Penny Marshall, and Jodie Foster) or successful screenwriting credits (Nora Ephron and Nancy Meyers). Very few women of color directed commercial features, either independently or for the major studios, during the decade. After her debut film *Rue Cases-Nègres* (*Sugar Cane Alley*, 1983) won the Silver Lion at the 1983 Venice Film Festival, Euzhan Palcy became the first Black woman to direct a studio feature with MGM's *A Dry White Season* (1989). However, this leap into the studio filmmaking pipeline was short-lived. In a 2019 *Los Angeles Times* interview, Palcy reflected on numerous meetings with studio executives for follow-up projects: "They would not touch my [own] stories because they were about Black people. They kept saying to me—to my face, but very nicely, not to insult me—that 'Black is not bankable.'" In order to tell stories about the Black experience, Palcy, like so many of her peers over the following decades, worked in television and independent film.[39]

With the exception of Bigelow, who went on to direct male-driven action films like *Point Break* (1991) and *K-19: The Widowmaker* (2002), the white female-led studio projects from this period were largely limited to family-oriented comedies or female-targeted genre movies such as Heckerling's *Look Who's Talking* (1989), *Look Who's Talking Too* (1990), and *Clueless* (1995); Marshall's *Big* (1988) and *A League of Their Own* (1992); Streisand's *The Prince of Tides* (1991) and *The Mirror Has Two Faces* (1996); and Ephron's *Sleepless in Seattle* (1993) and *You've Got Mail* (1998). Even as filmmakers Julie Dash, Cheryl Dunye, Rose Troche, Kelly Reichardt, Gina Prince-Bythewood, Karyn Kusama, Kimberly Peirce, and Sofia Coppola emerged from the 1990s and 2000s independent boom at the Sundance Film Festival, as discussed in later chapters, many struggled with gaining access to major studio projects and building sustainable directing careers.

Where the Girls Aren't: Tracking the Twenty-First-Century Employment Gap

American female workers still lagged behind their male peers in the mid- to late 2010s. Women entered higher education and started career paths in historically larger numbers than men, only to be stalled, stuck, or pushed off track along the way. Female students enrolled in two- and four-year postsecondary degree programs at higher rates than men, but increased rates of education did not translate into higher rates of employment and advancement. Women outpaced their male peers in enrollment rates for all US postsecondary degree plans by 44 percent to 56 percent in 2017.[40]

The lack of formal training or education is not the issue for the film industry.[41] Top-ranked film school numbers are not far off from national enrollment averages, with highly competitive programs like USC's Cinematic Arts reporting close to fifty-fifty gender parity in 2016 for both undergraduate and graduate programs. In 2018, Allyson Green, the dean of New York University's Tisch School of the Arts, reported "an equal number of women and men in our film programs" to *Variety*.[42] Even as colleges and universities, including my own university department, expand film and media curricula nationwide, a massive gap persists between film school training and feature film employment rates for female creative workers. Despite the increasing number of women educated and/or trained and ready to begin their careers in the film industry, significant barriers to entry into the professional pipeline remain.

Gender wage and promotion gaps hold women back at all professional levels of business, law, technology and engineering, academia, and media entertainment. At the highest levels, women made up merely 4.8 percent of Fortune 500 CEOs in 2018. This number represents growth from 0.8 percent in 2001, which translates to an increase from four to twenty-four women in top executives roles in the C-suite.[43] By 2015, the percentage of women in the labor force—56.7 percent at that time—was expected to decline in the coming decade.[44] Caretaking responsibilities for children, aging parents, and family life in general are incompatible with increasingly rigid workplace cultures and longer work weeks attributed to late capitalism's growing gig economy.[45] In spring 2020, as a result of the crippling public health and economic toll of the global COVID-19 pandemic, women began to leave the workforce or were pushed out in record rates compared to men in what some journalists deemed a "shecession."[46] Even in the broad context of this macrolevel employment data, the employment gap for women in the United States continues to widen.

Economist Myra Strober describes how the gendering of jobs, where specific work is labeled "masculine" or "feminine," creates a system of "occupational sex segregation." Such stratification develops over time, as "women are clustered at the lower levels, [with] men at the upper levels."[47] As men rise higher to management and executive ranks, women too often begin and remain in low-level clerical or administrative roles. The gendered nature of executive-level and above-the-line creative work represents an industry built on male-dominated structures and hierarchical systems of work that have long reinforced exclusionary job roles and rankings. From Silicon Valley to Wall Street, the media business to universities, a new wave of equity debates ignited around the gendered barriers keeping women professionals from employment and career advancement across the American workplace. As more women openly shared these experiences, myriad complex—and strikingly similar—stories emerged of ambitious, qualified, and highly skilled female workers hitting the glass ceiling or remaining on the "sticky" entry-level floor.

Employment Data Studies: What They Tell Us and What They Don't

A series of quantitative studies gained traction with journalists, activists, and scholars in the mid- to late 2010s by illustrating how few women held above-the-line positions on feature film projects, whether studio or indie financed. The Geena Davis Institute on Gender in Media; the Media, Diversity, & Social Change Initiative, University of Southern California; and the Center for the Study of Women in Television and Film, San Diego State University, all publish annual reports that evince dismal employment rates for women in financial and creative decision-making roles. First released in 1998, "The Celluloid Ceiling" annual study from UCSD's Martha M. Lauzen highlights that the percentage of all women working as directors, writers, producers, executive producers, editors, and cinematographers on the 250 top-grossing domestic films in 2019 was 20 percent versus the remaining 80 percent of positions held by men. The report breaks the data down by above-the-line and department head positions with women making up 27 percent of producers in contrast to directors (13 percent), writers (19 percent), editors (23 percent), and cinematographers (5 percent).[48] Even with small gains in each category from the previous year, the numbers are simply staggering.

Table 1.1 shows data from this study about the one hundred top-grossing domestic films between 1980 and 2019. A picture emerges over four decades showing the small numbers of female writers, producers, and directors with slight increases as compared to their male counterparts. That the needle barely moved for the handful of women in key creative positions—most notably an increase from one female director in 1980 to twelve in 2019—is the big takeaway for contemporary trade coverage and industry activism when presenting broad, macrolevel employment numbers with little to no other context. The most obvious conclusion is that change in gender parity since the 1980s DGA suit has been very slow.

Table 1.1. Women Employed on the 100 Top-Grossing Films: Domestic Theatrical Box Office

Above-the-line role	1980	1990	2010	2019
Directors	1%	2%	2%	12%
Writers	10%	7%	10%	20%
Producers	9%	19%	20%	26%

Source: Employment data from Lauzen, "The Celluloid Ceiling: Behind-the-Scenes Employment of Women on the Top 100, 250, and 500 Films of 2019," 5.

However, in examining the top one hundred films released domestically from this data set—specifically, the North American markets, United States and Canada—more closely, what does the opacity of box office data not account for? One of the first notable limitations in using box office numbers as a data set is that the list of top-grossing films is limited to American-*distributed* films but not American-*produced* films, specifically, only feature-length films, as previously highlighted by Natalie Wreyford and Shelley Cobb.[49] Because the data sets are based on snapshots of the top-grossing theatrical releases, films produced in other production contexts outside of US commercial feature filmmaking may also be included. In addition to documentaries, which often have a markedly different mode of financing and production, films coming from non-Hollywood national or regional contexts, such as state-supported industries with vastly different funding policies and production cultures, are not distinguished from the Hollywood films in the list.

Another limitation in comparing examples from 2019 of female-directed, -produced, and/or -written films is that the scale of each production and the scope of theatrical release strategy differ greatly. *Captain Marvel* was the top-grossing female-driven film that year, peaking at number five overall. Anna Boden and Ryan Fleck codirected and cowrote the script (along with Geneva Robertson-Dworet and likely additional uncredited writers due to the studio rewrite process discussed in the following chapter). As the first stand-alone female-led installment in Disney's Marvel Cinematic Universe (MCU), the project had an enormous production budget (reportedly $152 million), studio resources, and wide release opening in more than forty-three hundred theaters domestically in March. The next top-grossing female-driven release, ranked at number twenty-nine, was *Hustlers*, the Jennifer Lopez star vehicle directed and written by Lorene Scafaria. Premiering in September, the based-on-a-true-story drama about New York City strippers during the Great Recession had a production budget around $20 million and was distributed in 3,525 theaters by international mini-major STX Entertainment.

While both films proved commercial hits during their opening weekends, using box office rankings as a way to analyze gendered employment overlooks significant differences at each stage of filmmaking for both of these vastly different film projects and the individuals behind them. As Cobb asserts in her analysis about the structuring absences in data studies like "The Celluloid Ceiling": "Neither does the data tell us much, if anything, about who the women are, what films they make and how they navigate an industry that makes little space for them, although some of those stories are being collected and told elsewhere."[50] While some employment data studies increasingly are considering the intersectional factors—race, gender, sexuality, disability—in above-the-line employment disparities, reports like "The Celluloid Ceiling" do not.

Additional studies offer data variations on the lack of women in powerful creative and financial decision-making roles in Hollywood. For example, "Inclusion in the Director's Chair" from USC's Stacy L. Smith, Marc Choueiti, Kevin Yao, Hannah Clark, and Katherine Pieper highlights individual company hiring records from 2007 to 2019 to demonstrate a slow inclusion rate for all six major studios. Of the thirteen hundred top-grossing feature films distributed theatrically during this twelve-year period, Universal Pictures (fifteen female directors) and Warner Bros. (thirteen female directors) ranked highest in equitable gender representation while still illustrating shockingly low inclusivity.[51] While these statistics may show improvements in the number of women directing features ranked in the 250 top-grossing from 8 percent in 2018 to 13 percent in 2019, the long-term impact and sustainability of these institutional increases is not clear, nor is it obvious which filmmakers are benefitting from this increase.[52] Further context is needed to know why, for example, Universal hires more female directors than competitor Disney. These research studies would benefit from further scrutiny of employment numbers for important variables that are largely absent—for example, above-the-line talent, below-the-line workers, production company, production budget, prints and advertising, distributor, and release strategy and date.

Smith et al.'s report also evinces that as one ascends the Hollywood corporate ladder, the employment gap follows. In 2018, very few women occupied the so-called C-suite of chief officer positions for what was at the time the Big Seven (21st Century Fox, NBC Universal, Walt Disney, Sony, Lionsgate-Summit, Time Warner, and Paramount).[53] Of the ninety-five media executives running these entertainment groups in January 2018, 82.1 percent were men and 17.9 percent women, with only four positions held by women of color. Gender inclusivity peaked at the executive vice president, senior vice president, and vice president levels, which were made up of 41.2 percent women.[54]

However, the report's breakdown never moves beyond a big-picture view at the parent company level to offer more granular information about these different roles. As a result, a number of questions arise. How do each corporation's organizational structure and divisional hierarchies come into play? In what company divisions or specific groups are women more likely to rise to the executive level of SVP or VP—television divisions, film, or news? Are women more likely to be appointed to C-suite executive roles in traditionally gendered HR and communication roles compared to the male-dominated chairman or studio president roles, as demonstrated by Disney's organizational chart? Comcast's organizational chart in 2020 also raises questions: What does it mean for Bonnie Hammer to be chair of NBC Universal Content Studios compared to Donna Langley as the chair of Universal Pictures?[55] What if we look beyond the limited view of the major studios toward smaller production companies? How can Christina Oh in an executive role at Brad Pitt's production company, Plan B Entertainment, developing independent projects like *Minari* (2020, dir. Isaac Lee Chung), be understood in contrast to Courtenay Valenti, president of production and development at a major studio like Warner Bros., overseeing franchise installments of *The Lego Movie* (2014–) and *Fantastic Beasts and Where to Find Them* (2016–).[56] In other words, what does it mean to be a development executive at a major film studio in contrast to a small, independent production company? By only looking at the Big Seven, Smith et al.'s report leaves out an entire community of executives working many times outside of, and other times in collaboration with, studio film entertainment divisions. In turn, large, sweeping comparisons using a limited data set offer little insight into gender inequities across Hollywood beyond counting the number of women with executive job titles in the studio food chain.

Circulation and Limitations of Employment Data Studies

Many journalists and activists saw 2015 as a watershed moment, and perhaps a mandate, to launch a strategic push toward equity and inclusivity. Based on these widespread studies tracking employment, journalists increasingly reported on these egregious disparities in trade and popular publications—from Jessica P. Ogilvie with *LA Weekly*'s "How Hollywood Keeps Out the Stories of Women and Girls" to Kate Erbland with *IndieWire*'s "A Female Hollywood Producer Details How Industry Discriminates against Women"—stoking the flames of a slow-burning fire.[57] Rebecca

1.2. Viola Davis accepts her 2015 Emmy Award for Best Lead Actress in *How to Get Away with Murder* (2014–2020). In her speech, she called out the lack of roles for Black women in Hollywood. (Screenshot from 2015 Emmy Awards ceremony via YouTube.)

Keegan, one of a handful of journalists consistently tackling stories about gender equity in front of and behind the camera in Hollywood since the late 2000s, expresses a hopeful view in her *Los Angeles Times* article "Is 2015 the Tipping Point for Women and Minorities in Hollywood?" Keegan asserts: "I'd like to believe that something is different now—the crush of evidence of the industry's inequality is too big, the wrath of social media is too fierce to ignore. The tone and the tenor of the message has changed—at awards dinners and Hollywood luncheons—the topic of inclusion isn't the appetizer, it's the main course."[58]

Whereas Keegan sees a tipping point, I would describe 2015 as the year a new pressure point emerged, specifically on the subject of employment and compensation for women impacted by the increased circulation of these data studies. Public attention increased across various industry spaces as a means of putting pressure on the major Hollywood studios. Pressure came publicly at 2015 awards shows: In Patricia Arquette's Academy Awards acceptance in February, she highlighted the gender wage gap, and in her Emmy win in September, Viola Davis spoke of the difficulties for women of color in entertainment. In calling out the industry's diversity hiring practices, namely the lack thereof, Davis stated: "The only thing that separates women of color from anyone else is opportunity. You cannot win an Emmy for roles that are simply not there."[59] In using the spotlight of award seasons, both actresses leveraged their industry capital in that moment to criticize the stubbornly white male–dominated nature of Hollywood.

A pressure point also came from women filmmakers in less public-accessible spaces. At the Toronto International Film Festival (TIFF) during this period, industry-wide considerations of equity grew and expanded. Each year, the concurrent TIFF Industry Conference programs a panel or two to explore gender parity and inclusivity through a global lens, as discussed in more detail in chapter 4. Panelists include a mix of policymakers, filmmakers, executives, and academics discussing the dismal employment data for women in male-dominated film work worldwide. During a 2015 panel Q&A, an informal discussion about potential solutions emerged. At one point, Australian director Gillian Armstrong stood up in the audience and introduced herself. As the "sole female exception" of the Australian New Wave, Armstrong's debut feature *My Brilliant Career* (1979) premiered to critical acclaim at the Cannes Film Festival. She later made the move to Hollywood with films like Sony's *Little Women* (1994).[60] She passionately recounted experiences as a female director on set and in studio meetings. She described dismissive crew members who slowed progress on set each day to purposefully put the production behind schedule. When she called out the men for their behavior, she was asked if she was on her period. She detailed the challenge of getting the studio to greenlight *Little Women* and praised producer Amy Pascal as an ally. When she declared, "I am a woman and I am a director. This [fight] is about power and a female vision," audience members cheered and stood in applause. Armstrong's response was a striking example of how this swelling gender equity movement grew more visible inside industry events and generated an international dialogue, even if temporary, in these spaces for women.

Perhaps one of the most significant points of pressure resulted from the opening of an investigation by the US Equal Employment Opportunity Commission (EEOC). In May 2015, the American Civil Liberties Union sent letters to the EEOC, the California Department of Fair Employment and Housing, and the Office of Federal Contract Compliance Programs, calling for a federal investigation of the Hollywood studios for their discriminatory hiring practices. Written by Melissa Goodman, director of the LGBTQ, Gender, and Reproductive Justice Project at the ACLU of Southern California, and ACLU senior staff attorney Ariela Migdal, the letter sent shock waves through the film industry. Director Maria Giese instigated the review by the ACLU. In an extensive inquiry, the ACLU interviewed fifty women and reviewed employment data.[61] In its letter, the ACLU cited inequitable employment numbers for women and asked for "an investigation into systemic failure to hire women directors in violation of Title VII at all levels of the film and television industry."[62]

The letter did the job. The EEOC launched its own nearly two-year investigation interviewing women directors, which received extensive press coverage. In 2017, the federal commission concluded its investigation yet would not comment on its findings or release the report. As a result, the EEOC apparently began settlement talks with the major studios—although further information remains sealed, unless a lawsuit is ever filed.[63]

A new wave of public-facing pressure emerged during the 2018 awards season, significantly following the emergence of #MeToo and Time's Up. In the same weekend, Frances McDormand accepted the Independent Spirit Award for Best Female Lead and the Oscar for Best Actress in *Three Billboards Outside Ebbing, Missouri* (2017). In her Academy Awards speech, McDormand asked female nominees in each category to stand in the audience:

> Look around [at these women], ladies and gentlemen, because we all have stories to tell and projects we need financed. Don't talk to us about it at the parties tonight. Invite us into your office in a couple days, or you can come to ours, whatever suits you best, and we'll tell you all about them. I have two words to leave with you tonight, ladies and gentlemen: "inclusion rider."[64]

Significantly, this is the same weekend McDormand met with and struck a deal with Chloé Zhao to direct, write, and produce *Nomadland* (2020), with the actress to star and coproduce. After seeing the 2017 premiere of Zhao's *The Rider* at the Toronto International Film Festival, McDormand approached the director about the nonfiction book she had optioned, *Nomadland: Surviving America in the Twenty-First Century* by Jessica Bruder. McDormand's pivotal Hollywood position as a top-tier award-winning actress who has built a career moving between independent and studio projects paved the way for Zhao to join the $5 million road

1.3. Frances McDormand accepts the Oscar for Best Actress in *Three Billboards Outside Ebbing, Missouri* (2017) at the 2018 Academy Awards. During her speech, McDormand asked all the female nominees in the audience to stand and be acknowledged. (Screenshot from 2018 Academy Awards ceremony via YouTube.)

trip movie as writer, director, and coproducer.[65] This is a significant example of a well-connected and established star-producer creating opportunities for herself and an emerging independent filmmaker.

McDormand leveraged her Oscar speech to garner broad public attention for gender inequity—namely, calling out gatekeepers at major studios and production companies to develop and finance more female-driven stories. In a closing comment that spread wildly in subsequent press coverage, she identified legal contracts as a strategy toward equitable hiring. Matt Warren describes an inclusion rider as a "clause built into contracts of high-profile talent (actors, producers, directors, etc.) that stipulates greater rates of inclusion of underrepresented groups both *in front of* and *behind* the camera. Such groups include women, POCs, LGBTQ people and people with disabilities."[66] In other words, by implementing a rider with employment contracts, a certain A-list above-the-line individual can leverage their position during negotiations to ensure quotas for inclusive hiring with above-the-line and below-the-line roles. In subsequent months, while debates surrounding these riders continued, a handful of top-tier talent—including actors Michael B. Jordan, Regina King, and Captain Marvel herself, Brie Larson—pledged to employ inclusion riders to increase employment for women and people of color.[67]

Stacy L. Smith, director of USC Annenberg's Media, Diversity, & Social

Change Initiative, first advocated for inclusion riders for Hollywood film and television projects in a 2014 *Hollywood Reporter* op-ed. Smith reportedly worked with civil rights attorney Kalpana Kotagal and Annenberg Inclusion Initiative board member Fanshen Cox DiGiovanni to create legal language that later was included in an inclusion rider template. The National Football League's Rooney Rule served as the inspiration. Adopted by the organization in 2003 to address the lack of diversity in the NFL head coaching roster, the Rooney Rule requires every team to interview candidates of color when hiring head coaches and later evolved to include general manager and other staff positions.[68]

However, critical pushback against riders followed McDormand's 2018 speech. In a *New York Times* opinion piece, criminal defense and civil rights lawyer Rebecca Chapman warns that inclusion riders may only offer a "cosmetic fix" during one-off negotiations. This tactic shifts "the burden of equality, essentially requiring that the very parties who the riders are claiming to protect (the marginalized and disempowered—the silenced) do the work of enforcement."[69] What Chapman argues is that professionals of color are too often burdened with monitoring or reporting how well inclusion policies are enforced in ways that their white colleagues are not. Early calls for inclusion riders failed to address the layered nature of intersectional power dynamics in the entertainment industries, where negotiations and collaborations convene industry professionals with varying degrees of industry capital, experience, access, and other complex dynamics involved in negotiating employment that are nearly impossible to fully measure or quantify. Inclusion riders and other rhetoric may directly speak to white men "who in their absence, dominate inequality data," but the burden of employing legal initiatives and employment policy falls on the individuals who need protection the most.[70]

In a similar fashion, Time's Up, along with the USC Annenberg Inclusion Institute, introduced the "4 Percent Challenge" at the 2019 Sundance Film Festival.[71] Named after the data point that only 4 percent of the top one hundred grossing films in the 2010s were directed by women, the campaign asked major studios to pledge to hire one woman director in the next eighteen months. The list of individuals, studios, and production companies that signed the 4 Percent Challenge did so in a public and celebratory way through press releases and social media posts that went viral. Amplified further as a Twitter hashtag, the pledge was signed by Universal, Paramount, and Warner Bros., whereas other studios like Disney

The Growing List of Those Who Took the 4 Percent Challenge

Studios and Production Companies

Amazon Studios
Bad Robot
Legendary Entertainment
Makeready
MGM Studios
Moxie 88
Paramount Pictures, Paramount Animation and Paramount Players
STX Entertainment
Universal Filmed Entertainment Group (Universal Pictures, Focus
Features and Dreamworks Animation)
Warner Bros. Entertainment

1.4. The 4 Percent Challenge posted to the Time's Up website includes a list of film companies that pledged to hire one female director in the following eighteen months. (Screenshot from Time's Up website.)

either released company diversity policies already in place or pointed to upcoming production slates.[72] Shelley Cobb points out: "The commitment for one woman director to be announced before summer 2020 by each studio is at best tokenistic—although a token worth asking for when, in a number of recent years, certain studios have announced an entire year's slate of films with not one woman director in it."[73] Like so many of these initiatives, participants may have benefitted from the immediate social media buzz while also agreeing to a low-stakes commitment that was neither binding nor enforced.

Each of these examples—from brief, live broadcasts to lengthy, closed-door reports—aimed to disrupt the industry status quo and raise awareness of systemic gender inequities. In other words, the goal was to wake Hollywood up. This type of public shaming, or what Miranda J. Banks calls "data shaming," builds on the accelerated, repetitive circulation of employment data from quantitative studies coming from the Davis Institute, USC, UCSD, and other research centers and is then reported by trade and popular press, including headlines from the *Atlantic*'s 2018 "The Brutal Math of Gender Inequality in Hollywood" to the *Los Angeles Times*'

2020 "Female Directors in Hollywood Are Still Underrepresented, but the Gap Is Narrowing."[74] The reports offer easily digestible employment data and visualizations that translate to headlines, trade articles, or even back to scholarly presentations. At each point, filmmakers, journalists, and activists strategically mobilize gender disparity numbers as "bad data" by creating negative public relations with the goal of calling out gatekeepers and industry leaders for their responsibility. The logic is that bad press about an inequitable employment track record will shame the film and television studios, mount seismic pressure, and eventually force changes resulting in new inclusive institutional policies and cultures.

Data shaming works to create temporary pressure points in microlevel meetings and company cultures or through movements and organizations like Time's Up, using social media, press, and industry events to call attention to disparities at different stages of the filmmaking pipeline. However, the mobilization of broad, industry-wide statistics to measure the progress of parity often ends at identifying the problem. In other words, while data shaming may highlight the industry-wide problem of employment disparities, the discursive strategy offers little in the way of tangible solutions. Long-term impacts on hiring practices and employment policies stemming from this industrial strategy remain ambiguous at best without the ability to track any correlation between the accelerated circulation of employment data studies and individual studio hiring practices.

So where does the examination and circulation of data studies leave media industry studies scholars, moving forward? Quantitative reports offer significant contributions for identifying inequities—what Natalie Wreyford and Shelley Cobb assert play "an important part in consciousness raising" for Hollywood and other industries worldwide.[75] However, a broad data-driven approach reproduces an industry-wide view of employment with limited scope and a lack of context for unpacking the complexities of intangible systemic hiring practices, networking, power dynamics, and unique paths to career advancement. Only counting employment numbers, which often combine white women and women of color into the same category, offers a limited understanding of media workers' complex daily experiences working in independent and studio filmmaking. In her work on studio diversity initiatives and employment, Kristen J. Warner argues how counting bodies on screen or in the room to measure progress is not enough. She identifies these efforts toward inclusivity as a "plastic" or superficial view of complex industry dynamics, functioning more to gratify optics than to enact a genuine effort to create effective structural change.[76]

As important as employment studies have been to start mapping an uneven employment climate and contributing to the industry-wide awakening, what I aim to illustrate in a larger analysis of the filmmaking pipeline is that employment alone is not the silver bullet. A quantitative methodology offering macrolevel views of employment practices and inequitable hiring would be better situated in conversation with more in-depth qualitative methods such as discourse analysis, interviews, participant observation, and on-the-ground industry texts. I agree with Wreyford and Cobb, who argue that without personal accounts and industry context, "quantitative data showing varying participation by gender is open to misinterpretations, whether willful or accidental. Numbers on their own run the risk of contributing to neoliberal or postfeminist assumptions of women's disinterest, personal choice, or market preferences, as we have demonstrated."[77] While a qualitative approach serves as the foundation for this project, I place this methodology in conversation with quantitative studies throughout *The Value Gap*. While I incorporate examples of employment or other industry data throughout this book, I take care to frame the necessary industrial context so that these broad data complement and elucidate my on-the-ground analysis.

Measuring power in the entertainment business is more than counting the number of suits in C-suites or the number of women directors in a box office weekend. Power operates in complex tiers through subtle, uneven, and slippery ways—behind closed doors with many different gatekeepers and avenues to amassing and maintaining economic, cultural, and social capital. How can we understand the ways women navigate industry work cultures and production models that historically have left them little room at the table? Gender inequity operates through the intersection of deeply ingrained production cultures, industry myths, and institutional practices that reproduce gendered cultural and economic value that can leave women on the margins. It is important to situate industry-specific employment numbers alongside the complexities and imbrications of individual experiences, examined in the following section, in order to interrogate these historically and systemically rooted structures, practices, and cultures.

The Likability Gap and the Cool Girl Trap

The pressure to fit into the Hollywood boys' club can be intense and falls upon individual shoulders, particularly for emerging creatives still building their production credits and professional networks. Navigating the gender expectations, whether implicitly or explicitly stated, came up often in my conversations with women writers and producers around employment opportunities. Many of the LA-based creatives I followed constantly described selling themselves in order to demonstrate their "fit" for working within studio culture and compatibility with potential studio employers and creative collaborators.[78]

A significant barrier to entry in these tight-knit institutional spaces can come from what psychologists call "in-group bias." In a 2015 article, independent producer Mynette Louie writes openly about this dynamic for a broad audience on *New York Magazine*'s culture site *Vulture*:

> A powerful paradigm in the ego-driven, self-obsessed film industry is key players' desire to seek collaborators who are similar to themselves—not just in terms of taste and perspective but also culture, background, and yes, gender. . . . The "simpático" and "who you know" factors are very strong in the industry, though the people perpetuating them may not be aware that they often end up excluding new and "different" talent.[79]

Biases around "fit" and "likability" filter into hiring across all industries, as has been well documented in studies across psychology, sociology, management studies, and behavioral economics. Casually thrown around, terms like "cultural fit," "good fit," "simpático," and "one of us" are freighted with meaning around assumed shared identity and ideology. What follows are long-term consequences for creating inclusive workplaces across all levels and sectors of filmmaking by impacting women's rates of advancement in male-dominated institutions.

Madeline E. Heilman, Francesca Manzi, and Susanne Braun explain that "lack of fit perceptions are triggered by the perceived mismatch between what women are thought to be like and what people believe it takes to succeed in a male gender-typed occupation."[80] Heilman's scholarly work on gendered stereotypes, which I first encountered when reading Anne

O'Brien's in-depth work on women in media production, is a productive framework.[81] *Descriptive* gender stereotypes make assumptions about how women navigate high-pressure workplace cultures—lack of agency, lack of experience, lack of competence, lack of added value. Industry lore long reinforced biases about female screenwriters' ability to pen or female directors' interest in helming large-scale, expensive, male-driven action projects, as described in the following chapters. In contrast, *prescriptive* gender stereotypes place pressure on women to respond a certain way and adapt to current workplace cultures—what Heilman calls "should nots" for communication style, leadership, self-promotion, negotiation, and expressing emotions. She argues these should nots "include agentic attributes and behaviors associated with men. . . . Thus, women are prohibited from demonstrating the self-assertion, dominance and achievement orientation so celebrated in men." As a result, normative standards place women professionals in a double bind, with entrenched workplace bias setting them up to fail.[82]

Many of the women I interviewed working above the line recalled an awareness, often anxiety, that the "best" strategies for navigating their careers meant conforming to masculine workspaces. The tension between fighting descriptive stereotypes and conforming to prescriptive stereotypes—don't be a nag, don't be a bitch, don't be difficult, don't be too assertive, don't make a mistake, don't act like a man—left many female creatives I interviewed at a crossroads. Damned if you do, damned if you don't.

I first started to think about how film professionals understand and negotiate gender when I interviewed midlevel managers and executives working in Los Angeles and local Hollywood studio offices in Europe and Brazil for my first book, *Localising Hollywood*. Of the significantly few women I did encounter from 2010 to 2015, I usually snuck in a question about their leadership position at a major studio as the only woman in the room. At times, the question was met with resistance, dismissed, or coolly redirected to my research topic.[83] I also heard "I don't think of myself as a woman [insert job title]."[84] In many ways, my calling attention to gender conflicted with their dismissal of or struggle against the descriptive gender stereotypes that inevitably follow a "female vice president" or "female general manager." This refusal to internalize reductive labels about women in the workplace—difficult, sensitive, poor leaders— echoed ubiquitous contemporary postfeminist workplace advice in which the only thing holding women back is themselves. Yet, these responses offer insights into how some female executives manage the day-to-day power dynamics and gendered politics of the studio office.

How gender bias is perceived and addressed sometimes breaks down along generational lines. The women I interviewed in their mid-fifties and older, who began working in the industry in the 1970s or 1980s, often had a different perspective on progress and opportunity. One sixty-something independent producer-director credited her career longevity with "keeping my head down, being better than the men, and not letting gender define me."[85] This response echoed the experiences of other women in her generation who have talked about entering the workforce at the tail end of the women's liberation movement.

In a 2017 *New York Times* profile, former studio head Amy Pascal openly discussed similar survival tactics during her years working in Hollywood's male-dominated studio culture: "You're sitting in a business meeting, and you censor yourself because you don't want the men sitting all around you to think that you are upstaging them. You talk around your point. You find ways to make the men feel good even when they're wrong." After asking Pascal about her experience with sexism, the reporter describes the producer laughing in response: "You can't be a woman in Hollywood and not experience sexism. [The discrimination is] never overt."[86] On the one hand, reading between the lines suggests Pascal loosely acknowledging her experience in a male-dominated C-suite as the highest-ranking female executive at Sony Pictures Entertainment. On the other hand, the *New York Times* profile was one of the first public interviews Pascal gave after leaving Sony. Therefore, these comments should be read as balancing different priorities among reputation management, a professional move back into creative producing, and potentially any legal nondisclosure agreements with Sony upon her departure.

In her 1995 memoir, Lynda Obst recalls lessons learned during her thirty-plus-year career in Hollywood. Obst produced female-driven projects such as *Sleepless in Seattle* (1993), *One Fine Day* (1996), *Hope Floats* (1998), and *How to Lose a Guy in 10 Days* (2003). She describes unnamed peers at the time, which might include studio executives like Dawn Steel or producers like Denise Di Novi or Karen Rosenfelt, as "the first wave of powerful women in the movie industry. . . . Because we are the trailblazers, we are constantly confronting situations with which we are completely unfamiliar. We have neither a reference point as women here nor historical antecedents for the behavior expected of us. We are wearing a gender lens through which everything can become distorted. Let's take it off."[87] In echoing earlier comments from women interviewed about "keeping their head down," both Pascal's public-facing interview and Obst's memoir reflect a theme of survival and coping for their generation's second-wave feminist workplace experiences, particularly as the first wave of women moving into male-dominated creative and decision-making roles in the 1980s.

In addition to stories of pitching, deal making, and producing triumphs and disasters, Obst offers a series of recommendations for women working in Hollywood, ranging from adopting gender neutrality (taking off the "gender lens") to acknowledging perceived flaws of femininity ("winning is not a traditional female instinct" or "male bosses are afraid, often rightly, that our emotional reactions will lead them into bad deals").[88] She offers a "Ten Commandments for Chix in Flix" that includes: Thou Shalt Not Cry at Work, Thou Shalt Subdue Thy Sexuality, Thou Shalt Understand Thine Own Personal Style, Thou Shalt Entertain, Thou Shalt Not Appear Tough.[89]

The memoir's sections outlining advice for women in the 1990s film industry echo a wave of best-selling books released two decades later, and this insider Hollywood advice is steeped in a familiar postfeminist workplace culture that circulates across many industries.[90] Whereas earlier waves of feminism connected gender inequity to larger structural barriers (political, economic, health-care, technological, sociocultural), the postfeminist sensibility looks to "individualism, choice and empowerment" as sites of change for women.[91] In the face of the grim statistics about women in the workplace, an explosion of 2010s workplace guides—written by and aimed at mostly white, affluent women in high-profile positions with financial resources out of reach for the average American worker—call for individual actions to face the internal barriers holding women back. Most notably, in her 2013 book *Lean In: Women, Work, and the Will to Lead*, Facebook's then COO and former Google vice president Sheryl Sandberg offers strategies to overcome imposter syndrome and close the leadership ambition gap by adapting individual habits and behaviors, ranging from interpersonal communication to management styles.[92] By placing the onus on individual female workers to break the barriers holding back career advancement, Sandberg has been widely criticized for promoting a "trickle-down feminism" that glosses over larger systemic barriers like industry-wide discrimination, wage gaps, and intersectional issues of race, sexuality, class, and disability.[93]

I interviewed numerous female writers and producers in their thirties and forties, many of whom were early or midcareer and single, partnered, and/or parents, who negotiated their positionality somewhat differently against the current climate. Women of this age group were quicker to point to structural forces and systemic inequality at the root of Hollywood's gender disparities. The emergence of #MeToo and Time's Up shifted my research process and created a new sense of urgency to these conversations. By 2018, on the surface at least, these movements seemed to empower many of the women I followed in this age group to speak more openly and urgently with me about gender inequities and their own experiences in Hollywood's male-dominated spaces. A white studio screenwriter mused: "We talk about how [women] get into the room, but how do you stay in the room?"[94] To stay in the "room," many female creatives described the work involved in projecting ideal prescriptive gender stereotypes.

At the intersection of race and gender, women of color described additional pressure to overcome systemic discrimination. An established female editor of color working between New York and Los Angeles explained in a 2018 conversation in her office ongoing frustrations about the hurdles for hiring: "[Post-production] is super white and male. But it's like they hire friends of friends, you know what I mean? That's the thing. And I'm like, well, if they're going to hire friends of friends, why don't they hire the female friends that I have? . . . [On one production] I was the only [woman], and person of color, on that whole post crew." Because above-the-line talent both in front of and behind the camera holds the most visibility and public relations optics of all production roles, hiring more diversely across departments is too often treated as an afterthought. What is even more telling about the editor's experience is how the above-the-line A-list creative behind the project built a professional brand on investing in intersectional inclusion. The editor followed up in explaining how the film industry needs to rethink the value in hiring diversely: "This is what I don't want to hire: somebody who reminds me of myself because I already have this perspective. . . . That shows you that you have no curiosity about working with people who are different from you, have a different life experience, that it could maybe add another voice to the conversation."[95] What this editor points to is how the "one of us" mentality marginalizes and devalues white women and women of color. So much of the hiring and collaborating process stems from established networks and who can vouch for you. Therefore, in-group biases and definitions of who fits the job too often end up replicating the same mostly white male teams again and again in production and postproduction.

As Kristen J. Warner argues, Black women experience precarious conditions and systemic inequities in the film industry differently: "Some women have more access to opportunities than other women simply by virtue of their racial identity, and while all women certainly suffer under patriarchal labor regimes, some suffer less and some suffer more."[96] An emerging Black writer-producer stated: "If the door is open to me, I have a responsibility to kick ass and [keep it open]. If I kick ass, the next woman of color gets the opportunity. Start on the micro to change the macro." She proceeded to describe the tightrope she walks to progress in her career because Black women get even fewer chances to succeed and zero chances to fail.[97] The burden is twofold: recognizing the structural barriers that allow so few Black and Brown women to ascend to above-the-line roles while individually navigating largely white workplace cultures and interactions are burdens that weigh heavily on the creatives of color with whom I spoke.

A number of female creatives explained that "learning the rules" and "playing the game" still matter. Some believed that changing individual behaviors or interactions could significantly help advance their careers in hopes of achieving more financial stability and leverage. Anne O'Brien identifies similar workplace expectations in the Irish film and television industries. Women feel pressure to adhere to a tacit notion of "acceptable" femininity when keeping up friendly email communications or taking on care roles for coworkers.[98] While acknowledging a broken system rife with gender inequity and misconduct, many female creatives still steer through individual career trajectories and interpersonal dynamics by projecting acceptable femininity through self-presentation, likability, and self-protection.

One of the first points of scrutiny is physical appearance. The assumptions about a woman's clothing, hair, and body that come to signify her performance in the workplace circulate widely in public discourse. The simple, conservative pantsuit or coordinating blazer and skirt outfit emerged as the standard look in the US corporate workplace in the 1980s. In the case of US political campaigns, women are under intense scrutiny. As a result, the "female political candidate's uniform developed largely as a feminized version of the men's suit, chosen to demonstrate that women could fit into what was a male-dominated world."[99] On the campaign trail, candidates like Hillary Clinton and Alexandria Ocasio-Cortez received harsh criticism about whether their choices of pantsuits or blazers, makeup and jewelry, and hairstyles instilled necessary confidence in their leadership ability in ways that male opponents never would be scrutinized.

Hollywood workplace attire ranges widely from casual (crew on set, writers' rooms) to business (management and executives in corporate settings) to formal (red carpet events, award ceremonies, film festival premieres) based on industry sector, ranking, company culture, or type of event. No matter the context, norms of professional dress, hair, makeup, and other markers of normative cisgender femininity largely persist for many above-the-line female workers. One screenwriter talked extensively about monitoring her self-described "girly girl" appearance in the 2010s after experiences of not being taken seriously. Early in her career, she steered away from normatively feminine clothing (nothing too bright, too frilly, too pink, and no high heels) and carefully monitored her accessories and makeup: "I'm very aware of presentation and how you talk and how you enter a room."[100] Another writer reluctantly told the story of a male boss referring to her simply as "Barbie" in the office for years. What he and other coworkers laughed off as a nickname ultimately shamed the young creative by connotation—all plastic and no substance.

Likability came up in almost all of my conversations. Though not necessarily in industry parlance, the term was often used by female creatives to frame their approach to interacting with bosses and coworkers, whether male or female. A white writer for film and television in her forties routinely worked to establish her likability early in meetings: "I make it very clear from the beginning that I'm going to be easy to work with. I will take your notes. I will be thoughtful. I will be fun. I will not yell at you. . . . I think long-term it's going to serve [women writers] to be that person."[101] She described how brainstorming a story's potential directions and rewrites with executives and producers invited the chance to think on her feet, to showcase herself as the perfect collaborator—one who is "fun," "likable," "flexible," and "easy to work with." While characteristic of most employer/employee power dynamics, much of the filmmaking process involves presenting yourself as an enthusiastic, ideal team player to those who hold financial and creative power within the organizational hierarchy.

A female producer who wrote an article for *The Wrap* under the pseudonym "Ms. Jackson" had never thought of herself as a feminist before working in Hollywood. She blamed herself for the dismissive behavior of male coworkers, wondering if something she did earned their disrespect. So she tried to act like one of guys:

> Instead of flirting with male colleagues, we busted each other's balls. I quickly learned to tune out the usual locker-room chatter that men in this business seem to think is perfectly acceptable in mixed company, rather than chastising, when I felt uncomfortable. But with all the effort to prove I could hang (because I can), and even in situations when I made good points, it seemed that the men I worked with were still reluctant to hear me out.[102]

In the hope of advancing in this culture, the producer began to change parts of her personality to fit in with male coworkers. *The Wrap* is a trade publication with a largely industry-focused audience, and the producer's strategy to publish anonymously there offered a protective platform. She could speak broadly about gender dynamics at an unnamed production company without potential repercussions to her career or backlash that could occur if she went on the record about an employer and coworkers. The 2009 article also reflects a different discursive moment in Hollywood, where gender inequities based on personal accounts of women working in the film industry were not openly discussed in ways that would slowly increase a decade later.

Based on dual experiences as a veteran television writer-producer and media studies scholar writing about television production cultures, Felicia D. Henderson examines how race and gender play out in these industrial spaces through interpersonal dynamics. In discussing the ways in which white women and writers of color adapt to masculine spaces, she contends that "women writers must often let their laughter be heard as a strategy to combat being othered. A female writer who does not laugh along with off-color jokes about penis size may be labeled incapable of being 'one of the guys' and therefore 'not a good fit' with a predominantly male staff."[103] A woman's laughter thus operates as a performative strategy to defuse any potential negative reaction to a sexist or racist joke and assures creative collaborators of their ability to conform and fit within masculine work cultures.

The need for female writers or producers to conspicuously perform that they can "go along to get along" in the office requires shifting into a workplace persona. Such presentation on demand recalls the emergence of the "Cool Girl" in recent popular culture. From a much-quoted passage in Gillian Flynn's best-selling mystery novel and later 2014 Fox feature film, *Gone Girl*, the female narrator, Amy, describes the unrealistic expectations of modern femininity:

> Men always say that as the defining compliment, don't they? She's a cool girl. . . . Cool Girls are above all hot. Hot and understanding. Cool Girls never get angry; they only smile in a chagrined, loving manner and let their men do whatever they want. Go ahead, shit on me, I don't mind, I'm the Cool Girl. Men actually think this girl exists. Maybe they're fooled because so many women are willing to pretend to be this girl.[104]

The Cool Girl is the opposite of the "Difficult Woman" because she is chill and low maintenance, can take a joke and be one of the guys. Whether Scarlett Johansson, Olivia Wilde, or Jennifer Lawrence, Hollywood loves a beautiful (almost always white) Cool Girl personality.[105] She is likable, someone you want to be around. The Cool Girl's desirability comes not only from her physical attractiveness but also from her amiability and adaptability—which ultimately benefits and caters to the men around her. The theme is shape-shifting and tenacious.

Self-protection was another refrain across my interviews. I first met a thirty-something white indie producer, whom I will call "Megan," after a film she produced had premiered at a major festival. One of the first things she will tell you is that she did not go to film school. She worked her way up from an assistant position to crew until breaking into a producing role. She has an impressive number of produced credits for a creative her age. When I met her again at her Los Angeles office months later, she described a phone call with a difficult male executive from earlier that week. She apologized as she admitted she was having a hard time processing it: "I try really hard to never get emotional in my job. I literally this week had to mute a call because I started sobbing. I was just like, 'don't cry, don't cry, don't cry,' and then got back on. Ugh, it is like fucking hard. . . . I also think that's where there's a huge problem—you're not supposed to do that. You're supposed to keep that shield up, but that's so hard."[106] Megan berated herself for letting her guard down. Ultimately, she blamed herself for not managing both the male executive's yelling and her own reaction.

Anne O'Brien asserts that women navigating the male-dominated media industry landscape often internalize systemic gender discrimination: "If they failed to succeed, that failure was their individual responsibility, divorced from broader gendered, social or economic structure. Consequently, women internalized neoliberal forms of self-regulation with the transference of responsibility onto themselves to always adapt and to cope with normative-masculine and neoliberal structures and cultures of work."[107] Postfeminist workplace discourse permeated my conversations, as the women grappled with structural issues, inclusion, precarious employment, and internalized strategies for self-regulation in layered, weighted, and exhausting ways. Like Megan, many recounted similar personal experiences and described ways they adapted their approach, personality, or appearance to get a job or to manage a male-dominated creative team.

Joan C. Williams and Rachel Dempsey identify how this "fix the woman" narrative blames women for their own career problems or setbacks.[108] Structural and systemic barriers outside of an individual's influence are glossed over or downplayed in favor of a postfeminist empowerment narrative of progress through self-discipline and optimization. Alongside gender, the intersection of identities—race, sexuality, class, nationality, disability, religion—complicates the employment gap. Herein lies the paradox of addressing gender equity in the workplace: An impossible tension exists between fixing the individual *and* identifying and dismantling systemic barriers. By focusing on blaming individual workers, industry structures and business cultures remain intact and unchanged. In the case of the film industry, which is largely driven by freelance, precarious jobs on short-term projects, women film workers are given a Sisyphean task. Industry lore steeped in descriptive and prescriptive notions of gender labor only reinforce the status quo. Hearing women's experiences with gaining employment confirmed on a personal level what we already know on a structural level: a major task of female creatives continues to be convincing a room full of mostly straight, cisgender white men not only that a woman's professional experience matters but also that her creative voice and worldview have value.

As the following chapters explore in more detail, when a woman or creative of color does not fit into studio culture or is perceived as not experienced enough, or her female-driven film does not quite seem viable or bankable, too often the blame is laid on her individual ability or creative skill to adapt to the system, and not on the system's inability or, at worst, refusal to make space for her.

Conclusion

Four years after we first began a series of conversations, I asked a white studio screenwriter at the end of 2020 if anything had changed around hiring practices. She responded on a personal level that she was taking more meetings for female-driven projects than at any point in her more than decade-long career. However, on an industry-wide level, "the change is slow [and progress toward gender parity in employment] depends on the studio and the project. . . . A lot of education is happening inside companies [especially since the Black Lives Matter protests in summer 2020] and this knowledge gathering has changed hiring some."[109] She pointed to hiring shortlists and meeting invitations for studio projects that began to include a noticeable increase in women and people of color. We also talked about how companies like WarnerMedia (prior to the 2021 Warner Bros. Discovery merger and rebranding) had begun gathering internal employment data and releasing their own annual *Equity & Inclusion Report* in 2019. This was likely in response to the external quantitative studies discussed in this chapter that had come to drive industry discourse around gender equity in preceding years. This type of corporate report offers a new level of transparency on inclusive hiring practices, particularly as it breaks down employment percentages by race and gender. However, a colorful, celebratory layout featuring personal anecdotes from employees as "changemakers" and describing WarnerMedia (now Warner Bros. Discovery) as "investing in future talent" reads more for optics as a reactionary public relations campaign.

I heard similar reflections from many female creatives I followed at the start of the new decade. If trade headlines or data studies like then WarnerMedia's report offer any early insights, the number of white women and women of color hired in above-the-line studio roles anecdotally appeared to be slowly increasing. Significant pressure points around gender disparities and employment in the film industry emerged in the mid- to late 2010s, yet as I argue in this chapter, meaningful structural change in Hollywood needs to move beyond project-by-project thinking and instead make strategic and collaborative industry-wide efforts over a period of time. The evidence demands further inquiry, since it is too early to draw conclusions from small wins scattered across the filmmaking landscape.

In the meantime, the response to the employment issue from media parent companies and their major film divisions still proves reactionary, inconsistent, and at times contradictory. As part of a growing wave of pressure points around employment, Disney came under increased scrutiny in the late 2010s for not hiring women to helm flagship franchise projects after the acquisition of divisions like Lucasfilm and Marvel. By early 2019, then-CEO Bob Iger responded to the criticism about the Mouse House's low track record of female studio directors hired by citing that 40 percent of the upcoming film slate would be helmed by women, including *Captain Marvel* (2019, dir. Anna Boden and Ryan Fleck), *Frozen II* (2019, dir. Chris Buck and Jennifer Lee), *Mulan* (2020, dir. Niki Caro), *Black Widow* (2021, dir. Cate Shortland), and *Eternals* (2021, dir. Chloé Zhao). While hiring more female directors to helm blockbuster franchise installments can be positioned in the current industrial context as a meaningful public-facing gesture toward fixing inequitable studio practices, as discussed in later chapters, the win is a short-term fix that does little to address broader long-term corporate cultures and power structures in place.

During this period, a series of hirings and firings at the executive level of Disney-owned film divisions tells a more complicated story. Chief Creative Officer of Disney Animation and Pixar John Lasseter left at the end of 2018 after a history of sexual misconduct and harassment emerged—what the *Hollywood Reporter* described as "a pattern of alleged misconduct."[110] Considering the 2017–2018 timing, Lasseter's forced exit was undoubtably a result of the early #MeToo momentum, yet industry coverage at times downplayed the revelations as Disney returned to business as usual. Disney did not comment publicly on the allegations but instead praised Lasseter's "remarkable tenure" and contribution to the development of CGI animation.[111] Lasseter in an open letter called his behavior "missteps" whereas trade coverage from *Variety* described the Disney executive as a "liability" and "leaving the company under a cloud."[112] With her promotion to replace Lasseter, Jennifer Lee, the cowriter of *Wreck-It Ralph* (2012) and codirector of *Frozen* (2013) and *Frozen II* (2019), became the first woman to run Disney Animation Studios. In a similar situation the following year, Kevin Tsujihara resigned from his post as chair and CEO of Warner Bros. under allegations of sexual misconduct. Ann Sarnoff replaced Tsujihara to become the first woman to head Warner Bros. in another case of a "ceiling-breaking" promotion intended to facilitate the corporate transition and clean up after a male executive's scandalous departure.[113] However, this executive tenure was short-lived and the company announced Sarnoff's resignation in April 2022. New CEO David Zaslav made major organizational and leadership changes within the newly merged Warner Bros. Discovery. As Lucas Shaw reported in *Bloomberg* in July 2022, "gender and racial diversity, while a factor, would not be a top priority" for Zaslav and "his methods have resulted in a notable amount of homogeneity at the top of the new media giant."[114]

Disney acquired 21st Century Fox entertainment group from previous owner NewsCorp in 2019. The acquisition not only brought new film divisions Twentieth Century Fox, Fox 2000, and Fox Searchlight into the Disney fold but also, as one headline highlighted, the "Disney-Fox Deal Will Bring 7 Women Execs to the All-Male 'Mouse House.'"[115] However, in addition to dropping Fox from the name of each unit, every female executive running one of the newly Disney-owned film studios would be pushed out in the next few years. Between 2018 and 2021, a succession of female executives were asked to "step down," including 20th Century Fox CEO and chairperson Stacey Snider; president of Fox 2000 Elizabeth Gabler; and longtime head of Searchlight Pictures Nancy Utley, along with her cochair Stephen Gilula.[116] While changes in leadership are not unusual after a big acquisition or merger with a competitor in the media industries, the firing of notable female executives is striking in an industrial context, as Disney celebrated their own efforts to increase gender parity in the director's chair. The parent company's priorities around organizational restructuring resulted in a dramatic decline in women executives, whereas by 2021, men occupied nearly every C-suite and president of production position at Disney.

At the same time, Disney faced lawsuits regarding inequitable pay. In 2019, a group of ten former and current female Disney executives signed on to a class action lawsuit citing pay discrimination and pay secrecy violating California labor laws. Executives in the case report "rampant gender pay discrimination" where male colleagues made significantly higher starting pay and also moved, or skipped steps, along a promotional ladder faster than female peers.[117] Even as the case worked through the pre-trial information-gathering phase in spring 2021, the suit points to a significant disconnect between the conglomerate-owned major studios' public-facing responses to external pressure for more equitable hiring practices and the deeply ingrained internal corporate cultures, priorities, and hierarchies that continued to impact women working at different executive and management levels of Disney and its competitors.

CHAPTER 2

Script Market to Pitch Meetings (Development Gap)

Every year, the *Hollywood Reporter* (*THR*) organizes a series of roundtables featuring A-list and up-and-coming Hollywood talent that circulates widely across social media and digital platforms. Conversations convene with a small group of actors, directors, writers, cinematographers, or editors invited to reflect on the state of the industry and their respective creative fields. A fall 2018 screenwriters' panel included Paul Schrader, John Krasinski, Bo Burnham, Peter Farrelly, Eric Roth, and Tamara Jenkins. As a conventional conversation about the craft of screenwriting, the exchange covered villains, the cultural zeitgeist, bad scripts, and advice for writers. But, with only one woman on the panel, and no writers of color, a business-as-usual framework threw into relief the glaring lack of diversity in the wake of the #MeToo and Time's Up movements. Even as *THR* began to diversify for subsequent roundtables the following year, a long line of past panels routinely featured white men.[1] In an effort to create space for celebrating industry accomplishments behind the camera, *THR* visibly reinforced who actually gets a seat at Hollywood's power table to tell their story.

Elizabeth Martin describes her line of work, screenwriting, as "one of the least likely jobs ever. Only three hundred people a year get into the Writers Guild. You are five times more likely to become a major league baseball player in any given year."[2] For women and writers of color, the odds are even smaller and barriers to entry even more formidable. Women writers received credit on 19 percent of the 250 top-grossing domestic studio films in 2019 according to "The Celluloid Ceiling" study. Even when noting the numerous variables unaccounted for in such a range of feature films—particularly the lack of context for an intersectional range of players in front of and behind the camera, size of production budgets, and scope of theatrical releases—this small percentage from the data set equals roughly forty-seven scripts penned by women of the 250 top-grossing projects that year.[3]

Screenwriting is a tough business to break into—and an even harder one with which to build a sustainable career with a steady income. A key objective of this chapter is to explore the practices and cultures of filmmaking at its earliest stages of development primarily through the experiences of women writers and producers. Even as the emerging #MeToo and Time's Up movements brought public-facing pressure for gender equity and safe, inclusive workspaces in the film industry by the late 2010s, the major film studios' internal dynamics have in many ways remained slow to change. The development process can be slow, and any incremental improvements to the filmmaking pipeline in the earliest stages take time. Meanwhile, deeply ingrained gendered logic around the value and viability of female-driven films continued to shape the trajectory for women who originated and championed projects in the earliest stages during this period.

Development remains an understudied area of media industries work and by all means warrants further examination. The practice and ritual for developing a film project from concept to script highlight the immense work—and uncertainty—involved in gaining access to and successfully working within the Hollywood studio system. Industry lore—what Timothy Havens describes as "the conventional knowledge among industry insiders about what kinds of media culture are and are not possible"—shapes each stage of the development process.[4] Lore reinforces gendered logic that the film projects of female storytellers are too small. By focusing on three particular examples of lore—what stories women cannot sell, what stories they cannot tell, what stories they can tell—the development phase reflects the endless burden for women of proving their value in the creative workplace. Drawn from the experiences of writers and producers I interviewed, their perceptions illuminate the gendered power dynamics at play at the negotiating table.

Grounded in industry interviews, historical and contemporary trade and popular press coverage, and theatrical box office data, this chapter seeks to locate and examine key structural barriers to getting female-driven projects made at different points of development—script market, first-look deals, pitch meetings, writer's pay, rewrite jobs, and script notes. For the small percentage of women who do get into the room to pitch and sell film projects, what type of stories do they want to tell versus what kind of stories can they sell? How can we understand the struggle to sell female-driven films to industry gatekeepers and the work required to navigate and overcome this development gap?

The Development Process

A town full of dreamers, storytellers, and speculators, Hollywood loves to talk about itself. From *Singing in the Rain* (1952), following the tumultuous transition from silent to sound technology, to the intimate view of pitch meetings and casting calls in *The Player* (1992) and *La La Land* (2016), filmmakers have had a long tradition of turning the camera around to observe insider cultures and behind-the-scenes idiosyncrasies of the movie business. Stories about industry inner workings circulate widely beyond the scope of the soundstage and studio lot. From boardrooms to dinner parties, industry discourse moving inside professional circles and across institutional spaces reflects the desire to make sense of the complex practices and processes of a constantly evolving business. An axiomatic sensibility—"this is how things work"—is pervasive in the film industry, especially around the process of developing, pitching, and financing features.

Getting a feature film made involves years of selling your story again and again at every stage: the earliest rough concept to collaborators, the pitch to studio executives for financing, the marketing to target audiences. From development to greenlight, filmmaking, according to Janet Wasko, is a "project enterprise" involving an assignment or an unsolicited speculative script (typically beginning with a writer and/or producer), pitch meetings with development executives at a production company or major studio, script notes and rewrites, packaging (working with talent agencies to hire above-the-line roles such as the director and/or stars, if not already attached), and budget and financing. After receiving the official greenlight from a studio, a project moves into the production phase.[5]

Film projects rarely follow the same path, and only a small portion of scripts ever make it past the greenlight to move into production. As a so-called enterprise, development encompasses a number of key industry players in this critical phase of the filmmaking process:

- The creative producer may acquire the rights to a book, article, or other property, known as optioning, to be developed into a script with a writer and/or director involved.
- The screenwriter may work alone or with a producer and/or director on writing a treatment or speculative script.
- Agents and managers representing the writer or director send out the script to a development executive at production companies and/or film studios to secure a pitch meeting.
- Development executives and their teams review a vast array of materials to assess potential for a film project. The process might result in developing a concept or optioning a property in-house and hiring a writer to pen and polish the commissioned script. Alternatively, the development team reviews speculative scripts submitted for potential purchase and develop with the writer and/or producer.

Development executives serve as important gatekeepers and taste-makers for identifying, recommending, and shepherding potential new film projects inside their company. Both smaller production companies (for example, Forest Whitaker and Nina Yang Bongiovi's Significant Productions, Brad Pitt's Plan B Entertainment, Margot Robbie's Lucky-Chap Entertainment) and smaller to large film studios (for example, A24, Lionsgate, Warner Bros.) have development executives. This type of creative executive at a production company oversees both acquiring material and then the process of setting up a project in development to be made at a studio or network. In contrast, development executives at a traditional film studio typically acquire projects to coproduce with a production company and/or to distribute.

Specific industry-wide practices and studio cultures reveal deeply ingrained rituals and narratives about the process of filmmaking, particularly the complexities of development. Timothy Havens categorizes this type of industrial discourse as industry lore, "a catch-all term that refers to any *interpretation* among industry insiders of the material, social, or historical realities that the media industries face."[6] Building upon Michel Foucault's critical work on the ways that power produces social realities,

Havens looks at the conditions created by powerful transnational media conglomerates shaping how African American television programs are produced and circulated, specifically how long-held industry discourse that "Black television doesn't travel" globally has shaped programming decision making domestically. He argues, "The power of the cultural industries to produce reality operates on both popular and institutional levels, through distinct yet interwoven discursive practices."[7] Discourses about the viability of media function as a "regime of truth," driving decision making by powerful institutional players. Industry logic that determines a film project's value and viability operates as taken-for-granted knowledge among industry professionals and communities, who often benefit from these industry "truths." In turn, industry knowledge proves to be slippery and harder to identify.

On a broad level, lore serves as a productive conceptual lens for identifying and mapping widely held industry myths about female-driven films. On a more interpersonal level, and based on her work examining the television writer's room, Felicia D. Henderson offers insights into a process she calls "situational authorship," providing an illuminating lens through which to consider the collaborative writing and collective decision-making process that happens behind closed doors. Many writers I interviewed often work and move between both spaces, sometimes simultaneously developing different television and film projects. While the development and writing stages for television and film are distinct due to industry-specific business models, practices, and cultures, both require a form of "situational" collaboration, incubation, negotiation, and gatekeeping processes with entrenched gendered and racialized dynamics. Henderson contends that "in this space, ideas are negotiated, consensus is formed, and issues of gender, race, and class identities play out and complicate the on-screen narratives that eventually air on network and cable television."[8]

In a parallel to the collaborative culture of the writers' room, pitch meetings and the larger development process between above-the-line creatives and development executives unfold to reveal the complex ways that creative consensus and decision making as well as value play out in interpersonal dynamics for marginalized groups. The multifaceted work that women writers and producers must undertake requires navigating and tackling biases that limit female-driven projects and impact the creative exchange of ideas. Patterns began to emerge—stories women cannot tell and stories women can tell. The most common response to a female-focused pitch—indeed, one that every single creative reported hearing—is that women's stories are too small. As one seasoned female producer recounted: "I've heard those words spoken to me: 'She has no value.' Because when you're putting a movie together, as I've done many times. . . . I'm always trying to put women's stories on film. And I swear to God, time and time again, women have no value [in the eyes of executives]."[9] Perceptions of negligibility translate into an inability to open a global box office weekend or appeal to a more general, less targeted (read: white male) audience.[10] This powerful belief has reinforced twenty-first-century industry practices, devaluing and presenting obstacles for media produced about and by marginalized groups. As the following examples demonstrate, gendered lore throughout the entire development process discounts female-driven projects and reinforces an inequitable system built by and benefitting the interests of Hollywood's most powerful gatekeepers—white men.

What Can't She Sell? (Proof of Concept)

It should be no surprise that a gender gap persists in the development process. Female writers are not equally compensated, given access to writing jobs for male-driven projects, or offered development deals at the same rates as their male peers. Over time, these gaps widen and result in barriers to developing a long-term career.[11] This section considers the earliest stages of development, including the script market, development deals, pitch meetings, and pay quotes to highlight how female creatives must navigate these gaps.

The Script Market and Development Deals

For feature films, writers, producers, directors, and crew are typically hired on a project-by-project basis. Due to the systematic breakdown of Hollywood's assembly-line model and contract system, production work largely shifted to freelance employment by the second half of the twentieth century. The screenwriter became—and remains—a hired gun. As a result, a "write first, sell later" mentality has come to shape Hollywood screenwriting work and the labor market.[12] Developing a "spec" (speculative) script—unsolicited, original screenplay—demands frontloaded creative work and rests heavily on the shoulders of too often uncompensated writers who may never see a paycheck for their efforts. Furthermore, selling a spec script to a studio by no means guarantees the project will ever move into production. Accurate numbers for how many scripts are bought versus how many of these are produced are not available. Most writers and producers I spoke to describe the script market as a system where risk falls hardest on precarious individuals without a proven track record who are essentially gambling their careers with the odds of winning the lottery.

For more than half a century, the script market has historically benefitted emerging and established white male writers over women and writers of color. The rise of the big-paycheck script sales began in the 1960s, when William Goldman reportedly sold his original script *Butch Cassidy and the Sundance Kid* (1969) for $400,000, signaling what Margaret Heidenry calls the beginning of the modern spec market.[13] The mid-1980s into the 1990s witnessed an unprecedented spec market boom. Reported as major frontline news in weekly trade publications, bidding wars broke out among competing studios to buy the next big script, and this drove script prices higher than ever before for the most desirable properties of the moment. Examples include Joe Eszterhas earning $3 million for *Basic Instinct* (1992) and Shane Black receiving $1.75 million for *The Last Boy Scout* (1991).

Women writers did not benefit in the same ways as their male peers. In fact, at the height of the spec market, studios purchased close to two hundred spec scripts a year—on average, fewer than 14 percent were written by women.[14] After a bidding war in 1990, Kathy McWorter sold *The Cheese Stands Alone*, a romantic comedy script. Paramount Pictures paid her $1 million for the screenplay, with McWorter reportedly earning the highest fee ever paid to a female screenwriter at the time. After the widely reported sale, the film never left development hell. McWorter would sell seven screenplays over the next decade for fees in the high six figures; almost all of them were shelved and never made. Only her script for *The War* (1994) was produced and released by Universal Pictures.[15] While McWorter successfully sold multiple scripts, in a town where career longevity and reputation are built on produced credits, lucrative spec deals did not lead to a sustainable screenwriting career.

By the 2000s and 2010s, the changing industrial climate made it even harder for female-driven script sales, contributing to the stagnant number of women writing, directing, and producing top-grossing studio projects. A new wave of conglomeration resulted in big telecommunications parent companies consolidating the major film studios into their fold.

Comcast acquired all shares of NBC Universal in 2013. AT&T announced the purchase of Time Warner in 2016. After completing the deal in 2018, the telecom parent company spun off the newly reorganized and renamed WarnerMedia to merge with Discovery only a few years later at a major loss of $40 billion. Between 2009 and 2019, Disney undertook a strategic buying spree that included Marvel Entertainment, Lucasfilm, and 21st Century Fox. Major film divisions drastically scaled back development funds for spec scripts while reducing annual production slates to produce bigger-budget projects ranging from $100 million to more than $250 million.

The major studios began to release fewer films, averaging twelve to fifteen for each division per year. The films they did release consumed the lion's share of their resources with ever more rewrites, more reshoots, and more expensive marketing campaigns. Studio priorities shifted to the acquisition and expansion of lucrative intellectual property, like Star Wars, Marvel, and DC Comics, to mitigate the risk of massive investments in producing, distributing, and marketing these global event pictures. Such action-adventure or sci-fi blockbusters are intended to appeal to everybody (family-oriented, broad audiences) everywhere (global, day-and-date release) and extend across conglomerate divisions and platforms through television series, video games, soundtracks, merchandise, and so forth. What became clear in the 2010s—for industry gatekeepers and studio decision makers—was that the most valuable scripts shifted to big-budget action films reserved as star vehicles for a handful of highly paid male creative teams and stars, leaving very few opportunities for women in front of or behind the camera.

At the same time, the decline of the midbudget production left emerging and established screenwriters with fewer opportunities to pitch, sell, and develop original scripts.[16] Miranda J. Banks describes the contemporary studio climate: "Anxious executives are increasingly unwilling to take a risk and there is a lack of support of rising talent. . . . With no incentive for lower-level executives to buy scripts, only fear of accountability for a poor decision, few at the top are willing to take the risk."[17] As a result, the major studios stopped putting as many resources behind original midbudget projects for theatrical release, which Brooks Barnes describes somewhat dismissively as "mostly dramas and comedies from second-tier directors, cost[ing] $20 million to $40 million."[18] Midbudget projects long provided the few women and filmmakers of color a break into studio writing and/or directing work through adult-targeted dramas, comedies, and romantic comedies. Barnes's labeling midbudget directors as "second-tier" starkly underscores the film industry's production model hierarchy and how the studios discounted women and directors of color, their projects, and their audiences compared to the prized blockbuster model.

The first wave of (almost exclusively white) female directors in the 1980s and 1990s—including Gillian Armstrong, Kathryn Bigelow, Jane Campion, Martha Coolidge, Nora Ephron, Amy Heckerling, Penny Marshall, Susan Seidelman, Penelope Spheeris, and Betty Thomas—gained studio access and built their careers on primarily midrange, and largely female-driven, features. After her debut feature, *Smithereens* (1982), became the first US independent film to premiere in competition at the Cannes Film Festival, Susan Seidelman directed a succession of female-star vehicles, including *Desperately Seeking Susan* (1985) with Rosanna Arquette and Madonna and *She-Devil* (1989) with Meryl Streep and Roseanne Barr. In a 2014 interview published in *Flavorwire*, Seidelman discussed how the "death" of midbudget movies impacted her career:

> You could make movies in the ten-to-20-million-dollar budget range. . . . They didn't have to be huge blockbusters. They could be more adult-oriented, they didn't have to appeal to absolutely everyone in the world, and if it's good work then the studio was happy with making a good profit, but it was a different model. . . . And I think over the years, what happened is that things have gotten really polarized. . . . You have to make a billion dollars, right?. . . . They have to appeal to every demographic in every part of the world, so to make a $20 million movie that makes $60 million, why put their money there?[19]

The director struggled to make another female-driven studio feature after *She-Devil* and transitioned into television by the mid-1990s. Seidelman returned to independent film the following decade, but, as Christina Lane contends, "by the first decade of the twenty-first century, many of these indie women, now in their forties, fifties, or sixties, were not only 'too old' in the eyes of the ageist gatekeepers within Indiewood and Hollywood, but 'yesterday's news.'" Seidelman, who decades before had made the leap from indie to studio, navigated this period by employing what Lane describes as "DIY ethos" and "micro-strategies" for funding and releasing smaller-scale, female-driven projects like *Musical Chairs* (2011) and *The Hot Flashes* (2013).[20] Studio gatekeepers ignoring an entire generation of female filmmakers perhaps speaks to Hollywood's ageist brand of sexism. Seidelman and many of her peers became increasingly open and critical in public-facing interviews during the 2010s by speaking out against gender disparities through their own experiences. When shut out from directing studio features, Seidelman and contemporaries like Amy Heckerling and Martha Coolidge found work directing episodes of television series, a common running theme for female directors navigating inequitable hiring practices at various points in their filmmaking careers.

By the late 2010s, shifting studio priorities in a tumultuous moment of conglomeration and consolidation impacted entire studio divisions dedicated to developing midrange adult-oriented fare. The 2019 finalization of Disney's acquisition of 21st Century Fox led to major organizational and leadership changes. Disney dropped the name "Fox" from various holdings such as 20th Century Fox, Fox Searchlight Pictures, and 20th Century Fox Television. The new parent company unexpectedly shuttered Fox 2000, a twenty-five-year-old division specializing in modestly budgeted films largely targeted at female audiences.[21] Led by Elizabeth Gabler (from 1999 to 2019) and her team of five female executives, the Fox production unit was known for dramas and literary adaptations like *The Devil Wears Prada* (2006), *Life of Pi* (2012), *The Fault in Our Stars* (2014), and *Hidden Figures* (2016). Fox 2000 filled a gap between 20th Century Fox's big-budget tentpoles—the X-Men franchise (2000–2019), the *Planet of the Apes* reboot (2011–), *The Greatest Showman* (2017)—and Fox Searchlight's (later renamed Searchlight) smaller-scale, boutique fare—*Can You Ever Forgive Me?* (2018), *Battle of the Sexes* (2017), and *Wild* (2014). Journalist Nicole Sperling predicted from the unit's closing that "the sort of movies Fox 2000 trades in will wind up being the largest casualty: high-minded adaptations that now seem obvious in their success, but were risks to get made. They're movies that feature no capes, no toys, and no amusement park tie-ins."[22]

Actor-turned-producer-director Elizabeth Banks, in a 2019 interview with journalist Kim Masters, mourned the decline of the adult-oriented genres like the romantic comedy around the time she began working in Hollywood: "I grew up on rom-coms. . . . I thought I was well suited to rom-coms and I would have loved to play a romantic lead in a comedy movie and that has only happened to me once. . . . They sort of stopped making them."[23] Dissatisfied with the roles she was offered and wanting to still work on commercial projects, Banks made a rare move for on-screen talent to working behind the camera as a producer and director, helming modestly budgeted commercial franchise films like Universal's $29 million *Pitch Perfect 2* (2015) and Sony's $38 million *Charlie's Angels* (2019). Trade coverage like this Masters's interview or the *Hollywood Reporter* profile of Brownstone Productions, which Banks runs with her husband Max Handelman, likely helped to reframe her move to behind the camera.[24] Yet, the projects Banks directed reflect the risk aversion of the period in repurposing proven intellectual properties like *Charlie's Angels* or the development of a new directorial project announced in 2019, *The Invisible Woman*, as part of a slate of "filmmaker-driven projects based on the [Universal] monsters' legacies."[25]

Another studio practice in the film development process is the first-look deal between studios and producers. A first-look contract offers producers and their companies overhead and development funds for a fixed period. In exchange, a major studio has exclusive first access to projects and scripts in development before producers can go to competing studios. As described by *Variety*, these "pacts" are a "gold standard in Hollywood" and have long allowed studios to foster relationships with A-list producers and get first pick of new projects.[26] First-look deals peaked around the same time as the 1990s spec boom. Since the early 2000s, the major studios have gradually cut down by more than 40 percent on offering these pacts, opting instead to significantly decrease development spending and hire producers on a project-by-project basis. For perspective, in 1998, the major studios oversaw a total of 302 first-look deals with producing teams; in 2019, *Variety* reported only 105 ongoing deals.[27]

Not surprisingly, the overall decline in first-look deals impacted female producers the most. As illustrated in table 2.1, the number of female producers with deals dropped between 2003 and 2019—from fifty-four companies (or about 24 percent of the total) to seventeen companies (or 16 percent of the total). As far as the pacts reported in *Variety* since the mid-2010s, Universal and Warner Bros. led the industry in number of deals with female-led production companies, nine and three in 2019, respectively, compared to Sony, with one, and Paramount, with two. Disney and Fox together only had four pacts with female producers. Universal

Table 2.1. Studio First-Look Deals with Women Producers Attached (2003–2019)

Year	Number of Total First-Looks	Number of First-Looks: Female Producers	% of First-Looks: Female Producers
2003	225	54	24
2004	240	49	20.4
*2005	-	-	-
*2006	-	-	-
*2007	-	-	-
2008	180	32	17.7
2009	191	29	15.1
2010	159	21	13.2
2011	171	27	15.7
2012	176	25	14.2
2013	148	21	14.1
2014	154	18	11.6
2015	155	21	13.5
2016	151	22	14.5
2017	147	20	13.6
*2018	-	-	-
2019	105	17	16.1

*Data unavailable for 2005–2007 and 2018.
Source: Data compiled from *Variety*, "Facts on Pacts" annual report (2003–2017), and *The Hollywood Reporter* (2019).

and Warner Bros. have gradually increased their commitment to female-driven projects in an institution-wide effort. However, the numbers were still abysmal by the end of the decade. In contrast, male producers held the majority of these pacts in 2019: Disney had five; 20th Century/formerly 20th Century Fox, nineteen; Paramount, nineteen; Sony, seven; Universal, eighteen; and Warner Bros., including New Line Cinema, twenty. While the major film divisions negotiated development deals with A-list actors such as Ryan Reynolds at Fox or Leonardo DiCaprio at Paramount, the majority of first-look deals at this point were with established male writer-directors or producers.[28]

Between 2015 and 2019, pacts involving women producers with significant leadership roles or helming production units were largely made up of A-list actresses with their own companies (Eva Longoria/UnbeliEV-Able Entertainment, Charlize Theron/Denver and Delilah Productions, Margot Robbie/LuckyChap Entertainment), husband-and-wife teams (Elizabeth Banks and Max Handelman/Brownstone Productions, Zack Snyder and Deborah Snyder/Cruel and Unusual Films, Robert Downey Jr. and Susan Downey/Team Downey), and longtime established female producers (Mary Parent/Disruption Ent., Karen Rosenfelt/Sunswept Entertainment, Denise Di Novi/Di Novi Pictures, Allison Shearmur/Allison Shearmur Productions, Amy Pascal/Pascal Pictures, Sue Kroll/Kroll & Co. Entertainment).[29] For example, Banks and Handelman negotiated the multiple-picture deal with Universal Pictures after leveraging the surprising box office success of the first two *Pitch Perfect* movies in the modestly budgeted franchise, which the pair coproduced. Parent, Shearmur, Pascal, and Kroll spent years as studio executives before exiting and transitioning into producing deals. In other words, the women who do manage to acquire and/or maintain first-look deals with major studios remain deeply rooted in the studio system.

The transition of Banks, Robbie, Longoria, and Theron from in front of the camera to behind the camera, developing and producing female-driven commercial projects, is not an unusual strategy for navigating male-driven studio cultures. For example, Emily Carman argues how in the 1930s, female stars like Carole Lombard, Constance Bennett, and Claudette Colbert wielded a level of control over their careers as "part of an overlooked but significant trend of female independent stardom."[30] Silent film star-turned-studio executive and producer Mary Pickford held unprecedented power by the 1930s as a founding partner and vice president of United Artists.[31] Ida Lupino also made an exceptional transition from in front of to behind the camera as a writer-director working in the 1950s, whereas stars like Kim Novak and Marilyn Monroe launched their own production companies later in that decade.

With studio development deals in decline by the mid-2010s, A-list actresses like Jessica Chastain and Reese Witherspoon leveraged their industry capital and track records to launch production companies and push for female-driven projects through other avenues. Chastain, who started the all-female-led production company Freckle Films in 2016, has spoken widely in trade interviews and industry events about the ingrained gender inequities in the film industry in recent years. As a member of the Cannes Film Festival jury in 2017, she spoke critically at a jury press conference about gender disparities in the film industry:

> This is the first time I've watched twenty films in ten days, and I love movies. And the one thing I really took away from this experience is how the world views women from the female characters that I saw represented. It was quite disturbing to me, to be honest—there are some exceptions. . . . For the most part, I was surprised with the representation of female characters on-screen in these films. And I do hope when we include more female storytellers we will have more of the women I recognize in my day-to-day life. Ones that are proactive, have their own agency, and don't just react to men around them.[32]

The following year, Chastain and Freckle Films held a presentation for distributors to sell rights to the $75 million female-driven spy project *The 355* (2022) at the Cannes Marché du Film with attached lead actresses Lupita Nyong'o, Penélope Cruz, Marion Cotillard (later replaced by Diane Kruger), and Fan Bingbing in attendance. After widely publicized offers and negotiations, Universal Pictures secured the North American rights for $20 million.[33]

Witherspoon's most recent production company initiative, Hello Sunshine, launched in 2016 to produce female-driven media, including feature films *Where the Crawdads Sing* (dir. Olivia Newman, 2022) and *Your Place or Mine* (dir. Aline Brosh McKenna, 2022), as well as the television series HBO's *Big Little Lies* (2017–2019), Hulu's *Little Fires Everywhere* (2020), Apple TV+'s *Truth Be Told* (2019–) and *The Morning Show* (2019–), and Amazon Prime's *Daisy Jones & The Six* (2022). After a rapid succession of critically acclaimed projects, Hello Sunshine made headline news when the company sold for $900 million to a media company–backed private equity firm, Blackstone Group, in summer 2021.[34] On the one hand, Hello Sunshine notably blurs the line between film and television as well as traditional studios and streamers, which is increasingly a strategy for female-led production companies. For example, Regina King's Royal Ties Productions, Jennifer Lopez's Nuyorican Productions, and Jennifer Garner's Vandalia Films all have signed first-look deals with Netflix. Both Chastain's and Witherspoon's companies, on the other hand, can largely

2.1. Jessica Chastain participates in the 2017 Cannes Film Festival jury press conference after the awards ceremony. The actress-producer responds to a question about gender parity and the representation of women in the festival program. (Screenshot from TV Festival de Cannes 2017 "Post Palmares Press Conference" via YouTube.)

navigate these lucrative production and distribution deals based on the women's status as two bankable, A-list, white female stars with longevity. They have built their careers on the inside of the major studios in ways many women I spoke to, and most women of color, cannot.

One independent producer working in the industry for close to fifteen years pointed to the increasing gap in sustainability that begins with disparities in development deals: "I don't have an overhead deal. I don't have anybody invested in keeping me in the game besides myself. I don't know if it would be different if I were a guy to have another man look at me and be like 'I see myself in this scrappy young thing, and now I'm going to help you figure out how to keep going.'"[35] As the major studios maintain leaner development funds, buy fewer spec scripts, and invest less in up-and-coming talent, even established female creatives are given fewer chances to gain access to fewer opportunities in the studio system. As a result of the decline in spec sales, midrange-budgeted projects, and first-look deals, studios are not only taking fewer risks but also leaving fewer opportunities for emerging female talent.[36]

The Pitch Meeting

Descriptions of the film pitch as a development ritual vary depending on who is asked. A former independent producer and international sales agent I interviewed defined his entire career of selling film rights to international distributors as the "art of polished persuasion," as he saw pitching as a universal method everyone uses to get their needs met.[37] In her memoir, veteran producer Lynda Obst describes pitching as "transactional theater."[38] In the most oft-quoted definition, Steven Spielberg famously declared: "If a person can tell me the idea in 25 words or less, it's going to make a pretty good movie. I like ideas, especially movie ideas, that you can hold in your hand."[39] This type of casual pitching involves a quick exchange to convey the big-idea story and pique the interest of the listener in hopes of follow-up questions. Instead, this section focuses on the ritual of a formal pitch meeting set up at a production company or studio where a writer and/or producer presents a film project to development executives.

In conversations for this book, the ritual of pitch meetings came up a number of times, with stories ranging across successes, near misses, and utter failures. Characterized by a certain cadence, format, and structure, a pitch meeting is what John Caldwell identifies as a fully embedded deep ritual cloaked in private, intragroup exchange. Pitch meetings happen behind closed doors and involve proprietary exchanges, a reality that stymied any efforts to access these spaces for research purposes. As a result, I rely on personal accounts of pitching from writers and producers. Caldwell examines many of the embedded rituals across production spaces, and he warns scholars of treating "verbal producer self-disclosures or visual worker self-representations . . . as unmediated gateways to what is 'really' going on.'"[40] As such, I am interested in how creatives frame their experiences and the discursive patterns and conclusions that can be drawn.

A short pitch may be a ten-minute conversation offering a short plot synopsis that sets up the story world, characters, and central stakes or goal. A more detailed pitch can last an hour and involve laying out more-specific details for characters, story arc, and themes. What established writers deem "the whole song and dance" often involves more-elaborate conversations with executives about what a film would look like set at their company, with discussions of potential plot point changes or reimagining characters. More than simply laying out a concept or story, pitching is an industry ritual both performative in style and transactional in nature. For screenwriters in particular, these sessions may serve as a "writer for hire" interview for an in-house project in development or as an opportunity to pitch an original script. To even enter this "theater" requires connections and access to industry gatekeepers, particularly representation by a combination of agent, manager, and/or lawyer. Getting in the room with development executives at a production company or major studio represents more access than many aspiring writers will ever see.

Most of the women writers and producers I interviewed described "pitching while female," that is, the pressure and scrutiny experienced in meetings where development executives at production companies or studios vet creatives and their female-focused projects. Building upon the discussion of the likability trap in the previous chapter, female writers and producers must immediately work to convey multiple characteristics at once—experience, likability, capability, organization, in-demand buzz, and so much more. Building rapport with development executives during these conversations is an incredibly important part of the process. Established female screenwriters recounted how a big part of pitching for a writing assignment or selling a script is "shooting the shit," "getting to know each [other]," and "making sure you like each other."[41] Not only are you proving that you can work with the individuals in the room, but also that you can work within this institutional culture.

To negotiate the less visible aspects of dominant industry power structures, institutional cultures, and individual dynamics during studio meetings, many creatives find themselves grappling with long-held systemic beliefs about the worth of female-driven films. Writers and producers described strategically preparing extensive box office data as part of a pitch to anticipate "no value" comments. Because studio logic rooted in gendered economic value resounds in pitch meetings, a number of writers reflecting on the 2010s described an underlying pressure to show how they could do more for less money. A white female screenwriter recounted her experience developing a YA (young adult) action-adventure project; concerns over maintaining a small budget impacted not only how she wrote the story but also how she pitched the project. One strategy during meetings was to highlight how the project could be made for a "bargain" with a modest budget of less than $30 million using new talent, simple locations, handheld camera setups, and so forth. She noted: "You have to know how not to overspend at the script stage because you have to show how you can get it done for a lot cheaper. . . . The odds are already stacked against female-driven projects as it is."[42] Women must walk a tightrope in pitch meetings, convincing executives that a female-driven film will be small enough to finance but big enough to appeal to a wider (male) audience.

One of the most striking aspects is not the actual preparation or presentation, but the slippery, cultural work that happens inside the room for women—and even more for women of color. A pitch meeting represents how important power dynamics play out between freelance creatives and studio management behind closed doors in high-level industry spaces. As a formal vetting process, these meetings are conducted almost completely on the studio's terms. Pitch meeting invitations may be extended with short notice and require days of preparation, which may include practicing presentations from five minutes up to an hour or more, creating audiovisual slides and pitch decks, and conducting research on the specific company and tailoring a pitch toward their film slates and company priorities.

Writers or producers may initially meet with junior executives a few times before moving to additional conversations with their more senior bosses. A part of this process involves building support while working up the company chain of command to an executive with greenlight power. Most film treatments or scripts never move beyond development or even make it past the pitch phase. With personal and professional stakes high, producers and writers talk about the best strategy for increasing their odds that something will sell and eventually go into production. In conversations with me, screenwriters detailed the constant anxiety of having multiple projects spinning like plates in the air at all times because they never know which one will go forward. Writers recounted stories of working through Thanksgiving holiday to finish script rewrites or taking a pitch meeting only a few weeks after a difficult birth because they often cannot turn down the opportunity. One established studio writer described a period during which she gave forty pitches in a row—about a third for the same film—all without booking a job. Even as her career took off by the late 2010s and she began to book more studio projects, she explained in 2020, "I'm finally getting into the room where it matters but [there is the pressure] to keep delivering. I work steadily now and I even turn down work. But I still find myself overbooking jobs because of the precarity. The fear is that it can all go away any time."[43]

Developing spec scripts and crafting pitch presentations is a huge gamble. Screenwriters may invest months or years of constant, unpaid hustle with no guarantees of future financial rewards or employment. Writers can work on a script for a year or more when—after taking a dozen meetings, hundreds of pages of notes, and months of revisions—the studio kills the project. Some established writers can get paid handsomely for writing work that ends in development hell and is never made. Emerging writers speak to the immense amount of sweat equity required, investing uncompensated labor in a venture or product with hopes of future financial compensation and career rewards.[44] This process excludes many writers with economic limitations as well as childcare and family responsibilities that disproportionately fall on women in the United States, a topic that came up frequently in conversations. As one emerging writer said of the widespread inequities in the current system: "Like so much else of our wage gap in this country, writers' salaries have done the same thing—there are the mega earners and the people who can barely feed themselves."[45] Emerging writers have fewer opportunities and a more difficult path to building a sustainable career with a living wage. As a result, script development represents a high-pressure, high-stakes opportunity that requires white women and women of color to perform different forms of labor and for different levels of compensation.

Negotiations and the Pay Gap

Whether for A-list actresses or established writers, the pay gap is a central factor holding women back in the film industry. Trade publications widely reported on high-profile salary disparities between male and female costars, including Jennifer Lawrence and Amy Adams receiving lower compensation than male costars in *American Hustle* (2013, dir. David O. Russell) and Mark Wahlberg's exorbitantly higher payment of $1.5 million during reshoots for *All the Money in the World* (2017, dir. Ridley Scott) compared to Michelle Williams's shockingly low $1,000 salary.[46] When asked about the leaked salary details for Lawrence, then–Sony cochair Amy Pascal told *Variety* in early 2015: "I've paid (Lawrence) a lot more money since then, I promise you. . . . Here's the problem: I run a business. People want to work for less money, I pay them less money. . . . Women shouldn't be so grateful. Know what you're worth. Walk away."[47] In so many words, women should know and demand their worth or live with the consequences.

Pascal, who is clearly speaking in this *Variety* interview from a place of post–Sony hack (and pre-company exit) damage control from the leaked internal communications Lawrence spoke out against, places the responsibility on individuals to negotiate equitable pay. This assumption aims to absolve Sony as a film studio from labor issues like pay parity. Too often—from the entertainment business to corporate America—the structural pay gap is blamed on individual women and their negotiating skills. Such postfeminist discourse, like that embedded in Pascal's defensive remark, almost always places the onus for change on the women themselves. Pay equity for emerging writers to bridge the gender gap is not as simple as "Lean In" mantras suggest, especially without the attention and professional weight wielded by the A-list white actresses mentioned. The logic of only considering the actions of an individual employee ignores larger structural disparities as well as the various power players—agents, managers, studio executives, and top-tier talent—with their own priorities involved in these negotiations.

Pay disparities persist between white women and women of color working above the line. For example, Jessica Chastain reportedly worked closely with Octavia Spencer to secure a higher quote for Spencer for an untitled holiday comedy project produced by Freckle Films. Chastain wielded her leverage to negotiate a favored nations clause, or what SAG-AFTRA describes as "getting equal contractual treatment to others on the project—billing, accommodations, and any other contractual provision." Both actresses bundled their salaries together, and Spencer's quote increased by five times her previous salary.[48]

In an effort to decrease the gender pay gap across all industries, California passed a new employment law, AB168, in January 2018.[49] While studio executives can no longer require previous salary history when negotiating employment terms, there is still little industry-wide transparency around writer's quotes for feature films or television series. Deeply entrenched in the history of industry pay quotes and the negotiation process is the logic that women above the line are less valuable. An established white writer described the responsibility to fight for her deals and blamed studio cultures that are quick to shortchange female talent—"I'm still not getting parity with men at some places"—and she has walked away from deals when the studio would not meet her pay quote. As an in-demand writer working on projects in the $80–$150 million range, she was very aware of being one of very few women working at that budget level, an experience that is both isolating and confounds efforts to compare pay rates with other female screenwriters.[50]

In 2014, the Writers Guild of America released data from a quantitative study highlighting the median pay for screenwriters broken down by gender and race: white male writers ($133,500), all women writers ($118,293), all Asian writers ($115,817), all Black writers ($99,440), all Latinx writers ($84,200), and all Native and Indigenous writers ($152,500).[51] While this pay information clearly shows an inequitable divide between white men, women, and writers of color, it provides little insight into the intersectional differences among these groups, particularly for Black, Asian, Latinx, and Native and Indigenous women writers. Increasingly, the work in exposing intersectional pay disparity falls on the writers themselves. As one female writer explained: "Most studios are banking on the fact, literally, that [writers] don't talk to each other and we don't know what other people are getting. . . . There are clearly laid-out minimums but there is such a huge variation in what people can get. And you don't know if you're being screwed, because you don't know what everyone else is getting."[52] Another feature writer recalled talking with fellow female writers about their average salaries for assignments in order to understand not only what is a fair "Disney quote" or "Universal quote" but also if their deals included profit participation, bonuses for award nominations or winners of an Oscar, or box office bonuses.[53] Furthermore, in 2018, television writers began sharing salary information in an open Google spreadsheet, breaking down data points such as job title, gender, minority status, experience level, and studio name. Based on more than four hundred anonymous entries from television writers, a clear pattern emerges showing a significant pay gap between white women and women of color.[54]

In recent years, some writers have been taking the professional risk to speak more publicly in trade interviews about their experiences at the negotiating table. One of the most widely circulated examples emerged during development for the *Crazy Rich Asians* sequel. Adapted from Kevin Kwan's best-selling novel, the 2018 Warner Bros. film became a theatrical hit, grossing more than $238 million worldwide and leading the studio to develop the remaining two books in the series into a film trilogy. When the two screenwriters began separately negotiating their return to write the sequel, Warner Bros. reportedly offered Asian American writer Adele Lim around $110,000, compared to her white cowriter Peter Chiarelli's $800,000–$1 million quote range. For Lim, with more than a decade of television writing credits to her name, *Crazy Rich Asians* was her first feature job, compared to Chiarelli's nearly decade-long career in feature screenwriting. Her cowriter offered to split his fee before the studio came back months later with a higher offer, which in the end Lim declined.[55]

In an article for the *Hollywood Reporter*, journalist Rebecca Sun highlights the link between the lack-of-experience trap and pay disparities for women of color: "Less experience means lower pay, which means a lower quote, and with the supply of underrepresented talent outweighing demand, less leverage to negotiate for more—a vicious cycle."[56] Framing pay rates by "experience" obfuscates the historical systemic marginalization of white women and women of color, effectively blocking them from high-paying lucrative screenwriting work. A low-paying first- or second-feature job may be presented as a door-opening opportunity for more high-profile and high-paying work in the future. Hollywood's measuring stick of experience means that women always come up short—with women of color inevitably getting shortest shrift.

Trade publications and industry players were quick to celebrate the "groundbreaking" success of *Crazy Rich Asians*, a major studio project helmed by Asian American director Jon M. Chu with the first all-Asian studio cast since Disney/Buena Vista's adaptation of Amy Tan's novel *The Joy Luck Club* (1993, dir. Wayne Wang).[57] Yet, once the media property proved financially successful, the contradictions in whose contributions were valued and deemed irreplaceable became clear. For Warner Bros., *Crazy Rich Asians* is a closer fit to a media franchise–building strategy central to Conglomerate Hollywood's IP-driven priorities than a concerted investment in hiring and developing relationships with creative talent like Lim. In a *THR* interview, she suggested that the studios still consider women and creatives of color as "'soy sauce'—hired to sprinkle culturally specific details on a screenplay, rather than credited with the substantive work of crafting the story."[58] The case of *Crazy Rich Asians* reveals just how far the major studios have yet to go to commit meaningful *and* sustainable inclusion—that is, lasting beyond an individual project.

What Can't She Tell? (Proof of Experience)

One of the most elusive jobs for women screenwriters is the action blockbuster. More than twenty-five years ago, in *Script Girls: Women Screenwriters in Hollywood*, Lizzie Francke asked: "Where are the women writing Arnold Schwarzenegger or Jean-Claude Van Damme films? If a woman had written, say, *The Fugitive*, with Harrison Ford as a wrongly accused man on the run, we could believe that those women who are interested in such genres are getting a fair chance to play the field . . . and perhaps even bring a new dimension to this kind of tale."[59] Fast-forward to the late 2010s and a similar pattern existed. The major studios hired so few women to write and/or direct big-budget blockbusters that the so-called $100 million female directors club had only three members before 2018. A genre ceiling presents a significant barrier to career advancement, increased pay, and more prestigious projects. Because women writers and directors do not have experience with action movies, they are widely seen as too risky to hire for such projects. Rooted in a gendered logic around fluency and stakes with a handful of exceptions—Kathryn Bigelow, Lexi Alexander, and Patty Jenkins—until the late 2010s, such writing and directing assignments had historically been limited to men.

Experience can be used to restrict women writers and directors in ways that it does not for their male peers. Gendered logic persisted in the mid-2010s that women as a group lack the experience to helm big-budget projects. President of Lucasfilm Kathleen Kennedy commented on the difficulty of hiring female directors in 2016: "We want to make sure that when we bring a female director in to do *Star Wars*, they're set up for success. . . . They're gigantic films, and you can't come into them with essentially no experience."[60] As only one of a handful of women running a film division with a major media franchise at the time, Kennedy herself served as a powerful agent in reproducing these notions of risk and experience. Her comment in the *Variety* article—thoughtless and tactless coming from any executive but especially a woman—reflects the pervasiveness of this industry-wide lore. The "lack of experienced female filmmakers" is exploited as an on-the-record excuse for rationalizing the inability of Lucasfilm, and Hollywood at large, to shortlist and hire women to helm big-budget blockbusters. While Kennedy backtracked after the backlash, her comment remains illustrative of how "experience" is perceived differently when assessing male versus female directors and even more of how pervasive a rationale this is. The line between experienced and inexperienced is nebulous and it is too often enlisted to defend or justify studios' decision making despite their so-called commitment to inclusion.

In response to Kennedy's comment, journalist Scott Mendelson contended, "Hollywood has absolutely no problem giving young and inexperienced male filmmakers the keys to a franchise castle."[61] Examples of male directors with limited to no experience directing studio features, but still hired for major franchises including *Star Wars* installments, are legion. A number of male filmmakers were hired to lead $120–$200 million–budget rebooted franchises in the mid-2010s—Gareth Edwards with *Star Wars: Rogue One* (2016), Joseph Kosinski with *Tron: Legacy* (2010), Colin Trevorrow with *Jurassic World* (2015), and Jordan Vogt-Roberts with *Kong: Skull Island* (2017)—after having only one, or no, indie feature premieres at a major film festival.[62]

The genre lane for women storytellers remained a narrow one up until the late 2010s. Women writers have traditionally been expected to work in "less risky," lower-budget genres that focus on the intimate, interior lives of women's relationships and communities—or what Francke describes as "'feelings' films."[63] Until recently, most women writer-directors hired for studio projects worked almost exclusively on midbudget dramas, romantic comedies, and family comedies. Nancy Meyers became one of the most consistently working and commercially successful female filmmakers with star-driven projects like *Something's Gotta Give* (2003) and *It's Complicated* (2009). In a 2015 *Vulture* interview, Meyers recounted the nearly impossible challenge of women securing financing to direct big-budget projects: "Big movies are reserved for the guys, no one says it, but that's the way it is, right? Is it something about turning over $70 million to a woman or $50 million or $30 million or $150 million? . . . Let's not assume women don't want in on those kinds of movies. Women can direct dinosaurs. Believe me."[64] Meyers reported her struggles to get financing for *The Intern* (2015) starring A-list actors Anne Hathaway and Robert De Niro after she reportedly shopped the script around for years.

Emerging to established writers reflected on who got their start with women's stories only to be defined, or even confined, by the genre. Because writing partners Elizabeth Martin and Lauren Hynek established themselves early on through young adult and romantic comedy work, they were typically called in for pitch meetings to discuss assignments or spec scripts limited to lower-budget genre stories targeting female audiences. They asserted in 2018:

> We're still not really sought out to write guy movies. . . . Women-centric projects usually get a decent shot at a lady writer. But getting a woman on a guy project is very unusual. . . . We will not have

equality, even if we have equality in numbers, until women are writing *Teenage Mutant Ninja Turtles* or a *Fast and Furious*. We would love to write those. We don't even get interviews for those.[65]

To their point, few women are given the opportunity to develop and continue writing multidecade-running studio franchises like Paramount's *Teenage Mutant Ninja Turtles* and Universal's *Fast and Furious*. On the one hand, earlier in their careers, Martin and Hynek likely did not get meetings for big-budget action films without the produced credits, which are often used to gauge a track record and the potential for penning commercially successful projects. "Experience," on the other hand, functions as a slippery way to measure women writers' creative track record and future potential. What are the studio executives who hire writers really looking for? How much is "enough" experience, and how is experience quantified?

Rewrites

Some female writers have found a path to big-budget projects with rewrites. Script rewrites often happen when a studio brings in one or more established writers to redevelop a character, add comic elements, or polish a final draft. During a long Hollywood career as an actress and writer, Carrie Fisher had only one produced studio screenplay credit to her name: the adaptation of her book, *Postcards from the Edge* (1990). Yet, in the 1990s and 2000s, she worked uncredited on dozens of screenplays as one of the most sought-after script doctors in Hollywood.[66] Largely based on WGA rules, this work often is not credited. While Fisher transitioned from a successful acting career to writing, Maria Giese struggled to find directing work after graduating from UCLA with an MFA in directing in the 1990s. Even with an agent and production credits, including the UK feature *When Saturday Comes* (1996), Giese recalled that it was nearly impossible for her to get a directing job at a major studio or TV network. As a result, she took the work she could get—an uncredited script doctor.[67] For creatives like Giese, without the top-tier status and established career of someone like Fisher, the practice creates a hierarchy of working writers with creative contributions to a range of projects without the benefit of a visible career boost that comes from writing credits.

In a 2019 interview with the *Hollywood Reporter*, writer-producer Leslie Dixon describes working uncredited on more than thirty screenplay rewrites: "I have romantic comedies on my résumé [*Overboard*, *Just Like Heaven*] because I was a woman. I had an edge on being offered those things."[68] Dixon's experience rewriting rom-coms like *Runaway Bride* is not unusual for an established A-list writer. A common practice may involve a female writer hired to take a pass at a script revision, known as a "weekly" in the film industry, which may include rewriting a female character or romantic relationship story lines.[69] With the critical success of female-driven shows, BBC's *Fleabag* (2016–2019) and BBC America's *Killing Eve* (2018–2022), British actor-writer-producer Phoebe Waller-Bridge leveraged her characteristically dry humor and witty antiheroines into a writing job on the twenty-fifth James Bond installment *No Time to Die* (2021). After a rocky script development, British producer Barbara Broccoli reportedly called Waller-Bridge to take a pass at the script by punching up the humor, polishing dialogue, and offering alternative scene ideas. In joining a script process that already included director Cary Joji Fukunaga, Neal Purvis, and Robert Wade, she became the only woman on the writing team and the second woman with writing credits on a Bond film in the franchise's six-decade run.[70] Significantly, the rewrite work came during a specific industrial and cultural moment for Hollywood. During summer 2019, in light of growing pressure for more gender-equitable blockbuster practices, the creative team strategically negotiated an expensive development investment in modernizing a legacy franchise built on an out-of-date sexist playboy spy.

If a film project is moving quickly toward production or currently in production on a tight deadline, a writer may be hired on a weekly basis to complete major script revisions that involve generating new pages daily. One established female writer described the pressure of rewrite jobs as being "thrown into the deep end" of a swimming pool and needing to "present yourself as someone who can do everything." Weeklies can take five days or they can take months. For example, this type of job might involve fixing plot issues, action, or characters—men and women—for a script. One of the most extreme examples I heard was an assignment to rewrite a helpless, one-dimensional female character and keep her from falling into a damsel-in-distress trope. The screenwriter recalled:

> When there is a female protagonist [that needs rewrites], and they are trying to get a female writer for the project, this can sometimes create a narrative that the "only reason she got hired is because she

is a woman." But the truth is women [writers] who get on these projects have proven themselves. . . . I get hired because I deliver [and] I do repeat business working for the same people.

While being hired to complete a pass or for weeklies is lucrative for established screenwriters, the question remains whether this often uncredited work increases the number of marginalized writers gaining opportunities for future produced credits or to originate their own screenplays in the studio pipeline.[71]

In many ways, Chloé Zhao is an exceptional example of a female writer-director making the rapid leap from small-scale, low-budget intimate filmmaking to a large-scale, blockbuster-budget franchise. Her first two independent features—*Songs My Brothers Taught Me* (2015) and *The Rider* (2017)—were microbudget projects with crews of fewer than a dozen people and premiering to critical acclaim at the Sundance Film Festival and Toronto International Film Festival, respectively. Zhao secured a major follow-up offer to direct a new Marvel Cinematic Universe installment, *Eternals*. MCU's Phase 4 film slate includes *Eternals*, *Black Widow* (2021, dir. Cate Shortland), *Shang-Chi and the Legend of the Ten Rings* (2021, dir. Destin Daniel Cretton), *Black Panther: Wakanda Forever* (2022, dir. Ryan Coogler), *Thor: Love and Thunder* (2022, dir. Taika Waititi), and *The Marvels* (2023, dir. Nia DaCosta). Marvel's increased commitment to inclusion by hiring women and creatives of color above the line marks a shift in the Disney-owned division's established white male–dominated superhero strategy. Zhao, unlike other Phase 4 female directors DaCosta and Shortland, had a larger creative role with writing credits on *Eternals* that reportedly included significant script rewrites.[72]

In some cases, rewrite jobs offered the potential to push a handful of established screenwriters beyond the gendered budget ceiling at studios like Universal, Disney, and Warner Bros. Disney gave Allison Schroeder a call to help rewrite the mostly male-driven *Christopher Robin* (2018) after the critical and financial breakout success of her screenplay for the Fox 2000 historical drama, *Hidden Figures*, about Black female computer programmers working at NASA in the 1960s. The writing job allowed Schroeder to break into higher-budget studio films, and she developed a working relationship with the executives and producers. She was later hired as a writer on Disney's *Frozen II*, Warner Bros.' *Minecraft*, and various other big-budget features.[73]

In many ways, however, Zhao's and Schroeder's paths to blockbuster assignments are still largely the exception in the current industrial climate. Those early in their careers must vie for the right experience and opportunities in order to gain access to highly coveted work. Unlike inexperienced, unvetted writers, A-list writers are less likely to be required to provide script drafts without compensation. Daniel Bernardi and Julian Hoxter point to a shift in the development process contributing to a two-tiered system, whereby studios now hire inexperienced writers at cheap rates to complete first drafts or buy a spec script as part of a one-step deal. After the initial script deal, experienced writers are brought in, and paid at significantly higher rates, to complete revisions based on studio notes.[74] With industry-wide cost-cutting efforts in the development stage, studios are buying spec scripts from emerging writers at historically cheaper rates. An increasingly two-tiered employment structure benefits a small exclusive class of established well-paid writers whether they are selling spec scripts or hired for rewrites.

For example, Martin and Hynek pitched and sold a spec script to Disney for a live-action version of the animated feature *Mulan* (1998). Disney strategically grew its live-action film slate with a successful cycle of remakes—*Alice in Wonderland* (2010), *Maleficent* (2014), *Cinderella* (2015), *The Jungle Book* (2016), *Beauty and the Beast* (2017), *Aladdin* (2019)—by repurposing animated classics into one or more releases per year by the end of the 2010s. A live-action *Mulan* exemplifies how many Disney divisions went digging into lucrative media libraries to exploit existing intellectual property during this period.[75]

Pitching and selling the *Mulan* script to Disney was a savvy move and a major boost for Martin and Hynek even if they did not have creative input on the script after closing the spec deal. From there, the studio brought an established writing duo, Amanda Silver and Rick Jaffa, to rewrite multiple drafts of the script and receive top billing for screenplay credits. Silver and Jaffa had moved into writing big-budget studio franchise films, beginning with their script for Fox's *Rise of the Planet of the Apes* (2011). Disney hired New Zealand filmmaker Niki Caro to direct. Known for the female-driven dramas *Whale Rider* (2002), *North Country* (2005), and *The Zookeeper's Wife* (2017), Caro was the only woman to direct a Disney live-action project as of 2021. With a reported production budget at $200 million, she also became the first woman to direct a film with a budget at that level.

Because of its prominent casting of Asian and Asian American actors, *Mulan*, notably, was Disney's first live-action film developed and produced during the 2010s to feature both primary and secondary characters of color on screen. This reality speaks to a particular moment in industry-wide equity and inclusion concerns that focused on increasing the number of women in above-the-line roles even as the major studios still did not make space for larger and more complex considerations of how race and gender intersect on and off screen. Over the more than five years from the spec script sale in 2015 to the film's distribution in 2020, larger sociocultural and political conversations regarding the relationship between intersectionality in front of and behind the camera changed. By the late summer 2020 premiere of *Mulan*, the project was criticized for being out of step with the contemporary climate around intersectional inclusion. As a result, the film's release faced some backlash, as all of the key above-the-line roles were held by white women and men.

In an August 2020 *Film School Rejects* interview, Caro described how she takes "particular care in authenticity and specificity when working in cultures not my own. Every aspect of the filmmaking here was meticulously researched, and not just by me but across every department." She also addressed the criticism surrounding the lack of Asian creatives behind the camera by identifying what she saw as two issues at play: First, she asserted, "I resist the idea that you tell somebody who can tell what story. . . . An artist will express themselves, and the burden of responsibility is on the art. That will be judged—and should be judged." Second, she agreed that "more diverse people need to be allowed to tell stories. . . . It can't just be white people being hired to make movies, no matter what the subject matter is. The more this conversation is being had, the more that diverse artists are given opportunities."[76]

Some film critics criticized the studio development process of "writing by committee" as contributing to a Disneyfication of Chinese history and culture aimed at a larger global audience. Specifically, Justin Chang wrote for NPR: "I was more disappointed by how the script treats fairly intuitive cultural ideas—about a person's chi and the importance of family honor—as if they were difficult foreign concepts that needed to be repeatedly explained to the viewer."[77] This condemnation of the lack of cultural resonance echoes similar issues faced by the 1998 animated film and evinces Disney's long, complicated history of mishandling intersectionality across their live-action and animated film slate.

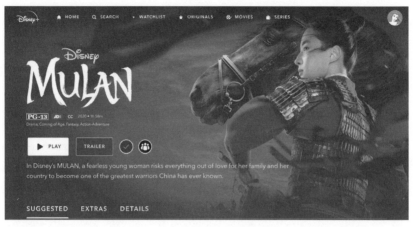

2.2. Disney+ home page for the live-action feature film *Mulan*, which premiered exclusively on the streaming platform in August 2020. (Screenshot from Disney+.)

The film faced additional challenges when Disney pushed the release date back multiple times from 2018 to 2020. With the global pandemic shutting down movie theaters worldwide in early 2020, Disney again delayed *Mulan*'s release from spring to late summer.[78] The gap between selling the script in 2015 and the film's 2020 release left Martin and Hynek in a difficult—but not unheard of—limbo as they waited to officially add those produced credits and to experience their big break. *Mulan* eventually skipped a wide theatrical release and, in August 2020, was released as a test model for the conglomerate's new streaming platform, Disney+.[79] In addition to the monthly subscriber fee, Disney+ members had to pay a premier VOD rental price of $30 to view the new release. Without publicly available box office data or Disney releasing subscriber viewing data, it remains unknown how successful this gamble was as well as how this lack of transparency might impact pay quotes and future employment opportunities for the writers and director.

Script Notes

Another part of the practice during both the pitch process and later during script revisions involves how to navigate receiving and incorporating studio feedback. Executives offer notes on all aspects of a script—from character motivations to casting suggestions. In her contribution to the collection *Double Bind: Women on Ambition*, Theresa Rebeck, who has written for television, theater, and film, describes her experience "taking notes":

The executives at the networks and the studios, none of whom are writers themselves, insist upon a systemic strangulation of the writing process called "note giving." Sometimes, after they have shredded your work with hundreds of notes, they might just decide that the whole thing doesn't work at all, and you have to throw the script out and start from scratch. They call this "blowing up a script." You are expected to do every note you are given, no matter how inane, no matter how much they are blowing things up. You are also expected to be really cheerful and appreciative while you do it.[80]

Rebeck, whom NBC hired, then fired, as showrunner for the short-lived television series *Smash* (2012–2013), which she created, characterizes executives wielding notes as a way for them to reinforce the power dynamic.

Writers and producers I interviewed cited recurring tropes in feedback for developing female-driven projects. If a female lead is forty-five years old, a note may ask for a younger character in her late twenties or early thirties. There might be a request to add a straight male love interest or spend more time focusing on the love story. One emerging screenwriter recounted a request not to make scripts "too feminine" or to "bring in more sex and violence, more testosterone." Another established screenwriter recalled the pushback she received after pitching an action film about female pilots. She described pitching the story in the 2010s to development executives: "The male executive asks, 'Who will ever believe the best pilot would be a woman?' After citing research on women having better abilities to deal with certain flight conditions, he responds, 'You can throw all the science at me but I won't believe [a woman as a pilot]. No disrespect.'"[81] The meeting ended shortly afterward. The message from that exchange—and subsequent meetings at other studios for this project—was clear: women do not belong in men's cinematic worlds. This reality was echoed by another screenwriter, who frustratedly discussed how pitching produces completely different outcomes for their male counterparts: "If I was pitching the exact same thing and I was a man then I would move further up the ladder. [There] is a statistical likelihood that when women talk we're less likely to be seen as expert or be believed."[82]

An emerging Latina screenwriter recalled her experience in the mid- to late 2010s pitching commercial genre projects featuring Mexican American female protagonists:

The part I heard early was the pushback that "nobody is interested in stories about Mexican women." . . . I was astonished [because] I thought for a long time I had a future in this industry. But the gatekeepers, the ones who greenlight, are saying you don't have a future. . . . This bias must be so strong that Latinos are such a risk. You are leaving millions on the table. It hurts as a screenwriter and as a Latina moviegoer. It is devastating to not see your community.[83]

Whether "nobody" implies an imagined white audience's lack of interest or merely expresses the white development executives' lack of investment in Latinx stories, the feedback reveals deeply held industry biases that devalue Latinas' contribution in front of and behind the camera. The screenwriter reported more traction and progress with two Latinx-led feature projects. One of the scripts she had been pitching moved into development with a production company in 2022.

A common recommendation mentioned by screenwriters was to refocus the story on a male character or to switch the protagonist's gender from female to male. An emerging white screenwriter working on an adaptation for a family-friendly fantasy project recalled an initial meeting with studio development executives: "I was told right up front that it had to have a guy protagonist. . . . [Because a female protagonist] will turn boy children off? Well, the project was killed because it had a girl protagonist and they straight up said, 'That's not what we do. We're not comfortable with that.'" After pressing a few more times for information from the female executive overseeing the project, she told the screenwriter off the record, "If this were about boys and stuff that boys like, I don't think we'd be having this conversation."[84] In many ways, swapping the gender of a main character from a female to a male role speaks volumes about a studio's priorities. The decision had come from a higher-up in the chain of command, a more senior male executive's office that did not see how a female-led story fit the company's brand or target audience.

This example illustrates a power dynamic much like Henderson's "situational authorship" whereby "the ideas of those who are othered effectively die on the vine. If the other wishes to survive, she or he quickly learns to present ideas that are acceptable to the more powerful writers in the room. It is this process that leads to the homogenization of ideas."[85] Henderson speaks to the messy interpersonal dynamic of throwing ideas around in a TV writers' room. Despite the industry-specific development processes for film versus television, the collaborative back-and-forth of suggestions from executives that lead to requests for revisions in multiple directions means the project almost always emerges transformed at the other end. Silencing points of view that do not reflect a dominant identity or the cultural perspective of those in more powerful positions not only "others" women and writers of color pitching their stories but also can erase the marginalized voices of the characters in the story when they are changed or cut out completely.

What Can She Tell? (Proof of Value)

In a 2015 *New York Times Magazine* feature about women working in Hollywood, filmmaker Shira Piven reflects on the value of female storytellers: "I feel that there is something going on underneath all of this which is the idea that women aren't quite as interesting as men. That men have heroic lives, do heroic things, are these kind of warriors in the world, and that women have a certain set of rooms that they have to operate in."[86] These rooms too often shrink a woman's experience down to one-dimensional tropes or stereotypes on the page—the nagging wife, manic pixie girl(friend), bitchy boss, funny best friend, and so on—in turn limiting the experiences, voices, and contributions of female filmmakers. With studio expectations fixed on traditional feminine categories from genre to gender roles, what kind of stories *can* women tell?

Biographical films, known in the industry as "biopics," have long been a staple of the Hollywood studio system. The twenty-first-century version of the prestige genre promises a platform for A-list male stars from Tom Hanks to Leonardo DiCaprio to enjoy career-defining roles and award-winning performances. Whether about a musician, a president, an academic, an engineer, or an astronaut in *A Beautiful Mind* (2001), *Walk the Line* (2005), *Lincoln* (2012), *The Theory of Everything* (2014), *The Imitation Game* (2014), *Breathe* (2017), *Steve Jobs* (2015), or *First Man* (2018), the contemporary biopic represents a prestige studio project reserved almost exclusively for white male stars. One female screenwriter described how the genre reproduces a cradle-to-grave formula that parallels the privileging of the Great Man Theory of history reminiscent of canonical university curricula. Behind each heroic journey through addiction, illness, war, or disaster, a beautiful, young, perfectly dressed wife or female coworker supports her male counterpart's destructive or vulnerable genius and his dreams of greatness.

I tracked a mid- to late-2010s cycle of films featuring exceptional women facing social injustices in their community or workplace. These female-driven biopics typically place heavy emphasis on stories of privileged white women who prove successful in tackling gender discrimination. Two examples of historical dramas challenging issues of gender equity and the wage gap include *Battle of the Sexes* (2017, dir. Jonathan Dayton and Valerie Faris) and *On The Basis of Sex* (2018, dir. Mimi Leder). *Battle of the Sexes* stars Emma Stone as Billie Jean King in the 1970s, when the professional tennis player led a fight against the gender pay gap for women players. Her efforts resulted in the formation of the Women's Tennis Association. At the same time, King beat self-proclaimed male chauvinist and former US champion Bobby Riggs in a media-hyped 1973 "Battle of the Sexes" tennis exhibition. *On The Basis of Sex* follows Ruth Bader Ginsburg, as portrayed by Felicity Jones, over a fifteen-year period—from 1950s Harvard law student, young mother, and wife to her struggles gaining employment in a New York law firm. After becoming a law professor, Ginsburg prepares, argues, and wins a landmark sex discrimination case in federal court during the early 1970s.

Through a conventional biopic lens, both protagonists face down a system rigged for inequality. Both films explore historical events happening a few years apart as two white women fight for equal opportunity to create lasting change against the backdrop of the women's liberation movement. Released in the midst of the emerging #MeToo and Time's Up movements and portraying groundbreaking events during an earlier tumultuous political period in the United States, the narratives benefit from timing. Yet, like many biopics, individual character growth is prioritized so that the personal overtakes the larger political struggle. Thanks to the tidy nature of Hollywood biopic hindsight, the stories efficiently follow exceptional individuals overcoming systemic inequities by their own strength and determination. Developed as intimate dramas for niche audiences with film festival premieres (Telluride and American Film Institute) and limited theatrical releases, *Battle of the Sexes* and *On The Basis of Sex* represent how contemporary female biopics are imagined on a smaller scale. Distributed by boutique studio divisions—*Basis* at Universal's Focus Features reportedly cost $20 million for production and *Battle* at Fox Searchlight cost $25 million—each hit its widest release at 1,957 and 1,822 screens, respectively.

In contrast, male-centered studio biopics released during the same period secured bigger budgets and wider releases. Positioned as high-profile projects about widely recognized public figures Freddie Mercury and Neil Armstrong, Twentieth Century Fox's *Bohemian Rhapsody* (2018) opened on four thousand screens and Universal's *First Man* (2018) on more than thirty-six hundred screens. The Fox production reportedly cost $52 million, whereas the Universal project had a $59 million budget. Universal secured the project with director Damien Chazelle and A-list actor Ryan Gosling attached. Fox undoubtedly invested heavily to secure licensing rights for Queen's string of hit songs. Pivotal scenes—Queen's performance at Live Aid and Armstrong leading the NASA launch—required a high level of investment in production and postproduction to reproduce live televised events. The scale of both projects reveals strategic studio choices that routinely privilege male-driven biopics as well as an industry-wide prioritization of whose creative and scientific achievements to celebrate.

Two female-driven biopic projects I followed closely—one released to critical and financial success and the other still in development—emphasize the negotiation to get women's stories immersed in male-dominated science and technology space made. Based on Margot Lee Shetterly's nonfiction book, *Hidden Figures* (2016, dir. Thomas Melfi) highlights the heretofore widely unrecognized history of Black women working for the NASA space program during the 1960s. The film follows Katherine Johnson (Taraji P. Henson), Dorothy Vaughan (Octavia Spencer), and Mary Jackson (Janelle Monáe) as they navigate the day-to-day work culture of the mostly white and hypermasculine Langley Research Center in Virginia. The three women work as "computers" in a segregated women's unit, performing mathematical calculations for NASA engineers and ultimately contributing to the launch of *Mercury-Atlas 6*, the first US orbital spaceflight, piloted by John Glenn.

Screenwriter Allison Schroeder cowrote the adaptation and described working closely with Shetterly, producer Donna Gigliotti, and executive producer Renee Witt to develop the project. *Hidden Figures* was Schroeder's first big feature job. She described how the creative team had "to work together to keep the movie on the rails." To secure the writing assignment, Schroeder pitched the film's producer with her insider knowledge of NASA from growing up near Kennedy Space Center in Florida, where her grandparents worked and where she interned in high school and college. The writer also pulled from both her college experiences as one of the only women in the room studying mathematics and economics at Stanford and her earlier career working in finance. Schroeder found that her firsthand experience proved an asset and that she could leverage this cultural capital throughout the development process because everyone in the room "respected my NASA credentials."[87] Her background later became part of the film's promotional discourse and featured widely in interviews at the time of the film's release. Schroeder asserted in our first conversation in 2017:

> If I had gone out on my own pitching a fictional story about Black women working at NASA, I probably would have been asked to change it to three white men. But because [Hidden Figures] was a true story about these real women, you couldn't change it. There was always a protection on this film. I have had other nonwhite characters in other projects changed to white characters or been asked to change women into men.[88]

Other writers and producers I talked to believe in general that having a woman in the room can make a difference in the development process. While female executives may internalize institutional culture or implement production priorities, they may also serve as powerful champions of women's stories. Elizabeth Gabler and her all-female executive team ran Fox 2000 prior to Disney acquiring Fox. The unit represented an outlier during this period and undoubtedly benefitted from having the support, resources, and protection of a boutique studio division nested inside a global conglomerate. Fox 2000's marketing strategy in 2015 for *Hidden Figures* included releasing a trailer during the summer Olympics broadcast and organizing special events at the Toronto International Film Festival. At TIFF, the film's spotlight included a music performance with Pharrell, who composed the music and served as a producer, and screening thirty minutes of the unfinished film, followed by a Q&A with the cast. After a limited twenty-five-screen theatrical opening at Christmas that year, the film gradually opened to twenty-four hundred screens the following month, earning first place in the domestic theatrical box office. After a few strong weekends, Fox 2000 expanded to its widest release—more

2.3. Musician-producer Pharrell Williams performing original songs from 20th Century Fox's *Hidden Figures*. The 2015 performance was part of a promotional event held at the Toronto International Film Festival prior to the 2016 theatrical release. (Screenshot from 20th Century Fox promotional featurette, "Achieving the Impossible," for *Hidden Figures* via YouTube.)

than thirty-four hundred screens in mid-January. Once *Hidden Figures* started to gain momentum during the 2016–2017 awards seasons—with Schroeder receiving an Academy Award nomination for best screenplay—the studio ramped up their official Oscar campaign.[89]

Schroeder described the main characters, Johnson, Vaughan, and Jackson, as "definitely the type of women I've been longing to see on the screen, and I've been writing them. I've been writing strong female characters like this for years, and either they just wouldn't see the light of day, they wouldn't get bought or they wouldn't get made, or they'd get changed in the development process."[90] During the revision process, the creative team reportedly fought to keep scenes featuring the group of Black female NASA employees as opposed to refocusing the story on one woman's story or giving more screen time to the white male engineers. The *Hidden Figures* script survived multiple revisions, with the story's focus remaining on the three Black women's experiences in the segregated workplace, but such loyalty to the vision is not always the case.

Studio notes can indirectly, or many times directly, suggest that Black female–led films are too small for a general (white) audience. Screenwriter Tracy Oliver, who wrote *Girls Trip* (2017, dir. Malcolm D. Lee), *The Sun Is Also a Star* (2019, dir. Ry Russo-Young), and the television series reboot of *The First Wives Club*, recalled the struggle of pitching films with Black female leads, as they could be seen as too "niche." In a 2017 guest column for the *Hollywood Reporter*, she summarizes feedback that she and other Black writers have heard across various studio meetings: "Great pitch, but we've already got the Black experience covered here," and "I know it's a show about women, but what about the men? We want to make sure they can see themselves in this."[91]

More conventional studio historical dramas set in the Jim Crow era (*Green Book* and *The Help*) or the contemporary American South (*The Blind Side*), each helmed by a white male director, have a history of sidelining Black characters. Instead of developing culturally specific and multidimensional portrayals of Black women in the United States, studios prioritize the emotional struggles and growth of the white protagonists. In the case of *The Help*, the story centers on the moral struggles of Skeeter (Emma Stone). In the "white savior" role, Skeeter recognizes discrimination against Black domestic workers in her small Southern town. Later efforts to shed light on what she found largely privilege her experiences and character growth over that of Aibileen (Viola Davis) and Minny (Octavia Spencer). Examples like *The Help*, *Green Book*, *The Blind Side*, and even *Hidden Figures* demonstrate how studios routinely hired white directors and writers to helm Black stories during this period. During a conversation with an LA-based independent producer during the late 2010s, she pointed to the structural disparities holding back female filmmakers of color, passionately arguing how systemic inequities begin with development and financing opportunities even in telling their own stories: "White men can tell anyone's story. They've had all the finances and power for over one hundred years. Women are told they can't direct or write because they don't have experience. . . . So much is not at the table for [women and filmmakers of color] while white men can do anything."[92]

In my conversations, various writers and producers recounted instances of studio pressure to make room for a male character's story in scripts centered on the experience of white women or women of color. As one producer pointed out, carefully navigating these script notes can make the difference between getting a film financed and never getting it made. An established female producer with extensive credits and festival premieres described the pushback she received when putting together a female-driven drama: "[Even with] a sizable female lead . . . by strategically casting a male role, you can get all the financing. The way women are valued in this industry is depressing and hard."[93] In the case of *Hidden Figures*, white actors Kevin Costner as Al Harrison, Jim Parsons as Paul Stafford, and Glen Powell as John Glenn served in key secondary roles as engineers or astronauts. In a pivotal scene, Costner's Harrison dramatically uses a sledgehammer to tear down the "whites only" sign to the women's bathroom as female computer programmers watch, effectively integrating the NASA bathrooms and showing support for Henson's character. These actions clearly place him in the "white savior" role, as *New York Times* critic A. O. Scott explains: "Mr. Costner, as usual, does what he can to give the white men of America a good name."[94] Casting Costner and Parsons, who participated in promotional and marketing campaigns, was undoubtedly a strategic decision to alleviate perceived risk and secure a wider release.

Despite what screenwriters Elizabeth Martin and Lauren Hynek hoped, the financial and critical success of *Hidden Figures* did not lead to a cycle of similar biopics. Their contributions to a Grace Hopper biopic, the second project I followed, had a different journey. A pioneering female computer scientist and navy admiral, Hopper developed the first software compiler and created the computer language COBOL. Known for the *LEGO* movie franchise, John Middleton's production company, Middleton Media, held the rights to the nonfiction book *Grace Hopper and the Invention of the Information Age* by Kurt Beyer. Martin and Hynek were hired for the writing assignment in December 2017 when Google was on board to fund the development of the script. In a period of increased public pressure to interrogate systemic gender discrimination in both Hollywood and Silicon Valley, the timing of the project seemed ideal.

Hopper's legacy, which contributes to modern-day computing practices, has received an overdue spotlight in recent years. Martin and Hynek reflected on the importance of Hopper's story, particularly as big technology and engineering companies continue to receive criticism for gender wage gaps, toxic work environments, biased algorithms, and exclusionary hiring practices:

> Here is this amazing smart woman who basically said technology doesn't have to be scary. That was her whole thesis: You shouldn't have to be a mathematician in order to understand how a computer

works and be able to interact with that. . . . She went out of her way to hire women and people of color and younger people and basically said, "You don't have to know how to do it yet. We'll figure it out."[95]

I followed the writing team throughout various stages—from landing the assignment to working with Middleton executives. The project partnered with Google, reflecting a clear fit for a technology company moving into media content creation while simultaneously working to manage widespread public perceptions of a sexist corporate culture and hostile workplace. Beginning in 2017, three former female Googlers filed a class action lawsuit against the tech giant for gender discrimination, including occupational segregation and an "extreme" gender pay gap.[96] The deal developed as Google faced accusations of gender bias and discrimination.

The script follows Hopper over a ten-year period, from her forties into her fifties, as she developed the compiler. Both Middleton and Google promoted the project as a way to highlight women's history in computer science. Compared to the previous success of similar historical dramas *Hidden Figures* and *The Imitation Game*, Hooper's exceptional story checked all the boxes. The biopic had the potential to serve as an awards-season vehicle for a forty-something star and highlight one woman's contribution to computing. Significantly, the Google deal fell apart before Martin and Hynek's contract was done, and they were not paid for this development work. Instead, the writers shopped the project around town along with the Middleton Media team. After several months of pitching, the Howard Hughes Medical Institute came on board and fully funded the script. As of summer 2022, the project has a director attached and Martin and Hynek are still involved as producers but not writers.[97]

Conclusion

In July 2021, *Variety*, the *Hollywood Reporter*, and other trade publications announced a feature film in development based on Megan Twohey and Jodi Kantor's *She Said: Breaking the Sexual Harassment Story That Helped Ignite a Movement*. The 2019 book recounts the Pulitzer Prize–winning journalists' investigation into Harvey Weinstein's decades of sexual abuse and harassment. *Los Angeles Times* columnist Mary McNamara praised the book:

And in many ways, *She Said* is more significant than *All the President's Men*, and not just because journalism is currently under siege, financially and politically, in a way it was not in the 1970s. . . . The alleged crimes of Harvey Weinstein are also the crimes of our culture, and they continue to be committed every day by many men all around the world.[98]

Carey Mulligan and Zoe Kazan lead the Universal Pictures and Plan B Entertainment project, portraying Twohey and Kantor, respectively. Significantly, *She Said* features female creatives in key roles, both above the line (director Maria Schrader and screenwriter Rebecca Lenkiewicz) and as department heads (cinematographer Natasha Braier and production designer Meredith Lippincott). The female-driven approach was clearly an intentional response to a female-penned book property and the current industrial climate. In stark contrast to the studio biopic conventions discussed earlier, female voices, from the source material to key creative roles, were the driving force on *She Said*.

The fall 2022 theatrical premiere date landed merely three years after the book's publication and five years after Twohey and Kantor's original *New York Times* article, "Harvey Weinstein Paid Off Sexual Harassment Accusers for Decades." The film industry has long been fascinated with retelling fictionalized versions of ripped-from-the-headlines, based-on-a-true-story investigations, particularly considering the proliferation of true crime stories involving female victims across film, television, podcasts, and so on. Even considering the studio development process for midrange dramas, *She Said* represented a swift and ambitious turnaround from book publication to film release. In many ways, the film signals how the Hollywood community was still coming to terms with the #MeToo revelations and, broadly speaking, its complicity in a culture profiting from powerful men like Weinstein. Because I am writing this prior to the film's theatrical release, I can only speculate whether the development, production, and reception of *She Said* will mark a turning point. However, it is worth considering if studios like Universal and its peers will continue to grapple on screen with Hollywood's history of sexual harassment, misconduct, and assault, or whether these events of the #MeToo movement will be placed firmly in the rearview mirror.

One established white LA-based producer pointed to the ways some interpersonal exchanges began to change in reaction to #MeToo and

Time's Up: "Before 2017, the call or solution was to hire more women. Treat them as you will but hire them. The treatment of women was never discussed because the hiring was for optics. Since 2018, what is happening [on set, in the room, in meetings] is talked about more."[99] Some writers and producers felt cautiously hopeful for an emerging cultural shift by the late 2010s, while others questioned whether the abrupt interpersonal-to-institutional changes—for example, handshakes instead of hugs at the end of meetings, subtle changes in tone or language inside pitch meetings—would amount to more than reactionary and temporary actions.

Despite major Hollywood studios and power players spending subsequent years making statements supporting women in the film industry and countless A-list talent delivering speeches and mobilizing around social media hashtags, women continued to navigate discriminatory and abusive behavior on sets, in offices, and in meetings into the 2020s. After throwing out a few so-called rotten apples, what happens next? Is the film industry actually invested in the long-term work necessary for dismantling this legacy of sexist, biased, and inequitable institutional cultures and practices? From the announcement of the *She Said* film project—and its timing so proximate to the actual events it portrays—Hollywood may once again run the risk of reducing structural complexities and power dynamics, which enabled abusers to remain in power for decades, into a neat and tidy narrative where the bad guy gets what is coming and everyone else can get back to work.

CHAPTER 3

Production Work and Gendered Cultures (Leadership Gap)

My interviews with female directors and producers provide powerful and persuasive accounts of the gendered pipeline and the challenges of securing and sustaining above-the-line film work. A white LA producer in her forties remembered how on-set gender dynamics were modeled in her first few assistant jobs, when every leadership role below or above the line—from director to department heads—was held by a man. Reflecting back two decades later, she commented how these early experiences altered her path: "I started in the industry at twenty to twenty-one years old in college. . . . I look[ed] at the roles available to me like 'Well, I could be a producer someday?' Because I didn't see women anywhere else, what other options did I have [in physical production]?"[1] This creative producer saw no models for women in leadership positions and ultimately questioned her ability to break into physical production without the female mentors and professional network so easily accessible, and visible, to her male peers. For many years in her twenties, she worried that her filmmaking ambitions were more of a pipe dream than a possibility, a fear that echoed across many conversations over many years.

Physical production provides one of the most visible, and enduring, examples of how occupational sex segregation and gender biases are ingrained in Hollywood business practices and cultures. In the 2010s, much of the early industry and popular attention around gender inequity focused on women's access to key above-the-line roles, despite the fact that these roles represent only one phase of the larger filmmaking process. This chapter both explicates and complicates long-held hierarchies and expectations around gender in film production. Grounded in a rich body of production studies and media industry studies scholarship that informs my research, I examine two distinct roles, the director and creative producer.[2] I am interested in an on-the-ground perspective of how gender dynamics play out for early- to midcareer women producing and directing independent and studio features in Hollywood, particularly how they grapple with and manage the film set in self-aware and complex ways. As a result, I focus on two above-the-line positions that originate and stay with a film project from development to distribution, in turn offering more of a bird's-eye view of interpersonal power dynamics at play within production cultures.

The masculine legacy for above-the-line work directly impacts how women understand their positionality and leadership, and these gendered dynamics impact their careers in different ways at different stages. How do industry dynamics for directors and producers shape their experiences, but also how do these women understand and navigate the gendered expectations of film work and available career opportunities? The first section briefly outlines inherent hierarchies and traditional gendered expectations at play between above-the-line and below-the-line production jobs. The next section explores the masculine legacy of the director from auteur theory as a popular film studies framework to the boy-wonder syndrome noted in trade press coverage. Female directors face a so-called double bind in needing to prove themselves in a position still largely dominated by white men. The third section explores the often misunderstood and invisible labor of the creative producer within the gendered framework of emotional labor and handling toxic individuals. Overall, female directors and producers must navigate masculine leadership expectations around creativity, emotions, and labor that serve to reinforce gendered norms long coded in women's film work. This chapter highlights the complex layers of value ascribed to different types of above-the-line production work and the experiences of the women who perform these jobs.

Above-the-Line and Below-the-Line Divide

A film's production budget offers an instructive guide into the hierarchical layers of film work. Even a cursory glance shows that a prominent line organizes the document by separating above the line—"upfront costs"—from below the line—"expenditures made during production."[3] Upfront costs sitting above the budget line are expenses related to top creative salaries for the director, producer(s), writer(s), and lead actors. Items below the budget line cover production and postproduction costs including salaries for the line producer, department heads—for example, cinematographer, editor(s), production designer—and crew.[4] On which side of the budget line someone's position lands can represent the financial compensation, job responsibilities, and degree of power and clout they carry into an individual film project.

The budget line also constitutes a distinct cultural hierarchy between the above-the-line "creative" contributions of director, writer, and producer and the below-the-line "manual" work of the crew. Vicki Mayer points to the different and inherent value distinctions between above-the-line and below-the-line positions, which reflect an ideological division of labor that has been ingrained in production work since the twentieth century: "Whereas the word *professional* in this discourse came to separate those who managed themselves from those who were managed by others, *creativity* more often demarcated intellectual from manual activities. Professionals located 'above the line' managed themselves and used their intellectual capacities, as opposed to tradespeople, artisans, and others 'below the line,' who used their manual skills under the control of managers."[5] If producing, writing, directing, and acting are deemed creative, intellectual management roles with various levels of agency and decision-making contributions, then the line demarcates the work of a large crew encompassing a wide set of skills, responsibilities, and contributions that range from the cinematographer and makeup artist to key grip and production assistant.

The gap between above the line (ATL) and below the line (BTL) reflects a well-established chain of command for on-set protocol, communication, and decision making during a film's physical production stage. With production budget increases come requirements for hiring more specialized workers, adding tiers and layers of physical production positions like multiple assistant roles across the different departments. For example, Ava DuVernay's first small-scale independent feature, *I Will Follow* (2010), reportedly had a $50,000 production budget and credited one editor (Spencer Averick) and one editorial assistant (Brennan Breyt). *Selma* (2014), her first studio project, reportedly cost $20 million and credited the film's editor (Averick) and an editorial department with nearly twenty positions, including a number of first assistant, second assistant, and assistant editors. Below-the-line jobs represent unique types of specialized, skilled labor where work assignments reside under the oversight and direction of a layer of supervisors, department heads, producers, and the director.

It is important to note how gendered labor value is constructed in relation to that line and the economic, cultural, and industrial ramifications. While above-the-line workers, regardless of gender, have additional layers of security, protection, privilege, and leverage that their colleagues below the line lack, production jobs on both sides of the line have a history of being coded as inherently feminine or exclusively masculine on a broad level. Entire departments like makeup and hair, costumes, and production design are still largely deemed and dismissed as feminine spaces.

One example of a below-the-line gendering is the costume designer. In her essay "Gender below-the-Line: Defining Feminist Production Studies," in *Production Studies: Cultural Studies of Media Industries*, Miranda J. Banks offers an extensive analysis of costume work in film and television by interviewing the department head who designs, develops, and directs wardrobe choices for all actors on a production. She examines how costume design is categorized and coded as feminine work and therefore devalued in the filmmaking process: "The invisibility of the costume designer's labor on screen, however, frequently means that they are marginalized on the set and in the press. For costume designers, it has not been a coincidence that their field, traditionally dominated by women, has also been underappreciated, undercompensated, and with imprudent disregard, labeled as 'women's work.'"[6] Not only is costume design expected to seamlessly blend into an actor's performance, but also the creative labor—itself representing traditionally feminized domestic labor—further marginalizes the largely female designer's contributions in the contemporary industry. The gendering of production work in both visible and invisible ways persists where the divide between ATL and BTL can further reinforce traditionally gendered categories of film work. As the following sections about directing and producing work reveal, socially and industrially coded patterns of confining women's contributions, opportunities, and value within physical production continue.

Masculine Legacy of the Director's Chair

In a media industries class I teach for undergraduate majors in my department, a significant lesson I scaffold at the beginning of the semester is making the gendered and racialized structures of the media industries visible. For example, I often use a simple exercise to illustrate the broad impact of the director's chair as a male-dominated space. I ask students to do a simple internet search using the term "film director" and share their findings in small groups. Inevitably, a homogeneous row of headshots populate the top of their Google searches. Scrolling across the faces of (primarily commercial Hollywood studio) directors from various industrial periods, students are quick to point out that only about five of the fifty faces in the top results are women or men of color. Setting aside differences in search engine results and algorithms for a moment, the faces of Martin Scorsese, Steven Spielberg, David Fincher, and their male peers serve as definitive search results for the contemporary film director.

A more in-depth conversation about barriers to inclusion and access follows. As a diverse group of twenty-somethings hoping to work in the media industries, my students often reflect on this eye-opening moment by questioning how a one-hundred-year-old industry has remained static and unchanged, why the storytellers are so similar, and why most do not see themselves in these filmmakers. This exercise works to illustrate what a legacy of film criticism, scholarship, and syllabi have already told us: white male storytellers have long controlled and defined creative filmmaking spaces. This section examines the vast gendered assumptions about film directors, spanning from film studies traditions to film set experiences.

Nowhere is the occupational sex segregation or the gendered hierarchy of film industry cultures more visible or structurally ingrained than in the artistically celebrated and exalted figure of the film director. While chapter 1 examines employment disparities in broad quantitative data studies for above-the-line and executive positions, this section considers how the masculine legacy of the film director still impacts scholarly, industry, and popular conversations. This tradition continues to reinforce the gendered expectations for directing, specifically film studies' auteur-driven narratives, trade publication coverage, and on-set interpersonal dynamics. In conversations I conducted with film directors and in discourse analysis of industry-facing published interviews, I sought a nuanced answer to the following question: How were filmmakers increasingly speaking about their experiences navigating masculine leadership conventions and reimagining production spaces in the 2010s?

From Auteur Genius to Boy Wonder Syndrome

Auteur theory—the notion that the director is a film's central author and creative force—maintains that an individual's signature style can be traced across their body of work. This school of thought originated in post–World War II France and the United Kingdom, specifically from the young editors of *Cahiers du Cinéma* and founders of the Nouvelle Vague/French New Wave including François Truffaut and Jean-Luc Godard. With the notable exception of Agnès Varda, this movement was largely a boy's club of critics and filmmakers. After migrating to the United States in the 1960s and taken up by American film critics like Andrew Sarris, auteur theory became a key scholarly and popular critical lens for viewing the film director's role within areas of US and global film studies. Critics championed a handful of directors like John Ford, Howard Hawks, and Alfred Hitchcock who, they argued, successfully developed a unique authorial signature and voice working inside the Hollywood system. However, in many ways, auteurism still reinforced the major film studios' hierarchical systems, with the director placed at the top, as the highly collaborative nature of filmmaking is condensed into individual and personal decisions credited to a lone, male author.[7] As Daniel Herbert, Amanda D. Lotz, and Aswin Punathambekar consider the theoretical framework's impact as a "long-standing" tradition in film studies, "auteurism prompted scholars to attend more to issues of textual form, style, and 'personality' rather than work practices, labor conditions, or industrial contexts."[8] Because traditional auteur studies do not delve into the industrial conditions shaping the director and their work, formal analysis of the film's text performs the heavy lifting of supplying authorial evidence.

An auteur-driven approach still prevails in some areas of the field as a tool for understanding the most critically acclaimed and stylistically innovative films coming from independent film circuits, Hollywood's major studios, and national industries in key regions of the Global South. The director-as-author approach continues to appear in university curricula and shapes the way some film classes are structured. It is not uncommon for film departments to offer semester-long courses on Alfred Hitchcock, John Ford, or Steven Spielberg. As an undergraduate film studies student in the early 2000s, I recall cutting my teeth on classes invested heavily in auteur theory to serve as a lens for understanding the tightly composed and layered shots in director William Wyler's Bette Davis star vehicles *Jezebel* (1938) and *Little Foxes* (1941), the high-contrast lighting characteristic of German Expressionist films like Fritz Lang's *Metropolis* (1927), and the distinct cinéma verité spirit of the French New Wave with Godard's *Breathless* (*À bout de souffle*, 1960).

This celebration of the director as author is reinforced in the "Best of" film list tradition, where the British Film Institute, American Film Institute, and other institutions or film criticism sites routinely publish the top films or directors of a specific period or of all time. In canonizing and categorizing "significant" films using "important" directors—lists that Orson Welles's *Citizen Kane* (1941) topped for many years—who is included and who is excluded? As Cynthia Chris details, this focus on individual authorship works to "elevate particular authors with large, coherent bodies of work over others who may be just as prolific but are, for various reasons, less acclaimed."[9] In other words, based on who gains access and opportunities to build a sustained body of film work, traditional auteurism reinforced a very white male canon that has contributed to the marginalization of filmmakers of color and of women's labor in film history.

Yet, employing auteurism to course-correct the traditionally white male film canon can also result in eliminating female filmmakers who persevered despite a male-driven system and industrial conditions that impeded and shaped their careers. J. E. Smyth questions an application for auteur theory in writing a revisionist film history: "How appropriate is it to reconstruct a woman's filmmaking 'canon' using the same exclusionary language that erased women from active participation in the earlier eras of US history? . . . Film historians schooled in conventional auteurism are committed to a hierarchy of work emphasizing directors as the definitive creative force in filmmaking, a position that masks women's wider presence in the industry during the studio era."[10] Furthermore, Deborah Jermyn questions: "Does the feminist film scholar thus become part of the problem, then, a colluder in the patriarchal structures that have informed the modeling of history, when she herself writes a history of a woman director that points to how the woman in question has been wrongly 'left out' of the (male-dominated) roll call?"[11]

The legacy of auteur theory and the celebration of a film's director above all other workers place unprecedented value on a role still largely dominated by men that, in turn, masks women's contributions in other areas of film history.[12] Despite decades of interventions and theoretical critiques of the white male auteur from feminist and queer studies, Black, Latinx, Asian, and Indigenous film studies, postcolonial studies, film history, and production studies, the legacy of auteurism persists in some areas of film studies as well as more broadly in the popular imagination through trade coverage and industry discourses exalting the next big director. The work to interrogate and dismantle a normative image of the director as a masculine position and filmmaking as a fantasy space for men must continue. The ongoing project by colleagues in film and media studies in decentering the white male director from syllabi and industry studies scholarship calls attention to the marginalization of women and people of color and how their labor and contributions remain at best understudied—or, at worst, invisible.

Auteurism still prevails not only in some areas of film studies but also, more much forcefully, among film critics and in popular discourse. Male directors experiencing their first taste of commercial and critical success in Hollywood are quick to be celebrated as the next "boy wonder." Despite emerging from distinct industrial moments, Steven Spielberg, Quentin Tarantino, and Christopher Nolan started their filmmaking careers at a young age only to be quickly championed as the creative geniuses and innovators of their generation.[13] This widely held regard for male directors, referred to as the "boy wonder syndrome," perpetuated romantic notions of up-and-coming filmmakers in 2000s and 2010s trade coverage.[14] After the release of *Juno* (2007) and *Up in the Air* (2009), *Variety* deemed Jason Reitman an indie wunderkind, whereas Damien Chazelle, who rose to film festival and awards acclaim with *Whiplash* (2014) and *La La Land* (2016), was celebrated as a Hollywood disruptor.[15]

In borrowing a much-overused and watered-down Silicon Valley designation for industry innovation and seismic change-making, white male directors continued to be romanticized as groundbreaking visionaries, obsessive mavericks, and committed artists. Despite the celebration around "disrupting" Hollywood's aesthetic and narrative norms, each new generation of celebrated boy wonders in fact actively reinforces the white male–dominated status quo. In her 2016 *Filmmaker Magazine* article, producer Katy Chevigny echoes what many women I interviewed identified as a double standard: "The slippery concept of artistic talent is shrouded in mystique that is often attributed to men. Throughout the arts, the words 'talented' and 'genius' are associated most commonly with men."[16] Hollywood is no stranger to categorizing and celebrating the stories of white men, both in front of and behind the camera, as extraordinary creators and inventors.

Genius not only is a label associated with male directors but it has also served to excuse or rationalize unprofessional or toxic behavior on film projects, or, as *New York Times* columnist Maureen Dowd contends: "Male directors who act out are seen as moody, eccentric geniuses. Women are dragons."[17] Revelations in the wake of the #MeToo and Time's Up movements included allegations of male directors who have a history of abusive behavior on set that continued over years or even decades. In a 2021 television interview, *Wonder Woman* star Gal Gadot reported instances of director Joss Whedon threatening her career after she raised issues about her specific dialogue or character on the set of the Warner Bros./DC Extended Universe's *Justice League* (2017): "Would he tell me what he told me had I been a man? I don't know. We'll never know. But my sense of justice is very strong. I was shocked by the way that he spoke to me."[18] As a writer-director-producer, Whedon built a bankable career in television and films and was widely praised for his work in the 1990s with *Buffy the Vampire Slayer* (1997–2003) and more recently Disney/Marvel installments such as *The Avengers* (2012) and *Avengers: Age of Ultron* (2015). Gadot's comments echoed those of cast members and crew members who worked with Whedon on earlier television series, particularly women and people of color, and detailed experiences of abuse on social media, including Ray Fisher who played Cyborg in *Justice League*. In many ways risking an emerging career for speaking out on Twitter against a studio power player, the Black actor described the director's "on-set treatment of the cast and crew of *Justice League* as gross, abusive, unprofessional, and completely unacceptable."[19] WarnerMedia launched an internal investigation concerning the accusations and reportedly took "remedial action" upon its conclusion in 2020. While WarnerMedia disclosed little to no details about investigation findings, Whedon stepped down as showrunner from the HBO series *The Nevers* (2021–) around the same time, though he continues to be listed as writer and executive producer.

Anthony Kaufman's 2019 *Filmmaker Magazine* article, "Where Are the Girl Wonders? Everywhere—But Who Noticed?," offers a critical perspective on the growing optimistic speculation that emerged by the end of the decade.[20] As studios slowly began to invest in developing and distributing more female-driven projects by the late 2010s, trade coverage reflected hopeful expectations that change was coming—with headlines such as *IndieWire*'s "Every Studio Film Directed by Female Filmmakers Coming Out in 2019 and 2020," the *New York Times*' "More Women Than Ever

3.1. Writer-director Greta Gerwig at a *Variety* press event in 2017 to promote her directorial debut, *Lady Bird*. (Screenshot from Variety Screening Series video via YouTube.)

Are Directing Major Films, Study Says," and the *Guardian*'s "Will 2020 Be a Turning Point for Female Film-Makers?"[21] In centering the growing industry discourse about gender disparities around studio film slates, trade coverage increasingly looks for hopeful signs in a search for progress. Even as female-directed and -starring independent projects—*The Farewell* (dir. Lulu Wang) with A24 and *Late Night* (dir. Nisha Ganatra) with Amazon—landed lucrative distribution deals after premiering at Sundance, Kaufman wondered why "few people seemed to take specific notice of this new wave of commercial 'wonder-women' filmmakers." In contrast to common boy wonder coverage, "industry trade coverage [of breakout female directors] largely failed to see the potential seismic shift going on here," focusing more on Amazon's acquisitions deals at Sundance or Disney's expansion of the Marvel Cinematic Universe.[22] Even in one of the most visible positions in filmmaking, he argued, women are still being overlooked in many ways.

Even as first-time or established female directors are celebrated, their achievements may be filtered through their relationships with men in Hollywood. Greta Gerwig emerged in the mid-2000s as a writer-actress collaborating within the small-scale DIY independent film circuit critics dubbed "Mumblecore" before starring in and cowriting the features *Frances Ha* (2012) and *Mistress America* (2015) with the filmmaker, and her partner, Noah Baumbach. More than two decades into her career, Gerwig wrote and directed her first feature, *Lady Bird* (2017), loosely based on her adolescence in Sacramento. The film received critical and awards season buzz in late 2017. In the marketing and publicity leading up to the film's December theatrical release and subsequent Oscar campaign, the Weinstein investigation news broke and #MeToo followed. In turn, during various broadcast and print interviews, Gerwig was asked about her own experiences as a woman in Hollywood. In an interview on WHYY's *Fresh Air*, broadcast in November 2018, host Terry Gross inquired about the "unmasking of men" happening as part of #MeToo and pressed Gerwig about working with Woody Allen on *To Rome with Love* (2012): "I'm just wondering as somebody who I think is very feminist oriented and has given a lot of thought to these things, what your thoughts are about that, having been in one of his movies?" After a tense back-and-forth about the heartbreak, difficulty, and fear of speaking to a rapidly evolving cultural moment, in which a clearly shaken Gerwig is caught off guard, the director steers the conversation back to *Lady Bird*: "I understand that this is something we need to talk about but I also have directed my first film that I wrote on my own and I want to talk about that."[23]

This painfully uncomfortable segment illustrates the challenges for both industry journalists and filmmakers grappling with the complexities of the unfolding #MeToo, particularly for industry professionals who in the past worked with or benefitted from association with accused abusers and predators like Allen. Yet the exchange also demonstrates how female directors as "girl wonders" are too often situated, aligned, or expected to speak for male collaborators, peers, and bosses in ways that men in return are not. As the following section explores, to reimagine, reconsider, and revolutionize the exalted and centralized position of the film director, a range of questions about the uneven gendered nature of film work remains: Who is bestowed with the title of auteur, creative genius, or wonder? Who receives credit, whose leadership is accepted, and whose labor is valued more? How does the hierarchy of production work reproduce an uneven system for female filmmakers?

Double-Bind Dilemma: The Leadership Gap

As one of only two working female directors during Hollywood's mid-twentieth-century studio period, Ida Lupino is an exception. In press materials for the release of her RKO film *The Hitch-Hiker* (1953), she articulated the tug-of-war as a woman taking on a male-dominated role and still allowing femininity to define her directing style:

I retain every feminine trait. Men prefer it that way. They're more co-operative if they see that fundamentally you are of the weaker sex even though [you are] in a position to give orders, which normally is the male prerogative, or so he likes to think, anyway. While I've encountered no resentment from the male of the species for intruding into their world, I give them no opportunity to think I've strayed where I don't belong. I assume no masculine characteristics, which can often be a fault of career women rubbing shoulders with their male counterparts, who become merely arrogant or authoritative.[24]

Keeping in mind the circulation and audience for this industry-focused press release, Lupino's statement undoubtedly reflects the working conditions and gender norms of her historical moment. Arguably, her response is a strategic one, as she presents her role as a female director in a clearly nonthreatening manner, conscious of the male-dominated studio system in which she actively wants to keep working.

Similar distinctions to those Lupino posed about female versus male leadership style in the 1950s continue to circulate and frame women's experiences in many contemporary American industries. Masculine styles of leadership, communication, collaboration, and decision making are still too often coded in gender normative ways. A 2007 Catalyst study, "The Double-Bind Dilemma for Women in Leadership: Damned If You Do, Doomed If You Don't," looked at women in leadership positions across the US workforce. Based on surveys and qualitative interviews with US managers and corporate leaders in a number of industries, the findings highlight how different stereotypical attributes for male leaders (strong, decisive, assertive) in contrast to those for female leaders (nurturing, emotional, communicative) lead to a double bind for women in the workplace. Women adopting masculine attributes are seen as competent but unlikable, while managers adopting feminine attributes were considered likable but less competent. In other words, women in leadership positions are commonly "held to a higher standard for competency" and typically "work twice as hard as men for the same recognition."[25] Female leaders across industries are constrained by being not too feminine and not too masculine. As the study's title bluntly indicates, female leaders are "damned if you do, doomed if you don't."

In a *Filmmaker Magazine* article, producer Kate Chevigny summarizes the common industry narratives about levels of competence and gendered leadership that circulate among those in positions of creative and financial power:

> You're also asking [the female director] to call the shots in a room that is mostly men, from the cinematographer to the dolly grip. In some ways, this aspect of the job—assuming and maintaining leadership of a crew—is the one that is the most traditionally masculine. She must be tough, smart, hardworking and determined. So you, the producer or investor, you're asking yourself: Will she be able to command that male attention? Will she be decisive enough? Will the crew respect her? Will she be able to pull this aspect off? Many secretly, and silently, feel that the answer is most definitely no.[26]

Women working across above-the-line roles are held to a different standard that not only plays out in inequitable hiring practices but also in gendered expectations on set. Doubt and uncertainty about female leadership qualities come down to this question: Can she (the director) pull it off, and what proof is required?

This predicament reflects what most female directors, as well as many producers, I spoke with recount from working on a variety of film productions at different budget levels. How women experience the leadership double bind in the director's chair varies from project to project, at different points in their careers, and as a result of their own intersectional identities and positionalities. However, three patterns emerge from my analysis of interviews and trade coverage: (1) prove you belong in the chair, (2) adapt to men's comfort level, and (3) beware of the studio as babysitter. These patterns illuminate the ways in which female filmmakers navigate gendered production dynamics. First, I was astonished to learn how many women I interviewed experience confusion on set about their status as the director. A white female director in her late thirties recounted a day when one of the film's independent financiers visited the production. He kept wanting to speak to "the guy in charge" and asking her to get him a coffee. She recalls the embarrassment of figuring out how to prove her leadership role in front her crew to a man who did not, or could not, believe she was the director: "It comes down to the way they talk to you. These types of interactions and how you manage them. . . . You have to choose your battles. There are bigger things that need to be fought for women directors."[27] She details similar anecdotes of dismissal or disbelief as common fare among her peer group and the justification for growing a "thick skin" to handle this "vicious business."

On the female-focused media site Refinery29 in 2016, Pamela Romanowsky depicts her experiences on set as a director as a constant "negotiation of power": "The huge number of people who ask me at lunch if I work in hair and makeup or the art department. It's not conscious, and I know they don't mean to be disrespectful, but they just don't include 'director' as one of the possibilities when they're trying to suss out what my job on set is. Even if I've already said it."[28] As illustrative of what the Catalyst study identifies as a "think leader, think male" mind-set, assumptions about men in charge often pervade all levels of film production. In echoing Romanowsky's account, many early- to midcareer women I interviewed recalled multiple instances of having to convince a male grip or female location manager that they are indeed in charge and calling the shots. These deep-rooted assumptions are immediate and habitual, dictating who can and cannot be a film director. What roles women are expected to inhabit on a film set adhere to more conventional ideas about feminine leadership and skill sets associated with fashion, art, and beauty industries.

Increasingly, female directors are calling out this double bind of having to prove themselves again and again. In a 2017 *Variety* interview, director and cinematographer Reed Morano states: "I think it's a common misconception that because you're a woman, you can't command a set and have people respect you, and for some reason, Hollywood is really far behind every other industry. It's getting better, it's just slow. I can't stress enough that there is an attitude too that women can't do action movies or superhero films or whatever."[29] In recent years, examples abound of female filmmakers sharing the challenges of securing directing jobs for big-budget, visual effects–driven features or of facing barriers when trying to direct action sequences on existing film projects. Argentine filmmaker Lucrecia Martel spoke about her experience on the director's short list for Marvel's *Black Widow* project in a 2018 master class at the Mumbai Film Festival. In a statement that may or may not have broken a signed NDA with Disney, Martel recalled her conversations with Marvel executives:

> What they told me in the meeting was "we need a female director because we need someone who is mostly concerned with the development of Scarlett Johansson's character." . . . They also told me

3.2. Director Cate Shortland and star-producer Scarlett Johansson on the set of Disney/Marvel's *Black Widow* (2021). (Screenshot from *Black Widow* promotional featurette "Go Big if You're Going Home" via Disney+.)

"don't worry about the action scenes, we will take care of that." I was thinking, well I would love to meet Scarlett Johansson but also I would love to make the action sequences. . . . Companies are interested in female filmmakers but they still think action scenes are for male directors.[30]

Marvel proceeded to hire Australian filmmaker Cate Shortland from a list of female directors to helm the MCU project, reportedly at the urging of Johansson, who also served as an executive producer.

Shortland and Johansson spoke often in interviews about prioritizing a more developed and dimensional portrayal of the female superhero. The character of Natasha Romanoff, aka Black Widow, appeared first in the MCU franchise in *Iron Man 2* (2010, dir. Jon Favreau) and was featured in multiple Avengers and Captain America installments from 2010 to 2019. Yet, Black Widow as a central part of the MCU ensemble proved to be an underserved and underdeveloped character. When Johansson hosted NBC's *Saturday Night Live* in spring 2015, one of the sketches asked, "Does Marvel not know how to make a girl superhero movie?" What followed was a trailer parody for a generic working-girl-looking-for-love-in-the-city film called *Black Widow: Age of Me* that called attention to disparities in the MCU while playing with larger gendered genre conventions of the rom-com. Popular press articles around the time of the 2021 premiere took a critical tone, describing Johansson's Romanoff prior to the stand-alone movie as "a thinly sketched character in the franchise" and "hyper-sexualized, sidelined, and treated as little more than support for the real (i.e., superpowered and super-suited) heroes."[31]

Hiring an independent, art house filmmaker reflects a slight shift in strategy for the Marvel Cinematic Universe. Shortland's previous character-driven features—Australian coming-of-age drama *Somersault* (2004), Australian-German-UK-coproduced WWII drama *Lore* (2012), and Australian thriller *Berlin Syndrome* (2017)—screened across the regional and international film festival circuit. After Marvel slowly began to hire a handful of independent filmmakers to helm MCU Phase 3 features—including Taika Waititi (*Thor: Ragnarok*, 2017), Ryan Coogler (*Black Panther*, 2018), and Anna Boden and Ryan Fleck (*Captain Marvel*, 2019)—the Phase 4 film slate noticeably included more women and directors of color leading new installments, including Shortland, Destin Daniel Cretton (*Shang-Chi and the Legend of the Ten Rings*, 2021), Chloé Zhao (*Eternals*, 2021), and Nia DaCosta (*The Marvels*, 2023). Shawna Kidman describes Disney's highly managed dynamic between the creative team and IP as "a shift in Hollywood's balance of power away from people and toward brands; in the franchise era, value came from studio-owned intellectual property, not from the contributions of individual artists or workers. To support this value shift, Disney advanced a discourse around authorship that I refer to here as 'corporate auteurism.' This updated and corporatized version of classic auteur theory prioritized managerial expertise over creative vision."[32]

The leap from a $5.5 million Australian independent project to a $200+ million Hollywood franchise installment is massive and reflects what Kidman describes as Disney's "corporate auteurism" strategy. Shortland had been reluctant to take the directing job and initially wanted to turn it down. In a 2021 *IndieWire* interview, she said: "I'd been making art-house films and hadn't the experience with fights, I kind of made short films exploring what I wanted to explore in this film in terms of physical movement and violence. . . . I cut together sequences from the last 30, 40 years of fights that I loved or moments of violence that I loved, even stalking or chase [scenes]. Then we could all look at that and talk about it."[33] Due to her lack of experience, she described working closely with second unit director Darrin Prescott, a role that oversees action-heavy sequences like fights, chases, and stunt work, as well as with visual effects supervisor Geoffrey Baumann and production designer Charles Wood, who all have multiple Marvel production credits to their names. When asked specifically about Martel's previous comments in trade and popular press interviews, Shortland gave a vague response about having the "opposite" experience and calling Marvel studio a "director-led environment," which aligns with the typical pro-Marvel responses expected of filmmakers and cast during such press tours.[34]

Studio institutional cultures are not the only variable of the production process factoring into a female director's handling of action sequences. In an interview with Kim Masters on KCRW's *The Business* podcast in 2020, Black filmmaker Gina Prince-Bythewood recalls her experiences finally moving into bigger-budget action films with the Charlize Theron–led comic book adaptation *The Old Guard* (2020) after nearly two decades of directing smaller features and television:

> It is a reality that there are very few women working in this space and there are a number of men working in this space who don't think women know what good VFX should be or good fighting. But I would say that a number of them haven't been in a ring before, which I have. I know what good fighting looks like so I am able to talk that way with them and when I start to point out things that don't look good or are wrong, you start to see that surprised look. But again you constantly have to prove yourself.[35]

Production protocols for action movies have specific genre conventions like the physical expertise required for choreographed fight sequences or the technical knowledge for setting up chase sequences heavy with explosions and stunt work. For decades, Hollywood has deemed these skills and knowledge to largely be the domain of men, explicitly and implicitly, and as spaces women do not have the interest or ability to join. As a result, until the late 2010s, female filmmakers with an array of experiences in these areas were mostly kept off hiring lists for these types of projects or required to routinely prove competencies on set in ways that male directors did not. Unconscious biases, sociocultural expectations, and industry norms all contributed to widely held ideas of who can embody—the specific gendered body—the role of film director.

Writer-producer Theresa Rebeck identifies a second obstacle for female leaders: the comfort level for men on set. In *Double Bind: Women on Ambition*, a collection of stories from female professionals across media,

3.3. Charlize Theron practicing fight choreography for *The Old Guard* (2020). (Screenshot from Netflix promotional featurette "*The Old Guard*: Combat Training" via YouTube.)

entertainment, sports, and business, Rebeck explains: "Comfort level, I came to learn, is Hollywood code for men who don't want to work with women. So women, who are suspect because there is this comfort level issue, have to work extra hard to play well with others and manage up, in addition to sucking everything up and understanding that things are going to be handed to the guys."[36] Female directors often report having not only to prove but also to negotiate their leadership style along every step of the production process. Masculine leadership expectations can shape work environments and entire group dynamics, especially for largely male crews who have never worked with a female director.

A director's role is to communicate and collaborate with on-screen talent, producers, and crew members from day-to-day tasks like shot setups and technical decisions to cohesively developing the overall vision of the story world across all departments. A midlevel, established white director reported that a surprising part of the job was addressing and adjusting to the comfort level of her male crew when she began working on midsized studio features. She was a studio "director for hire," and most of the crew had known each other for decades. She remembered grips not listening to her or gaffers deciding on their own when the end of the day would be, exhibiting "a real 9 to 5 clocking in and clocking out mentality."[37] Comparing the production experiences to walking a tightrope, she described the additional burden of managing below-the-line workers who did not trust her vision, did not respect her leadership style, and showed little interest in reporting to a woman in charge.

Negotiating a traditionally male-dominated workplace is not only *what* you are communicating but *how* you are communicating and ways you may or may not be perceived. Broad gender norms for female leaders in traditionally masculine roles often demand "softening" or adopting expected feminine attributes, including agreeability, likability, and an accommodating approach that indulges the comfort of men on set. A Black female director recalls questioning certain interactions on set as an act of self-protection: "It is so much harder as a woman director, a Black woman. I listen to what the crew says and [early on learned to] not always trust them. I learned this lesson the hard way." She described how high the stakes are for Black women working in spaces where they have so few opportunities that "we have to put on a face, perform not threatening so we can get to the next gig." Another emerging director of color remembered a production on which she had to work with "a really aggressive guy" and spent too much time going back and forth with him. At the time, she constantly wondered, "Am I coming off rude? I'm communicating information that he needs. I shouldn't worry about being rude or abrasive or harsh but I do. . . . That is frustrating and distracting [me from my job]."[38]

Accounts from well-established creative workers of color echo this struggle. In the 2016 *New York Times* article, "What It's Really Like to Work in Hollywood (If You're Not a Straight White Man," for example, Latinx actor-director-producer Eva Longoria stated:

> As a director, I definitely feel the boys' club. There's still that, "She can't possibly know what she's talking about." It's always been meant as a compliment, but [crew members] go: "You know what you're doing. Wow. You know lenses. Oh, my God, you know shots?" Yes, I know where to put the camera. You just go, "Do you say to the dude directors, 'I'm pleasantly surprised you knew what you were doing?'"[39]

Longoria established herself as an actress before making the switch to a behind-the-camera role a decade later. While this has been a path to becoming a director in different industrial periods, notably Lupino, Elaine May, Barbra Streisand, Jodie Foster, Penny Marshall, and, more recently, Elizabeth Banks, Greta Gerwig, Angelina Jolie, Olivia Wilde, Regina King, Halle Berry, and Rebecca Hall in the 2010s, the actress-turned-director path comes with its own demands for burden of proof, especially for women of color. The industry capital accrued from a successful career as a Latinx actress does not easily translate into directing jobs, particularly considering the extremely low percentages of Latinx women in all above-the-line positions. Over time, the expectation that a female director gauge whether male grips or gaffers or camera operators feel comfortable with a request or with her technical knowledge can be distracting and exhausting. These extra layers of emotional work draw time, energy, and focus away from an already intense and draining job of tight schedules, long hours, and high stakes.

How women navigate the industry's gendered ideals around leadership may fluctuate at different stages of their careers, particularly as directors become more established. Ry Russo-Young began directing in her twenties and emerged as part of Mumblecore. When making the leap to bigger productions in her thirties, she saw a shift with directing her first "real" commercial movie, specifically in learning about the dynamics of a woman leading male crew members. She recalled the move from working with a bare-bones indie crew to overseeing a larger, unionized team: "My job as a director is to ask for things . . . to be a kind of pain in the ass." She described doubting herself at times and struggling with how much she could ask from her crew: "I was feeling a lot of anxiety—for example, 'It is midnight and everyone is tired but I need two more shots. Will they be annoyed or angry [if I ask for more]?'" On her next project, the self-proclaimed feminist made a strategic decision "to stop worrying what other people think. I made the decision going in: my boss is the movie and I will do whatever the movie wants me to do to [make the best movie I can]. This was liberating."[40] Echoing what many of the filmmakers I interviewed shared, women often cite how larger structural barriers and gendered industry cultures manifest as postfeminist internalized struggles around individual behavior, tone, or approach. For example, Russo-Young and I discussed our frustration with the ways girls from a young age are socialized to be people pleasers and to make themselves smaller so others are more comfortable in any given space. In many ways, the limiting expectations about feminine leadership are not only incompatible with but also incongruous with successfully leading a production and fulfilling a creative vision.

A third part of the double bind relates to trust and competency, or what producer Mynette Louie described in her 2015 *Vulture* article as the "babysitting barrier." She explains that "a sort of 'babysitting' happens all the time with female filmmakers, who aren't granted the same level of trust in their executive decisions as their male counterparts," including producers or studio executives sitting in on director's meetings or overly monitoring the set.[41] Some female filmmakers I spoke with described having to contend with being underestimated and undermined by studio executives during the production process. A female director of color characterized her first studio project working with mostly men in front of and behind the camera as a "battle." She detailed excessive studio oversight on set and lack of creative control over the project, including losing script control on a project she originated and having no input into the film's final theatrical cut or marketing plans. While a controlled level of studio oversight is not unusual for filmmakers on their first studio project, she also spoke of how studio executives constantly "managed" her by visiting the set to monitor the production, hovering around, and cutting her out of important email exchanges. She pointed out matter-of-factly, "It is easy to be underestimated as a woman in [the studio] system. Navigating the system is difficult if you don't have leverage or leverage behind you that many women are never able to achieve."[42] Based on this experience, the director doubted she would pursue another studio directing job in the future and is refocusing her energies on smaller-scale independent features and documentaries.

Furthermore, an established director recounted a frustrating experience after landing a studio directing job for a young adult film. As a mid-budget genre cycle of YA romances adapted from popular novels—*The Perks of Being a Wallflower* (2012), *The Fault in Our Stars* (2014), *Everything, Everything* (2017), *Love, Simon* (2018), *To All the Boys I've Ever Loved Before* (2018)—proved commercially successful in the 2010s, more opportunities opened up for female directors on this type of project. The director struggled without "a lot of creative autonomy" on the script that went through multiple rewrites with different screenwriters. The head of the studio was not happy with the original ending (where the female protagonist takes action with a life-changing decision) and asked the director to reshoot an alternative ending (where fate brings the female protagonist's story to an end). The plan was to test both endings against each other for an audience and use the survey data to decide which version to release. At the test screening, the marketing team did not gather tangible data to measure how the two endings played beyond observing the audience's reaction. Instead, overriding the director's vision for the original ending, the studio released the film theatrically with the alternate ending and offered no real audience feedback or tangible data to back up the decision.

Many experiences of film directors working on midsized studio features parallel what Timothy Havens and Amanda Lotz identify as the "circumscribed agency" of media workers. Above-the-line professionals, like film directors, navigating the more controlled cultures inside a major studio operate as individual agents "whose autonomy is delimited by a range of forces including the cultures from which they come, the conventions of the media in which they work, and the priorities of their organizations and superiors."[43] In many ways, while this female director had creative autonomy in crafting a film that highlighted a day in the life of two people in New York City as she planned, studio mechanisms around final cut, identification of target audiences, and distribution and marketing models superseded. When I asked if she was worried about speaking openly about this experience, she said: "I didn't talk about it at the time. . . . I think it is ok to tell this story and I think a man would tell it." Very few directors hold the clout to retain final cut at a studio. Even in knowing about that practice, the director was disheartened because she felt she lost her creative voice. The alternative ending included a message she did not believe in, and she was frustrated with the message it sent to young female audiences.[44]

The Value of Producing

One of the least understood and most "nebulous" jobs in filmmaking is producing.[45] Producing does not have a clear formal or shorthand job description like many above- and below-the-line roles. Producers are not defined by one department, a specific skill set, or a designated phase of a film project. The confusion may be due to the laundry list of producer credits that appears in a film's credit sequence whether for big-budget studio features or low-budget independent projects. A film production often has multiple producers listed—creative producer, executive producer, coproducer, associate producer, line producer—each encompassing vastly different roles.

This section explores the role of the creative producer in the independent sector through the experiences of female producers during the 2010s. I should note that I am less interested in an expansive account of what a producer's day-to-day looks like. Instead, my examination of this specific above-the-line role focuses on how women understand their own positionality and experiences alongside ingrained film industry practices and cultures and how this understanding increasingly changed for many women interviewed in light of evolving gender equity debates. How producing work is valued or devalued in this system relates to what Miranda J. Banks describes as the ways production work is "socially constructed and industrially defined through gender."[46] Women make up a significant share of film producers, working more frequently and in bigger numbers than in writing and directing. By 2019, women made up 27 percent of creative producers for the 250 top theatrically grossing films released domestically, a small increase from 24 percent in 2000.[47] While female producers have a more sizable seat at the table than other above-the-line roles, this broad data set does not account for the vastly different types of creative producers and their experiences, specifically independent versus studio projects and range of budget levels.

Admittedly, locating and interviewing female producers was the first professional network I began to build and the one I was able to navigate the deepest and longest. In a classic case of snowball effect, many of my entrees into various areas of filmmaking came from producers introducing me into their network. I spoke with more than twenty female creative producers between 2016 and 2021. Experiences across this group ranged in age, race, socioeconomic level, location, education, and industry status—from an emerging producer a few years removed from her public university undergraduate film program to an established producer with dozens of credits and more than twenty-five years in the industry.

To be sure, entry into producing work varies across education level and first jobs. Many younger producers in their twenties who had entered the industry postcollege held film and media degrees, while some older women did not. For example, an established white female producer in Los Angeles proudly pointed to not having an undergraduate degree, having worked her way up from crew positions beginning in high school. Another female writer-producer of color graduated with an MFA from USC's Peter Stark Producing Program, a recognized pipeline to a studio development job. Another white female producer in her late thirties had attended NYU's prestigious film program and then launched her career from networking at festivals like South by Southwest (SXSW) and Sundance. The majority of women interviewed were located in the Los Angeles area, a handful in New York, and a few in major Midwest metroplexes like Chicago and Detroit. Based on available industry opportunities, professional community, and types of productions in each region, their experiences vary across budget size and scale of production. Some of the women operate independently as freelance producers, while others are employed at production companies, and many work—or worked—in other areas of the industry for festivals, nonprofit organizations, or film-adjacent roles that provide financial support and more stability than intermittent producing work alone provides. A handful of the female producers I interviewed previously or currently worked for established production companies, many of which were created and run by prominent white male producer-writers or actor-producers. I even spoke with a few producers who, for personal or professional reasons due to the lack of sustainable work, left independent producing completely over the course of my research.

The Creative Producer

To understand the distinct role of the creative producer, it helps to first define and distinguish it from other producing credits:[48]

- Executive producer: A film may have multiple executive producers who are involved in securing financing and may also contribute to different stages such as development, securing rights to source material, or casting.
- Coproducer: This person serves under the creative producer by supporting the daily logistics of the production process and working with heads of departments.
- Associate producer: Similar to the coproducer, the associate may work under the producer or contribute a key part in getting a production greenlit or finished. This credit may be granted to a development executive at the production company, a financier, or an on-screen talent.
- Line producer: The most senior member of the below-the-line production team who manages the daily operations, oversees the budget, and serves as the liaison to the producer.

Who receives a producer credit can be a murky and contentious process. An individual who contributes a creative or financial stake to a project may receive what is referred to as a "vanity" producing credit. One long-time LA-based sales agent and producer recalled his former executive boss explaining this type of credit: "Give them titles to make them happy." That is, producing credits can be given away as leverage to a financier or actor or to sway another key player needed in getting the film financed, completed, and/or released. A number of producers I spoke with criticized this legacy of passing out producer credits as a title that can be "borrowed," "manipulated," and given to someone who "legitimately did no work on the film." Unlike other key creative roles, the industry's flexible guidelines for who qualifies as a producer and what defines their contributions can devalue work that is already difficult to define and hard to locate in the final product.

In reality, the creative producer represents an all-encompassing role in filmmaking. As stipulated by the Producers Guild of America, the film's producer is "the person(s) most completely responsible for a film's production": namely, the one or two above-the-line creatives who receive the "produced by credit" by their name known as the "Producer's Mark" (p.g.a.).[49] As the film's shepherd, the creative producer guides a project across development, financing, packaging, pre-production, production, postproduction, and marketing and distribution. When asked to describe their roles, creative producers give answers ranging from "project manager" and "command center" to "wrestling an alligator every day" and the "least glamorous job" in production.[50] Alix Madigan, known for producing female-driven projects like Debra Granik's *Winter's Bone* (2010) and Lynn Shelton's *Laggies* (2014), describes her role in independent filmmaking as "the engine behind the movie, always pushing a project forward."[51] Producers like Madigan oversee all creative and financial aspects of a project—from start to finish—and often have multiple projects at different stages.

The act of hosting was a metaphor that emerged often in my conversations. A white independent producer based in Los Angeles compared producing to

being the first person at the party, and you're the person cleaning up after everybody leaves. Like you get there, you arrive early, you see the value in this story, the work. You're helping set everything up. You believe in [the project] so much, and then long after cut is called, and long after the film premieres wherever it's going to play, you're still the last person more than even the director. You're still dealing with it in terms of delivering it and handing it over so that it can be properly housed with a distributor. And it's the longest, longest road.[52]

She pointed out how the logistical role of producing is integral to each filmmaking stage, requiring years of commitment to, ownership of, and emotional investment in carrying a film project to the end. The road for an independent film lasts, on average, from three to five years from development to distribution, whereas studio projects might be made slightly faster depending on production and distribution schedules. Many of the women I interviewed emphasized the longevity and perseverance required for this long journey and the expansive responsibility for overseeing an entire project cycle. Because there is no phase of a film project that a producer does not touch, this ownership in the success or failure of an individual project weighed heavily in many of my conversations.

Producing work changes in many substantial ways as the film's budget increases. Alicia Van Couvering is an established producer who emerged as part of the DIY indie film community of Mumblecore filmmakers producing features for Joe Swanberg, Ry Russo-Young, and Lena Dunham in the 2010s. Because she has worked from all angles of filmmaking, including as a script consultant, line producer, and studio executive, she offered rich and unique insights. She described a noticeable shift as she moved up to produce bigger projects:

> Producing is 50 percent talent and 50 percent leverage. When I started, my value was the extent to which I could be a creative partner to the director, and my ability to actually pull it off—how to rent a camera, how to do the taxes. When there is more money involved, the second part isn't as important. In LA [where there is less of an indie film culture], it is not a thing to be both a physical and creative producer. [As the budget increases], your value comes more on politics and connections and not how good you are with making five extras look like a crowd.[53]

An independent creative producer on a $1 million budget operates as a jack-of-all-trades for both creative development and physical production. In overseeing a large studio budget of $100 million, line and associate producers take over more of the day-to-day physical production duties. At this budget level, creative producers are managing relationships and navigating studio politics along with supporting the director in crafting the final project. With bigger budgets, the stakes are higher, and it is not enough to be good at your job. Many producers confirm that being able to play the game, call in favors, put together financing, and maintain and grow a professional network inside major studios make a producer most valuable at this level.

Creative producers do not always make the leap along with their directors after a small successful independent project leads to their next, bigger-budget studio project. This move partly has to do with leveraging professional networks, locating and securing financing, and wielding the necessary power and experience to navigate major studio politics while protecting their director. Van Couvering described the difficulty for most indie creatives to make the budget and production culture jump to bigger studio projects:

> If you don't wield enough power to come between the filmmaker and somebody else—like if nobody is afraid of you or knows you well enough to call you, instead of going around you—it just becomes impossible to hang on to your position. . . . I've been on the other side of that conflict as a studio executive, where a producer is trying to hang on to their fee and their title, but they don't actually know how to produce at that level and they have nothing to fight with when very big players come after their position. The waves are big for folks who have never been in the water.[54]

On the one hand, regardless of gender, producers can hit a budget ceiling that prevents them from making the leap to bigger projects. Creative producers, particularly those working on independent projects below $2 million may be unable to ascend, getting stuck at the budget ceiling or left behind by collaborators moving up. Some who are unable to build a sustainable producing career may leave the industry entirely.[55] On the other hand—as discussed in the next chapter—the careers of male directors and their male producing partners are more likely to progress in tandem with higher-budget projects after a successful film festival premiere.

For many established producers with more than a decade of film and television credits, the issue has increasingly become the growing precarity of a position they fought so hard to achieve. In an August 2019 *Hollywood Reporter* story, "How Film Producers Became the New Expendables," journalists Tatiana Siegel and Borys Kit interviewed studio and independent producers who pointed to a precarious future path for the once so-called middle-class producer.[56] Even taking gender equity and inclusion initiatives into consideration, the question nonetheless emerges: Are creative producers expendable, or can a sustainable living come from an unstable and evolving twenty-first-century film industry?

In addition, female creative producers face a "leaky pipeline," a metaphor I borrow from research about the STEM fields that has found female academics encountering barriers in or falling through the cracks of the job pipeline due to larger structural problems around employment, funding, networking, evaluations, and awards.[57] Multiple producers cite larger structural problems with defining, valuing, and building sustainable producing work that contribute to female producers being impacted disproportionately. In hitting a budget ceiling when building a career in commercial feature filmmaking, a number of female producers found themselves needing to choose—do they stay and make it work, or do they leave the industry? With many unable to gain enough leverage and build powerful relationships with talent and executives to continue creative producing at a higher status level, they either specialize in physical production by becoming a line producer or continue struggling to cobble together enough independent projects in tandem with other paid gigs to maintain a sustainable producing career.

Producing as Emotional Labor

Patterns began to emerge from the numerous interviews I conducted for this book regarding what makes an effective or successful producer. The requirements for creative producing represent a dance with dualities— creative and financial, hard and soft skills, granular concerns and big pictures, day-to-day decisions and long-term oversight, passion and pragmatism. The qualities often associated with good producing align with traditional definitions of soft skills in the workplace such as problem solving, conflict resolution, flexibility, emotional intelligence, and effective communication, to name a few. Hard filmmaking skills include knowledge of technology, equipment, budgets and spreadsheets, and other tangible management experience or expertise that is still often socially coded as masculine. These perceptions of feminized labor roles are highly constructed and impact all levels and areas of film work. Gendered categories of film work between hard and soft skills extend below the line, whether with the physical nature of a crew position like gaffer or the technical expectations of the cinematographer as camera department head. Based on extensive interviews within the UK creative industries, David

Hesmondhalgh and Sarah Baker identify the widespread implications of this type of sex segregation: "the high presence of women in marketing and public relations roles in the cultural industries; the high numbers of women in production co-ordination and similar roles; the domination of men of more prestigious creative roles; and the domination by men of technical jobs."[58] If leadership is traditionally viewed through a masculine lens of hard skills, then soft skills—such as relationship building—are framed as a feminine trait. Women's contributions across different work-places and industries have routinely been associated with "superior" soft skills, whether due to normative "biological assumptions" about gender or structural divisions of labor related to domestic work and caretaking.[59]

Many producers recall having struggled with, at times even internalizing, such gendered notions of leadership at different points in their careers. In contrast to the masculine expectations for directing as fulfilling an author's creative vision, producing is a distinctly relational role, with community-specific emotional work baked into the job. This observation arose in reflections about how men and women produce differently in male-dominated production spaces. As one white female producer suggested: "Women are very good at caring about the world around them. It makes us better producers."[60] I heard similar expressions about women as better listeners or their intuitive assets as team players. Another established white producer warned her peers not to let their feminine leadership style get in the way: "Women have a harder time walking away from the responsibility of a project. Men instead say: 'I got paid this amount and I'm done.' Women aren't wired that way and have a harder time letting things go. Producing requires you to be a hard-ass. I have difficulty doing that and my male counterparts don't react that way."[61] Assumptions about a female producer's "wiring" to caretake and perform emotional labor carries the added burden of drawing and keeping boundaries. In contrast, their male peers do not struggle with such assumptions. Proficiency in managing relationships and other soft skills can be a double-edged sword.

In her extensive research on women's experiences working in media production as well as her own experiences working in the Irish media industries, Anne O'Brien posits that because women's contributions and labor are commonly rationalized as biological wiring or superior soft skills in ways that gender their role, the value of their labor "disappears within the production work."[62] Key to the vanishing act of producing work is emotional labor, which came up implicitly or explicitly in nearly every conversation. The widely used term is from sociologist Arlie Hochschild's seminal work *The Managed Heart: Commercialization of Human Feeling*, which has influenced how production studies scholars understand gendered production work and, in turn, has deeply impacted my own thinking.[63] Beyond the physical and mental labor required of women across workplace settings, Hochschild argues, emotional labor "requires one to induce or suppress feeling in order to sustain the outward countenance that produces the proper state of mind in others—in this case, the sense of being cared for in a convivial and safe place."[64] She contends that private emotional management transforms into emotional labor as it becomes a formal job requirement for niceties, sociability, and positive affirmation. In her examination of structurally gendered positions that skew heavily female, like flight attendants, Hochschild highlights how women are more likely to work as service economy workers in industries with expectations for emotional labor. Even with the distinctions between service work in the airline or restaurant industries and above-the-line creative work in the media industries, a striking connection can be drawn from the job-specific expectations of emotional labor by women in specific roles that reinforce larger "dynamics of power, status, and gender" at play.[65]

Film producers invest time and energy into building and maintaining relationships during production, particularly in supporting the "talent." In addition to helping create and ensure a physically safe production environment, every producer interviewed recounted how managing and working with above-the-line creatives like directors and actors in high-stress environments requires intense levels of trust and vulnerability on all sides. Whether "protecting the director's vision" or supporting their "emotional state" in a difficult moment, the creative process of producing represents care work and relationship management that can become unwieldy, and set boundaries can become lost. A white Los Angeles–based producer describes working with film directors over the course of production: "As a producer, emotional labor is everything. You have to be champion, cheerleader, watchdog. . . . You're sometimes mother, you're sometimes lover, you're sometimes [the] bully, you're sometimes a punching bag, like you try on every possible—from start to finish of a film—emotional mask because it is an emotional process."[66] Producers readily articulate that this expectation to embody whomever the director or actor needs in a particular moment or situation is vital to the creative collaborative process. Many admit they will do almost anything to achieve the best final product. Considering the immense weight one or two people must carry with all of these roles, what is so striking about this insightful observation is how the producer fulfilling this support work is compared to a sequence of masks to be worn, removed, and swapped depending on the emotional state and needs of others.

Producers describe the production phase as not merely ensuring that the project stays on track financially and creatively by moving forward on schedule but also placing others' physical and emotional needs before their own and making space for the filmmaker's process. Producers' work often entails hiding their own emotional state or needs. One established white producer, like most interviewed, related that the number one job is to protect at all costs the director's state of mind and feelings on set and in any creative negotiation with studio executives. In a matter-of-fact tone conveying a "this is how the film business works" example, this producer's experience reflected philosopher Ivan Illich's concept of "shadow work," what Hochschild describes as "the emotion work of enhancing the status and well-being of others . . . an unseen effort, which, like housework, does not quite count as labor but is nevertheless crucial to getting other things done." The comparison to the gendered space of domestic labor is manifest, aptly reflecting how many female producers recognize the present/absent nature of the emotional labor they perform: "The trick is to erase any evidence of effort, to offer only the clean house and the welcoming smile."[67]

Numerous producers, whether a few years or a few decades into their career, convey the joy derived not only from problem solving but also from community building and caretaking. For some producers, discovering new talent and mentoring first-time filmmakers is a real reward of working in the independent sector. A Los Angeles–based Asian producer who often works with female filmmakers of color framed her producing role as a "godparent." She explained, "What drives me as a producer [is] to be transported into worlds I haven't seen and tell stories that broaden one's compassion and other marginalized communities . . . not because I'm willing to fill a statistic. Maybe [because] I am a woman, a person of color, I get gratification in supporting diverse visionary new talents."[68] Other producers spoke passionately about working with female creative voices and felt strongly about making this contribution to gender and racial equity in their communities.

Patterns began to emerge around the ways the producers I interviewed expressed and categorized the fulfilling aspects of their work: "making people comfortable," "taking care of people," "abundance," "safety," "protection," "building meaningful relationships." These caretaking descriptors translate into a strongly held sense of responsibility for developing relationships and cultivating a supportive, nurturing environment on set—a cocoon that is not always available to the producers themselves. These patterns reflect what O'Brien identifies as "preserving activities," typically undertaken by female media producers in an effort "to make the team cohesive by being friendly, supportive, polite, and considerate."[69]

Additional expectations of the producer's relational roles are often categorized as the "therapist" or falling into the "mom trap." Over the extended interviewing period, I heard many war stories of this type of caretaking work—calls at two o'clock in the morning from a frantically sobbing A-list actress; battles with a dismissive male director who refused to relocate a scene from a crumbling abandoned warehouse despite real concerns for the crew's safety; so-called "psychotic" directors throwing verbal or physical fits that can ruin an entire day's production schedule and the morale on set among the cast and crew. The individual stories of sexual harassment or verbal abuse shared in confidence became even more poignant and alarming post-#MeToo.

As O'Brien argues, "Women are channeled into relational roles that require additional, invisible and undervalued emotional work, but for which they are never fairly compensated, nor is their work overtly acknowledged."[70] While women increasingly offer the emotional support—the work of listening, reassuring, validating, nurturing—in many industries, professions, relationships, and domestic spaces, this gendered labor is so deeply embedded that the lines between visible production duties and invisible emotional labor can dissolve. One female producer explained:

> I defined my role as a producer as "how can I help you?" For a long time, I thought the helpfulness would be rewarded and it would be acknowledged. I gave away huge ideas [and parts of myself]. I didn't believe I really had any value beyond that helpfulness, or at least, I didn't think any of my relationships would survive if I fought for that value. I kept thinking one day it would be appreciated, but in the end, it was just abused.[71]

Despite the emotional freight of these relational roles, some producers expressed difficulty reconciling the gendered expectations with the realities, namely, that the boundaries between being an effective and helpful producer can easily blur into feeling undervalued and/or exploited.

The producers of color I interviewed—about a third of the total women—emphasized additional (and invisible) layers of preservational work that come with navigating the white-dominated spaces that characterize much of the US commercial film industry, on set or in a production company. An emerging producer of color in Los Angeles compared working in production to riding a wave. Paralleling what many female creatives expressed in chapter 1 about the likability expectations in male-dominated spaces, the producer acknowledged the emotional management and labor necessary "to be able to keep growing your power and influence. You have to be able to ride a very sensitive wave. Black women in Hollywood are walking a fine line between getting their films made and not being called difficult."[72]

An often-cited example of the additional emotional work and subsequent risks for Black female producers seeking to navigate these gendered and racialized spaces occurred during an episode of *Project Greenlight* (2015) in the fourth season. The unscripted reality series portrays the behind-the-scenes filmmaking process of an independent feature film from development to final cut. Because the reality series follows actual filmmakers and crew, Effie Brown inhabited a dual role behind and in front of the camera: as the creative producer of the film production-within-the-reality show, shepherding the project through each filmmaking stage, and as a cast member appearing on the reality series. In an early episode, the producers and executives discuss in a meeting what director finalist(s) would best lead the film project. As the only Black woman or person of color in the room, Brown expresses her concerns about choosing the best director to handle with care and nuance the central character, a Black female sex worker, as the hiring decision was to be made by white executives, including Matt Damon, Ben Affleck, and Peter and Bobby Farrelly. As Brown defends her directing team pick—a Vietnamese man and a white woman—Damon shuts down the conversation by responding that diversity should not be a factor in the selection process: "When we're talking about diversity, you do it in the casting of the film, not the casting of the show." In other words, Damon echoes a long-held studio narrative that diversity is more important in front of the camera than behind it.

He specifically dismisses calls for inclusive hiring practices as a tactic to ensure diversity. A stunned Brown responds, "Wow, ok." The discussion opens up as the other white executives in the room consider who they think is best to deal with problems they acknowledge in a script written by a white male writer and yet still miss Brown's point completely. The scene cuts to a traditional talking-head interview with Damon, who reflects on the conversation by emphasizing that considering diversity when choosing a director would unfairly change the competition rules for hiring that judge "entirely on merit." As Kristen J. Warner argues in her work on color-blind casting and employment, discourses like "the best person for the job" relieves industry gatekeepers of having to address these inequities and only further masks exclusionary power structures. She contends: "They effectively neutralize arguments about systemic discrimination and inequality by displacing structural concerns in favor of questions about skills and talent. You're simply good enough to get the job or you're not."[73]

In a 2016 *Film Quarterly* "From the Editor," B. Ruby Rich writes about the reality television episode that went viral, specifically how a powerful white Hollywood star "mansplained diversity to [Brown]. . . . You don't go up against America's hero, Matt Damon, and walk away unscarred."[74] Brown later wrote openly about her experience on *Project Greenlight* for the *Hollywood Reporter* in 2020. As the film project's creative producer, she was paid to produce the movie but not paid to appear in the reality series: "That's exploitative. Sometimes I see it playing when I get on a plane and I haven't seen a single penny. They treated us secondary even though, unbeknownst to me at the time, the show was built around my experiences. I was the creative producer in charge and yet, I was still viewed as something less than my title, experience and treated as such." Brown also recalls how the series captured often behind-the-scenes or private, less visible moments of navigating the film industry as a Black woman:

A lot of the time, most of the time, there aren't cameras there when you are suffering microaggressions. Take Matt Damon out of it, this is happening every day. People just saw that one conflict, but there were others. . . . After I did *Project Greenlight*—and this is no secret—I suffered a huge backlash. I didn't work for a while. People didn't want to work with me because I spoke truth to power. People who speak up are usually marginalized and pushed back, called difficult, confrontational, you name it. I spoke up and got summarily smacked back down.[75]

In calling attention to the white power structures and systemic biases in Hollywood to a group of its gatekeepers, Brown was punished by being labeled as "difficult." Her career suffered: "It took five years to be released from that stigma. I'm CEO/Co-Owner of Gamechanger Films now, and I'm in a position of being invited to the table to help leverage the same access for all underrepresented groups—women, people of color, those with disabilities, LGBTQ, Indigenous, Latinx, Asian artists."[76] Notably, being hired in 2020 to run a film-financing fund created for and managed by women gave Brown the leverage not only to invest in more diverse storytelling but also to find the professional space and contemporary industry climate to speak more openly about the years of career setbacks she faced.

The emotional labor required to support creative talent is not limitless and it can eventually take a physical, mental, and emotional toll. Exhaustion and burnout can affect an individual project or it can surface at multiple points in a producer's career. When I visited an established white female producer who heads a successful production company for a prominent male hyphenate in Los Angeles during spring 2017, her exhaustion and frustration in that moment were so palpable and irrefutable that she apologized multiple times: "We [the producers] are giving everything and knowing we are never going to get as much back. What defines a producer: you will give more than everybody but you will never get the credit. You have to be ready for that." The "everything" is hard to quantify in terms of the hours and energy dedicated to a director's creative vision, talent's personal vulnerabilities, crew's personnel conflicts, and so on. For many, this caretaking role takes a toll during the production and beyond. Describing her job as 50 percent therapist, she wondered at the end of the day, "Who is going to take care of me?"[77]

Producer as Toxic Handler
In a study of how corporations manage employees' emotional pain caused by abusive bosses, layoffs, and institutional change, Peter Frost and Sandra Robinson locate a "certain breed of 'healing' manager" whom they call "toxic handlers." This type of senior manager "shoulders the sadness, frustration, bitterness, and anger that are endemic to organizational

life."[78] While creative producers operate in vastly different industrial and institutional spaces from traditional corporate managers, productive parallels emerge. Managerial positions carry the weight of a particular type of pressure and emotional work in which individuals are responsible for keeping a crew, project, and/or entire company afloat and moving forward in line with institutional priorities. Frost and Robinson assert: "In our current market-based and knowledge-driven world, success is a function of great ideas, which, of course, spring from intelligent, energized, and emotionally involved people. But great ideas dry up when people are hurting or when they are focused on organizational dysfunction. It is toxic handlers who frequently step in and absorb others' pain so that high-quality work continues to get done."[79] Through the work of defusing, mediating, and absorbing day-to-day conflict or stress, producers serve as the toxic handlers of film production. They "alleviate organizational pain" in the same five ways Frost and Robinson identify for corporate managers: (1) listen empathetically, (2) suggest solutions, (3) work behind the scenes to prevent pain, (4) carry the confidences of others, and (5) reframe difficult messages.[80]

While this inventory of tasks certainly applies to men and women in these types of managerial roles, the toxicity of the precarious, grueling, and cutthroat filmmaking culture emerges along a messy interpersonal spectrum and contributes to the gendered structural power dynamic increasingly being scrutinized by the late 2010s. Recalling the metaphor of changing emotional masks to fit the needs of the day, another established white creative producer described how some male directors expect "you to bend yourself into a funhouse mirror to what they need without them telling you."[81] On one end, producers note male directors' expectations to be "coddled," "carried," and "mothered" by having their biological, domestic, and emotional needs met in ways that their female peers do not. On the other end—and what the ongoing revelations after #MeToo continue to expose—are on-the-record accounts of toxic on-set and office cultures operating for decades in the film industry. Investigative journalists publishing headline-breaking stories are vital for Hollywood's long-needed reckoning with a history of excusing bad behavior, abuse, and misconduct as "business as usual" by those at the top if the result brings box office returns, awards, or career-making boosts. The previous lack of repercussions or public consequences on the part of the major studios, institutions, or collaborators has for decades allowed abusive men in power like executive Harvey Weinstein, producer Scott Rudin, and director-writer Joss Whedon to discriminate, abuse, and harass precarious individuals without the power to fight back or speak out.

In a 2015 *New York Times* interview, director Karyn Kusama points to the leeway afforded to men in positions of power: "There's an assumption that directors, showrunners, creators can be, and somehow benefit from being, tyrants. The assumption is that a man is a much better monster."[82] Men in the film industry have been allowed the emotional, physical, and verbal space—aka creative license—to be reactive, foster a toxic work environment, or lash out at talent and crew. Men wielding power, specifically those working successfully above the line, have perpetuated and benefitted from a system of toxic handlers who absorb and mediate their abusive behavior. One of the most nefarious aspects of the stories emerging from the #MeToo movement were the layers of enablers, from the assistant to the executive level, at film companies and on sets who react out of threat, fear, or indifference. Too many in the film industry have accepted the patterns of male directors', producers', and executives' destructive, abusive, and toxic behavior, or they have looked the other way or been silenced in fear of retaliation if they speak out. Yet, the high-profile individuals exposed since the late 2010s operate more as a game of Whac-a-Mole, taking out individual toxic players as outliers, and less as an interrogation of an industry's entire value system with a deeply ingrained abusive culture that manifests in innumerable ways.

My longitudinal process of collecting interviews spanning 2016 to 2021 captured this cultural shift on a personal, microlevel largely missing from industry press coverage beyond the handful of famous, well-positioned women who can afford to risk speaking out. The women I spoke with became more open and willing, without being prompted, to share their experiences as toxic handlers in what one described as a "bloodletting."[83] Every female producer recalled stories of working with and managing toxic male filmmakers and executives at some point in their careers. Many acknowledged the double standards for men, where anger is a privileged emotion, readily accepted and taken for granted as part of the creative process in film production. One middle-aged white female producer acknowledged that she is now processing experiences from her twenties and thirties differently in light of broader industry conversations about toxic and abusive work cultures. She tells a story about working with a "terrible" director: "He didn't listen to me because I was a woman. He was one of those 'bros' who says things about women on set. Misogyny and sexism appear in many forms. I'm only now recognizing things [from my past]."[84] Due to the ruthlessness of the film industry, as this producer signals, women have been expected to handle or ignore terrible working conditions as part of the process—in other words, who survives, stays. Another thirty-something producer of color had a similar revelation, which contributed to her leaving film production completely. "The culture is so pervasive that [a male supervisor and mentor] who has invested in my career and is helping me move up can make comments or gestures that are seen as innocuous on set," she explained, but made her feel gross, objectified, and devalued.[85] She recalled keeping quiet about instances of harassment due to the power dynamic: the older man's leverage as her supervisor and her precarious position as a young woman on the producer track without a solid professional network.

In addition to handling a director's bad behavior on a project, female creative producers also cited the complexities for what I call "navigating up" to studio executive. This topic often arose in conversations. The number one comment female producers at different stages of their career make is that because higher-ups at most studios are still mostly men, women must learn to handle a toxic spectrum—from microaggressions to verbal abuse—as part of the job. One example includes a white producer working with a production company run by "toxic boys" who routinely exhibited "biased" behavior in favor of male producers and constantly made degrading comments toward women in the office. Another producer of color, speaking upon condition of anonymity, described the experience of a female creative team landing a project with a major production company run by a multi-hyphenate household name white male producer only to be undercut and undermined at every stage of the project, reportedly because the A-list male executive felt threatened. What started as a project that promised to be the female creative team's big break turned into a nightmare as their project unraveled.[86]

During a routine negotiation for a project, an established white producer found out that "somebody was capital F Fucking me out of money," cutting her out of a deal for a project she had originated. In an effort to negotiate a "fair" amount of money—less than what the rights holders had contractually agreed to—she recalls a series of professional email exchanges in which questions about terms and money were volleyed back to her with questions about her feelings. The male executives turned the conversation away from compensation numbers and began to question her emotions and motives. When she countered their very low offer, in lieu of a continued negotiation, the producer was asked: "Why do you seem so angry? Don't you understand that we are such big fans of yours? Haven't we told you how great we think you are? All we want is for you to be happy—why are you making this all about money?" The more the producer tried to keep the exchange professional by moving the conversation back to the negotiation terms, the more the company representatives accused her of defensive and angry behavior. She recalled, "Only years later, and with the help of a therapist, did I realize I was stuck in a classic 'misogynist trap.' I was talking about the situation; they were talking about my temperament. The conversation felt like being caught in quicksand that I could not get out of."[87]

In this case, the producer found herself navigating the other party's destabilizing, gaslighting tactics in what should have been routine negotiation for pay. As Arlie Hochschild asserts, the gendered nature of anger operates to dismiss and demoralize women in different ways: "When women express an equivalent degree of anger, it is more likely to be interpreted as a sign of personal instability. It is believed that women are more emotional, and this very belief is used to invalidate their feelings. That is, the women's feelings are seen not as a response to real events but as reflections of themselves as 'emotional' women."[88] Even though the producer showed no explicit signs of antagonism and approached "the situation as a financial negotiator," the studio representatives made it about her "temperament," and as a result, dismissed her manner as irrational and unreasonable. Much like the "difficult" label, the possibility of feminine anger can become a threat to be weaponized against a woman in her efforts to silence men in the process of negotiating a financial deal or managing interpersonal conflict and can do long-lasting damage to her well-being and professional reputation.

Conclusion

For the 2018 documentary *Half the Picture*, director Amy Adrion and her team interviewed a diverse lineup of female directors with wide-ranging experiences in independent and studio filmmaking, including names who appear in *The Value Gap*—Ava DuVernay, Catherine Hardwicke, Gina Prince-Bythewood, Karyn Kusama, Kimberly Peirce, Patricia Riggen, and

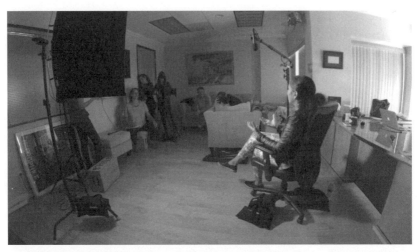

3.4. Director-producer Amy Adrion (left) on set interviewing director-writer-producer Gina Prince-Bythewood (right) for *Half the Picture*, Adrion's documentary about women directors (2018). (Screenshot from *Half the Picture*, 2018.)

Lena Dunham. Adrion conceived the documentary based on her own frustrations as a woman who faced similar barriers in building a filmmaking career in independent film in New York and Boston. Previously, she worked for writer-director Miranda July, completed an MFA in directing from UCLA, and won a Director's Guild of America student award for her thesis film. In a 2018 conversation, she described: "I had been swimming in these issues for over a decade. . . . I'd been reading all the headlines. Year after year of stats showing how it is almost impossible for women to have a career as director." After the ACLU announced an investigation into gender discrimination at major Hollywood studios in 2015, Adrion began to closely follow the issue with a journalist friend. Unable to secure funding or grants—"No one was going to finance [a film by a woman about female filmmakers] so I had to make it first"—she bought production equipment on credit cards ("we're still paying those off in 2018"), put together a crew from her UCLA graduate school network ("really talented women with small kids who can't hustle like they need to for jobs"), and began filming interviews with female directors. Only after filming twenty-five interviews did the project secure an equity investor and hire a full-time editor.

The small crew purposefully consisted of almost all women. Numerous behind-the-scenes shots appear in the documentary highlighting the women working in key physical production roles such as sound, lighting, and photography to capture Adrion as she conducts one-on-one interviews with filmmakers: "People think of [filmmaking as] the magical realm and that you need to have superhuman powers to be a filmmaker. We wanted to show a film set, and not something like *Thor: Ragnarok*, but wanted to give a behind-the-scenes look to visually represent the sisterhood—the informal network of women advising women who are trying to get there. [Everyone working on *Half the Picture*] is aspiring to careers these women in the interviews have."[89] As Anne O'Brien argues in her extensive work on women's experiences in media production, "the consequence of the gendering of roles, both horizontally and vertically, is that women working in screen production continue to exist within traditionally masculine structures where gender dictates the roles women are 'allowed' to assume and how they are permitted to play those roles."[90] The documentary highlights but also counters gender disparities in the filmmaking pipeline by centering women's visible contributions on an individual film production.

Half the Picture premiered at the Sundance Film Festival in January 2018 as industry and popular press coverage around gender equity in filmmaking shifted course. Leslie Felperin reflects on the documentary's Sundance premiere in the *Hollywood Reporter*: "It seems absurd that we've had to wait until 2018 for a film to address the essential question at the core of this inquiry: Why are there so few women film directors working today? What stands in their way? What forces conspire to keep them from working?"[91] As a result, *Half the Picture* benefitted from what the director described as "astonishing" timing at Sundance as the #MeToo movement escalated and the Time's Up organization emerged. At the same time, major international film festivals—including Cannes, Venice, Toronto, and Berlin, as well as more focused US festivals like Sundance—increasingly emerged as a site of criticism and reflection as contributing to these same equity and inclusion concerns. As will be discussed in the following chapter, festivals are vital to the larger filmmaking pipeline and for accessing career-building opportunities for directors and producers. The film festival operates as a vital industrial and cultural marketplace, and not surprisingly, similar disparities and biases that impact female filmmakers and their projects in development and production do not disappear in these later stages of the film process. Because gendered barriers to entry and access persist with festival programming and distribution deals, women working above the line must continue to navigate an uneven playing field well beyond finishing the production.

CHAPTER 4

Film Festivals and Markets
(Programming Gap)

Each May, the glitz and glamour of the global film business descends upon a resort town on the French Riviera. A mix of film professionals, from stars and filmmakers to journalists and studio executives, convenes at one of the most prestigious and exclusive industry events of the year, the Cannes Film Festival. Beloved international directors premiere their latest films, distribution deals are announced, and the opening night film feels like a wild-card choice between a French prestige drama or a Hollywood blockbuster. World premieres attract A-list talent from around the world dressed in the required formal attire of tuxedos and evening gowns. Because France's premiere festival represents a distinct business model closed off from the general public and serves as a reference point for the global film industry, Dorota Ostrowska asserts Cannes should be in its own category of scholarship.[1]

In her book *A Killer Life: How an Independent Film Producer Survives Deals and Disasters in Hollywood and Beyond*, American producer Christine Vachon recounts the importance of film festivals to independent filmmaking: "The whole world is at Cannes. There are other film festivals and markets, of course, and most often, the festival you take your film to is dictated by when your movie is done. If you finish in winter, you submit it to Cannes. Fall, you try for Berlin. Spring or summer, submit it to Venice."[2] Larger festivals attract some of the most powerful players, from studio moguls to A-list talent, with competing priorities and positions. For emerging to established filmmakers, acceptance into these major festivals is hypercompetitive, as a film premiere at one of these exalted events has the potential to launch or boost their careers. The largest of these annual events attract upward of hundreds of thousands of attendees spilling into the neighborhoods of Toronto and Berlin or taking over the entire towns of Park City and Cannes.

As early as Venice in 1932 and Cannes in 1946, film festivals have operated as a complex geopolitical, economic, and cultural site for the international film business. As film festival scholars often describe, early European festivals evolved from an Olympic-style display promoting national cinema into an international network of festivals serving a distinct set of audiences, traditions, perspectives, and cultures.[3] The festival space grew significantly in the twentieth century, with Berlin (also known as Berlinale), London, and Karlovy Vary in the 1940s and 1950s, the Hong Kong International Film Festival and early iterations of North American festivals like Toronto and Sundance launched in the 1970s, and the Shanghai International Film Festival and Busan International Film Festival beginning in the 1990s, to name a few.

The International Federation of Film Producers Associations (FIAPF) provides accreditation to Cannes, Toronto, Venice, and Berlin as top-tier international film festivals, all of which occur at different times of the year and vary in size, attendees, and competitiveness for entry. (Due to their status as prestigious competition categories, the three European festivals are popularly referred to as the "Big Three" or A-level.) This network of commercial festivals represents a powerful global marketplace that has come to encompass all phases of filmmaking—from financing to exhibition—in the twenty-first century.[4] Distinct from the public-facing festival screenings and awards, major business-oriented festivals coincide with formal or informal marketplaces. As a vital space for stakeholders working at each phase of the filmmaking pipeline, the "market" is where projects in development go to look for financing or to be packaged. Films in need of distribution deals are screened for sales agents and distributors. A film premiere may lead to a distribution deal, result in critical and industrial press coverage, or other potential career-making networking opportunities.

This chapter focuses on the film festival business as a series of industry gatekeepers for female-driven films and their filmmakers. Major international festivals are powerful institutions, tastemakers, and platforms for discovering, vetting, and promoting emerging cinematic voices, but women have historically been denied acceptance at many of the festivals at the same level as their male peers. During the 2010s, major European and North American festivals increasingly emerged as sites of contestation and mediation for evolving gender parity debates on a global scale. Specifically, business-oriented festivals have come under pressure to address internal gender inequity, from programming to executive leadership, as well as external expectations to develop more inclusive policies.

In *The Value Gap*, I am particularly invested in how the struggle for gender parity plays out in different spaces, by different voices, and with different results. As Dina Iordanova argues, "There is a consensus among scholars that media industries research needs to study how the film festival structures and narrates itself, what its components are, what constitutes the play of power between its participants, and how this is reenacted in the time and space of the festival and even beyond."[5] A robust body of film festival studies scholarship offers instructive categories—business/audience, open/closed, competitive/noncompetitive, commercial/independent, international/regional/local—that point to issues of access and gatekeeping, inclusion and exclusion, ingrained in infrastructure, operations, target audiences, and organizational mandates.[6] As massive global events, international film festivals operate through particular rules, cultures, and traditions, varying across institutions that are neither completely transparent nor immediately accessible.

As distinct microcosms of business activities across production, distribution, and exhibition, the film festival represents a fruitful longitudinal case study for tracking where evolving industry pressure collides with distinct institutional cultures. My research grew out of fieldwork and interviews conducted at four major festivals—Cannes, Berlin, Toronto, and Sundance—between 2013 and 2022. In attending festivals during this period and tracking trade press coverage and festival communication, I had a unique perspective on how film festivals, and the industry players attending, responded to real-time, rapidly changing conversations around gender bias, sexism, and misogyny in the film industry.

Each festival approaches the swelling pressure to hire, program, and support female filmmakers differently, ranging from dismissive deniability to actively engaged commitment to inclusive practices. The first section of this chapter examines the Sundance Film Festival at a particular moment, between 2010 and 2012, and the realities for female-driven films premiering in the US Dramatic Competition category. In general, female filmmakers and their films from this period did not experience the same career boost as their male Sundance "classmates," an equity gap known as the "post-festival chasm." The next section looks at internal institutional gatekeeping for female-driven films, including programming and leadership. During the 2010s, increased international criticism and scrutiny of the top festivals focused on widespread gender inequities in programming for competition or gala premieres. The third section discusses the film festival as a marketplace, specifically areas of inequity that have not been given the same attention as programming and leadership, such as awards, film critics and press coverage, and sales agents and distribution. The remaining section examines how, in parallel to the evolving #MeToo and Time's Up movements, festivals like Cannes, TIFF, and Sundance increasingly acted upon pressure for gender inclusion through a broad spectrum of initiatives and public responses. Building on earlier film festival studies that explore the history, operations, and experiences of festivals around the world, this chapter adopts a critical media industry studies lens to explore how the major international festivals are addressing their part in the film industry pipeline's gender gap and how these institutions responded to criticism in the 2010s.

Post-Festival Chasm

To describe the selection process for the Sundance Film Festival as competitive is a gross understatement. Although 3,853 feature films vied for consideration, Sundance 2020 programmers selected only 118 of those submissions.[7] Getting a feature film accepted to the festival places a project in front of programmers, journalists and critics, sales agents, distributors, and every other industry mover and shaker flocking to Utah each year. A handful of lucky filmmakers from the indie realm of lower budgets, scarcer resources, and fewer industry connections submit their films in the hope of career-making opportunities to follow. Even if an unknown filmmaker is plucked out of the pile, the programming process is opaque, and not all Sundance-selection stories and filmmakers' journeys have a happy ending. Even with a major festival premiere in one of the dramatic or documentary categories, female filmmakers too often find their career progress slows, stalls, or stops on the way to the next film project in ways that their male peers do not experience. This section examines the festival gender gap, or a post-festival chasm that Christina Lane compares to a career "plateau" where women's careers level out or drop off completely.[8] Building upon this conceptual framework, I compare a handful of filmmakers premiering in the same Sundance class in the early 2010s to illustrate the significant gap between acceptance rates for women in the US Dramatic Competition category in relation to their short-term and long-term career trajectories after the festival.

Started as the US Film Festival in the 1970s, the Sundance Institute took "creative and administration control" in 1985.[9] Steven Soderbergh's *sex, lies, and videotape* won the Dramatic Audience Award in 1989 and served as a major turning point for the festival and its distributor Miramax after becoming a commercial box office hit. By 1991, the officially renamed Sundance Film Festival emerged alongside a burgeoning American independent film industry. Synonymous with Hollywood power players, deal making, and discoveries, the Park City festival is the gold standard for launching the careers of independent multi-hyphenates, from Spike Lee to Quentin Tarantino to Rian Johnson.[10] By the 1990s, Christina Lane argues, Sundance had helped to foster a "'maverick' cinema . . . privileging young, white, male directors, and witnessing a massive corporatization and privatization of the independent and crossover Indiewood spheres."[11] The major Hollywood studios began to aggressively acquire independent films for theatrical distribution through newly created boutique divisions—Sony Pictures Classics (Sony) and Focus Features (Universal), formerly Fox Searchlight (Fox), as well as the now shuttered Warner Independent (Warner) and Paramount Vantage (Paramount) and the discarded shell of Miramax (Disney). With the backing of their parent companies with big pockets for buying festival films to strategically expand their film slates, the so-called Indiewood divisions invested heavily in a commercially minded, largely male-driven sensibility.[12] The distribution deals during this period became legendary, with first-time filmmakers negotiating multiple buyers at the festival.

Alongside, or more likely due to, higher stakes and larger distribution deals, "a renewed 'cult of the auteur' took hold," featuring a new generation of white male wunderkinds while simultaneously pushing female filmmakers further to Hollywood's margins after the festival. Writer-director Kelly Reichardt recalled this period of independent filmmaking in a 2020 *GQ* interview: "Independent filmmaking, or any kind of filming, was really not open and generous to women in any way. It was really like beating your head against a brick wall. People who somehow managed out of a fluke to get a first film made—trying to get a second film made was just really an impossible venture it seemed."[13] Premiering alongside Sundance breakouts *Clerks* and *Spanking the Monkey* that launched Kevin Smith's and David O. Russell's studio filmmaking careers, respectively, Reichardt's directorial debut also screened at Park City. Strand Releasing distributed *River of Grass* theatrically, which went on to win three Independent Spirit Awards, including Best First Feature. Reichardt waited twelve years before making her follow-up film, *Old Joy* (2006), in a textbook example of both the post-festival chasm and the extent to which women's voices were deprioritized or sidelined during this Indiewood period.

Lane describes how the industrial context by the early 2000s impacted female-driven films:

> The problem is that women who attempt to establish careers in an independent world now dominated by "mini-major" studios often hit a plateau after their first film. . . . What of the women who decide to direct the narrative features so valued by major film festivals and mini-major distributors? . . . What precisely are the hurdles for women filmmakers who try to parlay their "calling card" films into passkeys for further creative possibilities in the competitive age of mini-majors?[14]

Successful festival premieres are often compared to "calling cards," introducing emerging filmmakers to potential financiers and studio gatekeepers and, ideally, offering a way to leverage festival buzz into pitch meetings and future creative opportunities. Rose Troche's *Go Fish*, cowritten and coproduced with star Guinevere Turner, also premiered at Sundance in 1994. As captured in John Pierson's *Spike, Mike, Slackers & Dykes*, the Sundance premiere resulted in a lively bidding war ending when Samuel Goldwyn acquired the film for $450,000. Emerging as part of the New Queer Cinema movement of American independent filmmaking in the 1990s, the black-and-white lesbian comedy *Go Fish* became a "crossover hit" during its theatrical run.[15] Troche's two follow-up features did not meet the same critical and commercial success, and the filmmaker would spend the next two decades of her career working in television, a common experience for female filmmakers premiering at Sundance in the 1990s and 2000s.

Lane also points to Karyn Kusama's Sundance debut *Girlfight*, which won the 2000 Grand Jury Prize and directing prize. Acquisition of the directorial debut by Sony's Screen Gems label for $3 million led to splashy trade headlines recounting an aggressive bidding war among four competing distributors. On the one hand, *Girlfight* contributed to increased representation of female directors (40 percent) in the US Dramatic Competition program, leading to celebratory "Year of the Woman" press coverage.[16] On the other hand, the *Los Angeles Times* article "How 'Girlfight' Fell Flat on Its Face," published only a year later, asked, "How could a film burn so brightly, then flicker away without a trace?"[17] Despite female filmmakers who break through at Sundance and leave with distribution deals, many struggle, and continue to struggle, to maintain momentum. As was the case for female Grand Jury Prize winners before and after her, Kusama did not experience a steady career boost but instead struggled for the next two decades to build a sustainable career in Hollywood.[18]

Just as acceptance rates for female directors in the US Dramatic Competition category averaged 25 percent for the decade after Kusama's award-winning debut, familiar hurdles remained. The inclusion of women filmmakers fluctuated from 25 percent in 2010 and 2011 and 18 percent in 2012 to 43 percent in 2013 and 25 percent in 2014.[19] Beyond counting names on the program, a more complex story emerges from the early 2010s, one of inequitable boosts and uneven benefits experienced by female-driven premieres during and after Sundance. Based on analysis of the Sundance director classes in this category from 2010 to 2012, I consider how a series of gender gaps played out that include distribution deals, time to follow-up project, budget of the follow-up film, and collaborators along the way. While I cannot account for all variables that take place behind closed doors, festival programs, trade coverage, and personal and public-facing interviews reveal how films premiering in the same year and festival context impact male and female filmmakers in starkly different ways.

Drake Doremus's second and third features (*Douchebag*, 2010, and *Like Crazy*, 2011) premiered at Sundance back to back. Starring Felicity Jones and Anton Yelchin and budgeted around $250,000, the 2011 drama follows the long-distance relationship of a twenty-something couple struggling to stay together between their Los Angeles and London homes. As a generally well-reviewed festival premiere, Kenneth Turan offered

Table 4.1. Female-Driven Films in US Dramatic Competition at the Sundance Film Festival (2010–2012)*

Year	Director	Film	US Distributor	Widest Theatrical Release and Date	Follow-Up Feature
2010	Zeina Durra**	*The Imperialists are Still Alive!*	Sundance Selects	April 15, 2011 1 theater	*Luxor* (2020)
	Tanya Hamilton**	*Night Catches Us*	Magnolia Pictures	December 3, 2010 9 theaters	No follow-up as of 2021; directing for television
	Diane Bell**	*Obselidia*	Roadside Attractions	Data not available	*Bleeding Heart* (2015)
	Debra Granik**	*Winter's Bone*	Roadside Attractions	June 11, 2010 141 theaters	*Leave No Trace* (2018)
2011	Amy Wendel**	*Benavides Born* (retitled *All She Can*)	Maya Entertainment	Data not available	No follow-up as of 2021
	Maryam Keshavarz**	*Circumstance*	Participant Media/ Roadside Attractions	August 26, 2011 31 theaters	*Viper Club* (2018)
	Vera Farmiga	*Higher Ground*	Sony Pictures Classics	August 26, 2011 81 theaters	No follow-up as of 2021; credits from acting
	Dee Rees**	*Pariah*	Focus Features	December 28, 2011 24 theaters	*Mudbound* (2017)
2012	So Yong Kim**	*For Ellen*	Tribeca Films	September 5, 2012 3 theaters	*Lovesong* (2016)
	Ava DuVernay**	*Middle of Nowhere*	Participant Media	October 2, 2012 25 theaters	*Selma* (2014)
	Ry Russo-Young**	*Nobody Walks*	Magnolia Pictures	October 19, 2012 7 theaters	*Before I Fall* (2017)

*The US Dramatic Competition category selects sixteen films each year.
**Denotes director was also the screenwriter or co-screenwriter.
Source: Data from IMBD and Box Office Mojo.

glowing praise of *Like Crazy* in the first sentence of a *Los Angeles Times* article: "Drake Doremus has always been a bit of a prodigy, a filmmaker who combines the energy and enthusiasm of the 27-year-old he is with an old soul sensibility wise enough to value emotional honesty and capture it on film."[20] In fact, most festival film reviews largely foregrounded and celebrated Doremus. *IndieWire* labeled him "a filmmaker born to play the Sundance game" and who, according to *Rolling Stone*, "crafted a crazily inventive and totally irresistible tale of first love."[21]

In a very different scenario, Debra Granik, one of Doremus's female Sundance classmates from the previous year, came out with her second feature, *Winter's Bone*, in 2010. The rural Ozark-set mystery drama, often described as "rural noir," won Grand Jury Prize for Dramatic Film and launched Jennifer Lawrence to A-list status with a Best Actress Oscar nomination. Kenneth Turan opened his *Los Angeles Times* review with this description: "Intense, immersive and in control, *Winter's Bone* has an art house soul inside a B picture body, and that proves to be a potent combination indeed."[22] Turan's review of Granik's film appears just as positive as the review he would write for Doremus's *Like Crazy* the following year. Yet, what these examples highlight is the tendency of film critics to center white male directors as active, romantic agents in their reviews. One female director of color who had a film premiere at Sundance during the 2010s puzzled over this trope in Sundance film reviews: "Why are men always called geniuses? And I'm not. Why are my reviews not better based on the buzz? Why is my film not given the same consideration or recognition as my male peers?"[23] She recalled the frustration as her male Sundance classmates garnered press attention—or, as she put it, took up all of the space in a room.

Granik's and Doremus's features ended up with notably different distribution deals. *Like Crazy* won the Grand Jury Prize in 2011, and Paramount Pictures picked up theatrical rights for $4 million. The critical buzz helped to set Doremus on a filmmaking path along which he successfully produced and premiered a new project every two years during the remainder of the 2010s. In comparison, Roadside Attractions picked up US distribution rights for the $2 million–budgeted *Winter's Bone* for reportedly "low to mid-six figures," a stark difference from the deal Doremus secured the following year.[24] Notably featured in both Granik's and Doremus's films, Jennifer Lawrence saw her acting career take off during this period—evidence of how women on the screen can leverage a post-Sundance boost from which women behind the camera rarely benefit. After being cast in two big-budget franchises—Fox's *X-Men* reboot (2011–2019) and Lionsgate's *The Hunger Games* (2012–2015)—Lawrence became the highest paid actress in Hollywood by 2015.

A key challenge that female directors face is not only whether their films are acquired for distribution, but also *which* distribution company picks up their films. In a USC Annenberg Inclusion Initiative study looking at Sundance film selections from 2002 to 2014, Stacy L. Smith, Katherine Pieper, and Marc Choueiti find that female directors (70.2 percent) versus male directors (56.9 percent) secured distribution deals with independent companies compared to a higher number of men (43.1 percent) than women (29.8 percent) landing deals with more prestigious specialty boutique divisions.[25] Over this period, higher-profile, studio-owned distributors like Focus Features, formerly Fox Searchlight (now Searchlight), and Sony Pictures Classics routinely bought the rights to distribute male-directed films more often than those of their female classmates. Compared to smaller indie outfits that picked up Granik and other female-directed Sundance dramas during this period, studio specialty divisions come with deeper pockets for acquisition deals, marketing, and wider theatrical distribution. As a result, distribution deals varied widely and offered different launchpads for the Sundance classes between 2010 to 2012.

Another post-festival gap women disproportionately confront is the average number of years between a Sundance premiere and their next film project. One of the most cited examples of the post-festival chasm for women directors is the average six-year stretch before releasing a follow-up project. Despite garnering further critical acclaim and box office returns, Granik neither completed nor released a follow-up narrative feature until eight years later, with *Leave No Trace* (2018). Writer-director Dee Rees, who came off a critical and award-winning premiere with her first feature, *Pariah*, in 2011, also experienced a gap between projects. Developed from a short thesis project in her NYU graduate program into a feature script at the Sundance Labs, Rees's directorial debut is a coming-of-age drama about a young Black woman struggling with her queer identity. Universal's Focus Features picked up *Pariah* for reportedly around seven figures, making Rees an outlier from other female-driven Sundance premieres of this period.

In comparison, Rees's female Sundance classmates demonstrate more typical experiences of delayed acquisition and smaller theatrical distribution releases. Maya Entertainment picked up worldwide rights for an undisclosed amount for Amy Wendel's coming-of-age drama *All She Can* (previously *Benavides Born*) about a teenage Latina powerlifter in Texas. The acquisition deal, which happened more than three months after its festival premiere and a new cut of the film, led to a small, targeted release as part of a tour of "U.S. and foreign Latino-theme cinema to major markets nationwide."[26] In contrast, Participant Media initially acquired the North American rights to Maryam Keshavarz's Audience Award–winning *Circumstance*, a drama about a wealthy Iranian family and their rebellious teenage children, for six figures. Roadside Attractions then picked up the US distribution rights and the film was released in August 2011.[27]

Even though *Pariah* and *Circumstance* had similar limited theatrical releases, twenty-four versus thirty-one theaters, respectively, Rees gained traction from Sundance in ways her female classmates did not. She notably secured a blind script development deal with Focus, though the film and TV projects she worked on in subsequent years never left the development stage. While she was hired to direct a 2015 HBO Bessie Smith biopic starring Queen Latifah, Rees experienced a six-year gap between *Pariah* and her second feature, *Mudbound*, which premiered at Sundance in 2017. Rees reflects on the gap women experience in produced credits in the 2015 *New York Times* article, "The Women of Hollywood Speak Out":

I look at Woody Allen's prolific career of 30 or 40 films, and I'm watching the clock. . . . I'd love to work at a clip of a film a year. [Female directors] don't get the benefit of the doubt, particularly Black women. We're presumed incompetent, whereas a white male is assumed competent until proven otherwise. They just think the guy in the ball hat and the T-shirt over the thermal has got it, whether he's got it or not. For buzzy first films by a white male, the trajectory is a 90-degree angle. For us, it's a 30-degree angle.[28]

Even with noticeable gaps between follow-up projects, Rees and Granik, as working filmmakers, are in many ways considered exceptions compared to other female Sundance classmates, including Zeina Durra, Tanya Hamilton, and Wendel, none of whom made a second feature film in the following decade.

One of the most widely cited post-festival disparities comes from Sundance 2012. Ava DuVernay was the first Black woman to win the directing award, for her second feature, *Middle of Nowhere*.[29] Made for a $200,000 budget, the drama follows Emayatzy Corinealdi playing a woman who struggles to come to terms with her personal and professional path while her husband serves an eight-year prison sentence. Despite the film's critical acclaim and a mid-six-figure distribution deal with Participant Media, the festival did not launch DuVernay immediately into the studio space. As she told Manohla Dargis in a 2014 *New York Times* profile: "No one offered me anything [after Sundance]."[30]

In contrast, her Sundance classmate Colin Trevorrow arrived with his first feature, *Safety Not Guaranteed*, a $750,000-budgeted time travel romantic comedy starring Mark Duplass and Aubrey Plaza. FilmDistrict reportedly picked up distribution rights for more than $1 million. DuVernay's next job was to direct a Martin Luther King Jr. biopic, *Selma* (2014), produced by Brad Pitt's Plan B and distributed by Paramount Pictures. Trevorrow was hired to helm a reboot of Universal Pictures' *Jurassic Park* franchise, *Jurassic World* (2015). In a 2015 speech at *Elle* magazine's "Women in Hollywood" event, DuVernay recounted a conversation she had with Trevorrow about their Sundance follow-ups:

AV: And I said, "I got some good news. I got a big movie."
CT: Big movie. What do you mean?
AV: They're giving me $20 million dollars . . .
CT: $20 million dollars?
AV: . . . to make *Selma*, a film about Dr. King.
CT: Wow, that's amazing.
AV: He said, "I have some good news too." Really? What good news?
CT: I got a movie, too.
AV: Alright! We're doing this. What's it about?
CT: It's about dinosaurs. It's called *Jurassic World*. And it costs $150 million dollars to film.
AV: Great guy, Colin Trevorrow. Now after *Jurassic World* he'll go on and do *Star Wars*. And I'm happy for him.[31]

DuVernay followed up *Selma* (2014) with Disney's adaptation of Madeleine L'Engle's beloved children's book *A Wrinkle in Time* (2018) for her next feature, becoming the third woman (and first Black woman) to direct a $100 million studio project. While she leveraged smaller-scale indie projects into commercial studio filmmaking, DuVernay is an outlier in

4.1. Director Ava DuVernay in conversation on set with actor David Oyelowo, who stars as Martin Luther King Jr. in Paramount's *Selma* (2014). The behind-the-scenes footage comes from a Paramount promotional featurette about the film's production. (Screenshot from Paramount's marketing materials for *Selma* via YouTube.)

joining the small group of women who are big-budget Hollywood directors. Many women characterize the disparities in second feature budgets as lost years that further widen the gender gap of employment, pay, and career advancement for female directors. Kelly Reichardt's experience is the more common one, as she recounted to *GQ* magazine in 2020: "Just going to Sundance and watching my male counterparts get the budget I still haven't gotten on their second films and feeling like, 'Wow, a decade lost'—watching all those guys that I am in the same age of, watching their careers."[32] Her comments echo DuVernay's story and highlight how female directors are increasingly speaking more openly and publicly about their frustrations.

Trevorrow's leap from indie first feature to studio franchise follow-up was cited often in the trade press during the period, primarily with regard to how he landed the Universal gig. A well-connected male mentor introduced the emerging filmmaker to *Jurassic World*'s producer, who reportedly said, "There is this guy that reminds me of me."[33] A number of female creatives I interviewed referred to this as the "mini me" syndrome. Trevorrow became the poster boy for a line of first-time male indie directors hired to helm massive franchises with no previous studio experience.[34]

During the summer of *Jurassic World*'s release, a Twitter dustup occurred after the director responded to growing industry criticism that female filmmakers were not being hired to helm major blockbusters. He defensively tweeted:

> I want to believe that a filmmaker with both the desire and ability to make a studio blockbuster will be given an opportunity to make their case. I stress desire because I honestly think that's a part of the issue. Many of the top female directors in our industry are not interested in doing a piece of studio business for its own sake. These filmmakers have clear voices and stories to tell that don't necessarily involve superheroes or spaceships or dinosaurs.[35]

Trevorrow later apologized, but the tone-deaf comment reflects industry lore that dismisses real-world gender bias by accusing women of lacking ambition, experience, ability, or interest in helming what the studios have traditionally defined as male-driven genres.

For male directors and their female peers who do move on to the next independent project or break into working for the major studios, what happens to their creative collaborators who helped produce their "calling card" feature? Does a successful Sundance premiere raise the tide only for the filmmaker or include other collaborators in their boat? A central frustration I heard from female producers who shepherded indie projects to Sundance is how many are left behind after the post-Sundance boost. As explored in the previous chapter, female creative producers must navigate complexities from financing to distribution deals while working with male directors, financiers, and distributors with little public visibility and fewer accolades. I spoke separately with multiple women whose careers hit a plateau or slowed after successful Sundance premieres during the 2010s. The festival awards, critical success, and widely publicized distribution deals proved a boon to their young white male directors. One white female producer, who had two feature films premiere back-to-back at Park City, felt left behind by both male collaborators. She watched as these emerging directors immediately received offers to direct projects with budgets two to four times bigger. Another white female producer in her professional network recalls a similarly disheartening reality after experiencing the highs of multiple successful Sundance premieres:

> I started to have a personal crisis, because I was seeing a lot of the filmmakers that I worked with go on to great heights and so were

my [male producing] peers. . . . I was killing myself and watching my friends kill themselves to support unproven young, usually white male voices. And there was no reciprocity! Like, after we lifted them out of obscurity and got their first films made, there was no sustainability. They just dropped us and moved on.[36]

In both producers' cases, the male collaborators went on to direct additional films, with larger budgets and bigger stars either for an indie boutique division or for a major studio.

In my interviews, I encountered varied perspectives from independent producers versus executives on what the producer is owed versus what a director can realistically promise on a follow-up project. A former development executive responded critically to the expectations of any independent producer to be brought along by a first-time director with little leverage for their next project at a studio. Despite the impracticalities of this potential arrangement, a number of independent female producers expressed bitterness and frustration after "being left behind" by their first-time directors. As discussed in the previous chapter, expectations for the creative producer change dramatically from a small indie to a studio project, the latter of which requires experience and industry capital that many independent producers have not, and likely will not, acquire. Yet, a producer and former development executive also contends that when producers do get such opportunities, which can happen, they are often men bringing along their buddies:

I have seen lots of people brought along [to the next project, a bigger-budget studio], and it has always seemed like most often, they are male [even if they are not ready and don't know what they are doing]. I never felt like I got a free pass to not know what I'm doing. But I'd constantly stumble upon people who were stepped up quickly, not because they were qualified or were working hard to learn, but because the filmmaker simply liked having them around. "He's my guy."[37]

This former executive's comment reinforces a boy's club culture that can be re-created when homogeneous creative collaborative teams can move together along the indie-to-studio pipeline. Because male directors are more likely to move up to bigger-budget, higher-profile projects—and do so more quickly, as evidenced by the Sundance classes from these years—male creative producers may benefit from inequitable leaps. The festival gap remains a wide one for many female producers and directors and can shape future opportunities for years or even decades. These stories reveal the complex dynamics at play in not only getting accepted into a major festival but also in navigating that experience and then strategically building from it.

Festival Programming, Awards, and Power Roles

Business-oriented festivals serve a variety of stakeholders and are spaces in which filmmakers, distributors, publicists, programmers, policymakers, critics, journalists, corporate sponsors, local businesses, and general attendees often intermingle.[38] Cannes, Berlin, Venice, Toronto, and, on a smaller scale, Sundance prioritize industry players attending red carpet premieres and press junkets in a parallel to negotiating distribution rights surrounded by lucrative corporate branding and marketing campaigns. Beyond the press and public-facing festival screenings, the festival marketplace serves as a significant site of business for the global film industry. Cindy Hing-Yuk Wong contends:

> The markets at global film festivals are said to "ADD VALUE" to the festivals, allowing them not only to be showcases, but also to be channels through which films are made, distributed, and exhibited. They bring together the world of film, create a forum for competition, and, as in the case of film knowledge and selection, stratify it globally. In many ways, the markets are about the bottom line of the film business, and the traditional cultural aspects of film screenings and competitions are the more public faces of the festivals.[39]

The business festivals category, according to Mark Peranson, is distinct from smaller community-supported audience festivals, which are run mostly by seasonal and volunteer staff, support a variety of filmmakers from local to international, and cater to local public attendees.[40] In cases like TIFF, some bigger festivals are a mix of the two models, business and audience.

As both an industry-focused festival catering to delegates with strict accreditation and largely closed to the public, Cannes's exclusivity is central to its institutional brand, and the cultural capital accrues to the selected films. As a platform supporting French-language and international arthouse filmmakers, Cannes has long served as a launchpad for auteur-driven selections. After winning the Palme d'Or, the festival's top prize, Bong Joon-ho's *Parasite* (2019), Ruben Östlund's *The Square* (2017), Michael Haneke's *Amour* (2012), and Terrence Malick's *The Tree of Life* (2011) each played at other prestigious festivals before launching successful awards season campaigns. At the same time, Cannes has cultivated a long and cozy relationship with the Hollywood studios. From its beginning, the festival catered to the major studios, as evidenced by the decades of A-list talent attending red carpet premieres and posing for photo ops. The annual programming list includes staples of Hollywood fare, as big-budget star-driven projects like Dreamworks' *Shrek* (2001), Universal's *Robin Hood* (2010), Sony's *The Da Vinci Code* (2005), Warner Bros.' *The Great Gatsby* (2013), and Paramount's *Top Gun: Maverick* (2022) premiered as Out of Competition selections.

Programming for major international festivals like Cannes is more complicated than a selection and scheduling process. Jeffrey Ruoff contends that "programming . . . is not a matter of festival directors simply choosing the films they want to show. Even the most powerful European festivals—Cannes, Venice, Berlin—and North American festivals—Toronto and to a different extent Sundance—engage in delicate negotiations with filmmakers, distributors, and sales agents to secure the rights to premiere new works."[41] Many of these decisions are based on premiere and release strategies for each of the stakeholders involved to create momentum and produce critical and/or financial impact. Echoing a number of film festival scholars, Marijke de Valck and Mimi Soeteman identify a central function of film festivals as a "gateway to cultural legitimization."[42] Thomas Elsaesser categorizes a festival as "an apparatus that breathes oxygen into an individual film and the reputation of its director as potential *auteur*, but at the same time it breathes oxygen into the system of festivals as a whole, keeping the network buoyant and afloat."[43] Major festivals confer value on the selected films and filmmakers while reinforcing the prestige of their own brands as powerful platforms. If festivals are "multipliers and amplifiers," as Elsaesser contends, key questions persist around the inequities impacting female-driven films with regard to programming, leadership, and awards at major international festivals. Who is doing the amplifying?

Table 4.2. Leadership at Major International Film Festivals (2000–2022)

Film Festival	Festival Director	Title/Years
Berlin	Dieter Kosslick	Artistic Director 2001–2019
	Mariette Rissenbeek	Executive Director 2019–
	Carlo Chatrian	Artistic Director 2019–
Cannes	Thierry Frémaux	Artistic Director 2001–2007; General Delegate* 2007–
Venice	Alberto Barbera	Artistic Director 2011–
Sundance	John Cooper	Festival Director 2009–2020
	Tabitha Jackson	Festival Director 2020–2022
Toronto	Cameron Bailey	Artistic Director 2012–2018; Artistic Director & Co-Head 2018–2021
	Joana Vicente	Executive Director & Co-Head 2018–2021

*In 2007, Frémaux transitioned to the role of General Delegate, which encompasses both artistic director and lead management for the Cannes Film Festival.

The leadership of international festivals involves a range of individuals—artistic director, director of programming, staff positions on selection or programming committees. However, it is the artistic director who oversees festival operations and staff. The leadership role of the festival's artistic director for A-level competition and other major festivals has historically been male-dominated. As table 4.2 shows, a male artistic director led every single top-tier American and European film festival until 2019.

In addition to creative decision-making roles and overseeing festival programming committees, festival directors are the public face of the organization and its institutional culture in the most visible of a festival's "power roles."[44] As illustrated by trade publication coverage of the major international festivals, directors speak to the press and in many ways are the ambassadors of these organizations. Only in recent years—due to leadership changes and retirements—have major festivals begun to hire more women and people of color. TIFF appointed Joana Vicente as the festival's co-head and executive director working alongside Cameron Bailey in 2018, while Berlinale hired Mariette Rissenbeek as the executive director in 2019. Sundance promoted Tabitha Jackson from director of documentary program to festival director in 2020. Rissenbeek, Vicente, and Jackson were the only women (and only women of color) to direct or codirect major international festivals at the start of the decade. Notably, Vicente then left TIFF to become Sundance's CEO in September 2021 and Jackson left Sundance in 2022.[45]

Gender disparities characterizing the top-tier festivals in Europe and North America up until the 2010s do not necessarily reflect other, smaller industry-focused or regional festivals. While not the focus of this chapter, it is important to highlight how some smaller independent festivals have led the way with women in leadership positions. For example, South by Southwest Film & TV Festival (SXSW) in Austin is the premiere film festival running each March. What began primarily as a music festival in 1987 to highlight the entertainment and media industries in the Texas capital city has expanded in the past three decades into separate events for film, music, comedy, interactive, and education. Under the leadership of festival director Janet Pierson from 2008 to 2022, the SXSW Film Festival grew into a competitive international festival. Pierson worked in independent film distribution for decades, including closely with her husband John Pierson as a producer's rep. As a result, she helped to launch the careers of Richard Linklater, Spike Lee, Michael Moore, and Kevin Smith. As festival director, she championed independent filmmakers along with premiering studio movies and episodic television.[46] The festival was a springboard for the careers of female filmmakers Lena Dunham with *Creative Nonfiction* in 2009 and *Tiny Furniture* in 2010 and Olivia Wilde with *Booksmart* in 2019. As Dunham reflected during an interview at SXSW 2017:

> Janet Pierson is my champion. From the beginning, she has believed fiercely in both my work and the work of so many others who might have given up had they not been illuminated by her true and generous passion for anything new, exciting, and uncelebrated. If I hadn't found a home at SXSW (and a true home it was) for my film *Creative Nonfiction* in 2009, I never would have met the producers, actors, and collaborators who helped me make *Tiny Furniture* in 2010.[47]

SXSW also became a launching pad for studio genre movies like female-written and -led comedies *Bridesmaids* (dir. Paul Feig) in 2011, discussed in the following chapter, and *Trainwreck* (dir. Judd Apatow) in

2015.[48] What the case of SXSW highlights is not only that film festivals can serve as pivotal gatekeepers for independent female filmmakers for professionalization, mentoring, and networking, but also the importance of having women acting as linchpins in positions of power in these spaces.

Programming and Awards

One of the most glaring tensions can be found in the portrayal of women inside Cannes. From 2009 to 2019, the festival's marketing materials and film program offered two perspectives of a woman's place in the film industry, one from visibility and the other from absence. On the one hand, for eight years of the ten-year period, the annual festival's official posters prominently featured female stars.[49] From Juliette Binoche to Marilyn Monroe, images of primarily white American and European actresses graced giant posters hung on the exterior of the Palais des Festivals and as half-sheets adorning the city. A notable exception is the 2019 poster commemorating French filmmaker Agnès Varda. On the other hand, as indicated in the list of selected films inside each year's program, the festival has almost exclusively showcased male filmmakers for more than seven decades. During this ten-year period, female directors never made up more than 20 percent of films in the competition category and routinely less than 15 percent.[50] Whether commercial Hollywood genre fare or smaller, character-driven, state-supported European art cinema, the majority of films screened at Cannes are directed by men or, as *New York Times* critic Manohla Dargis contends, Cannes represents "the grand temple of the male auteur."[51]

Cannes came under increased scrutiny during the 2010s to improve the rates of acceptance for female-directed films, particularly for the In Competition films eligible for juried awards such as the most exalted prize, the Palme d'Or. In 2012, the French feminist collective La Barbe (The Beard) published an open letter in the French newspaper *Le Monde* to the Cannes Film Festival. The group admonished festival president Gilles Jacob, artistic director Thierry Frémaux, and the organization's male auteur-driven culture for not including one woman-directed project among the twenty-two films selected for competition that year. The letter scathingly warned: "Above all, don't let young girls imagine that they might one day have the audacity to direct movies and go up the steps of the Palais [des Festivals, the main venue] other than on the arm of a prince charming."[52]

An online petition then circulated, featuring prominent filmmakers, scholars, and feminist activists. In the following years, inclusion efforts were minimal, with Cannes increasing female-directed films in the competition category to one in 2013, two in 2014 and 2015, and three in 2016, 2017, and 2018.[53]

As Dina Iordanova argues, "Like most cultural phenomen[a], film festivals are multifaceted and riddled with inherent contradictions."[54] This is no more apparent than with Cannes 2015. After increased pushback for the lack of women programmed In Competition, festival organizers unofficially called Cannes 2015 the "Year de la Femme" (Year of the Woman). When the festival awarded her with an honorary Palme d'Or, Agnès Varda became only the second woman to receive the top award at the time. French filmmaker Emmanuelle Bercot's *La Tête Haute* (*Standing Tall*), an Out of Competition film, premiered as the opening night selection, while only two female-directed films—Valérie Donzelli's *Marguerite and Julien* and Maïwenn's *Mon Roi*—secured spots in the Competition category. With a largely female cast led by Charlize Theron, *Mad Max: Fury Road* (dir. George Miller) screened the second night as an Out of Competition selection to strong reviews like *Variety's* "*Mad Max: Fury Road* Gives Cannes a Testosterone Jolt with a Feminist Twist."[55]

However, the ways female attendees physically navigate festival spaces was the big story from 2015. Cannes famously requires formal attire to attend evening gala premieres for In Competition and Out of Competition films screened at the largest venue, the Grand Théâtre Lumière. A 1955 essay by André Bazin humorously compares the ritual of attending a Cannes premiere as a journalist, donning formal attire and attending extravagant premieres, to the pomp and circumstance of a religious order.[56] A troop of serious, impeccably suited male festival security guards strictly enforce the dress code of attendees. Nothing can prepare a first-time female attendee at Cannes for the critical gaze of the security guards as she ascends the red carpet past bleachers of press into an evening film premiere. A small scandal grabbed the fleeting attention of trade headlines and social media coverage when security denied entry into the premiere of *Carol* (dir. Todd Haynes) to a woman wearing flats and another in sandals.[57] In response, a Twitter dustup ensued with the hashtags #heelgate and #flatgate.[58] Although Frémaux responded defensively that heels are not required for gala screenings, the incident served as another example of tension between the masculine festival culture clashing with—even undermining—the organization's public-facing PR stance of celebrating and supporting women's presence at the festival.[59]

Cannes is not alone in structural gender disparities in the selection and programming process; Venice also made headlines in 2017 and 2018. For two consecutive years, the festival programmed only one female-directed film in competition. From the mid- to late 2010s, industry coverage increasingly called out the lack of female-driven films in the juried categories at these two festivals: among them, the *Hollywood Reporter* declared, "Venice: Festival Head Alberto Barbera Defends Lack of Women in Lineup (Again)," and *The Wrap* pronounced, "Cannes' Female Troubles: Women Directors Have Always Been Scarce."[60] Artistic directors for both Cannes and Venice, Frémaux and Barbera, respectively, blamed external factors for programming decisions in the 2010s.

First, both artistic directors claimed there was a lack of films directed by women. Frémaux told *Screen Daily* in 2016, "What percentage of filmmakers in the world are women? According to a recent report, it's 7 percent. I've been saying this for four years now but what you see in Cannes is a consequence, not the cause. More needs to be done in the film schools, the universities and the production houses, to favor women, and then you would see results."[61] Similarly, in a 2018 interview with the *Hollywood Reporter*, Barbera blamed the production pipeline for widespread gender disparities across festival programming, specifically that the problem lies at the "beginning of the chain, not at the end. . . . Give women the same possibilities that are given to men now, and this is something that is out of our hands. . . . Venice can't do anything about that. It's not up to us to change the situation. It came too late in the process of filmmaking."[62]

Indeed, that the barriers to access for training, development, and production phases disproportionately derail women filmmakers is the harsh reality at the core of this book. It is striking that public statements by institutional leaders like Barbera and Frémaux deflect their responsibility for structural inequities to other areas of the filmmaking pipeline as a way to absolve the festival sector of its gatekeeping responsibility as a powerful industry platform for distribution and exhibition. The lore about quantity does not add up. For example, out of the reportedly fifteen hundred films submitted for consideration to the Venice Film Festival in 2018, women directed 30 percent of them. One female-directed film in competition out of a total of twenty-seven selected results in an appallingly low rate of 4.7 percent. So, depending on the size of the submission pool, the logic that a dearth of women filmmakers is the problem quickly collapses.

The second excuse for inequitable programming blames female-driven film submissions for a lack of quality. Barbera considers selecting a film based on gender "offensive to the director. . . . I would prefer to change my job if I would be forced to select a film only because it's made by a woman and not on the basis of the quality of the film itself."[63] The Venice director publicly vocalized his refusal in 2018 to consider a gender quota when selecting the twenty-one films for the competition series. Frémaux told *Variety* that by programming the first or second films of young female directors, "I wouldn't be doing them a favor by putting their films in competition. [The critical scrutiny] can be very harsh."[64] The implicit argument is that they are not ready as filmmakers to show their films to Cannes's industry-facing audience. The few female-directed films programmed at Cannes in this period were often vetted by directors with established careers or by filmmakers with long-standing festival relationships returning for a second, third, or fourth time. As journalist Kate Erbland highlighted in May 2017, "It's telling that each of the women selected to compete with their latest works have been at Cannes before. They're festival approved, which means Cannes can tout an increased female filmmaker visibility without making visible the filmmakers who need it most—rising stars, fresh names, new talent."[65] Erbland referred to the three female filmmakers included In Competition that year—American director Sofia Coppola, Japanese director Naomi Kawase, and Scottish director Lynne Ramsay—each of whom had previously screened one or more films at Cannes.

When asked about how these artistic directors justify male-dominated programs, a former festival programmer for Sundance and other US festivals contended that the quality argument serves as a crutch to protect premiere festivals as elite institutional brands invested in maintaining an exclusive auteur boy's club. When asked about Barbera's widely circulated summer 2018 comments, she emphatically declared: "What bullshit! They don't have the numbers because they're just programming on 'quality,' as if these two things are mutually exclusive. And I have a really big issue with, one, not doing the work of looking for films [by women] and then, two, weighting the films as being less than [films directed by men]. I find myself trapped in that conversation over and over and over again."[66] In an attempt to minimize the responsibility of festivals, such narratives about lack of quality are blatant deflection tactics intended to silo the organization's role in the filmmaking pipeline at their convenience.

Erbland describes a premiere slot at festivals like Cannes as "a star-maker, or at least a foot-in-the-door-maker."[67] For the major international festivals with competition categories that come with sought-after awards, gatekeeping roles extend beyond festival leadership and programming. Thomas Elsaesser maintains that a significant function of the international film festivals is "to categorize, classify, sort and sift the world's annual film-production. The challenge lies in doing so not by weeding out and de-classifying, or letting the box office do its brutal work, but rather by supporting, selecting, celebrating and rewarding—in short, by adding value and cultural capital at the top, while acting more as a gentle gate-keeper than a bouncer at the bottom."[68] Every year, the competition festivals choose a jury president and members to attend screenings, participate in red carpet events, and vote on top prizes including the Golden Bear (Berlin), Palme d'Or (Cannes), Golden Lion (Venice), and Grand Jury Prize for US Dramatic (Sundance). In the case of TIFF, which does not have a juried competition category, public attendees cast votes for the People's Choice Award, regarded as the festival's top prize. Some recent winners—*Nomadland* in 2020, *Green Book* in 2018, and *12 Years a Slave* in 2013—launched successful award season campaigns after TIFF and ultimately went on to win the Best Picture Oscar.

The release of major international festival schedules drives a closely watched and much debated industry news cycle. Positioned as what journalist Nicolas Rapold describes as "its role as a gateway to the fall movie season," Venice competes with peer September film festivals like Toronto and Telluride as a coveted platform for premiering projects in hopes of competing in the fall and winter awards season.[69] World premieres of *Gravity* (2013, dir. Alfonso Cuarón), *La La Land* (2016, dir. Damien Chazelle), and *The Shape of Water* (2017, dir. Guillermo del Toro) led to additional international festival showings and prominent awards season campaigns that translated into Oscar wins and wider theatrical distribution.

Pierre Bourdieu's distinctions among types of capital—economic, social, and cultural—offer a foundational framework for looking at film festivals of various sizes, locations, formats, and so on. Symbolic value creation and cultural legitimization also come with festival awards. Marijke de Valck and Mimi Soeteman assert that "competition programs that award prizes are excellent ways of creating prestige. To the honor of being selected by a film festival for the competition are added the extended and formalized evaluation by an appointed jury, and most importantly, the critical attention such competitions bring in the media and press."[70] For competition festivals with juries, invited members often include a mix of actors, directors, screenwriters, and other established A-list players. For example, the 2018 Cannes jury for the In Competition section included Cate Blanchett, jury president (actor, Australia); Chang Chen (actor, China); Ava DuVernay (director-producer, United States); Robert Guédiguian (director, France); Khadja Nin (composer, Burundi); Léa Seydoux (actor, France); Kristen Stewart (actor, United States); Denis Villeneuve (director, Canada); and Andrey Zvyagintsev (director, Russia). Female jury members are routinely invited but rarely lead the juries for European festivals, which have appointed significantly fewer female than male jury presidents in the past two decades. From 2001 to 2019, Berlin appointed seven female presidents, whereas Cannes and Venice each had four.[71]

Of the juries in this nearly twenty-year period, very few awarded the top prize to female-directed films in competition between 2001 and 2019:

- Palme d'Or (Cannes)—0 women
- Golden Lion (Venice)—2 women
- Golden Bear (Berlin)—4 women
- Grand Jury Prize US Dramatic (Sundance)—6 women

Strikingly, Cannes juries awarded no female-directed films the Palme d'Or during this period. In fact, no female filmmaker won between 1994 and 2020. Jane Campion shared the top prize in 1993 when her film *The Piano* tied with Chen Kaige's *Farewell My Concubine*. And no female would win again until 2021 when Julia Ducournau captured the Palme d'Or with her film *Titane*. In many ways, the competition juries and awards reinforce a status quo whereby male-directed films benefit significantly more at each stage of the festival platform than those of their female peers.

As journalist Eric Kohn contends, programming has "a radical impact on the kinds of movies resonating on the festival circuit, and eventually, those with the potential to reach wider audiences."[72] In other words, selection and awards matter for the distribution cycle as these films move within industry circles and out to the public. Festivals as organizations absolutely have significant resource-controlling relationships in the media industries as power roles.[73] Film festivals exist as what Joseph

Turow identifies as a "linking pin" across production, distribution, and exhibition, between studios and filmmakers *and* journalists, distributors, sales agents, and potential investors and collaborators. The issue is not about lacking quality versus quantity but about *who* is judging the value and by *what* measures. Within the festival organizations, a central position of power comes from vetting, rewarding, and promoting the "best" film submissions that then impact which films circulate and which ones are written about for the next few years.

Value in the Festival Marketplace

In the 2013 documentary *Seduced and Abandoned*, actor-producer Alec Baldwin and director James Toback chronicle the challenge of financing a $10–$15 million project through conversations with prominent Hollywood actors, directors, and producers at the 2012 Cannes Film Festival. Both Hollywood insiders, Baldwin and Toback take meetings in private hotel suites and pitch a film project to Martin Scorsese, Francis Ford Coppola, Ryan Gosling, Jessica Chastain, and private investors. (Significantly, Toback was one of the first Hollywood directors named in fall 2017 at the beginning of the #MeToo movement as dozens of women shared experiences of sexual abuse and harassment.)[74] Early in the film, Baldwin, in voice-over, explains that commercial filmmaking requires spending 95 percent of the time looking for financing: "The movie business is the worst lover you have ever had. . . . You are seduced and abandoned over and over and over again." The documentary, which premiered at Cannes in 2013, is an exercise in highlighting the particular industry culture of and strategies for pitching ideas, cobbling together financing, and navigating day-to-day activities happening in a global film market. In other words, so much of the business activity occurring at Cannes and other business festivals that happens off the red carpet and outside of official screenings consists of buying and selling activities at "the market."

International festivals are a significant and often understudied site for acquiring the distribution rights for films at all stages, from script to screening. Value creation occurs across the festival marketplace in wildly uneven, and often inequitable, ways. This section focuses on two areas— press coverage and international sales agents and distribution. While earlier sections have broadly argued how gender inequities are ingrained inside event operations and cultures, key stakeholders working outside of festival organizations in the same industrial ecosystem have a significant part to play in women's experiences at the festival marketplace.

Press Coverage

An established female producer of color described how much of her work for a festival premiere requires a savvy knowledge of the circuit, a strategic plan for where her film fits, and how to sell her film in the context of that market. She recalled her first major festival experience in the late 2000s: "The work of wrangling the press circuit and positioning the film requires a whole machine. Publicist, sales agent, attorney . . . a team trying to create the right buzz and conversations with executives and companies around the film and filmmaker. There is a lot leading into the premiere and coverage [to attract the interest of] buyers and push to find distribution."[75]

A central part of positioning and launching a film premiere is press coverage. Major print and digital news outlets send journalists and critics to review films and cover business deals at the major festivals. In turn, film criticism and trade news are vital to generating the "right buzz." For example, a white male reporter I met at TIFF described a large part of his job as being on the annual festival circuit, gathering a "regular field report" from film premieres, cast and crew interviews, and the deals that happen. His coverage over the ten-day festival often contributes to a series of *Los Angeles Times* articles, interviews, reviews, podcasts, and other content released for months from the festival premiere through the theatrical distribution and awards season. Press coverage shapes narratives coming out of each annual festival, specifically the buzzworthy premieres. The circulation of this coverage has direct implications for the distribution and marketing campaign for these films from a few months following the premiere to more than a year later.

Which journalists and critics receive press access, or who is left out, has become a central point of criticism in conversations around the lack of diversity and inclusion at major festivals. By the late 2010s, a spotlight was placed on gender and racial disparities among film critics. In a USC Annenberg Inclusion Initiative study examining film reviewers for the top three hundred films from 2015 to 2017, using the rankings from the website Rotten Tomatoes, white male critics wrote 65.6 percent of movie reviews and male critics of color wrote only 13.1 percent. The percentage of film reviews written by women was low across the board and remarkably lowest for women of color, at 3.7 percent, in contrast to their white female counterparts, at 17.6 percent.[76] Specifically, in Europe's three biggest film markets—France, Germany, Italy—the numbers were slightly better in that women penned, on average, between 31 and 33 percent of film reviews from 2018 to 2019.[77]

Trade publications like *Variety*, the *Hollywood Reporter*, and *Screen International* release special daily print editions widely available for industry attendees, covering festival news, distribution deals, and film reviews. The gender gap is nowhere more evident than in these special festival editions. For example, the last page of *Screen International* festival editions between 2013 and 2018 featured a "jury panel" with film scores by a handful of international critics organized as a grid. Each critic awards a range of four stars (excellent) to zero stars (bad) for festival selections. Looking specifically at the jury panel for Cannes and Toronto from 2016 to 2017, *Screen International* included critics who were almost all male and largely white. Only one or two female critics were typically included in these trade jury panels across both festivals.

Karim Ahmad, the Sundance Outreach & Inclusion director at the time, described issues of access to the *Hollywood Reporter* in 2018: "The majority of the films getting wide-scale theatrical distribution are predominantly from white men. . . . When the array of critics covering those films are also white men, you perpetuate that vicious cycle. You create a system where diverse filmmakers don't have access to audience and distribution."[78] Most film festivals in the past only offered press accreditations to reporters and critics who already held a festival assignment with an established publication. Industry-wide disparities across publication rates are directly related to the film critics hired by major international and national publications to attend these festivals. In many ways, a parallel pipeline issue for print and digital journalism comes from the lack of diversity across newsrooms, impacting who covers the media and entertainment industries. Even if underrepresented journalists gain credentials for festivals, they can be shut out of press conferences or blocked from gaining key interviews if they are not working for major trade publications. An additional concern around access is that many locations where major industry festivals take place—Cannes, Park City, Venice—are not cheap destinations for travel. The cost of attending prohibits all but the most established and financially stable publications from sending journalists and critics to cover the event.[79] Both Sundance and TIFF began trying to address press credentials for their festivals by pledging to increase the number of writers from underrepresented groups by 20 percent. TIFF pledged 20 percent of press passes for underrepresented journalists—including women, people of color, LGBTQ+, and people with disabilities—for their 2018 festival, while Sundance pledged to give a minimum of twenty underrepresented writers access to their highest badge level, granting express lane entry into films.[80]

Distribution and the International Market

Another aspect of the film festival—and one of the least visible areas of business activity—is the path that a finished film premiering at a festival market takes to securing a distribution deal. Though this process varies from film to film, most of the actual business that takes place at major international festivals is in service to sales and acquisition. In her memoir, producer Christine Vachon describes the significance of attending the Cannes marketplace: "As the most important international festival, Cannes is the premier opportunity to broker these deals because everyone is here, wandering the Bunker. It's a clamoring, chaotic environment, a blizzard of themed tchotchkes, giveaway souvenirs, televisions previewing the schlock that makes up the majority of movies released every year and most of the films looking for financing."[81] Beyond the films screened as part of the festival's official selection or in sidebar "parallel" sections, such as Director's Fortnight or International Critic's Week that select their own separate programs, Cannes and Berlinale serve as important annual markets for buying and selling films in various stages of development for the global film industry.

A distinguishing aspect of business-oriented film festivals is that formal markets like the Marché du Film at Cannes or European Film Market (EFM) at Berlinale operate on site each year. These massive markets are housed in adjacent convention spaces and entire buildings, with floor after floor of media company booths. A walk through the Marché or EFM is an overwhelming sensory experience and requires access to specific industry credentials at different price points. Every open space from stair steps to walls is prime real estate for film marketing materials, company logos, and so forth. Producers, sales agents, and distributors take meetings and broker deals, as Vachon notes, or, as former international sales

4.2. Film marketing materials line company booths and walkways where sales agents and distributors take meetings inside the Marché du Film at the 2022 Cannes Film Festival. (Photo by author.)

agent Mark Horowitz asserted: "This is where the real festival happens."[82] One sees meetings between sales agents and distributors in company booths at the Marché or EFM or overhears a producer pitching the concept and pitch deck for a film in development at a café.

In contrast, another big international market, American Film Market, operates as a stand-alone event in Santa Monica each fall. Festivals with informal markets, like Toronto and Sundance, do not have the density of adjacent trade events where companies rent booths to build offices and advertising spaces. Instead, meetings and negotiations take place at less visible locations, typically outside official festival venues in rented office space at hotels or over dinner at nearby restaurants. Whether parallel with a formal or informal market, festival business at all major business-focused events ranges from films in development looking for financing to festival selections seeking to sell a mix of territorial rights and distribution windows.

A sales agent hired by the film's producer will meet with buyers whose job it is to acquire distribution rights for their company.[83] For example, an agent may arrive at Cannes or Berlin with a film or a film still in development—at the script stage of development or early in the production process with preliminary footage known as a "promo reel." The agent can negotiate a pre-sales deal for theatrical or television distribution that contributes to the financing needed to begin or complete the project. Another common deal is for a sales agent to broker a distribution deal for a finished film that is either premiering at the festival or screening at the market for buyers. Distribution deals may comprise US- or North America–only theatrical rights or worldwide theatrical rights. Or bigger distributors may acquire all media rights to a film, including combinations of theatrical, television, and/or digital rights. Typically, for independent films picked up by smaller US distributors that specialize in domestic releases, an international sales agent is hired to license theatrical or all media rights for the film on a territory-by-territory basis.[84]

The path to distribution varies for each project, and sales agents may visit more than one festival market to sell and market a film. It is instructive to consider the distribution deals for three female-driven films that premiered in January 2017 at Sundance. Ry Russo-Young's third feature film, *Before I Fall*, adapted from Lauren Oliver's best-selling young adult novel with a script by Maria Maggenti and Oliver, first screened at the Cannes film market in May 2016 for US and international buyers. As a result, Open Road Films acquired US theatrical rights, with Good Universe representing international rights on a territory-by-territory basis. The film premiered at Sundance outside of a juried category. From there, *Before I Fall* had a spring 2017 wide release opening with 2,346 theaters in the United States. The international release was handled by a mix of different companies: for example, IDC picked up regional distribution for Latin America and Elevation Pictures handled the Canadian release.[85]

In contrast, Janicza Bravo's dark comedy *Lemon* and Eliza Hittman's queer coming-of-age drama *Beach Rats* premiered at Sundance the same year without distribution in place. *Lemon* screened in the Next category, which the festival describes as "pure, bold works distinguished by an innovative, forward-thinking approach to storytelling."[86] After premiering in Park City, the film continued on the festival circuit, opening at the International Film Festival Rotterdam (IFFR) later that January and at SXSW in March. During Sundance that year, Bravo commented on the distribution gap between a festival premiere and a distribution deal as she and her fellow female classmates experienced it: "I hope that their movies sell. Because that they're [at Sundance] is great, but are they going to sell? And once they sell, how will they be distributed?"[87] In fact, *Lemon* did not secure a domestic release until months later at the start of SXSW when independent distributor Magnolia Pictures picked the film up for distribution. Bravo's film had a small theatrical release of thirteen theaters in September that year, and it is not clear if it was released internationally outside of the festival circuit. In the case of *Lemon*, a Sundance premiere along with playing other festivals in the annual circuit did not translate into immediate or wide distribution deals.

Beach Rats, Hittman's second feature, premiered in the US Dramatic Competition section to buzzy press and reviews, and she won the US Dramatic category directing award.[88] As Marijke de Valck and Mimi Soeteman highlight: "Nowadays, it is not uncommon for symbolic capital accrued from participation in the competition festival to be directly capitalized at the market taking place next door."[89] Formed in 2017 and known for edgy and ambitious arthouse and indie fare such as *I, Tonya* (2017), *Vox Lux* (2018), and *The Beach Bum* (2019), Neon picked up the film's North American distribution for all media, including theatrical and digital rights, during the festival.[90] After a film with buzz like *Beach Rats* premieres at a festival like Sundance, it can go on to screen at other top-tier festivals on the circuit. At the same time, international sales agents attend the corresponding market to sell territorial rights for theatrical and streaming. Mongrel International, the international sales arm of Canadian Mongrel Media, took the film to EFM in Berlin in February 2017 to license territory distribution deals, such as licensing rights to Mexican distributor Piano.

Producer Alix Madigan has premiered multiple female-directed films at festivals. She described the challenges of international distribution for these types of projects and the responsibility of sales agents in this culture: "The foreign film market is where real trouble lies [for female-driven films] and has such a huge effect on the business. So many powerful women are working in the business as sales agents. . . . Do we tap into those women to change the perception? This is a huge issue that needs to tackled."[91] Madigan's comment parallels what conversations with multiple longtime sales agents clearly evidence: women do work in larger numbers as sales agents at the festival marketplace. However, it is difficult to track the number of women working in international distribution as sales agents, particularly because agents can work for companies, on teams, or independently as individuals.

I did meet a surprising number of female sales agents at the Marché and EFM. For example, I talked with Mongrel's then–sales agent and executive Charlotte Mickie at the company's EFM booth in 2017. Companies like Mongrel specialize in selling arthouse and independent features and that includes representing female-driven films like *Beach Rats* at EFM and other film markets in order to sell territory-by-territory rights to international distributors. Mickie, who has worked as a sales agent for more than thirty years, attends markets like EFM and the Marché annually with the slate of films she represents to negotiate deals with buyers as well as to meet with prospective producers. Asked about the state of the market for arthouse films, markedly an area of the industry where women are more likely to be working above the line, Mickie recommended that I do my research while I can because the arthouse circuit is "a special world" and "I'm not sure it will exist in five years." A central topic of conversation at the film markets I attended between 2013 and 2017 focused on the state of the market since the late 2000s. The global recession hit this sector of theatrical distribution hard and impacted the business that international sales agents do at festival markets. Mickie pointed to the independent distribution business on the verge of collapse due to declining theatrical attendance, which led to struggling urban arthouse theaters, the decline of home entertainment, razor-thin margins from streaming deals to Netflix and Amazon, and a sharp decrease of television pre-sales deals with lucrative financing options.[92]

Whereas a number of producers I interviewed blame distributors and sales agents for the gaps in distribution deals for female-driven films, the sales agents point to the market, a common industry narrative for why female-driven and minority-driven projects do not or will not sell. Traditional industry lore about what films travel well internationally (action films starring white male stars) and do not travel well internationally (Black stories, comedies, female-driven films) can still shape how agents sell and what they think they can sell outside of North America.[93] Lore about international target audiences as well as about how sales agents and buyers perceive audience tastes are significant factors in the valuation of female-driven films in the global marketplace. In other words, these narratives work to place blame on what the market values and not on the complex negotiation process at play for sales agents and buyers making these deals.

The burden of proving the value of female-driven projects to distributors and sales agents was an issue raised about the festival marketplace in numerous interviews. Conversations with female producers, directors, and festival programmers who regularly attended the top five festivals during the 2010s point to the specific gatekeeping role held by international sales agents and distribution companies in determining the release of female-driven film projects. Furthermore, establishing value for an individual film means facing the added burden of increased competition for theatrical distribution in the late 2010s. From 2010 to 2019, the number of films released in the North American market (both Motion Picture Association members and nonmembers) increased from 563 to 835, respectively.[94]

An established white female producer recalled feeling low-balled and underestimated in an experience with the negotiation of a distribution deal in the 2010s. She asserted that the lack of different voices reinforces male-dominated taste cultures for buyers and distribution already pervasive in major film festivals:

> The culture of too many big festivals is emblematic [of Hollywood at large] where the conversation gets dominated by these powerful men who want to talk to other versions of themselves. These fucking guys! We can't escape them and they take up the space in the room. Where can women ever be centered? . . . Will I always have to ask a room of older white men to find value and be excited [about women's stories]?[95]

Distribution deals vary wildly based on how sales agents and distributors estimate a film will play as well as the brand and target audience of a distributor. Even when a film secures domestic and/or international distribution, theatrical release strategies fluctuate from film to film and involve a variety of stakeholders from vastly different markets with a range of priorities and no guarantees.

A Turning Point?

In May 2018, in a charged moment in the months following the emergence of #MeToo and Time's Up, all eyes were on the Cannes Film Festival. With global attention on the French Riviera, eighty-two women marched together in an unprecedented red carpet protest led by the year's jury president, actress Cate Blanchett. The group included fellow jury members Ava DuVernay and Kristen Stewart and other high-profile film

4.3. French news coverage of the eighty-two women participating in the 2018 Cannes Women's March. A speech by actress Cate Blanchett and filmmaker Agnès Varda followed. (Screenshot from TV Festival de Cannes "82 Women in Protest" video via YouTube.)

professionals, most notably French filmmaker Agnès Varda. The group stood in formal attire on the steps leading up to the Palais des Festivals to protest widespread gender inequity in the global film industry. The number eighty-two strategically symbolized the number of female directors who had premiered films at Cannes since the first festival in 1946, compared to their 1,688 male counterparts. Together, Blanchett and Varda gave a statement that included:

> We are writers, producers, directors, actresses, cinematographers, talent agents, editors, distributors, sales agents and all involved in the cinematic arts. We stand in solidarity with women of all industries. . . . We will demand that our workplaces are diverse and equitable so that they can best reflect the world in which we actually live. A world that allows all of us behind and in front of the camera to thrive shoulder to shoulder with our male colleagues.[96]

In one of the most visible spaces of global filmmaking—the festival red carpet—protestors aimed to call attention to the historic erasure and devaluation of women's labor and contributions in the industry.

In reality, despite the seeming spontaneity of this moment against the backdrop of a deeply formal and ritualistic festival culture, the Cannes

Women's March was the result of years of international organizing and activism. Organized in coordination with the French gender equity group Le Collectif 50/50, the march emerged from the evolving #5050x2020 movement. The movement originated as a transnational dialogue whose seeds were planted years earlier at industry panel discussions and meetings at festivals like Cannes and TIFF. In parallel, European state-supported film institutes slowly began to develop initiatives and policies toward gender-equitable practices.

For example, a leading gender equity activist and, at the time, Swedish Film Institute (SFI) CEO, Anna Serner, was a central public figure in calling industry and press attention to this issue by using festival event spaces. In a conversation with Serner in Stockholm in 2017, she recounted how networking at film festivals has been central in contributing to this movement. During her appointment as head of the SFI in 2011, Serner and her team restructured the national funding body toward a more equitable 50/50 divide for approving financing support by gender, and they reported meeting that goal by 2014.[97] She explained that the SFI's ability to make this action plan relied upon understanding the Swedish cultural and political context, which I would argue is missing from larger festival conversations and press coverage. Serner pointed to the state-run model common to the European film industry that supports national films with government funds as well as the "overall political agenda in Sweden" that also has resulted in voluntary gender equity in Parliament since the 1990s.[98]

Garnering press and social media coverage during Cannes and other international festivals was a strategy to shine an international spotlight, using Sweden as a case study for corrective policies. Serner first announced the SFI's 5050 initiative at a Cannes press conference in 2013, one of the first national film industries in Europe to make that commitment. At a small press conference, she described minimal press attendance and little attention, resulting in scant trade coverage. In 2016, Serner and the Swedish Film Institute organized a bigger panel at Cannes to discuss gender parity for female filmmakers beyond the national context. The panel included Swedish and French ministers of culture, each of whom oversees national film agencies in their countries, as well as female filmmakers from Sweden, Brazil, and Italy. She recalled: "Things had started to move in 2015, but [the gender parity movement] was still very recent in 2016 so we were really nervous about the event."[99] Though the SFI team anticipated a smaller crowd, they hosted an audience of close to two hundred, including international industry leaders and festival executives. In many ways, because festivals attract industry stakeholders from each part of the filmmaking pipeline, the different players invested in addressing equity and inclusion could amplify each other using the press following these industry events.

TIFF Artistic Director Cameron Bailey tweeted from the Cannes panel, praising the Swedish film head as the "new rock star of the film world, blazing trails in gender equality." During this period, Serner became a recurring panelist at the TIFF Industry Conference held alongside the festival each September. For example, the conference programmed at least one panel focused on equity and inclusion per year during the mid- to late 2010s. At "Women at the Helm: Because It's 2016!" panelists, including Serner, discussed the challenges female-driven projects face in individual markets like Sweden, Canada, and Australia, along with larger, interconnected issues of international financing and distribution. In attending TIFF annually between 2015 and 2019, I observed how the conference not only fostered dialogue with the participants in the room but also how these conversations often extended to social media and the press. For Serner, who has faced mixed reviews within Sweden, her annual participation on TIFF panels granted her star status as an international advocate for gender parity and a central figure in the international festival community. On the one hand, these festival panels helped to create a space where women in gatekeeping positions met to discuss these issues. On the other hand, a number of producers I spoke to criticized the siloing of equity and diversity conversations within the parameters of gender- or race-focused panels, resulting in a lot of the same people talking with little to no action taken.

The 5050x2020 movement coalesced in 2018 at a number of top-tier festivals to become a social media– and data-driven transnational effort, including the support of the US-based Time's Up organization and other state-run film agencies and international institutions. The Cannes Women's March goal of calling attention to inequitable programming at international film festivals happened as festival organizations agreed to sign the Programming Pledge for Parity and Inclusion. As part of the pledge, festival directors were invited to sign a voluntary commitment to gather and release data on film submissions and program selections by gender. Additionally, festival organizations were expected to publicly release names of selection and programming committee members and commit to more inclusive appointments to executive festival bodies. As part of an official Cannes press conference held two days after the march, Frémaux ceremonially signed the pledge. Other major international and regional festival leaders signed the pledge over the following year, including Venice, Toronto, Sundance, and Berlin.

On the one hand, for festival executives like Frémaux and Barbera, who so widely voiced their opposition to gender parity quotas over the previous decade, to volunteer to sign the pledge seems on the surface to indicate a pressure point at a steadily accelerating moment. Cannes in 2019 began to release a list of the selection committee for the first time, revealing more transparency than before around the eight-person team that now included four female members.[100] The individuals sitting on the committee to choose films in the competition category had long been shrouded in mystery and reflected the organization's general lack of transparency. In contrast, major festivals like Sundance and TIFF had routinely revealed their selection committees, with Toronto even highlighting the twenty programmers, their categories, and geographical territories in the annual festival program.

The Programming Pledge, on the other hand, did not require festivals to commit to gender equity in programming numbers by 2020 or, in fact, at any point. The external pressure coming from industry groups and key individuals operates largely symbolically and provides international festivals with the appearance of taking action. In a May 2019 press conference, Frémaux reiterated his refusal to implement hard quotas or aspirational goals for an equitable programming process: "No one has asked me to have 50 percent of films made by women. That would show a lack of respect." That year, female filmmakers helmed four of the nineteen films in competition, whereas women directed only 28 percent of the sixty-nine official selections. Shockingly, Mati Diop's *Atlantique* (*Atlantics*, 2019) became the first In Competition film ever directed by a Black Frenchwoman at Cannes.[101]

Sundance signed the 5050x2020 pledge under different circumstances. For years, the US festival had been in the process of working to improve gender equity not only for films programmed but also in selection committee ranks. In 2017, women directed 34 percent of films screened in all categories at Sundance. Three years later, female filmmakers made up 46 percent of selections in the four competition categories at the 2020

4.4. Share Her Journey rally at the 2018 Toronto International Film Festival. (Photo by author.)

festival—US Dramatic, US Documentary, World Dramatic, and World Documentary.[102] The US Dramatic Competition reached gender parity, with 50 percent female directors, with half of those films helmed by women of color. Furthermore, changes in festival leadership anticipated a new direction in 2018 with the promotion of senior programmer Kim Yutani to director of programming, replacing Trevor Groth, and Tabitha Jackson taking over from John Cooper as festival director from 2020 to 2022.[103]

The Toronto International Film Festival took a slightly different path toward addressing gender disparities. In contrast to external pressure placed on European peer festivals, the Canadian organization developed more of an internal mission or mandate for reaching gender parity across leadership hiring, festival programming, and filmmaker support. In 2017, the festival organization launched Share Her Journey, a five-year $3 million fundraising goal and programming initiative "to increas[e] participation, skills, and opportunities for women behind and in front of the camera."[104]

In many ways, the gender equity initiative benefitted from timing, launching at the festival in early fall before the accelerated emergence of #MeToo and Time's Up. As a former TIFF executive told me:

> The conversation about gender equity has been one that's been happening ever since I've been at TIFF, and it wasn't me that started it. It was already something that a lot of people were talking about. And then at the beginning of last year we made the decision that— we didn't announce it, so this is 2016—we decided that all of our talent development programs would have a minimum of 50 percent female participation.[105]

As part of Share Her Journey, TIFF created mentor and training opportunities for female creatives like the Micki Moore Residence for screenwriters. TIFF, like Sundance Institute's labs and Berlinale Talents, invests in and runs talent programs, development funds, and networking opportunities to support emerging filmmakers—most often women and directors of color. Since 2016, TIFF has boasted 50/50 gender parity for participants in all Talent Development labs and programs.[106] In contrast to festival leadership at Venice and Cannes blaming "the beginning of the chain," TIFF clearly positions not only the festival but also the organization as a gatekeeper with a powerful role in contributing to each stage of filmmaking. In many ways, TIFF is a uniquely and culturally Canadian organization, shaped by the state-supported film industry and specific government policies and programs regarding the equity and inclusion of marginalized communities, balancing catering to industry delegates and public attendees in one of the most diverse cities in the world.

Most TIFF staff I spoke to described their work as programming for the public—the more than four hundred thousand audience members buying tickets each year. When the campaign launched, Bailey told *Variety*: "We acknowledge that gender inequity is systemic in the screen industries, so change has to happen at every level. That includes getting more women into key creative roles."[107] Various areas of the festival did begin to integrate the Share Her Journey mission by 2018. Programming efforts for the TIFF Industry Conference also aligned with Share Her Journey and the two one-on-one sessions with industry leaders known as "Moguls" featured conversations with Dr. Stacy L. Smith (director of USC's Annenberg Inclusion Initiative) and Nina Yang Bongiovi (producer of *Dope*, *Fruitvale*

Station, Songs My Brothers Taught Me, Sorry to Bother You). Bailey signed the 5050x2020 pledge to get as much press attention as their peer institutions the first weekend of the ten-day festival. A Share Her Journey rally took place near the TIFF Bell Lightbox building on the morning of the festival's first Saturday. The TIFF rally was organized alongside the festival, open to the public, and featuring an array of speakers addressing gender inequity and sexism in the global film industry at large. The event, widely publicized through promotional emails and social media, included talks by Smith, actor and activist Geena Davis (Geena Davis Institute), Keri Putnam (then executive director of Sundance Institute), and filmmakers Amma Asante (*Belle, United Kingdom, Where Hands Touch*) and Nandita Das (*Firaaq, Manto*). A crowd consisting of independent filmmakers, journalists, and university students, as well as regular festival attendees, staff and volunteers, and more, expressed palpable energy and enthusiasm as it spilled onto King Street, the festival's busy main thoroughfare, serving as a stark contrast to the Cannes march a few months prior.

On the film-screening side, female TIFF programmers outnumbered their male counterparts thirteen to nine. Out of the 342 films screened from around the world in all fourteen festival categories, women directed 36 percent. A bird's-eye view of these festival-wide numbers suggests that TIFF's strategic efforts arguably led to more inclusive and equitable programming in the late 2010s. However, when breaking down each programming category, a closer perspective reveals distinctions in the female-driven films selected. For the high-profile, star-driven gala premieres in 2018, including Asghar Farhadi's *Todos Lo Saben*, Claire Denis's *High Life*, and Bradley Cooper's *A Star Is Born*, women only helmed six out of twenty selections, or around 30 percent.[108]

There is even more of a dramatic difference between the Discovery versus Masters selections, as TIFF's director of programming at the time, Kerri Craddock, explained to the *Hollywood Reporter*:

> Our Discovery section is almost at 50/50, men and women. But those are people with first and second films at the festival. You can always say it's easier for a woman to make her first film, and it gets harder as you advance in your career. Or you can say that's a sign of hope, that funders are more willing to give opportunities to women. And sadly, our Masters section is all men; there are no female filmmakers there. That really tells a story.[109]

Even with concerted efforts toward equitable programming, Craddock highlighted an issue with which many festivals still struggle. Categories delineating between early-career and established filmmakers, like TIFF's Discovery and Masters sections, often end up reinforcing the gender gap between experience, prestige, and leverage. As discussed earlier in this chapter with regard to Sundance, emerging female filmmakers face a tougher journey and take a longer time to secure financing for follow-up films, while their male peers build production credits and experience as well as festival acceptances and international reputations faster. As a result, the valuing of certain individuals in these spaces because of their longevity and industry status further reproduces and widens the festival gender gap, something that even festivals with intentional gender parity initiatives must address moving forward.

Conclusion

In early spring 2020, at the brink of the accelerating global pandemic, the film industry came to a devastating standstill. Movie theaters shuttered and film productions stopped abruptly as shelter-in-place orders went into effect around the world. Film festivals too began to rapidly respond. South by Southwest in March and Telluride in September cancelled their 2020 editions completely. Cannes, Sundance, and Toronto eventually announced scaled-back virtual or hybrid versions. In the case of Cannes, a postponed Marché du Film took place in late June as a virtual market. In place of film programming, the festival created a Cannes 2020 label designation for fifty-six films to carry when premiering at peer fall festivals. Toronto programmed a smaller lineup of fifty films to include a mix of in-person and virtual events. In contrast, Venice was the only major international festival to run a physical event.[110] Even as some summer and fall festivals managed to pivot to adapt their business models to a rapidly changing global health crisis and economic reality, the festival organizations took a financial hit in the process. Many festivals not only scaled back on programming but also on festival staff, with both Sundance and TIFF announcing layoffs in summer 2020 to reduce full-time staff by 13 and 17 percent, respectively.[111]

With the momentum for gender inclusion at all levels of festival operations and culture building by the late 2010s, the future of the film festival circuit remains uncertain. Cannes, Venice, TIFF, and Sundance all announced improvements in gender parity for 2020 programming. In the case of Venice, of the eighteen films in competition for the Golden Lion, thirteen were emerging filmmakers who had not previously competed and eight were female-directed.[112] However, bigger films with established directors chose to delay a film festival premiere and 2020 theatrical release. For example, Wes Anderson's *The French Dispatch*, originally set to open Cannes, was pushed to the following year's delayed in-person June festival. By giving all film selections a general Cannes 2020 certification, the festival dropped the usual category distinctions such as In Competition, Out of Competition, Un Certain Regard, and so forth. As journalist Kate Erbland contends, "It also means that Cannes, long disinterested in letting new female filmmakers into the highest reaches of its program, provided them with equal footing alongside the other filmmakers in the selection. At the same time, its blanket reference to an influx of 'discoveries' in this year's lineup takes this achievement down a notch."[113] For any pandemic-era festival, the shift from in-person to virtual or hybrid changed the valuation of selection, premieres, and awards.

Prior to the pandemic, major international festivals had been inching toward better gender parity in their programming numbers. In 2021, Cannes resumed an in-person festival and once again programmed long-running categories like In Competition, Un Certain Regard, and Out of Competition. Four female-directed features competed in the top category—*Bergman Island* (dir. Mia Hansen-Løve), *The Divide* (dir. Catherine Corsini), *The Story of My Wife* (dir. Ildikó Enyedi), and *Titane* (dir. Julia Ducournau)—matching the pre-pandemic record in 2019. A provocative and visceral French-Belgian coproduction thriller about a woman with a titanium plate in her head and a taste for cars and murder, *Titane* became only the second female-directed film to win the Palme d'Or in the festival's history. On the one hand, this was a significant win at a festival still grappling with gender disparities in leadership ranks and programming numbers. *Titane* came to Cannes with a distribution deal in hand after Neon acquired North American rights in September 2019. The festival award buzz gave the film a boost during its limited theatrical run and digital release later that year. On the other hand, the competition category included a total of twenty-four films with only four, or 16 percent, helmed by women. Three out of those four female directors were white French women. French filmmaker Ducournau was a known quantity, since her previous work—the short film *Junior* (2011) and her first feature,

Raw (2016)—had already appeared in parallel sections at Cannes. The programming committee's gesture toward gender parity clearly has its limits at this point, particularly on who is included and from where.

The 2022 festival rebounded back to capacity in a "business as usual" celebration for Cannes' seventy-fifth anniversary. However, familiar concerns surrounding gender equity emerged once again. While female-driven features appeared in Un Certain Regard, Director's Fortnight, and other side categories, women directed or codirected only four of the films in the competition category: *The Eight Mountains/Le otto montagne* (dir. Charlotte Vandermeersch and Felix van Groeningen), *Forever Young/Les Amandiers* (dir. Valeria Bruni Tedeschi), *Showing Up* (dir. Kelly Reichardt), and *Stars at Noon* (dir. Claire Denis). Riley Keough and Gina Gammell made their codirectorial debut with the collaboratively developed Indigenous coming-of-age story *War Pony* premiering in Un Certain Regard. In reflecting on the ongoing problems of inclusion and access, Keough told *Variety*:

> I'm curious as to how many women were in a position to submit to Cannes. How many women got the financing that they needed? From our own experience, that was very difficult, especially when we compare it to our male friends. . . . We know many first-time male filmmakers getting a lot more money than female first-time filmmakers we know. So there is a very profound mistrust in women leading. . . . I think it's very fundamental. . . . Women need the opportunities.[114]

Keough, who established herself as an actress prior to a move behind the camera, notably comes from an entertainment family as the granddaughter of Elvis Presley and daughter of Lisa Marie Presley. However, as recounted in interviews around the Cannes premiere, it still took seven years for Keough and Gammell as codirectors and coproducers to get *War Pony* financed and produced.

As this chapter has argued, this is not a Cannes-exclusive issue. *Screen Daily* published a 2021 report comparing fourteen A-level international festival competition categories over three years: 2018, 2019, and 2021. Not surprisingly, from Cannes to Venice and Tokyo to Shanghai, gender equity in programming still lags. And as the headline indicates, "Black directors make just 1% of competition films at major festivals"; the acceptance rate for Black, MENA (Middle Eastern North African), and Asian directors is even worse. Latinx and Latin American filmmakers not being included as a category is even more telling: this absence reinforces the fact that the diverse group's numbers are among the lowest at international film festivals.[115] In light of the 2010s' promising pressure points around film festivals, and despite the short-term improvements for women filmmakers at the start of the 2020s, there is much work left to be done not only specifically around gender but also toward marginalized and underrepresented groups in general. As major international festivals grapple with rebuilding and adapting to a (post-)pandemic future, gender equity and other intersectional-inclusive practices will demand further energy and attention.

CHAPTER 5

Distribution and Marketing
(Bankability Gap)

In a 2012 speech at the Women in Film Crystal + Lucy Awards, Meryl Streep used the platform to call attention to ways Hollywood sidelines female-driven content. From her position as one of Hollywood's most celebrated and revered actresses, she highlighted how the systemic lack of women working in key creative roles contradicts a wave of successful theatrical releases:

> This in spite of the fact that in the last five years, five little movies aimed at women have earned over $1.6 billion: *The Help*, *The Iron Lady*, believe it or not, *Bridesmaids*, *Mamma Mia!*, and *The Devil Wears Prada*. As you can see, their problems were significant because they cost a fraction of what the big tent-pole failures cost. . . . Let's talk about *The Iron Lady*. It cost $14 million to make it and brought in $114 million. Pure profit! So why? Why? Don't they want the money? Why is it so hard to get these movies made?[1]

Streep starred in *The Devil Wears Prada* (2006), *Mamma Mia!* (2008), and *The Iron Lady* (2011), each representing a type of budget-friendly star vehicle that defined recent decades in her A-list career. The actress pointed to the commercial success of this cycle of female-driven projects as illustrative of the bankability of small- to midrange cost-effective projects that routinely are overlooked for larger studio "tentpole failures."

Streep was not the only one in Hollywood questioning traditional practices regarding female-led projects. Since the mid-2000s, a string of female-driven commercial hits exceeded industry expectations at the box office. In response to big opening weekends, trade press coverage frequently referred to these films as "overperforming." But overperforming compared to what? Despite the average financial return for female-led small- to midbudget projects showing a healthy profit margin on investment, like the films above, studio logic during this period remained steeped in limited notions of the risks and gambles worth taking. Women clearly are a viable audience, and female-driven films prove commercially successful again and again. So, how do notions of bankability for theatrical releases continue to be constructed along gendered lines?

This chapter explores the industry myths around the bankability of women at the theatrical box office by looking at contradictions in how the film industry undervalues female-driven films and their audiences. Even if female-driven films manage to navigate the steep barriers during earlier filmmaking phases, as discussed in previous chapters, female creatives and their projects must overcome long-held beliefs related to value at the point of distribution. *New York Times* critic Manohla Dargis in 2009 explained the widespread industry discourse: "For years the received wisdom, both in the industry and the press that covers it, has been that women don't go to the movies and can't open movies."[2] Studios' gendered expectations reveal a significant disconnect across box office forecasting and actual performance that results in a real-world impact on marketing and distribution practices. As a result, for far too many female filmmakers, their projects may be discounted, thus derailing their careers.

Grounded in trade press coverage, box office data, interviews, and studio marketing campaigns, I employ discourse analysis to examine how industry myths discounting female-driven films persisted around theatrical releases throughout the mid-2000s to 2010s, even as a new, viable commercial cycle emerged. After the first section briefly traces earlier examples of the progress narrative "year of the woman" from the 1970s to 2000s, I examine what I call the "amnesia loop" around the celebration of (then quickly forgotten) box office release of female-driven films including Fox 2000's *The Devil Wears Prada* (2006), Warner Bros./New Line's *Sex and the City: The Movie* (2008), Summit's *Twilight* series (2008–2012), and Universal's *Bridesmaids* (2011) and *Fifty Shades of Grey* (2015). Trade press headlines were quick to hail the box office success of female-driven films and the value of their audiences only to dismiss their economic viability as an exception or anomaly.

The second section explores specific gendered ideas of risk and uncertainty around female-driven theatrical releases and disparities in how failure is measured. Female-driven projects can be "set up to fail" when the studios do not prioritize or put the resources into marketing and distribution, with female filmmakers taking the brunt of the blame. Female directors like Elaine May, Karyn Kusama, and Mimi Leder have been punished for poorly performing theatrical releases in ways their male counterparts have not, a status widely known as "movie jail."

The last section examines the recent cycle of "year of the woman" declarations generated by the so-called groundbreaking female-driven films within the superhero tentpole model. *Wonder Woman* (2017) serves as a striking example of contradictions within this discourse as the first female-directed and female-led studio superhero project of the Conglomerate Hollywood period. Moving from the risk of box office poison to rescuing Warner Bros. to the sequel's threat of ruining the theatrical business, this franchise was tasked with overcoming the structural weight of gender inequity from the glass ceiling to the glass cliff.

In contrast to the earlier chapters grounded in descriptive, qualitative interviews, the final chapter takes an industry-wide look at the discursive patterns and trade coverage circulating around the marketing and theatrical distribution of female-driven projects. What emerges is the broader perspective of female filmmakers and their commercial projects during this industrial period. Whether a box office hit or a disappointing release, gendered industry lore steeped in inequitable notions of risk continue to undervalue female audiences and female-targeted films despite every cyclical celebration of another so-called ceiling-breaking first in the film industry.

Box Office Success: The Amnesia Loop

Hollywood has a long history of "discovering" and forgetting the box office weight of female-targeted movies. Despite cycles of successful female-led movies in the twentieth century—most notably, the star-driven women's pictures of the 1930s and 1940s highlighted in chapter 1—the commercial viability and value of female-driven films has not been perceived as a stable, or consistent, business model for the major studios in recent decades.[3] The astonished recognition of their bankability reflects a familiar and well-worn terrain with the recurring "year of women" discourse.

During the 1970s, the women's liberation movement fought to pass the Equal Rights Amendment while women across their industry guilds in Hollywood organized to pressure the studios toward equitable representation and parity. Maya Montañez Smukler's extensive scholarly work traces the slow increase of women directing commercial narrative features. During the decade, sixteen women, including Joan Micklin Silver, Jane Wagner, and Elaine May, directed their first features.[4] A growing cycle of movies and television series featuring complex female leads served as a sharp contrast to the male-driven, antihero dramas and action blockbusters of the period. In a 1977 *New York Times* article, "Hollywood Flirts with the New Woman," Jane Wilson reviewed female-led, male-directed films, including *Alice Doesn't Live Here Anymore* (1974, dir. Martin Scorsese), featuring Ellen Burstyn; *Three Women* (1977, dir. Robert Altman), with Shelley Duvall and Sissy Spacek; and *Julia* (1977, dir. Fred Zinnemann), starring Jane Fonda and Vanessa Redgrave. She concludes with a familiar question—"Will such enlightenment last? The proof, ultimately, depends on the profit."[5] Wilson's critique presciently anticipated debates that would unfold over the next four decades about the major studios' wavering commitment to female-driven projects and the gendered value of the box office.

After a record four women were elected to the US Senate, the press deemed 1992 a turning point for women in politics.[6] Meanwhile, the film industry celebrated the 1991 release of *Thelma & Louise* (dir. Ridley Scott). The road-trip friendship revenge drama starring Geena Davis and Susan Sarandon and written by Callie Khouri sparked widespread debate at the time surrounding gender roles, feminism, and violence, as illustrated by the *Time* magazine cover story "Gender Bender over *Thelma & Louise*."[7] Expectations that *Thelma & Louise* would inspire a new cycle of female-led studio projects did not materialize. As Caryn James wrote in a *New York Times* response that year criticizing the lack of "meaty roles" for women:

> [The] narrow range of recent female characters suggests something more insidious at work, too: the *Thelma & Louise* backlash. The notoriety of *Thelma & Louise* should have inspired a slew of female-buddy, on-the-road, angry-women movies. Instead, *Thelma & Louise* tapped into such unexpected rage that it seems to have scared Hollywood to death. . . . But in Hollywood, where the belief in cosmetic solutions runs deep, paying lip service to women persists.[8]

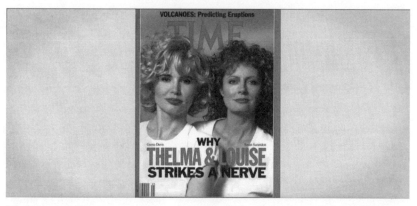

5.1. June 1991 *Time* magazine cover featuring *Thelma & Louise*, as discussed by Geena Davis in an interview for the 2018 documentary *This Changes Everything*. (Screenshot from *This Changes Everything*.)

In the 2018 documentary *This Changes Everything*, actress, producer, and activist Geena Davis refers to these moments of recognition and hype around her roles in female-led films like *Thelma & Louise* and *A League of Their Own* (1992, dir. Penny Marshall). Despite celebratory discourse that these films could "change everything" in Hollywood, Davis argues that this discourse did not bring sweeping change since the number of female-led films did not increase in the following years.

Even as the Academy Awards declared 1993 the year "Oscar Celebrates Women and the Movies," big categories like Best Picture, Best Director, and Best Screenplay (both adapted and original) had no female nominees. Mary Schmich declared, "Good Riddance to Year of the Woman," in a *Chicago Tribune* article dismissing the hopeful discourse as "a cute political slogan and a tidy sound bite. It was a great decoy. 'The Year of the Woman,' in the end, was more a diversion than a description."[9] Whether viewed as "lip service" or a "diversion," the Academy of Motion Pictures Arts and Sciences' gesture toward female representation and progress in front of the camera came off more as a pat on the head than an earnest call for industry-wide change. As Rebecca Ford and Mia Galuppo asked in a 2018 *THR* article reflecting on the 1993 Oscar theme: "Has anything changed in 25 years?"[10] Across industrial periods and sectors, this narrative emerges to highlight the presence of female-led or female-driven films that prevail despite male-dominated premieres, programs, and studio slates.

Yet, just as the bankability and cultural impact of female-targeted releases like *Thelma & Louise* were questioned in the previous decade, strikingly similar astonishment and celebratory lip service emerged again a few years later. A 1997 *New York Times* article began with the recognition: "After years of making action and adventure films for boys of all ages, studio executives are concluding that a new audience has emerged that is changing all the rules. Women." Quotes from surprised studio executives highlighted how the underserved female-over-twenty-five-years-old quadrant, in reality, drives ticket sales for the star-driven midbudget movies—*The First Wives Club*, *Jerry Maguire*, and *Michael*—released the previous year. In response, the president of Fox 2000 at the time, Laura Ziskin, acknowledged the film industry's realization about the influence women have on ticket sales: "We've been a testosterone-driven business for a long time. Now I'm looking more at an estrogen-driven business."[11]

By 2000, the "year of women" celebrations emerged across different sites of the independent and film festival scene with critically acclaimed premieres like Kusama's jury award–winning *Girlfight* at Sundance, discussed in the previous chapter. As Christina Lane points out: "Reporters had either forgotten or had never known that the Sundance Film Festival (formerly US Film Festival) had already celebrated the Year of the Woman in 1989, 1991, and 1993."[12] As Sundance improved gender equity in its programming, a series of think pieces appeared throughout the late 2010s pondering the same question again and again: Is this the (real) year of the woman?[13] A similar narrative framed the Toronto International Film Festival over the years—from Lone Scherfig's 2009 coming-of-age drama *An Education* to Lorene Scafaria's 2019 Great Recession–era stripper crime drama *Hustlers*—in a range of trade press and popular publications.[14]

As the American independent and film festival sectors made slow and uneven strides to address gender equity, Hollywood continued to grapple with the bankability of female-driven tentpoles with every new box office hit. Lynda Obst, veteran producer of female-driven studio projects has spoken publicly about this cycle of forgetting. Obst offered her impression in a 2011 *Salon* interview: "Studios have institutionally short memories when it comes to women's movies. . . . Every time a woman's movie does well, it's a brand-new fact. Every time we rediscover the female audience, it's astonishing."[15] Looking at the industrial period from the mid-2000s to early 2010s, cycles of discovery and visibility end in strategic forgetting and discounting of the economic and cultural bankability of women at the box office—or what I am calling the Hollywood amnesia loop: (1) Women Go to the Movies?!, (2) The Female-Driven Tentpole, and (3) The

Bridesmaids Effect? This cycle acknowledges, yet traps, financially successful female-driven films in a loop with few sustainable, industry-wide pathways forward for female-driven filmmaking during this period.

Women Go to the Movies?!

The major studios traditionally categorized audiences into four quadrants by age (under 25 or over 25) and gender (male or female).[16] However, Hollywood's most prized demographic in recent decades remained a narrow group—twelve-year-old boys to thirty-nine-year-old men. As one industry analyst remarked in a 2009 article in *The Wrap*, "There's a sense that Hollywood is attuned to a 13-year-old boy's mind. [Studio executives] pretty much know the fancies of a 13-year-old, and they can distribute films to that audience."[17] Bigger-budget movies that are expected to attract broader audiences, particularly as the global market became increasingly important by the 1990s, are described as wide and shallow. In contrast, the focused, midbudget genre movie is categorized as narrow and deep due to attracting a more targeted audience. Journalist Scott Mendelson describes how "the mid-budget, star-driven, concept-specific old-school movie, which was Hollywood's bread and butter of the studio system for a lifetime, is becoming an endangered species."[18] As the major studios released fewer films each year—albeit increasingly more-expensive franchises—the pressure increased exponentially for visual effects–driven, action-forward event pictures to open big the first weekend. There is no more obvious example than Hollywood's hard pivot in the 2000s toward expensive world-building with franchises like Warner Bros.' *Harry Potter*, Sony's *Spider-Man*, and Disney's *Pirates of the Caribbean* as well as their parent company's expansion with *Star Wars* and the Marvel Cinematic Universe in the 2010s. The pressure for expensive tentpoles to open big, strong, and globally means these films must make most of their theatrical gross in the first two to three weekends. Often deemed "the most coveted demographic in the industry," white male audiences were prioritized and targeted to turn the expensive blockbuster into a record-breaking box office event.[19]

During the mid-2000s and 2010s, a handful of journalists and film critics increasingly began to question the ways that Hollywood systems value female audiences. As Amy Ryan considered in a 2007 *Entertainment Weekly* article, "The industry is so busy trying to lure the young male quadrant away from their Xboxes and into the theaters that it's given up on trying to draw the rest of the potential movie-going audience."[20] Women and audiences of color largely existed at best as an afterthought, or, at worst, were ignored by an industry that prioritized young white male audiences. Manohla Dargis at the end of the decade mourned the decrease in female-targeted projects: "It's a vicious cycle. We're not going to movies because there aren't movies for us. Therefore we're not seen as a loyal moviegoing audience. . . . In the trade press, women audiences are considered a niche. How is that even possible? We're 51 percent of the audience."[21] In addition to making up more than half of the US population, women consistently constituted the majority of moviegoers, ranging from 55 percent in 2008 to 51 percent in 2018.[22] Female-targeted releases traditionally depended on a slow-building word-of-mouth strategy that was not expected to follow or adhere to a big opening tentpole weekend. Journalist Pamela McClintock categorized female-targeted projects as "dependable earners that open modestly and play long, rather than being big grossers right from the start."[23] However, by looking at how female-driven releases performed at the box office, this logic increasingly came to be challenged and contradicted, specifically during a pivotal cycle of commercially successful films released between 2006 and 2008.

The Devil Wears Prada (2006) was a game changer for Fox 2000. The production unit optioned film rights to Lauren Weisberger's breezy novel prior to its publication. The book, loosely based on the author's experience working as the assistant to *Vogue* magazine editor Anna Wintour, went on to become a massive best seller. Fox 2000 successfully used this development strategy (purchasing rights prior to publication) for many of its projects, as an estimated 75 percent of the unit's material was adapted. At a reportedly modest $35 million budget, *The Devil Wears Prada* opened domestically in 2,882 theaters on July 4 weekend against Warner Bros.' *Superman* reboot. The Fox 2000 film made front-page trade news as a "well-priced surprise hit" and a "counter-programming coup." Opening weekend ticket sales reflected an overwhelmingly female audience, with 66 percent total and 50 percent women over twenty-five, what McClintock attributed to *Prada's* playing "more female-centric than a mainstream romantic comedy."[24] In contrast, the larger 20th Century Fox film slate routinely targeted shallow and wide in 2006 by focusing on releasing installments of established franchises including *X-Men*, *Big Momma's House*, and *Ice Age*.

In many ways, the midbudget movie about a New York fashion magazine, starring Meryl Streep and a breakout role for Anne Hathaway, cemented Fox 2000 as an industry leader for female-targeted projects. After a regime change in 1999, Elizabeth Gabler took over Fox 2000. In a stark contrast to other Fox divisions, and other major studios in general during this period, women filled the ranks at Fox 2000, which led to the nickname "Foxy Fox." The unit's brand primarily focused on three types of projects: romantic comedies, prestige dramas, and literary adaptations (later expanding into family and YA). In Fox 2000's trade coverage, Gabler was described as a "stable, savvy shepherd of the mid-size label,"[25] and, in a *Forbes* 2008 issue offering a "broad tour of the C-suite," Gabler reportedly wielded the "Midas touch" with a commercial sensibility and reputation as a voracious reader with strong ties to the big New York publishers.[26]

As the film grossed more than $326 million worldwide, director David Frankel described the significance of the commercial success to *Variety* as follows: "The Holy Grail of this movie was to create an event movie for women."[27] Yet, the success of *Prada* also highlighted how unprepared publicly 20th Century Fox was for a commercial hit. The president of Fox's distribution division, Bruce Snyder, admitted his shock in a trade interview: "I never thought it would be this big. I've never seen a predominantly female movie open quite this large, unless it was a romantic comedy."[28] Trade coverage framed the film's success as a "wake-up call." Yet despite *Prada*'s successful theatrical run, the film was still largely written off as a fluke.[29]

The discovery that "women go to the movies!" emerged again in 2008 with Warner Bros./New Line Cinema's *Sex and the City: The Movie*, directed by Michael Patrick King (*SATC: The Movie*). Beginning as a newspaper column and later a best-selling book by writer Candace Bushnell, *Sex and the City* (1998–2004) became a critically and popularly acclaimed HBO original series. Set around the dating lives of four New York wealthy, white, single, thirty- to forty-something professional women, the show became a cultural touchstone during its initial broadcast. After benefitting from a syndicated run on the Warner-owned TBS network and strong DVD sales, Time Warner repackaged the TV property for the big screen.[30]

The smaller sibling division (New Line Cinema) of the major studio (Warner Bros. Pictures) released *SATC: The Movie* at the time of a wider

5.2. The product placement in *Sex and the City: The Movie* (2008) reflects a strategy of pink merchandising and gendered aspirational consumption. In this scene, Carrie (Sarah Jessica Parker) interviews her new assistant, Louise (Jennifer Hudson), at a Starbucks and discusses her Coach handbag rented from the online service Bag Borrow or Steal. (Screenshot from *Sex and the City: The Movie.*)

studio restructuring in 2008.[31] The parent company reorganized New Line Cinema from a stand-alone production unit specializing in genre and targeted audiences into a consolidated distribution label for Warner's mid-budget projects. This subsequently led to the division's "identity crisis" by the late 2000s.[32] New Line's president of marketing, Chris Carlisle, boasted to the *New York Times* prior to the release of *SATC: The Movie*, "We've positioned this movie from the beginning as 'the Super Bowl for women.'"[33] As a result, the film, with a reportedly $65 million production budget, benefitted from brand-driven marketing and the buzz of a "must see" event. Warner Bros./New Line released *SATC: The Movie* in 3,325 theaters domestically to become the studio's second-highest-grossing theatrical film that year after *The Dark Knight* (2008, dir. Christopher Nolan). In addition to the film's female stars, Sarah Jessica Parker, Kim Cattrall, Kristin Davis, and Cynthia Nixon, the marketing leaned heavily toward sponsorship deals and product placement featuring the "official spirits sponsor" Skyy Vodka, Bag Borrow or Steal, and Mercedes-Benz.[34] Hilary Radner argues that films like *Sex and the City: The Movie* and other "girly films" were "compatible with the demands for synergy within Conglomerate Hollywood. The emphasis on consumer culture facilitated the circulation of the neo-feminist paradigm as one that supported an array of media industries from fashion to music."[35] A traditional example of pink merchandising strategies used by the studios to target women with consumer products, luxury goods, and beauty products, the product integration that showed up in the film's dialogue, specific scenes, and creative marketing materials centers on normative gendered aspirational consumption.[36]

Despite developing the release as a midbudget event movie, the studio's $57 million opening weekend still came as a surprise. Trade articles routinely expressed shock, calling the theatrical success "unheard of" or an "unprecedented takeover." Opening weekend audiences consisted of 85 percent women, with 80 percent making up the female-over-age-twenty-five quadrant. Once again, McClintock highlighted how "the film's unexpected boffo performance mystified Hollywood and shattered the decades-old thinking that females—particularly older ones—can't fuel the sort of big opening often enjoyed by a male-driven event pic or family movie."[37]

The same *Variety* article included a quote from Warner Bros.' then-president of domestic distribution, Dan Fellman, as he clearly tried the spin the unexpected success of the female-driven event movie: "This has become a cultural phenomenon. What this shows is that given the right project, you can create a frenzy for the female aud, just like we are used to with boys and men."[38] The studio quickly moved into development for the sequel, *Sex and the City 2*. The second film follows the four friends on what could be described at best as a culturally insensitive and ignorant American-centric trip to the Middle East. Even with trying to replicate the event release model with similar product tie-ins and marketing tactics as the first film, the sequel resulted in a critically panned and financially underwhelming 2010 release. For the following decade, Warner Bros. proved unable to grow or uninterested in growing the media property in a new, sustainable direction, beyond the CW's short-lived teen prequel series *The Carrie Diaries* (2013–2014). The studio shelved the *SATC* franchise until releasing a new HBO Max series in 2021. *And Just Like That . . .* follows three of the four original characters—Carrie, Miranda, and Charlotte—navigating their fifties alongside new characters of color in a gesture toward a more inclusive ensemble than the cast who appeared in the extremely white original series. The revival was developed exclusively as an HBO Max original, reflecting a larger strategy of repurposing HBO properties like *SATC* and *The Sopranos*, which had a 2021 film prequel, to boost the new streaming platform's library with mixed results.

The Female-Driven Tentpole

After *Twilight*'s release in fall 2008, Summit built the best-selling young adult book series into a record-breaking global franchise. Described in *Variety* at the time as an "unlikely candidate for a blockbuster," the vampire teen romance featured no stars, no "definable" genre, and cost merely a reported $37 million to produce the first film.[39] However, Stephenie Meyer's four-book series—*Twilight* (2005), *New Moon* (2006), *Eclipse* (2007), *Breaking Dawn* (2008)—had a large, and growing, avid worldwide fandom. After moving to live with her father in a small town in Washington called Forks, Bella Swan meets and quickly falls in love with vampire Edward Cullen. Bella and Edward play out a Romeo and Juliet love story alongside battles with her over-protective father, rival vampires, and local werewolves. Written by Melissa Rosenberg, directed by Catherine Hardwicke, and produced by Paramount's former copresident of production Karen Rosenfelt, *Twilight* in many ways signaled a new period for the female-driven event film.

Paramount originally acquired the rights to adapt the book series for its MTV Films division in 2004, only for the project to languish in development before eventually landing with Summit in 2007.[40] *Twilight* marked a new period for the independent company. Launched as an international distributor, and later moving into cofinancing and producing, Summit evolved into a full-service studio by the mid-2000s, releasing twelve films per year around the time of acquiring the rights for *Twilight* from Paramount. Summit's theatrical release strategy included conventional marketing efforts for what the president of worldwide marketing compared in the *New York Times* to employing the superhero movie approach: "We took those tactics and used them for a female property."[41] Similar to how *Sex and the City* was designated the "Super Bowl for women," the film industry's equivalent for building buzz was to equate *Twilight* with a male-driven superhero event in order to denote the industrial value and box office expectations associated with male-targeted event films.

Much of the trade coverage leading up to the November release questioned whether *Twilight* would be a hit beyond the target female audience. The larger industrial discourse shifted from "Will women go?" to "What will make men go?" A review in the *Hollywood Reporter* considers what draws the two quadrants to the movie theater:

The box office question comes down to this: Every teenage girl in America, and presumably more than a few overseas, wants to see this movie. But do any guys? To a male, a vampire movie means blood 'n' guts and horror in the night. What's all this mushy stuff? The guess here is that girls determine what happens on Friday-night dates more than is recognized, so guys will have to tolerate a PG-13 vampire movie and crack jokes at all that mushy stuff.[42]

This review reinforces a dismissive hierarchy within American popular culture in which women's fantasy spaces of romance and pleasure are derided as "mushy" storytelling that men are required to "tolerate." Not only is this comment an incredibly reductive and heteronormative take on men's versus women's tastes, pleasure, and reception—one that indeed still drives how too many studios imagine audiences—but it also clearly highlights that women were not even the key valued audience for the "chick flick." Expectations for the commercial success of women-centric movies often came from being deemed a "crossover" movie that could appeal to male audiences. In other words, female audiences are good if you can attract them, but tracking male moviegoers is how studios measure the value of a legitimately bankable event movie.

As scholarship on the critical reception of the franchise widely notes, popular reviews at the time reflected this gender divide by widely panning the first film installment of the *Twilight* series.[43] A string of predictably dismissive remarks compared teenage female fans to "mobs" or "hordes" at the "mania-stirring" premiere as a "shrieking" and "rabid fan base."[44] As discussed in the previous chapter, men made up the majority of film critics working for major US publications during this period, a gender disparity that plays out across the mainstream reviews. While middle-aged men were clearly not the primary target audience for *Twilight*, many male reviewers centered their discomfort and disregard for the fans in ways that echo a long history of male tastemakers and gatekeepers dismissing and belittling young women's and girls' participation within—and their impact on—popular culture trends.

Summit spent reportedly $30 million in marketing to target the teen audience. For example, the first teaser trailer and song from the soundtrack premiered on MySpace in spring 2008, while the cast photo "first look" and other marketing landed exclusively on MTV.com. The cast appeared at a Comic-Con panel in San Diego, and the stars went on a multi-city mall tour in partnership with the store Hot Topic.[45] *Twilight* opened in 3,419 theaters to about $70 million domestically, eventually earning $407 million worldwide. Women overwhelmingly made up the first weekend audience (75 percent) with nearly half of female viewers (45 percent) twenty-five years of age or older.[46] Hollywood's unprepared reaction proved nearly identical to *Prada*—that is, *Twilight* reportedly "overperformed."[47] Once again a group of surprised male distribution executives responded in trade interviews. Chuck Viane, the president of domestic distribution for Walt Disney Studios, stated in the *Los Angeles Times*, "Everyone thought it would be in the low thirties. What you have is a tsunami in the marketplace called *Twilight*." Then Bruce Snyder, 20th Century Fox president of distribution, told *Variety*, "[Female audiences] are turning movies into event titles, making a pic's opening look more like a male actioner than a genteel female movie that would play out over a long period of time."[48] Studio executives, industry analysts, and journalists struggled to understand how young women—a demographic routinely considered "notoriously difficult to track and measure"—turned a midbudget romance into a blockbuster hit.[49]

Summit invested heavily into building the *Twilight* film franchise after the first installment became a box office hit. The remaining three books in the series were adapted into four additional films in rapid succession— *New Moon* (2009), *Eclipse* (2010), *Breaking Dawn—Part 1* (2011), and *Breaking Dawn—Part 2* (2012). *The Twilight Saga* resulted in a $3.3 billion global franchise. Due in large part to this success, Lionsgate acquired Summit in 2012 to form a new mini-major that found short-term, and mixed, success developing and releasing YA-focused, female-led franchises like *The Hunger Games* (2012–2015) and *Divergent* (2014–2016).

Even as Summit benefitted significantly from *Twilight*, the above-the-line talent instrumental to the first film experienced wildly different career paths. The two leads, Kristen Stewart and Robert Pattinson, both leveraged their roles as Bella and Edward into sustainable Hollywood careers spanning independent and studio projects. After a string of independent character-driven projects that played the international festival circuit, both actors starred in studio franchise reboots with Sony's *Charlie's Angels* (2019) and Warner Bros.' *The Batman* (2022). However, the *Twilight* director, Catherine Hardwicke, had a different experience. In a 2018 *Vanity Fair* interview, she recalled the film's budget restrictions impacting stunts, visual effects, and large set pieces. According to the filmmaker, Summit executives required a $4 million budget cut weeks before starting principal photography to keep the entire production from shutting down. Although the studio later called for reshoots of pivotal scenes, such as Bella and Edward's first kiss, Summit's initial approach for the first *Twilight* film was clearly focused on producing a scaled-back film on an ultimately tight budget of $37 million. During the film's European press tour, trade outlets broke the news that Hardwicke would not return to direct future installments and was replaced by Chris Weitz. In a press release, Summit cited the franchise's "aggressive time frame," with a new film to be released every year between 2009 and 2012, as the reason the director did not return. Even if Hardwicke's contract gave her first right of refusal, as she clarified in a 2013 interview, *Deadline Hollywood*'s Nikki Finke presented a different narrative from anonymous sources inside Summit. Summit executives reportedly considered the director "'difficult' and 'irrational' during the making of *Twilight*."[50] When a female director is labeled as difficult, the reputation can stick and have a longer negative impact on her career moving forward. Whether Summit fired Hardwicke or she left the franchise on her own, the contradiction between official studio PR narratives and whispered off-the-record accounts reveal a striking difference in terms of responsibility and blame.

Hardwicke is not the first woman helming a female-driven franchise to be replaced by a male director after turning a female-targeted romance into a commercial box office hit.[51] In 2012, Universal Pictures entered a bidding war to option the best-selling book series *Fifty Shades of Grey* (*FSOG*) by E L James, which began as *Twilight* fan fiction, minus the vampires.[52] The trilogy follows inexperienced Seattle college graduate Anastasia Steele's romantic entanglement with tortured billionaire businessman Christian Grey. The romance erotica series is known for sex scenes detailing the couple's BDSM (bondage discipline sadism masochism) and dominant-submissive relationship. Universal's boutique subsidiary Focus Features gave the film, starring Jamie Dornan and Dakota Johnson, a targeted Valentine's Day release date in 2015. Helmed by female British director Sam Taylor-Johnson, the first film installment became Universal's fourth-biggest opening weekend in a year of strong female-led box office results, including *Trainwreck*, *Mad Max: Fury Road*, and *Pitch Perfect 2*. Despite delivering an $85 million domestic opening weekend on a reportedly modest $30 million budget, Taylor-Johnson did not return for the next two films after creative differences with the book's author, whom journalist Kim Masters described as having "unprecedented control over everything from casting and wardrobe to dialogue."[53]

On the one hand, the reported dynamic reinforces how a creator or executive producer with enough power on a project, like James's creative control over *FSOG*, can be used to undermine or overpower a female director. The *FSOG* franchise, on the other hand, is just another example of a studio "trading up" for a male filmmaker when a female-targeted property, and the audience, proves valuable. Hardwicke and Taylor-Johnson, despite launching successful female-driven franchises, both had a difficult time securing follow-up projects and, as of 2022, have yet to direct another studio movie at the same level. Hardwicke opened up years later in trade interviews about not seeing the career boost she expected from *Twilight* that her male peers have had from equivalent successful tentpoles. Far from *Twilight* boosting Hardwicke's bankability, the director had to take a pay cut on her next project, *Red Riding Hood* (2011).

The Bridesmaids Effect?

Bridesmaids is an R-rated original comedy featuring a female ensemble cast, including Kristen Wiig, Maya Rudolph, Rose Byrne, and a breakout performance by Melissa McCarthy. Directed by Paul Feig, produced by Tina Fey and Judd Apatow, and written by Wiig and Annie Mumolo, the Universal midbudget project earned about $169 million from 2,958 North American theaters. *Bridesmaids* was celebrated as "summer's surprise blockbuster" and a "watershed" moment for women's comedy. Its commercial success, for many, defied the genre's traditionally male-dominated raunchy ensemble fare—the *American Pie* franchise (1999–), *Old School* (2003), *Superbad* (2007), the *Harold and Kumar* franchise (2004–2011), and *The Hangover* franchise (2009–2013)—and did so without proven stars.[54] Universal marketed the film as a crossover comedy, appealing to the male quadrant who made up 33 percent of the opening weekend audience.[55] The film succeeded in a genre entrenched in a long history of limited expectations and access for women in front of and behind the camera.

Specifically, the marketing strategy positioned *Bridesmaids* as the female version of *The Hangover*, the R-rated bachelor weekend comedy starring Bradley Cooper and Zach Galifianakis, which resulted in a 2009 breakout hit for Warner Bros. *Bridesmaids* theatrical posters prominently featured glowing praise from film critics with quotes such as "Chick flicks don't have to suck! *Bridesmaids* sets the bar for any R-rated comedy this year" or "Better than *The Hangover*."[56] The print and trailer campaigns, by centering gross-out comedy plotlines and referencing male-driven ensemble comedies, in many ways speak to long-held assumptions that "women aren't funny." One of the most egregious examples of this narrative appeared in a 2007 *Vanity Fair* article by Christopher Hitchens, who asked, "Why are women, who have the whole male world at their mercy, not funny? Please do not pretend to not know what I am talking about. . . . Why are men, taken on average and as a whole, funnier than women"?[57] Despite coming off as an offensive, tone-deaf opinion piece, this sexist assumption plagues women not only in the masculine coded film genre but also in the broader comedy industry at large.[58] By engaging in the "women aren't funny discourse," theatrical posters, trailers, and other promotional materials center an against-the-grain "chick flick" as a male-adjacent comedy. Universal's marketing worked to strategically downplay the film's focus on female friendships, love, and marriage characteristic of the traditional female-driven genre movie in order to prove its comedic chops. In other words, the marketing message implies that *Bridesmaids* is funny not because of but in spite of being a female comedy.

The $32 million female-led project became a commercial hit, first eliciting a round of surprised reactions followed by a wave of hopeful predictions. Journalists and industry professionals speculated about a potential "*Bridesmaids* Effect." Producer David T. Friendly, known for *Little Miss Sunshine* (2006), considered a series of outcomes in a 2011 column for the *Hollywood Reporter*: "If the *Bridesmaids* Effect really takes hold, imagine the possibilities. There's the comedy about the bachelorette party gone horribly wrong. There's the nightmare honeymoon from the woman's perspective. The *Bridesmaids* Effect allows entire genres to be reimagined. Chicks on horses. Women in space. Time-shifting gals."[59] Friendly's tongue-in-cheek comment addresses a somewhat patronizing "girls can do it all" tone, while simultaneously speculating on the potential impact by wondering if one individual film can in fact change industry-wide structures, cultures, and trends.

In contrast, Gabrielle Moss best articulated the implications of this discourse in an article for *Bitch Media*: "This all begs the question: what exactly does it mean to deliver on the promise of *Bridesmaids*? Does it mean bigger budgets for mainstream, non-romantic comedies with female leads? Or does it mean embracing more unknown female actors

bitchmedia

CULTURE   COMEDY   MELISSA MCCARTHY

The "Bridesmaids" Effect: How Did "Bridesmaids" Change Hollywood?

by Gabrielle Moss
Published on June 6, 2013 at 5:10pm

5.3. Example of a "*Bridesmaids* Effect" article, published by *Bitch Media* in 2013. (Screenshot from *Bitch Media*.)

for lead roles in comedies? Or utilizing the kind of plots that used to be considered off-limits for women's comedies?"[60] In contrast to Friendly's proposed outcomes, in which women can become bankable in any genre, Moss asks whether the success of one female-driven comedy can realistically translate to better roles for women in front of the camera. The celebratory discourse surrounding *Bridesmaids* reflected another phase in the amnesia cycle. What chance for industry-wide change, specifically sustainable and long-term, can a movie like *Bridesmaids* really offer for female-driven projects measured against historically male-dominated genres, roles, and audience expectations?

Martha Lauzen referenced similar queries that arose after Kathryn Bigelow became the first woman to win the Academy Award for directing the action drama *The Hurt Locker* (2008). As Lauzen argues: "Not only is the film industry notoriously resistant to change, but both *Bridesmaids* and Bigelow stand as victories in spite of their female identification, not because of it." In her critique "debunking" the early 2010s effect discourse, she poignantly predicts that "these victories are likely to be localized and short-lived"[61] Bigelow's win had immediately led to questions about her impact on the action movie and the potential to open doors for other female directors. It was a hopeful moment for female filmmakers, but a short-sighted one. With no immediate *Hurt Locker* effect, the action genre continued to be an exclusive boy's club into the following decade.

In my 2018 conversations with an established female producer, she reiterated her frustration with the gendered logic driving these commercial cycles: "*Sex and the City* and *Bridesmaids* were huge movies but films like that are called an aberration and treated as an exception by the major studios. Years later, little has changed."[62] This producer has had a handful of female-driven hits premiere at Sundance and later released by boutique indie division Fox Searchlight and mini-major studio Lionsgate. Despite the expected boost promised to the genre, she recalled the struggle at each filmmaking stage for the two modestly budgeted female comedies she was developing and producing in the immediate years following the release of *Bridesmaids*.

Wondering if there will be a "*Bridesmaids*' Effect" or a "*Hurt Locker* Effect" may not be asking the right question. Instead, the more appropriate question is: What individuals, if any, get credit for the success of a female-driven film, and in turn, whose careers benefit from this box office success? Female-targeted comedies and rom-coms have long been recognized as spaces that have opened up opportunities for female studio directors like Nora Ephron starting in the 1990s and Nancy Meyers, Anne Fletcher, and Sanaa Hamri during the 2000s. Yet, the handful of women directing female-targeted studio projects in this period were an exception, as their male counterparts still directed the majority of female-led romantic comedies at the time. As producer David T. Friendly humorously noted: "Still, getting female-driven comedies to the big screen has been as hard as selling Disney an X-rated movie. And one has to wonder how many will get made without a champion like *Bridesmaids*' Judd Apatow behind them."[63]

In a more critical manner, Melissa Silverstein, journalist and founder of Women in Hollywood, pointed to a sense of legitimacy and leverage that proven above-the-line male directors and producers bring to female-driven studio projects:

Women producers, writers and directors and others have been beating their heads against a wall trying to get women's films made, yet it took this film [*Bridesmaids*] produced and directed by men to make Hollywood realize this fact. . . . I don't think we would be having the same conversation about the film if it had not been produced by Judd Apatow and directed by Paul Feig. There was no big outcry for more female-led PG-13 musicals following the huge success of *Mamma Mia*. That movie is not too far behind *Bridesmaids* with a domestic gross of $144 million.[64]

On the one hand, the involvement of established above-the-line male collaborators—Feig and Apatow—no doubt helped to mitigate the risk and contributed to the film's momentum from development to distribution.[65] On the other hand, if there was an immediate boost for female talent or female-driven comedies after *Bridesmaids*, bankability was rewarded individually to above-the-line talent. Melissa McCarthy went on to work again with Feig in Twentieth Century Fox's *The Heat* (2013) and *Spy* (2015), as well as reuniting with Kristen Wiig in Sony's commercially disappointing gender-swapped *Ghostbusters* (2016). Universal Pictures went on to release a handful of commercially successful female ensemble comedies in the following years—the *Pitch Perfect* franchise (2012–2017) and *Girls Trip* (2017)—but nothing to signal a significant development or production strategy shift industry-wide.

As Kristen J. Warner contends:

> There is a taken-for-granted attitude to how scholars and popular culture critics imagine women audiences as a viable demographic who have always been considered valuable to content producers. Embracing this kind of revisionist history allows us to elide conceptual and definitional obstacles and, in turn, ignore the material circumventions that women have faced and navigated to attain the inches of progress in value gained. Progress narratives are encouraging nuggets of hop[e]. However, seductive success stories should not blind us to the historical disenfranchisements that continue to inform popular misunderstandings that affect how "successful" films and television series about women are discussed, as they are considered exceptions and not the rule.[66]

Warner makes an important point about understanding box office wins within a larger historical context of the contested viability and valuation of "women-centered media" and female audiences in the twenty-first century. Progress narratives like "the effect" that aim to celebrate the commercial success of female-driven fare can too often elide or erase the systemic barriers and industrial obstacles that female filmmakers have to navigate in order to even get a film produced, let alone have an exceptional breakout hit.

In other words, the celebration around bankability is a short-lived part of the overall box office amnesia loop. This type of short-term recognition, highlighting the commercial success of a single film, female filmmaker, or cycle, operates more as a stopgap reaction than a door-opening measure toward larger institutional and industrial shifts. The amnesia loop gestures at the systemic gender inequities, specifically that female filmmakers are not hired and their films are not financed, produced, or distributed at the same rate as those of their male peers. The mistake was to expect a celebration of visibility and progress, which represented nothing more than a fleeting recognition of bankability during this period, to directly translate into material, long-lasting changes for an individual genre, filmmaker, or studio slate.

Box Office Failure: Movie Jail

So what happens when female-driven films prove disappointing, or even bombs, during theatrical distribution? This section explores another layer of how risk and failure are gendered and how female filmmakers often have one chance to succeed or fail in Hollywood, a consequence widely known as "movie jail." Even as women may not benefit from a lucrative hit as equitably as their male peers, blame for a failed release lands unevenly on female-driven projects and even harder on its female filmmaker by limiting or delaying future opportunities.

A film is considered "underperforming" if opening weekend returns do not reach the studio's projected estimates. A disappointing theatrical release becomes a box office bomb when it not only falls below expectations but also fails to return production, distribution, and marketing costs, resulting in major financial losses for the studio. In February 2020, in the earliest months of the pandemic, Warner Bros. released *Birds of Prey and the Fantabulous Emancipation of One Harley Quinn*, a loose spin-off to the male-driven comic book film *Suicide Squad* (2016, dir. David Ayer). As part of the DC Extended Universe (DCEU) franchise, Warner Bros. expanded the story arc of Harley Quinn into a stand-alone female-led ensemble project directed by Cathy Yan, starring and coproduced by Margot Robbie, and written by Christina Hodson. While projected for a $45 million domestic opening, the film in the first weekend earned $33 million and drew critical headlines like *Variety*'s "*Birds of Prey* Lays an Egg at the Box Office" and the *Hollywood Reporter*'s "Box Office: *Birds of Prey* Flies off Course with $13M Friday."[67] The disappointing weekend led the studio's distribution division to recommend a display change for major exhibitors like AMC, Regal, and Cinemark. As a result, the film's title was shortened and displayed as *Harley Quinn: Birds of Prey*.[68] In a trade interview that spring, Yan pointed to the "undue expectations on a female-led movie, and what I was most disappointed in was this idea that perhaps it proved we weren't ready for this yet. That was an extra burden that, as a woman-of-color director, I already had on me anyway."[69] Yan was the first Asian American and woman of color to helm a comic book franchise movie and only the second woman to direct a DCEU installment, which, following Patty Jenkins's record-breaking *Wonder Woman* release, proved a fraught task. Despite the film's breaking even during its global theatrical run, *Birds of Prey* was seen as a female-driven failure more than a DCEU or comic book movie failure.

The burden to defy expectations that female directors like Yan carry is nothing new. Elaine May's *Ishtar* (1987) continues to be one of the most-cited industry examples of box office failure—so much so that the film's name remains synonymous with movie flop decades later. *New York Times* critic A. O. Scott traced a string of recent flops to the "summer of *Ishtar*" discourse that followed summer 2013, maintaining that *Ishtar* "has entered the lexicon—along with *Heaven's Gate*, *Waterworld*, and *Howard the Duck*—as shorthand for large-scale cinematic unsuccess."[70] The stakes for *Ishtar* were set exceptionally high. May was only one of a few women writing and directing studio projects in the 1970s and 1980s, including her hit comedies *A New Leaf* (1971) and *The Heartbreak Kid* (1972). Under Columbia Pictures and starring Warren Beatty and Dustin Hoffman, *Ishtar* proved to be one of the most expensive failures during this period; with a budget of reportedly $55 million, its domestic theatrical gross was only $14 million. Rumors of careless and excessive production spending and on-set tensions leaked prior to the theatrical release, culminating in a critical *New York Magazine* cover story stating, "*Ishtar* has been regarded as a potential *Heaven's Gate*—the classic $44 million bomb that brought about the downfall of a movie studio."[71] The film opened with bad press and vitriolic film reviews and never had a chance to recover.

In retrospect, the film began to have a reassessment by the 2010s in light of the gender equity debates and May's pioneering contributions as one of the few female directors working in this studio era. Yet, the blame and career damage landed solely on May as screenwriter and director, who had a history of tension with the studios on her two earlier projects.[72] She garnered a reputation as unreasonable and difficult, a too often gendered accusation that plagues a number of female filmmakers whose leadership styles, expertise, and creative vision are questioned. May continued to work occasionally as a writer in Hollywood, penning a handful of screenplays like *The Bird Cage* (1996) and *Primary Colors* (1998). However, the blowback from *Ishtar* irrevocably damaged her directing career. May was placed in metaphorical "movie jail" and had not directed another studio feature as of 2022.

As two of the most-cited contemporary examples of women placed in movie jail, Mimi Leder and Karyn Kusama each spent more than a decade struggling to return to feature film directing. Prior to her movie jail sentence, Leder built a directing career in network television series like *China Beach* (1988–1991) and *ER* (1994–2009) before moving on to helm two successful action blockbusters, *The Peacemaker* (1997) and *Deep Impact* (1998). Her transition into feature directing was a significant move, since few women helmed studio tentpoles in the $50–$80 million–budget range in the late 1990s. Despite a proven track record, Leder's next project, starring Helen Hunt, Kevin Spacey, and Haley Joel Osment—Warner Bros.' inspirational drama *Pay It Forward* (2000) about the impact of good deeds— was a critical and financial failure. Leder's opportunities to direct another feature all but disappeared until the 2018 Ruth Bader Ginsburg biopic *On The Basis of Sex*. In a 2015 *New York Times* interview, Leder openly acknowledged: "*Pay It Forward* was not a box-office success and I went to movie jail for quite a long time. I excel in television. I've directed nine pilots and six of them went to air, so my television career was flourishing, but I couldn't get arrested in features. Saying this sounds like sour grapes, but it isn't: It's very different for women filmmakers than it is for male filmmakers."[73]

Despite continuing to work as a television director for critically acclaimed series like Showtime's *Shameless* (2011–2021) and HBO's *The Leftovers* (2014–2017), Leder waited for almost two decades before returning to feature filmmaking. In a 2014 *Indiewire* interview, she described the painful path of finding work after *Pay It Forward* as an exhausting climb out of movie jail.[74] While Leder is one of the most well-known examples of movie jail and publicly open about her experiences, it is important to highlight that she consistently worked for the next fourteen years directing television movies and episodes, with significant creative contributions to prestige drama series like *The Leftovers* and later Apple's *The Morning Show* (2019–). Furthermore, that Leder spoke out critically in interviews about the experiences of female studio directors while continuing to work in series television and did not necessarily appear to face career-ending repercussions is telling. Unlike directors sent to movie jail whose careers never fully recover, she clearly maintained the degree of leverage that comes with a three decades–long career and the support of a professional network.

As the release of *Pay It Forward* derailed Leder's career, Karyn Kusama's career experienced a lift after the critically acclaimed Sundance premiere of her directorial feature debut, *Girlfight* (2000), discussed in the previous chapter. Kusama's well-documented trajectory moves from Sundance breakout to movie jail within only a few years of her directorial debut. Kusama's follow-up project was a 2005 feature film adaptation of *Aeon Flux*, the early 1990s MTV cult animated series. The project was greenlit during Sherry Lansing's tenure as Paramount's chairperson. After Lansing's departure from the studio, a regime change significantly impacted the theatrical version of *Aeon Flux*. Kusama delivered a cut of the post-apocalyptic sci-fi blockbuster, starring Charlize Theron, to the new Paramount leadership, who reportedly dismissed it as a "$50 million art movie." As a result, the studio took the reportedly $62 million–budgeted project away from Kusama in postproduction and recut the film down to a paltry and incoherent seventy-one minutes. Despite Paramount later bringing her back to complete the editing and to help fix the final theatrical cut, she was not allowed to be alone with her editor during the process. Similar to the studio babysitting of female directors discussed in chapter 3, Kusama recounted the level of mistrust she experienced in a 2016 *Buzzfeed News* interview: "This is where gender plays a part. This is where big personalities and power and influence really make a difference. Because I just didn't have anyone who could advocate for why it was important that they treat me better. There are so few playbooks to go by in my situation [as a female director]."[75] *Aeon Flux* earned $25.8 million domestically and $53.3 million globally the first weekend, and Paramount deemed the release a massive flop. Kusama's journey paralleled what journalist Matthew Hammett Knott describes as "an impossible standard [where] executives are seemingly just waiting for [women] to make a mistake, at which point they can be deemed unsuitable, unreliable and unhireable."[76] The Paramount experience resulted in Kusama struggling to land a follow-up job.

Taking the brunt of the blame, Kusama acquired only one directing credit during this period—an episode of the Showtime series *The L Word* (2004–2009). After the critical and financial success of Fox Searchlight's *Juno* (2007), screenwriter Diablo Cody's next project, *Jennifer's Body* (2009), was a female-focused teen horror project budgeted at $16 million. To escape her movie jail status and land the director's job, Kusama reportedly had to convince Fox Atomic's unit head Peter Rice. Starring Megan Fox and Amanda Seyfried as high school friends in a toxic relationship, *Jennifer's Body* follows the duo as Fox's character becomes inhabited by a man-eating demon. Cody, Kusama, and Fox each spoke publicly in late 2010s interviews about the studio's mismarketing and mishandling of the film. As a subversive take on the traditional male-focused teen horror genre with dark comedic moments, the female-driven project was intended for young women who too often have been sexualized and victimized in earlier iterations of the horror genre.

However, the studio's marketing campaign deliberately targeted a young male audience by foregrounding Megan Fox's sexual appeal and desirability. For example, versions of the theatrical poster feature Fox wearing a short, plaid schoolgirl skirt with a tight, revealing red tank top and high-heeled red sandals as she sits atop a school desk with legs loosely crossed and a cool, alluring look on her face. The chalkboard behind her includes excerpts from film reviews repeatedly calling the movie "sexy," "slick," and "smart," and Fox as "dangerously hot." Notably, Seyfried, who is arguably the film's protagonist (as she ultimately stops her best friend's killing spree and takes revenge on those responsible for the possession), is completely absent from the theatrical poster. The marketing campaign sidelines female audiences to target young men by centering Megan Fox's sexual appeal and downplaying the film's exploration of toxic friendship and the power dynamic between the two main characters. As a result, *Jennifer's Body* played poorly with young women while also experiencing

5.4. *Jennifer's Body* (2009) star Megan Fox and screenwriter Diablo Cody reflect on the film's mismarketing and biased reception on an *Entertainment Tonight* segment in 2019. (Screenshot from *Entertainment Tonight*, "*Jennifer's Body* Reunion" segment via YouTube.)

backlash from male audiences and critics. The film grossed only $6.8 million domestically the first weekend.

Much like the aftermath of *Aeon Flux*, Kusama returned to movie jail and did not direct another feature until *The Invitation* (2015), a critically acclaimed $1 million, low-budget independent project that led to more television-directing work and the Nicole Kidman–led drama *Destroyer* (2018). On the one hand, Kusama, like Leder, not only managed to keep working in different sectors and on a different scale of projects in stops and starts, but she also spoke openly about her experiences working on studio movies. Kusama's opportunity to reflect in detail about both female-driven projects during the 2000s contributed to critical reassessment of and later cult status for *Jennifer's Body* as a biting critique of teenage girlhood. On the other hand, much of this industry press attention in the late 2010s that was featured in the *New York Times*, *Buzzfeed News*, the *Guardian*, and elsewhere was published in a different industry climate. Reassessing the halted careers of female directors and female stars became more common in the wake of #MeToo and Time's Up. In addition to a reevaluation of Kusama's career, the studio's release strategy for *Jennifer's Body* as well as the sexualization and sexist treatment of Megan Fox in the press were also examined under sharper scrutiny a decade later due in large part to the changing industry climate around the treatment of women in the entertainment business.

Producer Lynda Obst articulated the gendered double standard in a 2017 *Hollywood Reporter* article: "There are different rules for women. If a woman makes one bomb, she's done. (Men are forgiven two at least if they've also had a big hit.)"[77] Two, three, or more box office failures or flops do not kill a male director's employability or studio career.[78] These double standards also may limit the studio opportunities that female directors are willing to take as they must mitigate the risk of potential movie jail against their long-term career opportunities and ambitions. In a 2021 conversation on the popular podcast *WTF with Marc Maron*, Patty Jenkins discussed a short-lived experience when Marvel hired her to direct *Thor 2* in 2011, which was later released as *Thor: The Dark World* in 2013. Jenkins ultimately walked away from the project: "I knew it couldn't be me [to fail]. It couldn't be me that had that happen. If they hired any guy to do it, it wouldn't be a big deal, but I knew in my heart that I could not make a good movie out of the story they wanted to do."[79] Jenkins's 2003 directorial debut *Monster* was a critically acclaimed drama starring Charlize Theron in her Oscar-winning role as serial killer Aileen Wuornos. However, Jenkins struggled to land another feature film project. She directed a handful of television episodes before Warner Bros. hired her to lead the long-gestating *Wonder Woman* project discussed in the following section. It should be noted that Jenkins's 2021 reflection about her short stint on a Marvel project came at a different time in her career, after she had already directed two Wonder Woman movies. In other words, she had gained significant leverage and a more protected position from where to speak out than in the previous decade.

Where men in the director's seat are given the benefit of the doubt and measured in potential and opportunities to prove themselves, women can be dismissed after one shot, deemed box office poison, and relegated to movie jail. *New York Times* co-chief film critic Manohla Dargis highlighted the gender double standard that plays out with theatrical releases from women and directors of color. She referred to indie darling Wes Anderson, whose $50 million–budgeted *The Life Aquatic with Steve Zissou* (2004) for Disney's division Touchstone Pictures proved to be a box office flop domestically and internationally. She pointedly argued:

Do you think that a woman would have been able to get forty million dollars to make a puppet movie the way that Wes Anderson has been able to make, bringing to bear all the publicity and advertising budget of Fox [with *Fantastic Mr. Fox*]? After two movies that didn't make a lot of money? I think this is true for a lot of black filmmakers too—they're held to a higher standard. And an unfair standard. You can be a male filmmaker and if you're perceived as a genius—a boy genius or a fully-formed adult genius—then you are allowed to fail in a way that a woman is not allowed to fail.[80]

Yet, Anderson worked steadily throughout the 2000s and 2010s, following up the *Life Aquatic* with *The Darjeeling Limited* (2007) and *Fantastic Mr. Fox* (2009), even as the two succeeding projects underperformed at the domestic theatrical box office.

Notable examples of white men failing upward into bigger blockbuster projects include Zack Snyder, who rode the financial success of the Warner Bros./Legendary Pictures ancient Greek battle blockbuster *300* (2006) into a lucrative studio directing career. Despite a rapid succession of three follow-up projects with Warner Bros.—*Watchmen* (2009), *Legend of the Guardians: The Owls of Ga'Hoole* (2010), and *Sucker Punch* (2011)—each proving financially and critically disappointing, Snyder continued to release a new project every one to three years for the next two decades. He helmed the Superman reboot *Man of Steel* (2013) starring Henry Cavill. Warner Bros. brought him back for additional DCEU franchise installments, such as the much-maligned releases *Batman v Superman: Dawn of Justice* (2016) and *Justice League* (2017), Warner Bros.' response to Disney/Marvel's globally successful Avengers ensemble movies. The production history of *Justice League* was reportedly a tumultuous one. According to Tatiana Siegel's account in *Rolling Stone*: "Executives at [Warner Bros.], headed up at the time by former chief Kevin Tsujihara, felt the film had major issues, including that it was convoluted and still too long at more than two-and-a-half hours. The movie was deemed 'a disaster' and a 'full-on failure.'"[81]

When Snyder left *Justice League* for personal reasons, the studio passed the project for completion to Joss Whedon. The film proved a disappointing box office failure even with a $93 million domestic opening weekend.[82] In 2020, Warner Bros. announced that Snyder would return to the project and recut the 2017 film, known as the "Snyder Cut," to premiere on then–AT&T parent company's new streaming platform HBO Max at the cost of $70 million.[83] A 2022 *Rolling Stone* article about the emergence of the controversial Snyder Cut later revealed the complicated power struggle between the studio executives, the director, and a "toxic social media movement."[84] Despite Snyder's increasingly tumultuous relationship with Warner Bros., the opportunity to shoot additional footage and recut a new director's cut is a striking example of the long-term relationships male directors enjoy with studios. Investment in men's potential, despite inconsistent box office track records, is a luxury most female directors are never given at any budget level.

Year of the (Wonder) Woman!

With great fanfare at CinemaCon, the annual trade show for film exhibition, John Fithian, president of the National Association of Theatre Owners, predicted that "2015 will rock at the box office because it will be the year of women." He pointed to Disney's live-action version of *Cinderella*, Universal's first installment of the erotica romance *Fifty Shades of Grey* trilogy, and Lionsgate/Summit's latest film in the young adult dystopia *Divergent* series *Insurgent*. This successful wave of female-driven theatrical releases extended into summer with Universal's Elizabeth Banks–directed *Pitch Perfect 2* and the Amy Schumer star vehicle *Trainwreck*. Coming as a surprise yet again to the major studios, *Variety*, the *Hollywood Reporter*, and other prominent trade publications responded with celebratory stories reflecting an industry congratulating itself for a financially lucrative film cycle. Each of these releases opened without A-list marquee stars to a domestic opening weekend between $52 and $85 million. The majority of the midrange-budgeted productions reportedly cost between $29 to $40 million, with the CGI-driven *Cinderella* and *Insurgent* exceptions at $90 and $110 million, respectively. Trade and popular press think pieces followed, with titles such as "At the Box Office, It's No Longer a Man's World"; "This Year, Women (and Girls) Rule the Big Screen"; and "Female-Driven Movies Make Money, So Why Aren't More Being Made?"[85] Much like the "*Bridesmaids* Effect," the return of the "year of the woman" discourse raised questions about female-driven projects and their filmmakers around bankability and wider implications, or potential, for an industry-wide shift.

Conglomerate Hollywood-era studios exploiting reliable intellectual properties, franchise expansion, and cinematic world-building as a central strategy slowly began to encompass a few female-driven big-budget studio projects developed and released in the mid- to late 2010s. Following an industry-wide investment in remakes, reboots, and sequels, the major studios found mixed success with refreshing or expanding media properties in their libraries, which included Disney's live-action remakes *Cinderella* (2015), *Beauty and the Beast* (2017), and *Mulan* (2020);Warner Bros.' comic book adaptations *Wonder Woman* (2017) and *Birds of Prey* (2020); and Disney's *Captain Marvel* (2019), *Black Widow* (2021), and *Eternals* (2021).

Wonder Woman is illustrative of how a mid-2010s rebooted "year of the woman" celebration grappled with notions of gendered risk on a bigger scale. For the three decades prior to the 2017 film, studio executives widely categorized female-led comic book movies as box office poison based on a handful of disappointing theatrical releases. To build on the commercial success of the Christopher Reeve *Superman* films (1978–1987), franchise producers developed a female-led *Supergirl* starring Helen Slater with Faye Dunaway and Peter O'Toole in 1984. Along with terrible reviews, notably Roger Ebert panning it as an "unhappy, unfunny, unexciting movie," *Supergirl* failed to take its female superhero seriously and resulted in a notorious box office flop.[86] As opposed to the Warner Bros. *Batman* films (1989–1997), in which the few women on screen were relegated to love interests (Kim Basinger as Vicki Vale and Nicole Kidman as Dr. Chase Meridian), villains (Michelle Pfeiffer as Catwoman and Uma Thurman as Poison Ivy), or sidekicks (Alicia Silverstone as Batgirl), female-led superhero projects did not emerge until the mid-2000s. Both Warner Bros.' *Catwoman* (2004), starring Halle Berry, and Fox's *Elektra* (2005), starring Jennifer Garner, proved to be underperforming spin-offs of earlier, successful male-driven releases. For the following decade, female-centric comic book movies were widely categorized as box office poison and not a priority for the major studios. *Women and Hollywood* posted a leaked email exchange, courtesy of the 2014 Sony hack, between Sony's and Marvel's chief executives. Ike Perlmutter, Marvel's head at the time, categorized *Catwoman* as a "disaster" and said that, for *Elektra*, "the end result was a very, very bad idea." This track record held weight in Hollywood as confirmation of an industry-wide understanding of the female-driven superhero as not bankable and too risky.[87] From the release of *Iron Man* in 2008 to *Wonder Woman* in 2017, every single studio superhero project starred male characters helmed by male directors.

In this industrial climate, Warner Bros. struggled for decades to move a Wonder Woman project out of development.[88] By the time the newest project was announced and moving toward production in the mid-2010s, industry publications began to speculate whether potential directors would include a woman.[89] Few women were included on potential director lists that floated around the studios for big-budget projects during this period, another revelation from the Sony hack emails. For example, leaked emails between Sony executives and producers for an Angelina Jolie–led Cleopatra project in development included a list of twenty-three potential directors with only one woman—acclaimed New Zealand director Jane Campion of the Palme d'Or–winning *The Piano* (1993), *The Portrait of a Lady* (1996), and the series *Top of the Lake* (2013–2017).[90] If it took the top prize from Cannes and nearly thirty years of directing experience to make the studio's short list of directors in the 2010s, what chance did any other women have of making it onto that list?

Because of the poor track record for female superhero films, director Lexi Alexander discussed the pressure placed on a potential female director helming *Wonder Woman* in a 2014 *Fast Company* interview: "Imagine the weight on my shoulders. . . . How many male superhero movies fail? So now, we finally get *Wonder Woman* with a female director, imagine if it fails. And you have no control over marketing, over budget. So without any control, you carry the fucking weight of gender equality for both characters and women directors. No way."[91] It is unclear if Alexander was on Warner Bros.' short list for hiring a director. Either way, based on her experience directing the Marvel comic book adaptation *Punisher: War Zone* (2008), distributed by Lionsgate domestically, she understood the challenges that *Wonder Woman*'s female director would need to navigate working in this masculine space. Indeed, Alexander pointed to how industry logic ingrained in economic viability inevitably poisoned the project with gendered expectations of failure before even leaving the development phase.

The story of Diana Prince went through a number of transformations on the path it took to the big screen—despite Wonder Woman being one of the most recognizable superheroes of the twentieth century. Developing a contemporary Wonder Woman project was a decades-long process with a number of competing iterations from films to television series in development.[92]

- 1996: Ivan Reitman was attached to a Wonder Woman project that never left development.
- 2004: Patty Jenkins pitched a Wonder Woman project to Warner Bros. after the release of her critically acclaimed indie *Monster* (2003).
- 2006: Joss Whedon developed a *Wonder Woman* film but walked away from the project the following year.
- 2007: George Miller, who would go on to helm the acclaimed female-led *Mad Max: Fury Road* (2015), developed and later scrapped in 2008 his Justice League project, which would have prominently featured Diana Prince.
- 2011: David E. Kelley, known for creating television series, including *Ally McBeal* (1997–2002) and *Big Little Lies* (2017–2019), aimed to revive the Amazon princess for television and produced a pilot for NBC that was not picked up.
- 2014: Warner Bros. announced a Wonder Woman project led by Canadian director Michelle MacLaren, best known for television work.
- 2015: MacLaren left the project, and Patty Jenkins replaced her as director. This was Jenkins's first feature film job since her directorial debut in 2003.
- 2016: Gal Gadot first appeared as Wonder Woman in *Batman v Superman: Dawn of Justice*.
- 2017: *Wonder Woman*, starring Gadot, premiered in theaters worldwide and plans for a sequel were announced later that summer.

The various stops and starts for developing a feature-length film based on this iconic superhero are not uncommon in the studio development world. Whether due to studio leadership, economic limitations, creative conflicts, or licensing issues, this troubled production history contributed to the narrative of *Wonder Woman* as a major gamble for Warner Bros. even before the struggling project left development by 2015.

In the press leading up to the June theatrical release, *Wonder Woman* continued to be framed as a risk both inside the studio and within the industry at large. For example, a promotional tweet highlighting a cover story in the *Hollywood Reporter* described the film as a gamble due to Jenkins's limited feature film experience: "#WonderWoman: Warner Bros. is gambling $150M with a filmmaker whose only prior big-screen credit was an $8M indie."[93] While *THR* rightfully received pushback on Twitter for the headline, early discourse around the film focused on gendered risk. Kevin Lincoln pointed out in *Vulture*, "As the first female-fronted superhero movie of the Marvel era, as well as the first to be helmed by a female director, *Wonder Woman* also carries with it the (unfair) prerogative of proving the international viability of female-oriented tentpoles."[94] The Warner Bros. project carried the burden of proving bankability not only for female superhero movies but also for all potential female-driven big-budget projects in Hollywood moving forward.

A female studio screenwriter I interviewed multiple times over the course of researching this book spoke often about how the studios too often "shortchange" female-driven projects and underestimate women working above the line. Based on her experience with prestige projects and franchise films, she shared her frustrations: "*Wonder Woman* had an impossible hill to climb. So often female-driven films are set up to fail by the studios—the budgets are too high or not high enough, not enough time spent in pre- or post-production, not spending enough on marketing the film. And who do you think gets blamed?"[95]

In the case of the theatrical marketing strategy, Warner Bros. planned a shorter campaign and noticeably slower rollout of paid promotional materials as compared to other, male-driven films in the DCEU franchise. In *AdWeek*, Chris Thilk examined the difference in paid TV spots for *Batman v Superman: Dawn of Justice* and *Wonder Woman*. The former had fourteen television spots circulating two months prior to the film's March 2016 premiere compared to the latter's four spots released a month and a half from its release.[96] Comparing official trailers posted to Warner Bros.' YouTube channel, promotion for *Justice League* included twice as many trailers leading up to its fall 2017 release.[97] While both male-driven films featured tested characters, larger production budgets, and significantly more brand partnerships, the contrast to *Wonder Woman*'s marketing reach was a telling example of how studio resources were expended in relation to box office expectations, the most valued properties, and the most desirable audiences.

Originally projected for a $65–$75 million domestic opening, *Wonder Woman* reportedly shocked Warner Bros. by bringing in more than $100 million theatrically the first weekend in North America.[98] The film out-grossed each of the three previous DCEU films at the domestic box office. A review of a steady stream of major publications between May and August

5.5. A pivotal scene in *Wonder Woman* (2017). Diana heroically moves across the no-man's-land of the battlefield in order to draw fire from the German army and save a village. (Screenshot from *Wonder Woman*.)

2017—including the *Washington Post*, *Los Angeles Times*, *New York Times*, *Hollywood Reporter*, and *Variety*—shows that an identifiable narrative shift occurred. As the first weekend box office data arrived, *Wonder Woman* was described as "overperforming" for a female-driven tentpole and an "unusual exception" as a summer blockbuster.[99] Yet, as record-breaking box office numbers continued to hold into the following weekends domestically and internationally, the discourse around the release transformed a major risk into a savior that "rescues" the superhero genre, DCEU franchise, and, potentially, the future opportunities for female filmmakers.[100]

Trade coverage widely applauded Patty Jenkins for "cracking" or "breaking" the ceiling in a moment when the industry slowly began to recognize publicly how few women are hired to direct big-budget studio projects, such as the *Washington Post*'s "How *Wonder Woman* Director Patty Jenkins Cracked the Super-Hero Movie Glass Ceiling."[101] As seen in the *New York Times*' "*Wonder Woman* Could Be the Superhero Women in Hollywood Need" or in *THR*'s "What *Wonder Woman* Really Means for Female Directors," questions and speculation about the long-term impact for women in Hollywood quickly followed. Furthermore, headlines such as *Variety*'s "How Patty Jenkins Saved the DC Extended Universe" viewed *Wonder Woman* as a corrective for the dark tone and uneven storytelling weighing down earlier installments in the franchise, including Zack Snyder's contributions.[102] After strong critical praise and financial returns, Warner Bros. chairman Toby Emmerich described the DCEU prior to *Wonder Woman*, noting that because of the "disdain or downright loathing for earlier releases *Batman v Superman* and *Suicide Squad*, the franchise was struggling in 2017."[103] Warner Bros. invested heavily in rebooting Batman and Superman projects as part of the DC Extended Universe franchise in order to create a cinematic universe to rival Marvel with mixed results.

After the global success of the *Wonder Woman* release, Patty Jenkins began what the *Hollywood Reporter* called in the fall 2017 an "unusually lengthy and tough negotiation" for a reportedly seven-figure salary plus significant back-end residuals to direct, produce, and cowrite a sequel.[104] Warner Bros. began promoting the much-hyped sequel, *Wonder Woman 1984* (2020), early in production with surprise footage at the 2018 Comic-Con International in San Diego and a new trailer at Comic-Con Experience in São Paulo, Brazil, the following year.[105] The studio announced a decision to move the DCEU franchise in a new direction with a new phase of female-driven superhero projects led by female directors of color, including Warner Bros./DC's Cathy Yan/*Birds of Prey* and Ava DuVernay/*New Gods*.[106] During the same period, Disney's Marvel Studios announced upcoming projects in Phase Four of the Marvel Cinematic Universe at the 2019 Comic-Con International. As a markedly more inclusive lineup, the film projects included female-driven *Black Widow* directed by Cate Shortland, *The Eternals* (later changed to *Eternals*) directed by Chloé Zhao, a *Captain Marvel* sequel directed by Nia DaCosta, and a female-led *Thor: Love and Thunder* directed by Taika Waititi.[107]

The upcoming slate marked a significant shift in the established male-dominated superhero strategy by incorporating women and people of color in front of and behind the camera. In a series of superhero films developed within the emerging climate of #MeToo and Time's Up, both studios clearly aimed to seize upon industry-wide conversations with intentional optics about diversifying big-budget filmmaking that also neatly fit into existing franchise-building efforts. On the surface, this strategic shift to hire white women and female directors of color, as well as to center female protagonists, is clearly a response to criticism of the gender and racial disparities within the biggest studio franchises. As hopeful and celebratory as Warner Bros. and Disney actors and executives were during these announcements at various promotional events, this new phase replicates older studio practices relying on established male-driven intellectual property.

Originally scheduled for earlier 2020 releases, *Wonder Woman 1984*, *Eternals*, and *Black Widow* all saw their theatrical release dates pushed back due to the uncertainties caused by the global coronavirus pandemic. Warner Bros. delayed the release date of Jenkins's sequel multiple times until finally announcing an unprecedented and shocking hybrid release plan. In November 2020, after multiple delays, WarnerMedia made a surprise announcement that the $200 million sequel would be released domestically day-and-date in theaters and on HBO Max on December 25. In a move some considered to be the dumping of a lucrative franchise installment and potential box office hit to streaming, then–Warner Bros. chair and CEO Ann Sarnoff spun the new distribution strategy, and the company's clear business decision, in the press as a way "to super-serve our fans."[108] Two weeks later, Warner Bros. made another shocking announcement: that the studio's entire 2021 film slate would premiere simultaneously on HBO Max and in theaters. The unexpected decision, which *Deadline* called a "seismic windows model shakeup" and *Variety* described as a "shocking move," angered top creative talent on a number of these films due not only to the changing distribution strategy but also to the loss in potential back-end profit.[109] Because studio leadership did not inform most of the top talent of these projects prior to the press announcement, WarnerMedia faced scathing public criticism from film-makers like Christopher Nolan and Denis Villeneuve for prioritizing sub-scriber numbers over maintaining strong creative relationships.

The day-and-date decision was largely seen as both a reaction to the studio's failed theatrical release of Christopher Nolan's *Tenet* in September 2020 and a corrective to build then-WarnerMedia's mishandled and poorly branded new streaming platform. HBO Max's rocky launch in summer 2020 included subscriber confusion around HBO Go versus HBO Now versus HBO Max apps as well as former parent company AT&T's battles to negotiate carrier deals with Amazon and Roku. In many ways, *Wonder Woman 1984* and the Warner Bros. 2021 film slate were sacrificed to the parent company's ambitions to attract streaming subscribers with a more exclusive media library and to compete against Netflix and other platforms in a moment of instability in the theatrical and streaming businesses. The sequel arrived to mixed reviews and grossed a disappointing $152 million worldwide, compared to the 2017 film's $821 million. How-ever, HBO Max subscriptions responded, totaling 17 million by the end of 2020 and peaking at around 70 million worldwide by fall 2021.[110]

In the December print issue of the *Hollywood Reporter*, Warner Bros.' distribution change was described as "upend[ing] Hollywood's future."[111]

Most strikingly, two illustrations featuring Wonder Woman accompany the cover story. At the beginning of the article, a slightly disheveled Diana Prince holds over her head a massive globe that depicts the famous Hollywood sign. In contrast, the magazine's cover image shows Wonder Woman's Amazonian sandaled foot in the process of stepping on, with the anticipation of crushing, a modest, twentieth-century-style movie theater. Key questions about the franchise emerge from comparing these two images: Is Wonder Woman saving or ruining the Hollywood business? Furthermore, how did a lucrative female-driven property go from a risky gamble to rescuing the female superhero genre and its studio to ruining the Hollywood business in a short span of fewer than four years?

Common metaphors describe women overcoming barriers to gender parity across many male-dominated workplaces, as if the women are themselves superhero projects. Successful women are often depicted as individually breaking ground, busting the glass ceiling, opening doors, and seismically changing industry infrastructure due to their own strength, merit, and drive. As with Jenkins helming the first globally successful female-driven superhero movie, female filmmakers have superhero expectations placed on them to individually overcome the systemic gendered obstacles ingrained in the Hollywood studio system. Such high stakes—whether for female filmmakers battling to work in a male-driven genre or a single female-driven property faced with saving its parent company in a time of crisis—are comparable to what many in the business world call the "glass cliff," a situation in which women CEOs are brought in to lead struggling companies during a crisis when the risk of failure is higher and the margin for error nonexistent. A term coined by Michelle Ryan and Alex Haslam, the glass cliff reflects how these female executives' "positions are precarious, because they're happening in difficult times. So the idea is to evoke this idea of women teetering on the edge, and that their fall, or their failure, might be imminent."[112]

Wonder Woman as a character and a franchise bears the burden to save the day. Despite the range of reviews, from mixed to disappointed, the sequel's move from a wide theatrical release to a focused digital release illustrates a moment of crisis for then–parent company AT&T and its film studio Warner Bros. If Wonder Woman (2017) supposedly broke a glass ceiling and Wonder Woman 1984 teetered on the glass cliff, what happens for the next cycle of female-directed, female-led, and female-targeted tentpoles moving forward? Despite the critical and financial success of the first installment, and the ultimate sacrifice of its release for the sequel, the case of *Wonder Woman*'s trajectory reflects a site of struggle for female-driven tentpoles navigating the inequities around gendered bankability, failure, and risk.

Conclusion

In fall 2021, a messy public battle over *Black Widow* between the film studio and female star exploded when Disney reactively changing the film's distribution strategy. Scarlett Johansson filed a lawsuit against Disney for breaching her contract with the new day-and-date plan.[113] As discussed in chapter 3, *Black Widow* is the first female-driven Avengers spin-off, and Johansson is an integral part of the MCU as Natasha Romanoff. The lawsuit represented a legal "complaint for 1) intentional interference with contractual relations; and 2) inducing breach of contract." The lawsuit claims that Disney broke her contract when changing from an exclusive wide theatrical release to a hybrid release model in theaters and on Disney+, which, in turn, caused her to lose out on significant back-end compensations. Disney did not renegotiate contractual terms when shifting from a traditional distribution strategy to an experimental day-and-date release during the pandemic. The case publicly questioned what a number of journalists and analysts also asked: Is pivoting to include the premier VOD release of a $30 film rental alongside theatrical distribution solely a reaction to uncertainties around movie theater attendance due to Covid? Or is this shift a way to shore up higher subscription numbers for a fairly new platform as part of Disney's efforts to compete with Netflix's massive global market share? In a rush to attract Disney+ subscribers over protecting talent relationships in the restructuring of traditional distribution windows, who loses?

This legal action represented an unprecedented power move by one of the highest-paid A-list actresses in Hollywood, and a number of trade outlets wondered if this complaint would open the door to additional cases from above-the-line talent. Disney's official response was to criticize Johansson's move as "callous" in the light of a pandemic, a characterization women's industry groups and activists called out as a sexist and "gendered character attack."[114] This PR blunder, largely credited to the leadership team of new (and ultimately short-lived) CEO Bob Chapek, who lacked previous experience working with top talent on the content side of Disney, reflected at best a media conglomerate clumsily adjusting to studio business practices in a tumultuous period. The case was settled out of court, and Disney was reported to be developing future projects with Johansson by late 2021. Yet the suit raised major questions about how studio contracts and talent compensation will be handled or adapted to new windowing models in the future as the lines between theatrical and streaming continue to blur.

As part of a cycle of female-led superhero projects released at the beginning of the decade amidst collapsing and uncertain studio distribution models, *Black Widow* and the struggle over its release reminded me of the culture writer Jenna Wortham's reaction to *Wonder Woman*'s release. In summer 2017, in an episode of the *Still Processing* podcast she cohosts with fellow *New York Times* writer Wesley Morris, Wortham questioned the tension between studio commercial logic and the pressure to cultivate inclusive filmmaking practices:

> I don't know if it is ever going to be possible to make a version of a female star or female action star or female superhero that has to exist in this already existing [male-dominated] infrastructure. Because it's not built for them. It was never built to house them, it was built to accommodate them. It was built, sure, to make room for them at the table a little bit. But it's never going to be their table. It's never going to be their dish. They're always going to be a side dish. They're never going to be the main course.[115]

Wortham makes a compelling case. The Wonder Woman franchise and subsequent female-driven superhero projects developed and released during the late 2010s to early 2020s served less as an example of the major studios responding to building pressure for more equitable tentpoles and more about how female filmmakers and audiences fit into existing industry infrastructure, studio priorities, and definitions of value.

With films like *Wonder Woman*, *Black Widow*, and *Eternals*, female filmmakers have gotten opportunities that were out of reach in the previous decade. This increase in hiring at top budget level is an important landmark in and of itself and moves the major studios in the right direction. Employment, studio experience, and bigger budgets are marking a significant shift for a handful of women navigating the future of female-driven tentpoles. But questions remain for this new cycle of more inclusive and gender-equitable franchise reboots and expansions coming from Disney/Marvel, Universal, and Warner Bros./DC. Do they have the potential to shift not only studio distribution and marketing practices but also the perceived bankability of female-driven projects beyond their value as part of the male-driven IP and to male audiences? Will female filmmakers and their female-driven projects be given the room to experiment, to innovate, or even to fail?

Yes, these opportunities are absolutely game-changing for the select few women working above the line. Yet, these opportunities remain uneven and at times unstable as Lucasfilm hired Patty Jenkins to direct a new Star Wars installment only to remove the project from the production schedule less than a year later, and Warner Bros. cancelled Ava DuVernay's DC spin-off *New Gods* while still in development.[116] Can this new phase of superhero installments continue to challenge changing industry structures and cultures for female-driven filmmaking? At this stage of the Conglomerate Hollywood era in the early 2020s, women are still asked to make room, fit into, and bend to the will of established intellectual property, franchises, and tentpoles production and distribution cultures of existing male-dominated systems. As Wortham emphasized back in 2017, Hollywood may have made room for a few women and creatives of color, but when will they be able to bring their own stories to the table, and how long will they have a seat?

Gendered Value in a Changing Media Marketplace

At the end of 2021, *IndieWire* published its annual list of female-directed studio films, with journalist Kate Erbland offering a hopeful outlook for the upcoming slate: "Despite the unpredictability of 2020 and 2021, female filmmakers continue to make great strides."[1] I also felt cautiously optimistic as the start of 2022 brought a new slate of female-driven studio films. Projects ranged from first-time directors to veterans helming their second, third, or fourth projects, established IP and original scripts, different genres and budget levels, more diverse casting, and a mix of theatrical and streaming releases. Sony boasted eight female-led projects, including Gina Prince-Bythewood's *The Woman King* and Olivia Newman's *Where the Crawdads Sing*, and Universal Pictures promised three female-led projects, including Kat Coiro's *Marry Me* and, as discussed in an earlier chapter, Maria Schrader's *She Said*. Releases like Universal's Jennifer Lopez romantic comedy vehicle *Marry Me*, strategically aimed to build upon the star-producer's 2019 commercial hit *Hustlers*, helmed by Lorene Scafaria, also reflected a major studio investing in a familiar and previously tested female-targeted genre at the start of the new decade.

This type of celebratory trade coverage illustrates how nearly seven years after I started conducting research for this book, studio employment numbers still remain a central discursive tool for measuring progress toward achieving industry-wide and institutional gender parity.[2] The release of pandemic-era employment reports like UCSD's "The Celluloid Ceiling" and USC's "Inclusion in the Director's Chair" in early 2022 also reflect this continued investment in a "consciousness-raising" effort.[3] Counting the number of female studio directors continues to reinforce employment as *the* priority and *the* end goal for Hollywood. Headlines ranging from the buoyant "Women and POC Filmmakers See Sustained Growth as Directors of Top Films Despite Pandemic" to the more measured "Streamers More Likely to Hire Female Directors, While Women of Color See Little Growth at Studios: [USC] Study" demonstrate how varying conclusions can be drawn from the so-called incremental progress underscored in these data studies.[4] As Chris Lindahl pointed out in *IndieWire*: "The industry is continuing to make gains when it comes to hiring women directors and directors of color, but Hollywood is still a long way off from parity."[5] In the case of the USC study, with only three films by female directors of color—Chloé Zhao's *Eternals* (Disney), Liesl Tommy's *Respect* (MGM), and Nia DaCosta's *Candyman* (Universal/MGM)—in the fifty top-grossing theatrical releases for 2021, these incremental studio employment gains disproportionately benefit white women, value theatrical release over streaming, and largely leave women of color behind.[6]

As I've argued throughout *The Value Gap*, just getting a seat at the table is not enough for women to progress individually in creative and financial leadership roles or structurally in strengthening the studio system pipeline. Staying at the table, contributing to organizations and overhauling work cultures in meaningful ways, and making more room for women and other historically underrepresented and marginalized creatives to follow—these are the long-term goals to be accomplished and celebrated. A key objective of this book project is to offer a longitudinal, methodologically multifaceted examination of the barriers that female-driven films face in conglomerate Hollywood by considering how industry lore circulates and reinforces gendered perceptions of value and risk. In considering the tensions between what John Caldwell identifies as "corporate macrostrategies and human microstrategies," it becomes painfully evident that larger industry cultures and business operations contribute to exclusionary, privileging, and discriminatory practices that female filmmakers face individually and collectively.[7] Significantly, the stories, experiences, and anecdotes gathered from the interviews I conducted offer individual, human faces and personal counterpoints to the broad, sweeping trade headlines and statistics-driven data studies that have shaped so much of the contemporary discourse around gender equity and inclusion in Hollywood. In many ways, I saw our conversations for the book as offering female producers, writers, directors, and other film professionals an opportunity to share their stories and contribute their voices in a protected and safe space.

I organized *The Value Gap* to explore different stages of the filmmaking pipeline in order to demonstrate how every sector and phase of the process contributes to the challenges and roadblocks women face in entering and pursuing sustainable careers.[8] Focusing on only one part of the filmmaking process continues to ignore or underplay an entire pipeline full of gaps, cracks, or weaknesses that need more than temporary fixes or repairs to stop the leaks. Important career-making and career-breaking points occur along every juncture from development to distribution—or pitch to premiere as the book's title denotes—for women at all levels of filmmaking and every point of their careers. I argue that scholars, journalists, activists, decisionmakers, and gatekeepers need to keep looking beyond the entry point of employment to other points where pressure can be placed, exerted not as a temporary release valve but to strategically locate ways to rebuild and reimagine the industry as a more equitable ecosystem from the inside out. Ultimately, what *The Value Gap* contributes to larger scholarly and industry conversations is a framework to examine, and ultimately dismantle, how gender inequities operate simultaneously and in tandem across three levels—individual, intersectional, industrial—through everyday filmmaking practices and real-world lived experiences as well as slippery cultural practices and recycled discursive narratives.

The Value Gap is by no means a definitive or all-encompassing analysis of women working in the contemporary film industry. I faced limitations by relying on established professional networks, many of which are still largely comprised of cisgender white women referring me to more cisgender white women. Even as I sought out directors, writers, and producers of color, conversations with emerging to established Black, Asian American, and Latinx creatives only further reinforced how the gendered pipeline issue reproduces itself along racialized and classed lines. In focusing specifically on women working above the line, I examined particular points of the filmmaking process directly impacting their ability to develop, produce, and distribute female-driven projects. There are key collaborative roles—whether in development, pre-production, physical production, post-production companies, or distribution and marketing—that deserve much more attention. Due to the limited scope of this research and the constraints of a book-length study, I also did not address a number of forces—talent agents and agencies, managers, unions and guilds, public relations firms, advocacy groups, talent development labs and mentoring programs, for example—that play important roles in a female-driven film's life cycle and female creatives' individual career paths. And, finally, by narrowing my focus to Hollywood studio and independent industry players, I acknowledge that questions remain about how female filmmakers beyond the US and outside the English-language US market tackle and navigate similar barriers and disparities in their own industries. What potential research questions open up when addressing areas of transnational collaboration and activism in relation to or beyond a Hollywood lens?

In this concluding chapter, I highlight the developing dynamics and larger forces emerging at the end of my research period—i.e., in 2020 and 2021—and also certain related industrial trends and institutional cultures unfolding in parallel media industry spaces. In the first section, I explore the transformative impact of the COVID-19 pandemic on film workers and their projects in early 2020, which was quickly followed by a new wave of momentum in the Black Lives Matter movement that brought additional pressure on the major film studios. The next section looks at how gender equity and inclusion debates are playing out within a rapidly evolving television and streaming landscape. While I began this project focusing on feature films, a significant shift occurred over the course of my research period that challenged earlier distinctions between film and television business models. Conglomerate film and television divisions have increasingly integrated their operations, resulting in a group of above-the-line film professionals crossing traditional boundaries and creating new spaces for female-driven storytelling. The final section of the chapter offers a brief snapshot of Hollywood's gender parity debates at the end of 2021. The implosion of the Time's Up organization serves as a lens, poignantly, for understanding the complex and contradictory promises of industry-wide efforts and the powerful players involved. In contrast, follow-up conversations with a handful of women I interviewed over the course of this project offer a more personal perspective on this unique industrial moment. While this group of emerging and established filmmakers have felt the impact of pressure points and parity initiatives on their careers differently—from disappointment and disillusionment to advancement and fulfillment—together they represent the continued determination to enact tangible systemic change for all women working in Hollywood.

A Period of Devastation and Reckoning

March 2020 marked a major turning point in Hollywood annals when the COVID-19 pandemic shut down the film industry overnight.[9] In an unprecedented development, movie theaters closed, film festivals were cancelled or delayed, physical production stopped, and studios sent staff and executives to work remotely from home and furloughed others.[10] Film production and theatrical distribution halted completely as the United States and countries around the world, aiming to prevent the further spread of the virus, entered lockdown and ultimately a prolonged quarantine. Because women made up 55 percent of the jobs Americans lost by early summer, press coverage labeled the economic downturn that followed the "shecession" as women were fired, furloughed, or left work to care for children or family members. The pandemic set back American women's employment numbers to levels not seen since the 1980s.[11]

The economic impact was felt widely, particularly for the large body of freelance film and service workers ranging from below-the-line crew to movie theater employees. For women working at different stages of the pipeline, a new set of questions emerged around women's work in the film industry: Whose employers and job roles allowed and supported working from home? Who stayed employed, and who lost jobs and income? Who took on childcare or other care work?

As a media industry scholar and teacher, I too grappled with the sudden workplace upheaval and the best way to convey instability and uncertainty to students aspiring to enter the media industries. The pandemic also forced me to rethink research methods for the fieldwork-in-progress and the remaining interviews needed to complete this project. Whereas I had relied on on-site, in-person interviews and participant observation up to that point, upcoming research trips were cancelled, establishing new contacts became increasingly difficult, and I pivoted to Zoom and phone meetings to complete follow-up interviews. In scheduling another round of conversations with primary interviewees from 2020 to 2021, I had the opportunity to check in and hear how a small group of writers, producers, directors, and editors were adapting to new working conditions in real time.

Film workers in physical production, regardless of gender, were affected significantly by the pandemic. Yet, women carried the additional burden of holding on to hard-fought individual gains and industry-wide momentum during a period of unprecedented precarity.[12] The question quickly shifted from "where are women working in the film industry?" to "how will the pandemic impact women's work and livelihood in the film industry?" One independent producer located in the Midwest described a project that was about to begin principal photography instead being delayed for almost a year. An LA-based line producer lost incoming work as productions shut down. She had to subsist on limited unemployment benefits for months.

Even as the major studios temporarily, or at times indefinitely, delayed films slated for production or theatrical distribution, development continued. I talked to writers and producers who refocused their efforts, pushing film projects down the development path as production companies and studios continued to schedule Zoom pitch meetings and hire writers to polish and complete scripts in progress early in the pandemic. One studio screenwriter was surprised by how much work she was being offered for feature projects and was happy to take Zoom meetings from home since it meant she could avoid a regular commute across the notoriously bad traffic in Los Angeles. Another writer found an unexpected job on an animated film. Without the constraints of live-action features, she talked about how animated projects were thriving since they could move forward more easily with the creative team collaborating remotely. An editor continued to work on a big, expensive series for a major streamer because the studio producing the show supplied her with editing equipment at her house, allowing her to collaborate daily with the rest of the editing team virtually, through email and video meetings.

For many women at different levels of filmmaking, the COVID-19 pandemic shed a light on the growing divide between precarity and privilege in Hollywood. For working women with childcare or other caretaking responsibilities, the uncertainty of the global health crisis revealed in glaring ways how vital, and how uneven, support systems for families are in the United States. An editor located in the Los Angeles area was able to maintain long days cutting episodes of a drama series on deadline because her husband, a teacher also working remotely, cared for their young child.

In a Zoom call from a makeshift office in her bedroom, a screenwriter recounted how her parents moved in with her family at the beginning of the pandemic to form a "bubble" and provide childcare while she and her partner worked. The tolls taken by job losses, lack of social support and financial security, and health impacts are expected to resonate for years to come. The long-term effects undoubtedly will lead to new disparities for women entering and working toward sustainable careers in filmmaking beyond the pandemic. After recent hopes of closing the gaps for women working in Hollywood, the start of the new decade disproportionately impacted women at all levels of filmmaking and will require aggressive, macro-industry-wide and micro-institutional efforts for more inclusive policies to address the industry's post-pandemic landscape.

Ushering in a second major turning point, the growing wave of Black Lives Matter protests in summer 2020 signaled an urgent public moment of reckoning around systemic racial injustice and discrimination in the United States. Weeks of marches began in cities across the country to protest police violence and brutality, including the highly publicized murders of George Floyd in Minneapolis and Breonna Taylor in Louisville by police officers. Major studios and other film institutions quickly released corporate statements, posted social media support, and announced donations in support of the BLM movement and related racial justice organizations. For example, Disney reportedly pledged $5 million in donations to social justice nonprofit organizations, including the NAACP. Universal Pictures' parent company Comcast promised $75 million in donations and $25 million in ad time "to groups that fight injustice and inequality."[13] Netflix announced funding efforts to support broad equity and inclusion initiatives that included a $5 million fund to train and mentor female filmmakers. This was followed in 2021 by the establishment of a $100 million five-year fund for organizations supporting employment opportunities for underrepresented communities.[14]

Yet, Hollywood's strategic—and, many argue, opportunistic—response rightly received criticism and backlash for superficially seizing on a political moment.[15] The legacy studios and their conglomerate parent companies pledging support to the Black community contradicted years of failing to act on increased pressure for more inclusion and diversity efforts in front of and behind the camera, as well as more diverse hiring practices from entry to executive levels. Industry analyst Richard Rushfield's June 2020 newsletter, *The Ankler*, gathered all the photos of executives running major media company divisions and C-suites, manifestly evidencing that the major studios and their parent and sibling companies are still run largely by white men.[16]

Widely publicized responses to the Black Lives Matter movement by the major studios are in reality short-term reactions that reveal the lack of a solid plan of action for desperately needed long-term institutional change.[17] The question remained whether the role of Hollywood institutions and power players in publicly supporting this political moment would result in the same corporate optics and shallow promises as in the past. In the wake of the 2020 racial justice reckoning in the United States, a number of industry and popular publications responded to the slew of Hollywood studios' monetary donations, hiring promises, and mentoring initiatives with rightful skepticism. Headlines ranged across *Variety*'s "Hollywood Shells Out for Diversity, but It Costs Much More than Money"; the *Los Angeles Times*' "Hollywood Says Its Antiracism Push Is Not a 'Fad.' Is the Industry Keeping Its Promises?"; *IndieWire*'s "In 2020, Hollywood Reckoned with Its Past—and Present—When It Came to Diversity"; and *KCRW*'s "Retired Hollywood Workers: Industry Isn't Diversifying as Fast as It Should Be over Past 50 Years."[18] Specifically, Jay Tucker critically questioned the impact of this new wave of studio diversity initiatives in *Variety*: "Hollywood's response certainly evokes a sense of wonder: The scale of these initiatives and the speed with which they are rolling out have captured our attention, and collective praise, for all the right reasons. But these valiant efforts arguably fall short of soothing decades of legitimate, repeated and ongoing concerns about diversity and inclusion throughout the industry."[19] In other words, journalists and industry critics clearly had seen the major studios do this dance before and rightfully questioned their sincerity and long-term commitment.

The following year, at a scaled-back and socially distanced Academy Awards ceremony, Chloé Zhao won best director for her third feature, *Nomadland* (2020). Coproduced by and starring Frances McDormand, the intimate drama follows a widow in her sixties trying to build a nomadic life in her van while traveling the United States in the aftermath of the Great Recession. From the *Los Angeles Times* headline, "Why Chloé Zhao's Historic Best Director Oscar Win Matters" to CNN's "Chloé Zhao Has Made Oscar History," trade and popular press headlines widely celebrated the first woman of color, and only the second woman ever, to win an Oscar for directing.[20] The female-driven film beautifully unfolds with visually lush

American landscapes and McDormand's quietly complex and interior performance of an older woman too rarely portrayed on screen. In light of the growing pressure for more intersectional inclusivity across Hollywood workplaces, some looked to this win as a signal of a changing tide. However, the Oscar win sits at a moment of increased criticism not only due to the Academy's historically white membership and voting record but also to Hollywood's consistently messy and uneven grappling at various levels with its own contemporary marginalization of and discrimination toward people of color in front of and behind the camera.

In no way diminishing the artistic merit of *Nomadland*, or the significance of an Asian female director winning the Oscar, the reaction to Zhao's win is what I find most revealing. Zhao was already on a studio filmmaking trajectory after Disney/Marvel hired her three years prior to direct the superhero adaptation *Eternals* (2022).[21] In celebrating Zhao for "blazing a trail for women" and emphasizing "her achievement is historic many times over," the long-recycled discursive framing once again credits and celebrates the individual filmmaker who, due to her undeniable talent and creative track record, overcame the odds in spite of those systemic barriers to shatter racialized and gendered ceilings.[22]

Once again the question was posed as to whether Zhao's win was an individual one or if her trajectory into blockbuster filmmaking with *Eternals* would have ramifications for the directors coming behind her. Hollywood loves to hold up the myth of meritocracy when celebrating an underdog story, especially when the industry can celebrate and give itself credit in the process.[23] Even as I point to this familiar question, discussed in previous chapters, I also want to avoid placing the burden of breaking glass ceilings and systemic gendered disparities on Zhao's shoulders just as Hollywood has done with Patty Jenkins, Kathryn Bigelow, Ava DuVernay, and other pioneering women navigating the contemporary studio system and, more recently, the rapidly expanding streaming landscape.

The Seductive Promise of Scripted Television and Streaming Originals

In focusing *The Value Gap* on the contemporary feature filmmaking pipeline, this project did not address the rapid growth of scripted television series and a new generation of Silicon Valley- and conglomerate-owned streaming platforms. Parallel questions arose during my research period from 2016 to 2021 around how increased opportunities for scripted original series and the resources coming from streaming platforms, not to mention the future of distribution windows, might address or duplicate structural gender inequities still characterizing much of the major studios' pipelines. Similar industry discourse regarding the pressure for gender equity and inclusion circulates within other areas of the contemporary media industries. As a result, female-led scripted series for broadcast, cable, and premium pay TV, and streaming platforms offer a fruitful area for future inquiry, particularly the promises and pitfalls of female-driven storytelling during this transitional industrial moment.

The early 2020s marked an industrial climate in which continuing pressure on the major studios' intermittent efforts toward gender equity collided with distribution windows in enormous flux. In an effort to compete with the head start and sizable market share gained by Big Tech's first-generation streamers Netflix and, to a lesser extent, Hulu, Amazon Prime Video, and Apple TV+, conglomerate parents of the legacy studios raced to launch new streaming platforms between 2019 and 2021—Walt Disney's Disney+, Comcast's Peacock, then-Viacom's Paramount+, then-AT&T's HBO Max. New opportunities to develop film and television properties emerged in the rush to fill streaming libraries with original content and expand subscriber numbers. It is important to highlight how new avenues for developing, producing, and releasing television series had already been expanding in previous decades. After the expansion of original programming on cable networks (FX, AMC, TNT, TBS, etc.) and premium pay networks (HBO, Showtime, Starz) in the 1990s and 2000s, FX's CEO John Landgraf famously deemed the saturation of scripted series as "peak TV." The television landscape expanded into the next decade as an estimated 532 and 493 original scripted series premiered in 2019 and 2020, respectively, on broadcast, cable, premium pay TV, and streaming platforms.[24]

The considerable number of scripted series developed, financed, and produced at this point prompted questions during my research about whether more opportunities in the television industry were developing for female-driven storytelling and above-the-line employment. A number of female creatives I interviewed pointed to the strategic work by Ava DuVernay, Reese Witherspoon, and other well-connected creatives whose careers reflect not only the increasingly common tactic of moving between film and TV but also the potential to use their leverage to produce female-driven series. For example, *Queen Sugar* (2016–2022), a rural Louisiana–set Black family drama series following the Bordelon siblings, was a coproduction of DuVernay's Array, Oprah Winfrey's Harpo Films, and Warner Horizon Television, and it aired on the cable network OWN. The *Queen Sugar* creative team strategically committed to hiring independent female filmmakers without experience in episodic television to oversee individual episodes. Notably, Julie Dash (*Daughters of the Dust*, 1991) and Cheryl Dunye (*Watermelon Woman*, 1996) were hired to direct multiple episodes. Despite critically acclaimed features premiering in the 1980s and 1990s, making them foundational and groundbreaking voices in Black independent film, both Dash and Dunye faced decades of gendered and racialized barriers that slowed down, or halted, the careers of Black women in their generation. More broadly, an impressive lineup of female filmmakers whose careers stalled after their first features premiered to critical acclaim at the Sundance Film Festival helmed *Queen Sugar* episodes:

- Patricia Cardoso (*Real Women Have Curves*, 2002)
- Tina Mabry (*Mississippi Damned*, 2009)
- Tanya Hamilton (*Night Catches Us*, 2010)
- Maryam Keshavarz (*Circumstance*, 2011)
- Aurora Guerrero (*Mosquita y Mari*, 2012)
- So Yong Kim (*For Ellen*, 2012)
- Kat Candler (*Hellion*, 2013)

Many of these filmmakers faced a post-festival chasm after Sundance with no follow-up feature work or delayed opportunities for directing, further reinforcing the film festival pipeline issue examined in chapter 4. After gaining experience working in series television, every female filmmaker listed above, with the exception of Keshavarz, continued to work consistently directing television episodes for a range of series into the early 2020s.

In a 2017 *Los Angeles Times* article about the second season of *Queen Sugar*, DuVernay explained wanting to remove the barriers women face to gain jobs and experience in episodic television by hiring "some of the greatest independent filmmakers to come out of the festival circuit in the last 10 years."[25] The first-time television directors received mentorship and guidance from preproduction to postproduction, which is not always the case with work-for-hire television production jobs. Reportedly, for a few emerging independent filmmakers, directing a *Queen Sugar* episode granted them a crucial stepping-stone and career-changing production credits that led to a Directors Guild of America membership, which in turn came with eligibility for future employment opportunities on other DGA shows.[26] *Los Angeles Times* journalist Meredith Blake described the scripted series realm as "a kind of filmmaking collective and talent incubator."[27] The hope is that experience begets more experience, and employment can lead to future employment. The *Queen Sugar* strategy for hiring and training white women, queer women, and primarily women of color served as a way to circumvent traditional gatekeeping processes by attempting to boost accomplished female filmmakers over the barriers halting their progress in the filmmaking pipeline.

In another well-publicized example, Reese Witherspoon's production company Hello Sunshine developed and produced a number of female-led scripted drama series for HBO (*Big Little Lies*, 2017–2019) and Apple TV+ (*The Morning Show*, 2019–; *Truth Be Told*, 2019–), as well as a limited series for Hulu (*Little Fires Everywhere*, 2020) and Amazon (*Daisy Jones & The Six*, 2022). In a 2019 article in the *Hollywood Reporter*, Witherspoon recalled her frustration working for the major studios:

> I was in this position where I was making studios a lot of money, and I had for years and years, and they didn't take me seriously as a filmmaker. Somehow, they didn't think that 25 years of experience could add up to some inherent knowledge of what movies work and how to keep them on budget. . . . And you think about the kind of guys who come out of Sundance and get gigantic jobs off of one, like, "Oh, I see the potential."[28]

Even as an actor-producer operating at a privileged and well-connected level in the industry, Witherspoon has spoken in interviews about hearing gendered lore about lack of experience, ambition, and value that drove her to start producing. She made a strategic move behind the camera as a producer of *Wild* (2014, dir. Jean-Marc Vallée) and *Gone Girl* (2014, dir. David Fincher) after acquiring the rights to the best-selling source novels by Cheryl Strayed and Gillian Flynn, respectively. Headlines in the late 2010s—the *New York Times*' "Reese Witherspoon's Second Act: Big-Time Producer" and the *Hollywood Reporter*'s "How Reese Witherspoon Took Charge of Her Career and Changed Hollywood"—that lauded the

A-list producer-actress and her female-led production team reproduced a striking post-feminist discourse about Witherspoon's individual determination to overcome male-dominated studio systems.[29] After rebranding as Hello Sunshine in 2019, the company grew from film and television projects into podcasts, newsletters, digital videos, live events, and an expanded book club.

Adapted from Liane Moriarty's best-selling book, the ensemble television drama *Big Little Lies* starring Witherspoon, Nicole Kidman, Laura Dern, Zoë Kravitz, and Shailene Woodley was a big critical and commercial hit for Hello Sunshine and HBO. The first season was criticized for being led by two men—writer-showrunner David E. Kelley and director-executive producer Jean-Marc Vallée. As Melissa Silverstein noted, "It was a really bad look to have all of these men behind the camera while continuously advocating for the importance of telling women's stories." In response, British filmmaker Andrea Arnold (*Fish Tank*, 2009; *Wuthering Heights*, 2011; *American Honey*, 2016) was brought in to helm the second season's seven episodes. Further proof that even female-led prestige series do not operate outside Hollywood's deeply ingrained gendered production cultures and creative tensions, *IndieWire* reported that Kelley and HBO network executives "took the show away from" Arnold. Resulting in what Chris O'Falt described as a "strange editorial tension," Vallée took over in postproduction, closely supervised Arnold completing reshoots, and oversaw the season's final cut.[30] While Arnold did not speak publicly about her experience on *Big Little Lies*, the social media response to the *IndieWire* revelation hit a nerve at a particular moment in summer 2019 as growing pressure for gender parity in Hollywood grew. An outpouring of support followed for Arnold on Twitter calling to #ReleaseTheArnolCut, while everyone involved with the series remained strategically quiet. In a July 2019 statement to the *Hollywood Reporter*, HBO representatives aiming for damage control affirmed, "There wouldn't be a season two of *Big Little Lies* without Andrea Arnold."[31]

As Danny Leigh asserted in *The Guardian*, the story of *Big Little Lies'* second season "tells a grim story about the continued trials of women directors. . . . [But] the picture is complicated by the roles as executive producers of Kidman and Witherspoon, each unlikely to have known nothing of Arnold's crisis. Neither has commented. . . . Still, the gender dynamics at play feel clearer if you simply tweak the question asked in that first episode from What Have They Done? to Would They Have Done

It to a Man?"[32] Whether or not writer-showrunner Kelley or HBO executives promised final cut to Arnold as reported is not known. While it's not unusual for a television director to work closely under the supervision of the showrunner, Arnold's distinctive cinematic style earned her the directing job, and her involvement was heavily highlighted in the promotion and marketing of the new season. Unfortunately, the promise of hiring an established independent female director with a distinct visual style and celebrated creative voice was undermined and squandered in order to reportedly maintain continuity with the male director-producer's season one signature.

In the end, Arnold was a director for hire on a female-targeted project that privileged the creative control of the above-the-line male creatives. Behind the symbolic progressive gestures and accolades that come with supporting female-driven projects and hiring a woman director, competing institutional priorities were likely at play for this HBO series. For context, the late 2010s was a tenuous moment during WarnerMedia's (known as Time Warner at the time) rocky acquisition by AT&T when HBO was under pressure to reproduce another season of the A-list female-led blockbuster series. An article by David Sims in *The Atlantic* warned that the ramifications of a new telecommunications owner would be "The End of an Era for HBO—and for Television."[33] In many ways, *Big Little Lies* likely reveals another example of corporate priorities, institutional production cultures, and a powerful male creative duo at odds with the network and the series' outward-facing commitment to gender parity and progressive values.

Hello Sunshine's next female-led television projects demonstrated a shift to include more women in key creative positions. Hulu's *Little Fires Everywhere* was an adaptation of Celeste Ng's novel with writer-showrunner Liz Tigelaar, executive producer-director Lynn Shelton, and director Nzingha Stewart. Apple TV+'s *The Morning Show* boasted all but one female executive producer, including Witherspoon, Jennifer Aniston, Mimi Leder, and showrunner Kerry Ehrin. Established female director-producers helmed the majority of the first two seasons, including episodes from Leder, Shelton, Michelle MacLaren, and Lesli Linka Glatter. *The Morning Show* pivoted during development to address the unfolding events of #MeToo in broadcast news, resulting in a major narrative arc for the series. Created as a star vehicle for Witherspoon and Aniston, the latter in her first return to series television since *Friends* ended in

2004, Apple TV+ reportedly paid $240 million for two seasons and twenty episodes in an effort to launch their new streaming platform in 2019. Despite the lukewarm critical response, the series gained a high profile, with big paydays for both stars and directing gigs for a number of in-demand female creatives.

Witherspoon's company once again made headlines in August 2021 when Hello Sunshine was sold for more than $900 million to a media company backed by a private equity firm, Blackstone Group.[34] As John Koblin asserted three years earlier in a *New York Times* company profile: "The rise of Hello Sunshine—with projects centered on strong, complicated women—syncs up perfectly with the #TimesUp movement, which counts Ms. Witherspoon as a major player, and gives evidence that the risk-averse Hollywood establishment may have learned something."[35] The production company benefitted from strategic branding as a studio for prestige female-driven dramas led by A-list talent and established television writers, showrunners, and executive producers. Witherspoon and her collaborators leveraged their combined decades of studio relationships and insider industry knowledge to build a valuable media company that benefitted not only from the changing tides around gender parity and inclusion but also from the rapid emergence of new streaming platforms looking to build their libraries and attract subscribers with talent-tested prestige series.

As Netflix, Amazon, Hulu, and later Apple TV+ began to invest heavily in original programming in the 2010s, legacy studios' streaming ventures—Disney+, HBO Max, Paramount+, and Peacock by the late 2010s/early 2020s—began to develop their own exclusive slates in response. Questions circulated whether streaming could be a new gateway for female creatives. A central discourse surrounding content development related to the so-called streaming wars speculated whether historically marginalized communities in the media industries, namely women, creatives of color, LGBTQ creatives, and creatives with disabilities, could stand to benefit when the low supply of content met high demand to fill new pipelines.

As the leader of the pack, Netflix launched into developing and producing original series early and aggressively. The first phase of English-language programming—including *House of Cards* (2013–2018) and *Orange Is the New Black* (2013–2019)—aimed to reproduce the prestige and critical acclaim bestowed upon previous "peak TV"–era cable and premium network dramas to drive subscriber rates with exclusive, buzz-worthy series. In order to adapt to the media industries' "differentiation-as-survival-strategy," Joshua Glick argues that "from early on, Netflix cultivated a liberal public image, which has propelled its investment in social documentary and also driven some of its inclusivity initiatives and collaborations with global auteurs and showrunners of color."[36] One strategy included the Big Tech streamer investing heavily in development deals to attract established talent. In addition to feature film development deals with star-producers similar to those discussed earlier in the book, Netflix negotiated big paydays within the television industry for a handful of Black female showrunners who built their careers in broadcast and cable television, including Shonda Rhimes with ABC (*Grey's Anatomy*, 2005–; *Scandal*, 2012–2018; and *How to Get Away with Murder*, 2014–2020), Mara Brock Akil with UPN/The CW (*Girlfriends*, 2000–2008), the CW/ BET (*The Game*, 2006–2015) and BET (*Being Mary Jane*, 2013–2019), and Courtney A. Kemp with Starz (*Power*, 2014–2020; *Power Book II: Ghost*, 2020–2021; and *Power Book III: Raising Kanan*, 2021–). In a highly publicized example, Rhimes signed a four-year mega-deal estimated at $100 million with Netflix in 2017 that was later renewed in 2021. Around the same time, she ended the fifteen-year relationship between broad-caster ABC and her Shondaland production company that had created the ratings hit Thursday scheduling block known as #TGIT/Thank God It's Thursday. Numerous trade publications, quick to applaud Netflix's investment both in inclusive storytelling and in facilitating creative and financial opportunities for women of color, celebrated this new deal as a progressive strategy by the streaming platform.

On the one hand, the lucrative move allowed Rhimes and her production company to gain financial resources and creative storytelling flexibility outside of a more traditionally rigid broadcast network model. She could now develop and produce female-focused content with bigger budgets and wider, more targeted audience potential. On the other hand, this type of expensive creator deal revealed Netflix's increased dependency upon luring away established network talent. Moreover, it signaled a move in the larger chess match between Big Tech and the closely integrated conglomerate-owned legacy film and TV studios over talent, established IP, and audiences. Netflix's efforts to woo Rhimes undoubtedly resulted from the viewer data gathered from licensing older seasons of Shondaland ABC dramas in the 2010s that brought strong viewing numbers for syndicated streaming runs of *Grey's Anatomy* and *How to Get Away with Murder*.[37] After licensing multiple syndicated seasons, Netflix benefitted from the popularity and bingeability of these types of older broadcast network shows—Warner Bros. Television's *Friends*, NBC Universal Television's *The Office*, and Disney/ABC Signature's *Grey's Anatomy*—which proved a boon to subscription rates and domestic viewing numbers as the company simultaneously jumped into an aggressive international expansion of the platform and an investment in original local-language programming. Netflix's existing agreements for these network shows began to end just as the conglomerate-owned streamers launched in the late 2010s to early 2020s. As a result, the legacy studios banked on audiences following their re(discovered) favorite programs when their rights reverted—*Friends* to then-AT&T-owned HBO Max, *The Office* to Comcast-owned Peacock, and *Grey's Anatomy* to Disney-owned Hulu.

In hopes of luring television creators like Rhimes to develop new programming, Netflix wanted to maintain exclusive access to this new cycle of original programming. This exclusivity promised a way around the messy licensing agreements with the legacy studios, bound by a set length of time and territorial market limitations characteristic of traditional international television distribution. Based on Julia Quinn's best-selling romance book series set in Regency London, *Bridgerton* (2020–) was one of the first series Shondaland produced under the new deal. The revisionist historical romance series proved to be one of the streamer's most-watched English-language shows by 2021, according to the company's limited publicly available viewing data.[38]

Courtney A. Kemp, who grew the Black-led commercial hit series *Power* into multiple television spin-off series at the premium network Starz, made the move to Netflix in 2021. She spoke openly in trade press interviews and industry panels about the specific challenges she faced as a Black female showrunner not being recognized in the television business in contrast to her white peers. In a 2021 profile in the *Hollywood Reporter*, journalist Mikey O'Connell asked Kemp, whose *Power* was a commercial hit for Starz, why the industry ignored a massively successful Black show? She responded:

> The fact that you're asking me the question is the answer. I've been in multiple rooms full of showrunners and WGA members—before the pandemic, of course—and heard, "Oh, you're a showrunner?

Power? Never heard of it." If your own peer group has never heard of your show, and it's been on for six years and it's the biggest hit on your network, it can't just be because they're not looking for it. It has to be a combination of factors.[39]

By 2020, *Power* became Starz's most-watched show ever, averaging 10 million viewers per episode between broadcast and streaming audience numbers.[40] Even as Starz invested further in the *Power* franchise with four spin-off series, Kemp moved to develop new programming for Netflix. Around the same time, she expressed frustration in a 2021 interview with the lack of turnover for television executives to allow for more inclusion inside financial and creative decision-making spaces: "People making decisions at the top haven't shifted entirely. Things have changed kind of, they're going that way, and things are changing, certainly. You know there's Bela [Bajaria, Netflix's TV head]; there's Pearlena [Igbokwe, chairman of the Universal Studio Group]; there's Channing [Dungey, chairman of Warner Bros. TV]. It's happening. But . . . I would like to see even more change just at the top ranks."[41]

In previous years, trade coverage highlighted female Netflix executives who had ascended to key leadership positions at a moment when the major studios were under increased scrutiny for their male-driven leadership circles. For example, an October 2019 *Fortune* magazine cover story for the "50 Most Powerful Women in Business" issue deemed Netflix executives Bela Bajaria (then VP, Local Language Originals), Melissa Cobb (VP, Kids and Family), Channing Dungey (then VP, original series), Cindy Holland (then VP, original content), and Lisa Nishimura (VP, independent film and documentary features) the "Streaming Warriors: The Team Leading Netflix into Its Biggest Battle Yet."[42] While the five executives served as a counterpoint to the industry's history of a male-dominated executive pipeline, it should also be noted that many of these women—notably Bajaria, Dungey, and Cobb—built their careers at legacy film and television studios before joining Netflix in the 2010s. (Dungey only remained at Netflix for two years before being hired away as CEO and chairwoman of Warner Bros. Television Studios.) A question remains whether the number of female executives working in the media business at large is significantly increasing in the early 2020s, particularly inside streamers like Netflix. Or are women at the executive level making lateral moves between companies? Is Netflix identifying, developing, and promoting women to executive positions or merely poaching established leaders from the legacy studios in a strategy similar to that of offering lucrative deals to powerful creators like Rhimes and Kemp?

Kristen J. Warner argues that, in strategically attracting established creatives and studio executives, "our favorite streaming platforms—from Netflix to Disney+ to HBO Max to Amazon—rely on the same tastemakers and gatekeeping strategies as their legacy media counterparts, ultimately resulting in the veneer of difference at the level of content while employing the same techniques to ensure success is in play."[43] She warns against the disruptor narrative that had come to exalt Netflix and other streamers with promises of circumventing Hollywood's deep-seated racialized and gendered disparities. Warner draws a compelling parallel between Tom Streeter's seminal work examining the "blue skies rhetoric" of cable television's utopian transformative potential for American society and the contemporary celebratory discourse surrounding the disruptive promise for scripted original series developed inside a new generation of streaming platforms. In the case of landing mega-deals with established and prolific TV creators to lure away Rhimes from ABC or Ryan Murphy from Fox and FX, Warner contends that "the streamers are not innovating; they're exploiting existing channels for content. And, between the costs of retaining these auteurs in eight- and nine-figure development deals and producing their content, there's just not much room left for people who are not as 'tested' or who must be scouted as possibilities."[44]

A 2021 internal Netflix study aimed to highlight company efforts in hiring more female creatives to develop and helm their original film and TV programming. The report concluded that 23 percent of original feature films from 2018 to 2019 were directed by women. Taking the company-produced report at face value, the number of female directors at Netflix is higher than at many of the major networks and film studios. Yet, once again, claims drawn from internal, and opaque, proprietary data not made available publicly raise further questions surrounding, among other things, intersectionality, experience level, existing industry connections, type of film projects, budget level, representation of women as a whole in front of and behind the camera, marketing and promotional support, and future employment opportunities. While these numbers are promising, a more informed long-term view will be required at all levels of a network or streaming platform to understand how "game-changing" opportunities celebrated in the early 2020s actually pan out for the TV staff writers, showrunners, or executives two to five or even ten years down the road.

Netflix's stock price significantly dropped in early 2022 after the company reported losing two hundred thousand US subscribers. The streaming platform responded with a wave of layoffs and budget tightening in different areas. As reported in the *Los Angeles Times* that spring: "Some of the cuts impacted social media teams, writers and editors who aimed to elevate diverse content and talent."[45] For example, layoffs hit experienced female journalists of color working at Netflix's promotional publication *Tudum* particularly hard. As a result, the company's public-facing policies and demonstrative efforts to support diversity and inclusion came under scrutiny.[46]

Even as Netflix and other streaming platforms crafted gender equity and inclusion into their 2020s branding and public-facing corporate strategies, questions remain: What impact, if any, will these efforts have in developing and supporting a more inclusive streaming ecosystem? Who ultimately benefits from the rise of the mega-streaming deals at the top and what happens to the remaining 99 percent of Netflix's filmmakers and television creators?

Where Do We Go from Here?

In the span of a few weeks in 2021, Time's Up CEO Tina Tchen, chair Roberta Kaplan, and the majority of the board of directors, including Shonda Rhimes and Eva Longoria, resigned. Fewer than four years after its widely lauded and optimistic launch, the nonprofit organization quickly moved from splashy promotion by Hollywood A-list players on red carpets and award show broadcasts to headlines revealing serious conflicts of interest for the organization founded in an effort to support survivors of sexual harassment, misconduct, assault, and other discriminatory workplace practices.[47] Most notably, a sexual harassment investigation that forced New York Governor Andrew Cuomo to resign also exposed that Tchen and Kaplan had offered his administration guidance in the handling of these allegations and feedback on what became a damaging op-ed targeting a female accuser. As a result, who benefitted from Time's Up's powerful players and resources came under intense scrutiny.

What began as a series of working committees made of largely well-connected women in business and entertainment quickly grew into a traditional, nonprofit structure with a board of directors, president, twenty-five-person staff, and advisory board. Even as organizational efforts aimed at Hollywood industry cultures grew to encompass pay equity, employment parity, and safety guidelines, including calls for hiring and training intimacy coordinators for on-screen sex scenes, the policy priorities became too broad and reactive, and stretched the relatively small group too thin. Time's Up staff anonymously began to speak to the press about the toxic workplace culture and internal inequities surrounding their own pay and compensation. Subsequent industry and popular press coverage painted the nonprofit as a chaotic workplace without a clear institutional mission. Time's Up boldly aimed to challenge a wide array of male-dominated industry structures and institutional cultures, only to be run by women who remained in, and benefitted from, those same political and entertainment power circles. Despite the founding mandate and public-facing rhetoric, the organization in reality replicated many of the insidious workplace dynamics and disparities it was created to address. By September 2021, in a shift described as "an evaluation and transition period," Time's Up came under the guidance of Monifa Bandele, interim president and CEO.[48] By November, the organization had laid off Bandele and the majority of its twenty-five-person staff and released an extensive report identifying central institutional concerns around conflicts of interests, leadership failures, and an unclear mission and purpose.

The seventy-one-member advisory board made up of largely well-connected, influential activists and Hollywood power players that included Jessica Chastain, Reese Witherspoon, Natalie Portman, Brie Larson, Tessa Thompson, America Ferrera, and Kerry Washington was also dissolved. Many of the A-list women who served on the board of directors and advisory board saw their careers flourish during this short-lived period of Time's Up and undoubtedly will be protected personally and professionally from the organization's tarnished reputation.

Once again, the question that emerged was not *what has Hollywood learned?* but *who will ultimately benefit from this industrial moment and movement?* Whether the organization can rebuild and regain its influence, momentum, and credibility seems highly unlikely after flaming out so brightly and publicly. As of this writing in 2022, the future of the Time's Up movement and organization is nearly impossible to predict. Referred to widely in trade coverage as a "major reset," a new iteration of Time's Up may be on the horizon, but it is just as likely to never return with equal force or momentum. The future for Time's Up remains at best on a long road to building a viable path forward and at worst might result in squandering decades of hard-earned industry-wide momentum and good will in fewer than four years.

The short-lived initial run of Time's Up offers a convenient frame for the timeline of *The Value Gap*. The key industrial period explored in this book from 2016 to 2021 can also largely be described as "an evaluation and transition period" in recognizing and addressing questions around gender disparities and inclusion efforts in Hollywood. *The Value Gap*, in many ways, serves as a broad, sweeping account of the contemporary film industry and society at large leading up to and during this transformational moment. Hollywood has only recently begun to publicly recognize and acknowledge the deeply rooted inequities ingrained in white male–driven institutions. Therefore wrestling with meaningful structural solutions for intersectional gender parity will take time, as the fate of Time's Up remains uncertain. The disproportionate mainstream attention given to an organization like Time's Up or equivalent buzzworthy initiatives such as the 4 Percent Challenge to address and offer a corrective for deeply ingrained systemic issues ultimately proved to be short-sighted.

So, what has really changed by the early 2020s in terms of intersectional inclusion in the filmmaking pipeline? On the macro level, the recent employment data and studio film slates, discussed earlier in the chapter, signaling incremental increases for women working above the line, indicate that not much has changed systemically. On the micro level, a number of the women I spoke to regarding Hollywood's gender progress ranged from cynically hopeful or ambivalent to conflicted or frustrated. In a conversation with an LA-based producer of color at the beginning of 2021, she described in frustration that "there is still resistance in the agencies and production companies," whereas many of these so-called gains for women have been "shallow gestures and small victories."[49]

An emerging Latinx screenwriter described the period from 2020 to 2021 as an important turn in industry conversations around inclusion: "Things are starting to change. Some of the VPs and Junior VPs I'm seeing [in meetings and hiring announcements in the trades] are women and people of color. Hopefully they will move up and bring more women with them." While she recognized some "progress" made in hiring and funding projects by women of color, she found the pace of change "frustrating," especially with her own career: "Do I even have a future in this industry? Will I ever cross the threshold?" This thirty-something screenwriter, like many of the women of color in emerging above-the-line roles I interviewed for this book, participated in a number of studio pipeline programs and talent development labs during the 2010s. These development and mentoring initiatives ranged from nonprofit professional programs like the Sundance Institute's Screenwriters Lab, American Film Institute's Directing Workshop for Women, and Film Independent Screenwriting Lab, to studio-run programs like Sony Pictures Diverse Directors Program, the former Fox Global Directors Initiative, and the Universal Writers Program.

I spoke with writers and directors who participated in these programs and saw value in terms of building professional networks, learning professionalization within the industry, workshopping film projects, and developing mentor and peer relationships. Yet, despite an investment in relationship and reputation building, these experiences did not often translate into the promised employment or career boosts. Women who completed multiple programs described feeling stuck at the apprentice level. The Latinx screenwriter above applauded an increase in the last five years in types of initiatives for supporting women creatives, but "real change is not just initiatives. You need to hire us. We've already done the work, you need to give us jobs and you need to keep us in the pipeline. . . . I told my manager I'm not doing any more diversity initiatives or labs [for a while]. I have done so many. If I were a white guy, I'd have been in year five [of a steady career] with my name in *Variety*."[50] Similar to what Kristen J. Warner and Alfred Martin have written about television writers' experiences in network diversity programs, initiatives at NBC, CBS, and other networks provide more short-term professional opportunities for apprenticing and shadowing than material and sustainable pathways to staff positions on a television show.[51] Moving forward, a close examination of post-2020 film studio and TV network development and mentoring initiatives, including a longitudinal study of participants and their career trajectories, will offer a productive space for media industry scholars to examine whether this new wave of institutional promises is resulting in tangible, inclusive hiring and promotion practices.

An established white studio writer-producer offered a "slightly hopeful" assessment of her experience:

> My career really took off after 2018 and I am getting more opportunities. [And there is] a push happening toward hiring more women

and people of color than five years ago . . . especially on the television side where writers' rooms are striving for more parity. . . . But [is it] happening in features? And what type of features? . . . We have to fill the pipeline with people who can originate with a project from the beginning [and keep them] in the pipeline.[52]

Her comment brings to light a number of questions addressed throughout this book around the continued value of female-driven stories, voices, and audiences in a vastly shifting media landscape. In contrast, I asked two screenwriters in early 2022 if anything had changed for women writers with the increased pressure points around gender equity. One writer responded:

The risk aversion of the industry means no. A lot of people have the desire for change. They want to be supporting the next voices [women and writers of color] but they need a hit. So they need to go for someone who had a hit before. . . . Old white men feel like they are being targeted and not wanted but they are still the ones getting hired. We *are* getting more interviews, but it doesn't turn into paid work or jobs. . . . The new conglomerate, more corporatized business model is the biggest obstacle to meaningful progress.[53]

In an industrial moment that continues with an uncertain theatrical market and distribution windows, IP expansion and "safe" studio releases are winning out over original, untested film projects. Parameters of risk, viability, and experience still largely shape notions of value in the film industry. Even as more women are building sustainable filmmaking careers in the studio pipeline, a question remains about not only what stories they can tell and what stories they can sell in the future but also how female-driven films will be valued as the divide between theatrical and streaming widens and the future for the midbudget business model remains bleak.

As we move into the 2020s, we can look back on the previous decade as one that brought about more revelations than revolution, fewer seismic shifts and a series of industry-wide pressure points still largely in progress. But for the women I interviewed over this period, the story is extremely personal, from the individual films pitched, developed, produced, and distributed to the festivals, initiatives, events, and panels organized and attended. What gathering and amplifying individual experiences of above-the-line workers reveals is how stories within and outside professional networks reflect the challenges and struggles but also the joys and validations that are found in the filmmaking process. Whether resulting in progress and promotions or setbacks and dead ends, the multifaceted industrywide systemic campaign to develop more equitable practices, opportunities, and work cultures for female filmmakers is still in motion and in many ways is just getting started.

Acknowledgments

I began thinking about the contemporary commercial shift in female-driven films about fifteen years ago as a graduate student in the Department of Radio-Television-Film at the University of Texas at Austin. I can credit graduate film seminars with Janet Staiger and Tom Schatz for laying this foundation as much as all of those visits to the Alamo Drafthouse and lively conversations with my PhD cohort. However, the inspiration for this book probably came much earlier as a young girl watching Classical Hollywood movies from musicals to melodramas on weekend afternoons with my dad. We chatted about film industry trivia and the people behind the camera as much we gushed over our love of Rosalind Russell, Katharine Hepburn, Lauren Bacall, Vivien Leigh, and all of the dynamic leading women of that era. Our movie dates are still so special to me and a significant part of shaping me as a media industries scholar.

The research journey toward completing this book took many twists and turns—a new area of study, numerous fieldwork trips and conversations, a new job and a move back to Texas, a pandemic upending so much and leading to a pivot in the project's scope from international to domestic. More than anything, I want to thank the dozens of women who generously shared their experiences and expertise throughout the six years I conducted interviews. From the very early stages when this book was a kernel of an idea to the final stages of the manuscript, Elizabeth Martin, Lauren Hynek, Allison Schroeder, Rebecca Green, Jennifer Cochis, Ericka Frederick, Christina Varotsis, Angela Lee, Emily Greene, Ry Russo-Young, Alicia Van Couvering, and many, many more offered incredible insights into their work and careers in the film industry. Without the women, whether attributed or anonymized, whose stories I gathered and careers I followed, this book would not be possible. I cannot thank them enough.

I began the early stages of this book as an assistant professor at Oakland University. Thank you to my Cinema Studies (now Film Studies and Production) and English Department colleagues who supported and encouraged my early fieldwork. To Andrea Eis, the incomparable feminist filmmaker and my dear friend and mentor: thank you for your constant belief in me that no matter what, I will persist, and for all of the newspaper clippings for my book research. A big thank you to Brendan Kredell for introducing me to TIFF and the Film Festival Research Network and for building a student program together that I am deeply proud to have been a part of; to Erin Dwyer for being my lady movie matinee buddy and my inspirational Detroit feminist-at-large; to Erin Meyers and Kathy Battles for being all-around amazing lady colleagues and friends. A big thank you to my research assistant Nicole Diroff, who helped with interview transcribing in summer 2018.

By joining the faculty in the Department of Media Arts at the University of North Texas in 2019, I found my academic home. Thank you to my Media Arts colleagues for your generosity, support, cheerleading, compassion, and laughs over a tumultuous few years as I settled into my new department—Harry Benshoff, Eugene Martin, Jacqueline Vickery, Jennifer Porst, Tania Khalaf, Melinda Levin, Jennifer Gómez Menjívar, Xiaoqun Zhang, Brenda Jaskulske, Jason Balas, Stephen Mandiberg, Frances Perkins, Phyllis Slocum, and Travis Sutton. Jac, Jen, Harry, Tania, Melinda, Eugene, and Jenny—all of the coffees and happy hours and dinner conversations and pep talks filled me up, and I am forever grateful for your friendship. Thank you to all of my amazing Media Arts students for your engaging conversations about the contemporary media business that contributed so much to my writing process. A massive thank you to our incredible department staff, especially Marielena Resendiz and Lesa Statler, for all the help figuring out scheduling, finances, and travel, and for letting me raid your candy dishes. I am so appreciative of Kat Huerta-Ortega, my amazing research assistant from 2020 to 2022. It was such a pleasure to work with you, and I cannot wait to see where your filmmaking journey takes you. In the College of Liberal Arts and Social Sciences, I am immensely grateful to Steve Cobb and Andrea Miller for being champions of junior faculty and for chasing down additional funding to support gathering research materials, copyediting services, and travel.

The travel, research, and writing necessary to complete a book of this scope was possible due to generous funding from a number of granting bodies and institutions. At Oakland University, I received funding from the Cinema Studies Program and English Department, the University Research Council's Faculty Research Fellowship and New Investigator Research Excellence Award, and the PI Research Academy Program. At the University of North Texas, I am grateful for funding from the Department of Media Arts, College of Liberal Arts and Social Sciences, and Faculty Success and Office of the Provost, including the CLASS Scholarly Creative Award, CLASS Small Grant, and Junior Faculty Summer Research Grant. Finally, I want to thank the National Endowment for the Humanities immensely, for the funding award that allowed me to take a research leave and complete my fieldwork and the final manuscript.

Early versions of concepts and case studies appeared in *Feminist Media Studies* as well as in edited collections by Susan Liddy (*Women in the International Film Industry: Policy, Practice and Power*), Paul McDonald (*Routledge Companion to Media Industries*), and Derek Johnson and Daniel Herbert (*Point of Sale: Analyzing Media Retail*). I also presented excerpts from chapters-in-progress at the Society for Cinema & Media Studies conference, Console-ing Passions Feminist Media Studies Conference, Doing Women's Film and Television History Conference, CARLA 2020: A Global Digital Conference on Diversity and Inclusion in the Film and TV Industry, and the Film Festival Research Network. Thank you to all the editors, reviewers, panelists, and colleagues for their invaluable feedback during these initial stages of writing.

I could not have dreamed of working with a more supportive or passionate publishing team than the University of Texas Press. Thank you to my series editor Tom Schatz for believing in this project and seeing the potential from the proposal stage. Your endless enthusiasm, editorial guidance, and keen perspective on the contemporary film business made this book so much better and stronger. It has been a great pleasure working with you again. Thank you to Sarah McGavick who supported and shepherded this project during the proposal and contract phase, especially for the early feedback on chapter structures. And a massive thank you to Jim Burr, who inherited this book during the manuscript and review phase and guided it swiftly into production. I would also like to thank Mia Uribe Kozlovsky, Lynne Ferguson, Sally Furgeson, and Sue Gaines for a wonderful experience during the production process. I am grateful to the UT Press Faculty Board for their support of this project from the proposal pitch to the greenlight for publication. Thank you immensely to the external reviewers at both the proposal and manuscript stages whose suggested revisions greatly strengthened the foundation of this book. And a special thank you to Reviewer #2, who suggested the absolutely perfect title change. And thank you to my incredible copyeditor Annalisa Zox-Weaver, for your insightful and engaging revisions for the early proposal chapters and first draft of the manuscript.

Anyone who knows me understands how much I cherish my academic community. Y'all have shaped me as a scholar and enriched my life in so many ways. I am forever grateful for my UT mentors and the profound impact they had—Janet, Tom, Joe Straubhaar, and Shanti Kumar; Paul McDonald, Tim Havens, Aswin Punathambekar, Serra Tinic, Amanda Lotz, Tamara Falicov, Alisa Perren, Kevin Sandler—thank you for your mentorship, guidance, support, and all-around scholarly brilliance. Miranda Banks, your work has been such an inspiration for this project. I cannot thank you enough for helping me sketch out the book outline over coffee at SCMS and workshopping the entire project during a visit to Detroit. Anne O'Brien: reading your book was a lightbulb moment that I credit with helping me build a stronger conceptual framework for women's work in production. Jonathan Gray: thank you for your publishing wisdom and the early feedback and guidance you gave on the book proposal.

Thank you to my dear media studies friends: Matt Payne, Kevin Bozelka, Emily Carman, Racquel Gates, Katherine Haenschen, Kevin Sanson, Manuel Aviles-Santiago, Derek Johnson, Daniel Herbert, Kevin Ferguson, Ethan Tussey, Alfred Martin, Alyx Vesey, Colin Tait, Suzanne Scott, Elizabeth Ellcessor, Melanie Kohnen, Jade Miller, and Swapnil Rai. I look forward to getting back to in-person conferences and bourbon hours very soon. Ross Melnick, you have been a huge champion and generously given me advice at every step. Thank you for the lovely LA dinners and long chats on our respective commutes. Mark Horowitz and Bryan Sebok, thank you for always offering a place to land on my visits, talking through film festivals and distribution with me, and lively dinners debating the state of film over rosé (of course). To my BC ladies, Erin Meyers, Faye Woods, Amanda Klein, Anna Froula, Melissa Lenos, Kirsten Strayer, Karen Petruska, Dana Och, and Kristen Warner—I will be forever grateful for this devoted group of incredible women. Kristen and Dana, thank you for Sunday afternoons watching romance movies, low-key travel adventures, and always knowing exactly what my brain needs to hear in the moment.

I am so grateful to be back in Texas near my family for this new chapter. To my lovely in-laws, the Donoghue family, thank you for your encouragement and support. You have always made me feel so special. To the Wranosky family, thank you for all of the wonderful dinners, puppy play time, and helping us get settled into DFW. Words cannot express how grateful I am for my Brannon family. Jessica, thank you for all the academic life advice and sharing in the excitement and frustrations that come with it. You are truly an inspiration, and I am so proud of my incredible historian sister, Dr. Brannon-Wranosky. Emily and David: I am truly blessed to have such loving, supportive, and generous parents. Thanks to the miracle of FaceTime, you have been with me on every adventure at every stage of this project. This book carries so many of the feminist values and empowering lessons you taught me throughout my lifetime. Your unconditional love and encouragement are the reason I am here today.

And always, for my Brian. My favorite person in the entire universe. You are always there with words of inspiration, wisdom, and comfort, coffee and tacos, long runs and lake walks with Charlie Holiday, plane tickets and a packed bag for the next adventure, protecting the space I need for my independence, and helping me when my stubbornness has finally passed. Your partnership, friendship, and infinite love have carried me through every season from stormy to sunny. I cannot wait to write the next chapter together.

Notes

Introduction. Mind the Gaps

1. The producer's name has been changed.

2. "New Study Charts the 'Post-Festival Chasm' for Women Directors," *Women and Hollywood*, June 3, 2015, https://womenandhollywood.com/new-study-charts-the-post-festival-chasm-for-women-directors-219df79b77a9/.

3. Interview by author, Emma, independent producer, April 2015.

4. Sam Frizell, "Sony Executives' Salaries Leaked in Devastating Hack," *Time*, December 2, 2014, https://time.com/3615160/sony-hack-salaries/; Kevin Roose, "Hacked Documents Reveal a Hollywood Studio's Stunning Gender and Race Gap," *Splinter*, December 1, 2014, https://splinternews.com/hacked-documents-reveal-a-hollywood-studios-stunning-ge-1793844312.

5. Jennifer Lawrence, "Why Do I Make Less Than My Male Co-Stars?" *Lenny Letter*, no. 3, October 13, 2015, https://www.lennyletter.com/story/jennifer-lawrence-why-do-i-make-less-than-my-male-costars.

6. Interview by author, publicist, PR firm, Los Angeles, February 2016.

7. Sony used a string of underperforming films—*After Earth* (2013), *White House Down* (2013), *How Do You Know* (2010)—as further justification for firing Pascal.

8. Rebecca Keegan, "Is 2015 the Tipping Point for Women and Minorities in Hollywood?" *Los Angeles Times*, December 11, 2015, https://www.latimes.com/entertainment/movies/la-ca-mn-1213-tipping-point-essay-20151213-story.html; Jessica Ogilvie, "How Hollywood Keeps Out the Stories of Women and Girls," *LA Weekly*, November 16, 2015, https://www.laweekly.com/how-hollywood-keeps-out-the-stories-of-women-and-girls/; Maureen Dowd, "The Women of Hollywood Speak Out," *New York Times*, November 20, 2015, https://www.nytimes.com/2015/11/22/magazine/the-women-of-hollywood-speak-out.html?smid=tw-nytmag&smtyp=cur&_r=1.

9. Dowd, "Women of Hollywood."

10. Stacey L. Smith, Marc Choueiti, and Katherine Pieper, "Inclusion in the Director's Chair? Gender, Race, & Age of Directors across 1,100 Films from 2007–2017," Annenberg Inclusion Initiative, January 2018, 8–9, https://assets.uscannenberg.org/docs/inclusion-in-the-directors-chair-2007-2017.pdf; Martha D. Lauzen, "The Celluloid Ceiling: Behind-the-Scenes Employment of Women on the Top 100, 250, and 500 Films of 2018," https://womenintvfilm.sdsu.edu/wp-content/uploads/2019/01/2018_Celluloid_Ceiling_Report.pdf; Stacy L. Smith, Marc Choueiti, and Katherine Pieper, "Inequality in 800 Popular Films: Examining Portrayals of Gender, Race/Ethnicity, LGBT, and Disability from 2007–2015," Annenberg Inclusion Initiative, September 2016, https://annenberg.usc.edu/sites/default/files/2017/04/10/MDSCI_Inequality_in_800_Films_FINAL.pdf.

11. Lauzen, "The Celluloid Ceiling," 2.

12. Rebecca Rubin, "Former Hollywood Assistant Posts Sexist Email She Received from Her Boss," *Variety*, August 10, 2017, https://variety.com/2017/biz/news/former -hollywood-assistant-posts-sexist-email-1202523582/amp/; David Sims, "Can Hollywood Kill the Casting Couch?" *Atlantic*, June 13, 2018, https://www.theatlantic.com /entertainment/archive/2018/06/sag-aftra-union-casting-couch-deal/562643/.

13. Jodi Kantor and Megan Twohey, "Harvey Weinstein Paid Off Sexual Harassment Accusers for Decades," *New York Times*, October 5, 2017, https://www.nytimes .com /2017/10/05/us/harvey-weinstein-harassment-allegations.html; Ronan Farrow, "From Aggressive Overtures to Sexual Assault: Harvey Weinstein's Accusers Tell Their Stories," *New Yorker*, October 10, 2017, https://www.newyorker.com/news /news-desk/from-aggressive-overtures-to-sexual-assault-harvey-weinsteins-accusers -tell-their-stories.

14. Kim Masters, "Amazon TV Producer Goes Public with Harassment Claim against Top Exec Roy Price (Exclusive)," *Hollywood Reporter*, October 12, 2017, https://www.hollywoodreporter.com/news/general-news/amazon-tv-producer-goes -public-harassment-claim-top-exec-roy-price-1048060/.

15. "#MeToo: A Timeline of Events," *Chicago Tribune*, February 4, 2021, https:// www.chicagotribune.com/lifestyles/ct-me-too-timeline-20171208-htmlstory.html.

16. Time's Up, https://www.timesupnow.com/.

17. Cara Buckley, "Powerful Hollywood Women Unveil Anti-Harassment Action Plan," *New York Times*, January 1, 2018, https://www.nytimes.com/2018/01/01 /movies/times-up-hollywood-women-sexual-harassment.html.

18. Katy Chevigny, "Can She Pull It Off? (Or, How to Hire Women Directors)," *Filmmaker Magazine*, February 17, 2016, https://filmmakermagazine.com/97378-can -she-pull-it-off-or-how-to-hire-women-directors/#.XQgbJNNKj-a.

19. 5050x2020 website, https://www.5050x2020.fr/; Stewart Clarke, "French Stars, Executives Back Gender-Equality Initiative," *Variety*, February 28, 2018, https:// variety.com/2018/film/news/french-stars-executives-back-equality-1202713095/.

20. Helen Meany, "Waking the Feminists: The Campaign That Revolutionised Irish Theatre," *Guardian*, January 5, 2018, https://www.theguardian.com/stage/2018/jan /05/feminist-irish-theatre-selina-cartmell-gate-theatre; Lian Bell, "Waking the Feminists One Year On—Change, in Stages," *RTÉ*, February 10, 2017, https://www.rte.ie /culture/2016/1110/830647-wakingthefeminists-one-year-on/.

21. Marcela Xavier, "The Campaigners Challenging Misogyny and Sexism in Brazil," *Guardian*, December 3, 2015, https://www.theguardian.com/global-development -professionals-network/2015/dec/03/sexism-misogyny-campaigners-brazil-social -media; Júlia Barbon, "42% das mulheres relatam ter sofrido assédio sexual, aponta Datafolha," *Folha de São Paulo*, December 28, 2017, https://www1.folha.uol.com.br /cotidiano/2017/12/1945636-42-das-mulheres-relatam-ja-ter-sofrido-assedio-sexual -aponta-datafolha.shtml.

22. See Susan Liddy, ed., *Women in the International Film Industry* (London: Palgrave Macmillan, 2020); Susan Liddy, ed., *Women in the Irish Film Industry: Stories and Storytellers* (Cork: Cork University Press, 2020); Anne O'Brien, *Women, Inequality, and Media Work* (London: Routledge, 2019); Susan Liddy and Anne O'Brien, eds., *Media Work, Mothers, and Motherhood: Negotiating the International Audiovisual Industry* (London: Routledge, 2021); Shelley Cobb and Linda Ruth Williams, "Calling the Shots: Women and Contemporary Film Culture in the UK, 2000–2015," https://

womencallingtheshots.com/; Natalie Wreyford, *Gender Inequality in Screenwriting Work* (London: Palgrave Macmillan, 2018); Leslie L. March, *Brazilian Women's Film-making: From Dictatorship to Democracy* (Urbana: University of Illinois Press, 2012); Jack A. Draper III and Cacilda Rêgo, eds., *Woman-Centered Brazilian Cinema: Film-makers and Protagonists of the Twenty-First Century* (Albany: SUNY Press, 2022); Skadi Loist and Elizabeth Prommer, "Gendered Production Culture in the German Film Industry," *Media Industries Journal* 6, no. 1 (2019): 95–115; Deb Verhoeven, Bronwyn Coate, and Vejune Zemaityte1, "Re-Distributing Gender in the Global Film Industry: Beyond #MeToo and #MeThree," *Media Industries Journal* 6, no. 1 (2019): 135–155.

23. Courtney Brannon Donoghue, *Localising Hollywood* (London: British Film Institute Press, 2017).

24. Interview by author, cofounder of Alliance for Women Directors, phone, January 2017.

25. Christina N. Baker, *Contemporary Black Women Filmmakers and the Art of Resistance* (Columbus: Ohio State University Press, 2018); Christina N. Baker, *Black Women Directors* (New Brunswick, NJ: Rutgers University Press, 2022); Miranda J. Banks, "Gender below-the-Line: Defining Feminist Production Studies," in *Production Studies: Cultural Studies of Media Industries,* ed. Vicki Mayer, Miranda J. Banks, and John T. Caldwell (New York: Routledge, 2009), 87–98; Emily Carman, *Independent Stardom: Freelance Women in the Hollywood Studio System* (Austin: University of Texas Press, 2016); Shelley Cobb, "What about the Men? Gender Inequality Data and the Rhetoric of Inclusion in the US and UK Film Industries," *Journal of British Cinema and Television* 17, no. 1 (2020): 112–135; Jane Gaines, *Pink-Slipped: What Happened to Women in the Silent Film Industries?* (Urbana: University of Illinois Press, 2018); Hilary Hallett, *Go West, Young Women! The Rise of Early Hollywood* (Berkeley: University of California Press, 2013); Erin Hill, *Never Done: A History of Women's Work in Media Production* (New Brunswick, NJ: Rutgers University Press, 2016); Christina Lane, "Just Another Girl outside the Neo-Indie," in *Contemporary American Independent Film: From the Margins to the Mainstream*, ed. Chris Holmlund and Justin Wyatt (New York: Routledge, 2004), 193–209; J. E. Smyth, *Nobody's Girl Friday: The Women Who Ran Hollywood* (Oxford: Oxford University Press, 2018); Maya Montañez Smukler, *Liberating Hollywood: Women Directors and the Feminist Reform of the 1970s American Cinema* (New Brunswick, NJ: Rutgers University Press, 2018); Shelley Stamp, *Lois Weber in Early Hollywood* (Oakland: University of California Press, 2015).

26. Jennifer Holt, *Empires of Entertainment: Media Industries and the Politics of Deregulation, 1980–1996* (New Brunswick, NJ: Rutgers University Press, 2011); Henry Jenkins, "The Cultural Logic of Media Convergence," *International Journal of Cultural Studies* 7, no. 33 (2004): 33–43.

27. Tino Balio, *Hollywood in the New Millennium* (London: BFI Press, 2013); Brannon Donoghue, *Localising Hollywood*; Derek Johnson, *Media Franchising: Creative License and Collaboration in the Culture Industries* (New York: New York University Press, 2013).

28. Michael Nordine, "Nina Jacobson's Full Sundance Producers Brunch Keynote Speech," *IndieWire*, January 27, 2019, https://www.indiewire.com/2019/01/nina -jacobson-sundance-producers-brunch-keynote-speech-1202038685/?fbclid= IwAR1c4dqisW5azbIZBC7Bc6ajWA5sPPWxXUw9AxYa9YYKBpWThg0lrCqVcyU.

29. Gillian Doyle, *Understanding Media Economics*, 2nd ed. (London: Sage, 2013);

Janet Wasko, *How Hollywood Works* (London: Sage, 2003); Daniel Bernardi and Julian Hoxter, *Off the Page: Screenwriting in the Era of Media Convergence* (Oakland: University of California Press, 2017).

30. Interview by author, studio screenwriter, phone, August 2017.

31. For scholarship on the romantic comedy, see Tamar Jeffers McDonald, *Romantic Comedy: Boy Meets Girl Meets Genre* (London: Wallflower, 2017); Claire Mortimer, *Romantic Comedy* (London: Routledge, 2010); Maria San Filippo, ed., *After "Happily Ever After": Romantic Comedy in the Post-Romantic Age* (Detroit: Wayne State University Press, 2021).

32. Hilary Radner, *Neo-Feminist Cinema: Girly Films, Chick Flicks, and Consumer Culture* (London: Routledge, 2010); Ashley Elaine York, "From Chick Flicks to Millennial Blockbusters: Spinning Female-Driven Narratives into Franchises," *Journal of Popular Culture* 43, no. 1 (2010): 3–25; Suzanne Ferriss, "Fashioning Femininity in the Makeover Flick," in *Chick Flicks: Contemporary Women at the Movies*, ed. Suzanne Ferriss and Mallory Young (New York: Routledge, 2008), 41–57; Angela McRobbie, "Post-Feminism and Popular Culture," *Feminist Media Studies* 4, no. 3 (2004): 255–264; Diane Negra, "Quality Postfeminism? Sex and the Single Girl on HBO," *Genders* 39 (2004), https://www.atria.nl/ezines/IAV_606661/IAV_606661_2010_52/g39_negra.html; Kim Akass and Janet McCabe, eds. *Reading Sex and the City* (London: I. B. Tauris, 2004); Deborah Jermyn, *Sex and the City* (Detroit: Wayne State University Press, 2009).

33. Radner, *Neo-Feminist Cinema*, 2.

34. Owen Gleiberman, "The Rom-Com Is Dead. Long Live the Rom-Com," *Variety*, February 22, 2019, https://variety.com/2019/film/columns/why-rom-coms-need-to-go-beyond-tropes-to-survive-1203145823/.

35. Karen Hollinger, *Feminist Film Studies* (New York: Routledge, 2012), 47.

36. Shelley Cobb, "Black Women, Romance and the Indiewood Rom Coms of Sanaa Hamri," in *Indie Reframed: Women's Filmmaking and Contemporary American Independent Cinema*, ed. Linda Badley, Claire Perkins, and Michele Schreiber (Edinburgh: Edinburgh University Press, 2016), 154–168.

37. On the "death of the rom-com," see Alexander Huls, "The Romantic Comedy Is Dying, but Cinematic Romance Is Thriving," *Atlantic*, January 24, 2014, https://www.theatlantic.com/entertainment/archive/2014/01/the-romantic-comedy-is-dying-but-cinematic-romance-is-thriving/283252/; Wesley Morris, "Rom-Coms Were Corny and Retrograde. Why Do I Miss Them So Much?" *New York Times*, April 24, 2019, https://www.nytimes.com/2019/04/24/magazine/romantic-comedy-movies.html; see also Maria San Filippo's edited collection, *After "Happily Ever After": Romantic Comedy in the Post-Romantic Age*.

38. Kevin Maynard, "Screen's Smart Women Face Delicate Dilemmas," *Variety*, January 13, 2002, https://variety.com/2002/film/awards/screen-s-smart-women-face-delicate-dilemmas-1117858475/; Nicole LaPorte, "Can Chicks Get in the Pic Mix?" *Variety*, June 25, 2006, https://variety.com/2006/film/news/can-chicks-get-in-pic-mix-1200337193/.

39. Interview by author, independent producer, phone, August 2018.

40. Pamela McClintock, "*Twilight* Takes Bite Out of Box Office," *Variety*, November 23, 2008, https://variety.com/2008/film/box-office/twilight-takes-bite-out-of-box-office-1117996354/; Pamela McClintock, "2008: The Year That Broke the Rules," *Variety*, December 12, 2008, https://variety.com/2008/film/features/2008-the-year

-that-broke-the-rules-1117997294/; Pamela McClintock, "Women Take Center Stage at Summer B.O.," *Variety*, April 26, 2010, https://variety.com/2010/film/box-office/women-take-center-stage-at-summer-b-o-1118018273/.

41. John Thornton Caldwell, *Production Culture: Industrial Reflexivity and Critical Practice in Film and Television* (Durham, NC: Duke University Press, 2008); Timothy Havens, Amanda D. Lotz, and Serra Tinic, "Critical Media Industry Studies: A Research Approach," *Communication, Culture & Critique* 2 (2009): 4–6.

42. Caldwell, *Production Culture*, 5.

43. Daniel Herbert, Amanda D. Lotz, and Aswin Punathambekar, *Media Industry Studies* (Cambridge, UK: Polity, 2020), 50.

44. Vicki Mayer, "Bringing the 'Social' Back In: Studies of Production Cultures and Social Theory," *E-compós* 12, no. 3 (2009): 1.

45. Timothy Havens, "Towards a Structuration Theory of Media Intermediaries," in *Making Media Work: Cultures of Management in the Entertainment Industries*, ed. Derek Johnson, Derek Kompare, and Avi Santo (New York: New York University Press, 2014), 40–41.

46. Kristen J. Warner, "Strategies for Success? Navigating Hollywood's 'Postracial' Labor Practices," in *Precarious Creativity: Global Media, Local Labor*, ed. Michael Curtin and Kevin Sanson (Oakland: University of California Press, 2016), 172–185; Nancy Wang Yuen, *Reel Inequality: Hollywood Actors and Racism* (New Brunswick, NJ: Rutgers University Press, 2016); Darnell M. Hunt and Ana-Christina Ramón, "Hollywood Diversity Report 2020: A Tale of Two Hollywoods," UCLA Division of Social Sciences, 2020, https://socialsciences.ucla.edu/wp-content/uploads/2020/02/UCLA-Hollywood-Diversity-Report-2020-Film-2-6-2020.pdf.

47. Natalie Wreyford and Shelley Cobb, "Data and Responsibility: Toward a Feminist Methodology for Producing Historical Data on Women in the Contemporary UK Film Industry," *Feminist Media Histories* 3, no. 3 (2017): 108.

48. Interview by author, independent producer, Los Angeles, July 2017.

Chapter 1. The Gendered Workplace (Employment Gap)

1. Janice Min, "Letter from the Editor," *Hollywood Reporter*, December 15, 2010, 16.

2. Janice Min, "*The Hollywood Reporter* to End Rankings for Women in Entertainment Power 100," *Hollywood Reporter*, November 11, 2015, http://www.hollywoodreporter.com/features/hollywood-reporter-end-rankings-women-839046.

3. Carman, *Independent Stardom*; Mark Garrett Cooper, *Universal Women: Filmmaking and Institutional Change in Early Hollywood* (Urbana: University of Illinois Press, 2010); Gaines, *Pink-Slipped*; Hallett, *Go West, Young Women!*; Hill, *Never Done*; Karen Ward Mahar, *Women Filmmakers in Early Hollywood* (Baltimore, MD: Johns Hopkins University Press, 2008); Smukler, *Liberating Hollywood*; Smyth, *Nobody's Girl Friday*; Shelley Stamp, *Lois Weber in Early Hollywood* (Oakland: University of California Press, 2015).

4. Mahar, *Women Filmmakers*, 2.

5. Stamp, *Lois Weber*. In their biographical entry on Normand as part of the Women Film Pioneers Project, Simon Joyce and Jennifer Putzi emphasize the "absence of definitive information" to confirm which and how many films she directed during the 1910s. "Questions of attribution remain open for most of the films . . . with directorial credit often given to Sennett, Chaplin, or 'Fatty' Arbuckle,

her frequent co-star following Chaplin's departure, and they may never be answered, since the popularity of Keystone meant multiple re-edited prints and re-issues." Even as women like Normand moved into the directorial role, their contributions were often not documented or given instead to male collaborators. See Simon Joyce and Jennifer Putzi, "Mabel Normand," in *Women Film Pioneers Project*, ed. Jane Gaines, Radha Vatsal, and Monica Dall'Asta (New York: Columbia University Libraries, 2013), https://wfpp.columbia.edu/pioneer/ccp-mabel-normand/.

6. Stamp, *Lois Weber*, 4.

7. Hallett, *Go West, Young Women!*, 219.

8. Mahar, *Women Filmmakers*, 2–3, 7; Thomas Schatz, *The Genius of the System: Hollywood Filmmaking in the Studio Era* (New York: Pantheon Books, 1989).

9. Gaines, *Pink-Slipped*, 193.

10. Kyna Morgan and Aimee Dixon, "African-American Women in the Silent Film Industry," in *Women Film Pioneers Project*, ed. Jane Gaines, Radha Vatsal, and Monica Dall'Asta (New York: Columbia University Libraries, 2013), https://wfpp.columbia.edu/essay/african-american-women-in-the-silent-film-industry/; see also Christina N. Baker's chapter "Recognizing the Pioneers," in her book *Black Women Directors* (New Brunswick, NJ: Rutgers University Press, 2022): 4–29.

11. Hill, *Never Done*, 165.

12. Judith Mayne, *Directed by Dorothy Arzner* (Bloomington: Indiana University Press, 1994); Smyth, *Nobody's Girl Friday*; Lizzie Francke, *Script Girls: Women Screenwriters in Hollywood* (London: BFI Press, 1994).

13. Allyson Nadia Field, "Dorothy Arzner," Women Film Pioneers Project, https://wfpp.columbia.edu/pioneer/ccp-dorothy-arzner/; Mayne, *Directed by Dorothy Arzner*; Smyth, *Nobody's Girl Friday*, 20–22, 240.

14. Smyth, *Nobody's Girl Friday*, 20.

15. Hill, *Never Done*, 188–191; Mahar, *Women Filmmakers*.

16. Smyth, *Nobody's Girl Friday*, 155.

17. Carman, *Independent Stardom*, 8; Smyth, *Nobody's Girl Friday*, 239.

18. Carman, *Independent Stardom*, 4, 8.

19. Carman, *Independent Stardom*, 13.

20. Smyth, *Nobody's Girl Friday*, 96–98.

21. Hill, *Never Done*, 5.

22. Hill, *Never Done*, 4.

23. Janet Staiger, "The Package-Unit System: Unit Management after 1955," in David Bordwell, Janet Staiger, and Kristin Thompson, *The Classical Hollywood Cinema: Film Style & Mode of Production to 1960* (New York: Columbia University Press, 1985), 330–331.

24. Douglas Gomery, *The Hollywood Studio System* (New York: St. Martin's Press, 1986); William M. Kunz, *Culture Conglomerates: Consolidation in the Motion Picture and Television Industries* (Lanham, MD: Rowman & Littlefield, 2007).

25. "The Many Loves of Howard Hughes, Part 2: The Many Loves of Ida Lupino," *You Must Remember This*, podcast produced by Karina Longworth, July 10, 2014, 36:49, http://www.youmustrememberthispodcast.com/episodes/youmustrememberthispodcastblog/the-many-loves-of-howard-hughes-part-2-the-many.

26. Thomas Schatz, "Desilu, *I Love Lucy*, and the Rise of Network TV," in *Making

Television: Authorship and the Production Process, ed. Robert J. Thompson and Gary Burns (New York: Praeger, 1990). For a detailed historical account of women writers in the postwar television industry, see Annie Berke's *Their Own Best Creations: Women Writers in Postwar Television* (Oakland: University of California Press, 2022).

27. Brannon Donoghue, *Localising Hollywood*, 28.

28. Thomas Schatz "The New Hollywood," in *Film Theory Goes to the Movies*, ed. Jim Collins, Hilary Radner, and Ava Preacher Collins (New York: Routledge, 1993); Paul Monaco, *The Sixties: 1960–1969*, History of the American Cinema series (New York: Charles Scribner's Sons, 2011).

29. "Breaking Down the Gender Wage Gap," Women's Bureau, United States Department of Labor, https://www.dol.gov/wb/.

30. Lynda Obst, *Hello, He Lied and Other Truths from the Hollywood Trenches* (New York: Broadway Books, 1996), 11.

31. Smukler, *Liberating Hollywood*, 2.

32. Smukler, *Liberating Hollywood*, 81, 160.

33. Stephen Galloway, *Leading Lady: Sherry Lansing and the Making of a Hollywood Groundbreaker* (New York: Crown Archetype, 2017); Smukler, *Liberating Hollywood*, 279–280.

34. US Department of Justice, Title IX, https://www.justice.gov/crt/title-ix.

35. Maya Montañez Smukler, "Liberating Hollywood: Thirty Years of Women Directors," UCLA Center for the Study of Women (January 2011) 6–7, https://escholarship.org/uc/item/3pd5t9m6.

36. Nancy Mills, "Plight of Women Directors Improved—but Not Much," *Los Angeles Times*, November 17, 1986, https://www.latimes.com/archives/la-xpm-1986-11-17-ca-3890-story.html.

37. Smukler, *Liberating Hollywood*, 8–9, 10–12.

38. Smukler, *Liberating Hollywood*, 272. For a detailed account of the DGA lawsuit, see Smukler's *Liberating Hollywood*, 262–271.

39. Akiva Gottlieb, "30 Years after Making History with 'A Dry White Season,' Director Euzhan Palcy Looks Back," *Los Angeles Times*, February 1, 2019, https://www.latimes.com/entertainment/movies/la-ca-mn-euzhan-palcy-dry-white-season-20190201-story.html.

40. National Center for Education Statistics, "Postsecondary Enrollment Rates," https://nces.ed.gov/programs/coe/indicator_cha.asp.

41. It is important to note that many working film professionals do not have a film-related degree or a complete postsecondary education. In fact, a college degree is typically not a requirement for working in the production sector.

42. Malina Saval, "Film Schools Open Path to Hollywood Diversity," *Variety*, April 27, 2016, https://variety.com/2016/film/spotlight/film-schools-diversity-hollywood-1201760991/; Stephanie Prange, "Top Film School Deans Use #MeToo Scandal as Teachable Moment," *Variety*, February 15, 2018, https://variety.com/2018/film/news/metoo-becomes-teachable-moment-at-film-schools-1202700827/.

43. Pew Research Center, "Women CEOs in Fortune 500 Companies, 1995–2018," January 14, 2015, http://www.pewsocialtrends.org/chart/women-ceos-in-fortune-500-companies-1995-2014/; Susan Chira, "Why Women Aren't C.E.O.s, According to Women Who Almost Were," *New York Times*, June 21, 2017, https://www.nytimes.com/2017/07/21/sunday-review/women-ceos-glass-ceiling.html?smprod

=nytcore-ipad&smid=nytcore-ipad-share&referer=https%253A%252F%252Ft.co
%252FvdcHlJJQio.

44. Pew Research Center, "Labor Force Participation Rate Has Declined," January 30, 2017, http://www.pewresearch.org/fact-tank/2017/01/31/women-may-never -make-up-half-of-the-u-s-workforce/ft_17-01-30_womenlaborforce4/; Ellen Pao, "This Is How Sexism Works in Silicon Valley," *New York Magazine*, August 21, 2017, https://www.thecut.com/2017/08/ellen-pao-silicon-valley-sexism-reset-excerpt .html; Ariane Hegewisch, "The Gender Wage Gap: 2017," Institute for Women's Policy Research, September 13, 2018, https://iwpr.org/iwpr-issues/esme/the-gender-wage -gap-2017-earnings-differences-by-gender-race-and-ethnicity/.

45. Dionne Searcey, "For Women in Midlife, Career Gains Slip Away," *New York Times*, June 23, 2014, https://www.nytimes.com/2014/06/24/business/women-leave -their-careers-in-peak-years.html?_r=0; Jack Peat, "Women 'Damned Either Way' on Maternity Leave," *London Economic*, May 31, 2017, https://www.thelondoneconomic .com/lifestyle/women-damned-either-way-maternity-leave-47921/.

46. Alisha Haridasani Gupta, "Why Some Women Call This Recession a 'Sheces-sion,'" *New York Times*, May 9, 2020, https://www.nytimes.com/2020/05/09/us /unemployment-coronavirus-women.html.

47. Maya H. Strober, "Towards a General Theory of Occupational Sex Segregation: The Case of Public School Teaching," in *Sex Segregation in the Workplace: Trends, Explanations, Remedies*, ed. Barbara F. Reskin (Washington, DC: National Academy Press, 1984), 144.

48. Lauzen, "2019 Celluloid Ceiling," 2.

49. Wreyford and Cobb, "Data and Responsibility," 111.

50. Cobb, "What about the Men?" 117.

51. Stacy L. Smith, Marc Choueiti, Kevin Yao, Hannah Clark, and Katherine Pieper, "Inclusion in the Director's Chair: Analysis of Director Gender & Race/ Ethnicity across 1,300 Top Films from 2007 to 2019," January 2020, https://assets .uscannenberg.org/docs/aii-inclusion-directors-chair-20200102.pdf.

52. Lauzen, "2019 Celluloid Ceiling."

53. These data were collected prior to two major media acquisitions going into effect in 2019: AT&T buying Time Warner and Disney buying 21st Century Fox. Additionally, Warner Bros. replaced CEO Kevin Tsujihara with Ann Sarnoff in 2019.

54. Smith, Choueiti, and Pieper, "Inclusion in the Director's Chair? 2007–2017," 8–9.

55. Richard Rushfield, "Class Photos," *The Ankler*, email newsletter, June 12, 2020.

56. Plan B and Warner Bros. Organizational Charts, *Variety Insight* database.

57. Ogilvie, "How Hollywood Keeps Out the Stories of Women and Girls"; Kate Erbland, "A Female Hollywood Producer Details How Industry Discriminates against Women," *IndieWire*, July 8, 2015, https://www.indiewire.com/2015/07/a-female -hollywood-producer-details-how-industry-discriminates-against-women-60505/.

58. Keegan, "Is 2015 the Tipping Point?"

59. Viola Davis, Emmy Awards broadcast, September 20, 2015.

60. Devika Girish, "Rediscovering Australia's Generation of Defiant Female Directors," *New York Times*, July 26, 2022, https://www.nytimes.com/2022/07/26/movies /australia-women-directors.html.

61. Rebecca Keegan, "Female Film Directors Are on Outside Looking In, but Will ACLU Flip the Script?" *Los Angeles Times*, May 13, 2015, https://www.latimes.com/entertainment/movies/la-et-mn-aclu-gender-discrimination-hollywood-20150513-story.html.

62. "ACLU Letter on the Exclusion of Women Directors," *New York Times*, May 12, 2015, https://www.nytimes.com/interactive/2015/05/12/movies/document-13filmwomen.html. Title VII refers to the 1964 Civil Rights Act, which states: "It shall be an unlawful employment practice for an employer . . . to discriminate against any individual with respect to his compensation, terms, conditions, or privileges of employment, because of such individual's race, color, religion, sex, or national origin." See American Association of University Women, https://www.aauw.org/what-we-do/legal-resources/know-your-rights-at-work/title-vii/.

63. Rebecca Keegan, "The Hollywood Gender Discrimination Investigation Is On: EEOC Contacts Women Directors," *Los Angeles Times*, October 2, 2015, https://www.latimes.com/entertainment/movies/moviesnow/la-et-mn-women-directors-discrimination-investigation-20151002-story.html; David Robb, "EEOC: Major Studios Failed to Hire Female Directors; Lawsuit Looms," *Deadline Hollywood*, February 15, 2017, https://deadline.com/2017/02/hollywood-studios-female-directors-eeoc-investigation-1201912590/.

64. Julie Kosin, "Frances McDormand Just Brought Down the House with Her Oscars Speech," *Harper's Bazaar*, March 5, 2018, https://www.harpersbazaar.com/culture/film-tv/a19081077/frances-mcdormand-oscars-speech-transcript-2018/.

65. Tatiana Siegel, "Making of 'Nomadland': How Frances McDormand and Chloé Zhao Created a Story That 'Crossed Cultural and Generational Lines,'" *Hollywood Reporter*, February 22, 2021, https://www.hollywoodreporter.com/movies/movie-news/making-of-nomadland-how-frances-mcdormand-and-chloe-zhao-created-a-story-that-crossed-cultural-and-generational-lines-4133719/.

66. Matt Warren, "From the Archives: Eight Important Things You Need to Know about Inclusion Riders," *Film Independent*, June 18, 2018, https://www.filmindependent.org/blog/from-the-archives-eight-important-things-you-need-to-know-about-inclusion-riders/.

67. Cara Buckley, "Inclusion Rider? What Inclusion Rider?" *New York Times*, June 19, 2019, https://www.nytimes.com/2019/06/19/movies/inclusion-rider.html.

68. Stacey L. Smith, "Hey, Hollywood: It's Time to Adopt the NFL's Rooney Rule—for Women," *Hollywood Reporter*, December 15, 2014, https://www.hollywoodreporter.com/news/general-news/hey-hollywood-time-adopt-nfls-754659/; Kalpana Kotagal, Stacy L. Smith, Fanshen Cox DiGiovanni, and Leah Fischman, "Inclusion Rider Template," USC Annenberg Inclusion Initiative, March 2018, http://assets.uscannenberg.org.s3.amazonaws.com/docs/inclusion-rider-template.pdf; "The Rooney Rule," National Football League website, https://operations.nfl.com/inside-football-ops/diversity-inclusion/the-rooney-rule/.

69. Rebecca Chapman, "Sorry, Hollywood. Inclusion Riders Won't Save You," *New York Times*, April 3, 2018, https://www.nytimes.com/2018/04/03/opinion/hollywood-inclusion-rider.html.

70. Cobb, "What about the Men?" 128.

71. Rachel Montpelier, "4% Challenge: Inclusion Initiative & Time's Up Aim to

Boost Number of Women Directing Top Films," *Women and Hollywood*, January 28, 2019, https://womenandhollywood.com/4-challenge-inclusion-initiative-times-up -aim-to-boost-number-of-women-directing-top-films/.

72. Gregg Kilday, "Universal, MGM Studios Accept 4 Percent Challenge to Hire Women Directors," *Hollywood Reporter*, January 29, 2019, https://www .hollywoodreporter.com/news/universal-becomes-first-studio-accept-4-percent -challenge-1180949.

73. Cobb, "What about the Men?" 128.

74. Miranda J. Banks, "The Room Where It Happens: Showrunners and Diversity Mandates," Media Industries Conference, King's College London, April 18, 2018; Derek Thompson, "The Brutal Math of Gender Inequality in Hollywood," *Atlantic*, January 11, 2018, https://www.theatlantic.com/business/archive/2018/01/the-brutal -math-of-gender-inequality-in-hollywood/550232/; Anousha Sakoui, "Female Directors in Hollywood Are Still Underrepresented, but the Gap Is Narrowing," *Los Angeles Times*, January 2, 2020, https://www.latimes.com/entertainment-arts/business /story/2020-01-02/women-directors-working-reaches-highest-level-in-a-decade-but -still-underpresented.

75. Wreyford and Cobb, "Data and Responsibility," 108.

76. Kristen J. Warner, "Plastic Representation," *Film Quarterly* 71, no. 2 (2017), https://filmquarterly.org/2017/12/04/in-the-time-of-plastic-representation/.

77. Wreyford and Cobb, "Data and Responsibility," 125.

78. Tomas Chamorro-Premuzic, "Is Hiring for Culture Fit Another Form of Unconscious Bias?" *Fast Company*, December 21, 2018, https://www.fastcompany.com /90282111/is-hiring-for-culture-fit-another-form-of-unconscious-bias.

79. Mynette Louie, "A Female Producer Explains 4 Ways Women Get a Raw Deal in Hollywood," *New York Magazine*, July 7, 2015, https://www.vulture.com/2015/07/how -hollywood-discriminates-female-filmmakers.html.

80. Madeline E. Heilman, Francesca Manzi, and Susanne Braun, "Presumed Incompetent: Perceived Lack of Fit and Gender Bias in Recruitment and Selection," in *Handbook of Gendered Careers in Management: Getting In, Getting On, Getting Out*, ed. Adelina M. Broadbridge and Sandra L. Fielden (Northampton, MA: Edward Elgar, 2015), 92.

81. O'Brien, *Women, Inequality, and Media Work*, 61–62.

82. Madeline E. Heilman, "Gender Stereotypes and Workplace Bias," *Research in Organizational Behavior* 32 (2012): 123–124.

83. Interview by author, Rio de Janeiro, Brazil, August 2010; interview by author, Madrid, Spain, January 2011; interview by author, Madrid, Spain, June 2013; interview by author, Los Angeles, March 2014; interview by author, Rio de Janeiro, Brazil, August 2014.

84. Interview by author, managing director of a major studio office in the European market, June 2013; interview by author, vice president of international production at a major Hollywood studio, Los Angeles, March 2016.

85. Interview by author, producer-director, phone, January 2018.

86. Brooks Barnes, "Amy Pascal's Hollywood Ending, Complete with Comeback Twist," *New York Times*, July 8, 2017, https://www.nytimes.com/2017/07/08/business /media/amy-pascal-sony-pictures.html?smid=tw-share&referer=https://t.co /fEkqsw4pqt%3famp=1.

87. Obst, *Hello, He Lied*, 179.

88. Obst, *Hello, He Lied*, 183.

89. Obst, *Hello, He Lied*, 191–193.

90. Katy Kay and Claire Shipman, *The Confidence Code: The Science and Art of Self-Assurance—What Women Should Know* (New York: HarperCollins, 2014); Sallie Krawcheck, *Own It: The Power of Women at Work* (New York: Crown, 2017); also see Laura Vanderkam, *I Know How She Does It: How Successful Women Make the Most of Their Time* (New York: Portfolio, 2015); Tiffany Dufu, *Drop The Ball: Achieving More by Doing Less* (New York: Flatiron Books, 2018).

91. Rosalind Gill, "Postfeminist Media Culture: Elements of a Sensibility," *European Journal of Cultural Studies* 10, no. 2 (2007): 149; Yvonne Tasker and Diane Negra, "Introduction: Feminist Politics and Postfeminist Culture," in *Interrogating Postfeminism: Gender and the Politics of Popular Culture*, ed. Yvonne Tasker and Diane Negra (Durham, NC: Duke University Press, 2007), 22.

92. Sheryl Sandberg, *Lean In: Women, Work, and the Will to Lead* (New York: Alfred A. Knopf, 2016). A central argument across many industries to explain gender inequity in the workplace is the so-called ambition gap. This narrative has long been used against women in the film industry to explain away their absence from leadership and management roles. Ambition is a polemical point of discussion in recent popular publications exploring the gender gap. See Rebecca J. Rosen, "The Ambition Interviews: A Table of Contents," *Atlantic*, December 19, 2016, https://www.theatlantic.com/business/archive/2016/12/the-ambition-interviews-a-table-of-contents/510848/.

93. Elaine Blair, "Anne-Marie Slaughter's 'Unfinished Business,'" *New York Times*, September 23, 2015, https://www.nytimes.com/2015/09/27/books/review/anne-marie-slaughters-unfinished-business-women-men-work-family.html.

94. Interview by author, screenwriter, Los Angeles, July 2018.

95. Interview by author, female editor, Los Angeles, June 2018.

96. Warner, "Strategies for Success?" 172.

97. Interview by author, writer-producer, phone, August 2017.

98. O'Brien, *Women, Inequality, and Media Work*, 72–75.

99. Vanessa Friedman, "It's 2018: You Can Run for Office and Not Wear a Pantsuit," *New York Times*, June 21, 2018, https://www.nytimes.com/2018/06/21/style/female-politicians-dress-to-win.html.

100. Interview by author, screenwriter, phone, August 2017.

101. Interview by author, screenwriter, Los Angeles, July 2018.

102. Ms. Jackson, "Investing in Women: Why Hollywood Won't Do It," *The Wrap*, June 20, 2009, https://www.thewrap.com/investing-women-why-hollywood-wont-do-it-3792/.

103. Felicia D. Henderson, "The Culture behind Closed Doors: Issues of Gender and Race in the Writers' Room," *Cinema Journal* 50, no. 2 (Winter 2011): 152.

104. Gillian Flynn, *Gone Girl* (New York: Crown, 2012), 222.

105. Anne Helen Petersen, "Jennifer Lawrence and the History of Cool Girls," *Buzzfeed*, February 28, 2014, https://www.buzzfeed.com/annehelenpetersen/jennifer-lawrence-and-the-history-of-cool-girls.

106. Interview by author, producer, Los Angeles, April 2017.

107. O'Brien, *Women, Inequality, and Media Work*, 90.

108. Joan C. Williams and Rachel Dempsey, *What Works for Women at Work: Four Patterns Working Women Need to Know* (New York: New York University Press, 2014), 10.

109. Interview by author, screenwriter, Zoom, December 2020.

110. Kim Masters, "John Lasseter's Pattern of Alleged Misconduct Detailed by Disney/Pixar Insiders," *Hollywood Reporter*, November 21, 2017, https://www.hollywoodreporter.com/news/general-news/john-lasseters-pattern-alleged-misconduct-detailed-by-disney-pixar-insiders-1059594/; Gregg Kilday, "John Lasseter to Exit Disney at End of the Year," *Hollywood Reporter*, June 2, 2018, https://www.hollywoodreporter.com/news/general-news/john-lasseter-exit-disney-at-end-year-1069547/.

111. Skydance CEO David Ellison hired Lasseter to run the animation studio in 2019 after he left Disney. Lasseter oversees animated film and television projects such as the 2022 *Luck* (dir. Peggy Holmes), which was distributed under a multi-year deal with Apple TV+. Rebecca Keegan and Carolyn Giardina, "John Lasseter's Second Act," *Hollywood Reporter*, July 27, 2022, https://www.hollywoodreporter.com/movies/movie-features/john-lasseter-skydance-animation-luck-1235186710/.

112. Brett Lang, "Jennifer Lee, Pete Docter to Run Disney Animation, Pixar," *Variety*, June 19, 2018, https://variety.com/2018/film/news/jennifer-lee-pete-docter-head-disney-animation-pixar-1202851411/.

113. Tatiana Siegel and Kim Masters, "'I Need to Be Careful': Texts Reveal Warner Bros. CEO Promoted Actress amid Apparent Sexual Relationship," *Hollywood Reporter*, March 6, 2019, https://www.hollywoodreporter.com/movies/movie-features/i-need-be-careful-texts-reveal-warner-bros-ceo-promoted-actress-apparent-sexual-relationship-1192660/; Erik Hayden, "Ann Sarnoff Named Warner Bros. CEO in Surprise Pick," *Hollywood Reporter*, June 24, 2019, https://www.hollywoodreporter.com/news/general-news/ann-sarnoff-named-warner-bros-ceo-surprise-pick-1217672/.

114. Ryan Faughnder, "Warner Bros. Head Ann Sarnoff to Leave Company amid Discovery Merger," *Los Angeles Times*, April 5, 2022, https://www.hollywoodreporter.com/movies/movie-features; Lucas Shaw, "Warner Bros. Discovery Leadership Team Draws Ire over Diversity," *Bloomberg*, July 28, 2022, https://www.bloomberg.com/news/articles/2022-07-28/warner-bros-discovery-leadership-team-draws-ire-over-diversity.

115. Sisi Cao, "Disney-Fox Deal Will Bring 7 Women Execs to the All-Male 'Mouse House,'" *Observer*, December 15, 2017, https://observer.com/2017/12/disney-fox-deal-will-bring-7-women-execs-to-the-all-male-mouse-house/.

116. Brent Lang, "Stacey Snider on Life after Fox: 'My Job for the Last Year Has Been Chairman of Human Emotions,'" *Variety*, October 23, 2018, https://variety.com/2018/film/news/stacey-snider-fox-exit-interview-1202988981/; Pamela McClintock, "Emma Watts Steps Down as 20th Century Studios Chief," *Hollywood Reporter*, January 30, 2020, https://www.hollywoodreporter.com/movies/movie-news/emma-watts-steps-down-at-20th-century-1274899/; Mike Fleming Jr., "Elizabeth Gabler's Fox 2000 to Shutter as Disney Takes Over," *Deadline*, March 21, 2019, https://deadline.com/2019/03/elizabeth-gabler-fox-2000-to-shutter-as-disney-takes-over-1202580356/; Matt Donnelly and Brent Lang, "Searchlight Pictures Co-Chairmen Nancy Utley and Stephen Gilula to Step Down," *Variety*, April 20, 2021, https://

variety.com/2021/film/news/nancy-utley-stephen-gilula-resign-searchlight-pictures
-1234955922/.

117. Brooks Barnes, "Pay Discrimination Suit against Disney Adds Pay Secrecy Claim," *New York Times*, March 18, 2021, https://www.nytimes.com/2021/03/18/business/media/disney-pay-discrimination-lawsuit.html.

Chapter 2. Script Market to Pitch Meetings (Development Gap)

1. Stephen Galloway, "'Screenwriting Is Really a Bastardized Form': The Writer Roundtable," *Hollywood Reporter*, November 15, 2018, https://www.hollywoodreporter.com/features/screenwriting-is-a-bastardized-form-writer-roundtable-1160626; Rebecca Ford, "Heroes of Horror, Sci-Fi and Supervillains: The Genre Roundtable," *Hollywood Reporter*, July 18, 2018, https://www.hollywoodreporter.com/features/fanboys-fangirls-are-loudest-voice-genre-roundtable-1127307; "Producer Roundtable," *Hollywood Reporter*, July 18, 2018, https://www.hollywoodreporter.com/news/watch-thrs-full-producer-roundtable-judd-apatow-amy-pascal-seth-rogen-jason-blum-eric-fellner-ridley-1081439.

2. Interview by author, Elizabeth Martin, screenwriter, phone, August 2017.

3. Lauzen, "2019 Celluloid Ceiling."

4. Timothy Havens, *Black Television Travels: African American Media around the Globe* (New York: New York University Press, 2013).

5. Janet Wasko, *How Hollywood Works* (London: Sage, 2003), 32–37.

6. Havens, "Towards a Structuration Theory of Media Intermediaries," 50.

7. Havens, *Black Television Travels*, 3.

8. Henderson, "The Culture behind Closed Doors," 152.

9. Interview by author, producer, Los Angeles, July 2017.

10. In a stark contrast to the female-driven films of contemporary Hollywood, films of the 1930s and 1940s studio era with female stars and appealing to female audiences were a valuable business model during that period. European stars like Greta Garbo and Marlene Dietrich were important for the international market as the major studios increasingly expanded their business operations globally. As discussed in chapter 1, the women's picture was one of the most bankable genres for Hollywood through World War II, leading female stars like Bette Davis, Katharine Hepburn, and Barbara Stanwyck to dominate the domestic box office.

11. Lauzen, "2018 Celluloid Ceiling."

12. Margaret Heidenry, "When the Spec Script Was King," *Vanity Fair*, February 8, 2013, https://www.vanityfair.com/culture/2013/03/will-spec-script-screenwriters-rise-again.

13. Heidenry, "When the Spec Script Was King."

14. "The Spec Scripts and Women," *Women and Hollywood*, June 21, 2013, https://womenandhollywood.com/the-spec-scripts-and-women/; Scott Myers, "Gender as Represented in Spec Script Deals: 1991–2015," *Go into the Story*, April 13, 2016, https://gointothestory.blcklst.com/gender-as-represented-in-spec-script-deals-1991-2015-1cceba3c4ca0.

15. Francke, *Script Girls*, 100; Nina J. Easton, "A Woman in the Upper Reaches," *Los Angeles Times*, October 16, 1990, https://www.latimes.com/archives/la-xpm-1990-10-16-ca-2617-story.html.

16. Dana Kennedy, "Screenwriters Adjust to Being Bit Players Again," *New York*

Times, December 9, 2001, https://www.nytimes.com/2001/12/09/movies/film
-screenwriters-adjust-to-being-bit-players-again.html; Bernardi and Hoxter, *Off the Page*, 78.

17. Miranda J. Banks, "Oral History and Media Industries: Theorizing the Personal in Production History," *Cultural Studies* 28, no. 4 (2014): 550.

18. Brooks Barnes, "In Blockbuster Era, No Room at the Box Office for the Middlebrow," *New York Times*, November 23, 2019, https://www.nytimes.com/2019/11/23 /business/media/in-blockbuster-era-no-room-at-the-box-office-for-the-middlebrow .html.

19. Jason Bailey, "How the Death of Mid-Budget Cinema Left a Generation of Iconic Filmmakers MIA," *Flavorwire*, December 9, 2014, https://www.flavorwire .com/492985/how-the-death-of-mid-budget-cinema-left-a-generation-of-iconic -filmmakers-mia.

20. Christina Lane, "Susan Seidelman's Contemporary Films: The Feminist Art of Self-Reinvention in a Changing Technological Landscape," in *Indie Reframed: Women's Filmmaking and Contemporary American Independent Cinema*, ed. Linda Badley, Claire Perkins, and Michele Schreiber (Edinburgh: Edinburgh University Press, 2016), 71–72.

21. Gregg Kilday, "Elizabeth Gabler's Fox 2000 to Shutter amid Disney Reorganization," *Hollywood Reporter*, March 21, 2019, https://www.hollywoodreporter.com/news /elizabeth-gablers-fox-2000-shutter-disney-reorganization-1196298.

22. Nicole Sperling, "Why Hollywood Is 'Shocked and Devastated' over Fox 2000's Imminent Death," *Vanity Fair*, March 29, 2019, https://www.vanityfair.com /hollywood/2019/03/disney-fox-2000-elizabeth-gabler.

23. "Actress, Producer, Director Elizabeth Banks on Making It in the Mainstream," *The Business*, podcast hosted by Kim Masters, KCRW, March 29, 2019, https://www .kcrw.com/culture/shows/the-business/elizabeth-banks-on-directing-producing-and -blazing-a-trail-in-the-big-leagues/actress-producer-director-elizabeth-banks-on -making-it-in-the-mainstream.

24. Rebecca Keegan, "Elizabeth Banks, Max Handelman Re-Up Deals at Universal and WBTV, Talk 'Charlie's Angels' Reboot and 'Shrill' Abortion Scene," *Hollywood Reporter*, June 12, 2019, https://www.hollywoodreporter.com/news/general-news /elizabeth-banks-max-handelman-rebooting-charlies-angels-shrill-1217370/.

25. Justin Kroll, "Elizabeth Banks to Direct, Star in 'Invisible Woman' for Universal," *Variety*, November 26, 2019, https://variety.com/2019/film/news/elizabeth -banks-invisible-woman-universal-1203417107.

26. Dave McNary, "Fact on Pacts: Studios Have Few First-Look Deals with Women," *Variety*, October 25, 2017, https://variety.com/2017/biz/news/studios-first -look-deals-women-1202598087.

27. Peter Bart, ". . . Cuts Are Making Backlots Look Leaner & Meaner," *Variety: International Weekly* (August 11–17, 2008), 1; Tatiana Siegel and Borys Kit, "How Film Producers Became the New Expendables: 'There's Panic and Confusion,'" *Hollywood Reporter*, August 15, 2019, https://www.hollywoodreporter.com/features/why -hollywood-studio-film-producer-deals-are-disappearing-1231089.

28. Tatiana Siegel and Borys Kit, "How Film Producers Became the New Expendables."

29. Dave McNary, "Facts on Pacts: Sony Ups Roster Despite Recent Challenges,"

Variety, March 11, 2015, https://variety.com/2015/biz/news/despite-recent-troubles-sony-packs-on-the-first-look-deals-1201450041/; "Facts on Pacts: Studio-Producer Deals Retreat as Sony, Warner Bros. Pull Back," Variety, March 24, 2016, https://variety.com/2016/film/news/studio-producers-deals-1201736686/; "Fact on Pacts: Studios Have Few First-Look Deals with Women." Amy Pascal landed a lucrative multiyear producing deal with Sony as part of a settlement after her firing. When the deal expired in 2019, Pascal signed a new first-look deal with Universal.

30. Carman, *Independent Stardom*, 2–3.

31. Tino Balio, *United Artists, Volume 1, 1919–1950: The Company Built by the Stars* (Madison: University of Wisconsin Press, 2009), 136–140.

32. Gwilym Mumford, "Jessica Chastain: The Portrayal of Women in Films Is Disturbing," *Guardian*, May 30, 2017, https://www.theguardian.com/film/2017/may/30/jessica-chastain-women-cannes-disturbing-palme-dor.

33. Brent Lang, "Jessica Chastain Spy Thriller '355' Sells to Universal," *Variety*, May 12, 2018, https://variety.com/2018/film/news/jessica-chastain-spy-thriller-355-sells-to-universal-1202808145/.

34. Brent Lang and Rebecca Rubin, "Reese Witherspoon's Hello Sunshine Sold for $900 Million to Media Company Backed by Blackstone," *Variety*, August 2, 2021, https://variety.com/2021/film/news/reese-witherspoon-hello-sunshine-sold-1235032618/.

35. Interview by author, independent producer, Skype, September 2017.

36. Dave McNary, "Studios Cut Production Deals," *Variety*, October 27, 2012, https://variety.com/2012/film/news/studios-cut-production-deals-1118061274/; McNary, "Fact on Pacts: Studios Have Few First-Look Deals with Women."

37. Interview by author, Mark Horowitz, former sales agent and producer, Los Angeles, April 2017.

38. Obst, *Hello, He Lied*, 37.

39. Justin Wyatt, *High Concept: Movies and Marketing in Hollywood* (Austin: University of Texas Press, 1994), 13.

40. John Thornton Caldwell, "Cultures of Production: Studying Industry's Deep Texts, Reflexive Rituals, and Managed Self-Disclosures," in *Media Industries: History, Theory, and Method*, ed. Jennifer Holt and Alisa Perren (Malden, MA: Wiley-Blackwell, 2009), 203.

41. Interview by author, screenwriter, Skype, August 2017.

42. Interview by author, screenwriter, Los Angeles, July 2016.

43. Interview by author, screenwriter, Zoom, November 2020.

44. Miranda J. Banks, *The Writers: A History of American Screenwriters and Their Guild* (New Brunswick, NJ: Rutgers University Press, 2016), 7.

45. Interview by author, screenwriter, Skype, July 2017.

46. Catherine Shoard, "Michelle Williams 'Paralysed' by News She Was Paid $1000 While Male Co-Star Got $1.5 Million," *Guardian*, April 3, 2019, https://www.theguardian.com/film/2019/apr/03/michelle-williams-paralysed-by-news-she-was-paid-1000-mark-wahlberg.

47. Dave McNary, "Amy Pascal Talks Getting 'Fired,' Sony Hack and Angelina Jolie Emails in Candid Interview," *Variety*, February 11, 2015, http://variety.com/2015/film/news/amy-pascal-sony-angelina-jolie-obama-hack-the-interview-1201431167/.

48. Lisa Respers France, "How Jessica Chastain Got Octavia Spencer Five Times

the Pay," *CNN*, January 26, 2018, https://www.cnn.com/2018/01/26/entertainment
/octavia-spencer-jessica-chastain-pay/index.html; Jude Dry, "Octavia Spencer Says
Jessica Chastain Helped Her Get Five Times Her Salary: 'She Is Walking the Walk,'"
IndieWire, January 24, 2018, https://www.indiewire.com/2018/01/octavia-spencer
-jessica-chastain-pay-equity-women-1201921282/; SAG-AFTRA, "Favored Nations,"
SAG-AFTRA official site, https://www.sagaftra.org/favored-nations-4.

49. Margaret Heidenry, "How Hollywood Salaries Really Work," *Vanity Fair*, February 12, 2018, https://www.vanityfair.com/hollywood/2018/02/hollywood-movie
-salaries-wage-gap-equality.

50. Interview by author, screenwriter, Zoom, October 2020.

51. Darnell M. Hunt, "Renaissance in Reverse?" *2016 Hollywood Writers Report*,
Writers Guild of America, March 2016, https://www.wga.org/uploadedFiles/who_we
_are/HWR16.pdf.

52. Interview by author, screenwriter, Los Angeles, July 2017.

53. Interview by author, screenwriter, Los Angeles, July 2018.

54. Julia Carrie Wong, "TV Writers Circulate Anonymous Spreadsheet to Fight
Gender Pay Gap," *Guardian*, January 25, 2018, https://www.theguardian.com/tv-and
-radio/2018/jan/24/tv-writers-women-men-pay-gap-anonymous-spreadsheet.

55. Rebecca Sun, *Crazy Rich Asians* Co-Writer Exits Sequel amid Pay Disparity Dispute," *Hollywood Reporter*, September 4, 2019, https://www.hollywoodreporter.com
/news/crazy-rich-asians-screenwriter-adele-lim-exits-sequel-pay-disparity-dispute
-1236431.

56. Rebecca Sun, "Why Hollywood's Pay Gap for Women of Color Is Wider,"
Hollywood Reporter, January 17, 2018, https://www.hollywoodreporter.com/news
/why-hollywoods-pay-gap-women-color-is-wider-infrequent-golden-opportunities
-1075057.

57. Ryan Faughnder, "'Crazy Rich Asians' Could Be Groundbreaking for Hollywood," *Los Angeles Times*, August 14, 2018, https://www.latimes.com/business
/hollywood/la-fi-ct-crazy-rich-asians-warner-bros-20180814-story.html; Pamela
McClintock, "'Crazy Rich Asians' Becomes Most Successful Studio Rom-Com in 9
Years at the U.S. Box Office," *Hollywood Reporter*, September 3, 2018, https://www
.hollywoodreporter.com/news/crazy-rich-asians-becomes-successful-studio-rom
-9-years-1139353.

58. As paraphrased in Sun, *Crazy Rich Asians* Co-Writer Exits Sequel."

59. Francke, *Script Girls*, 137.

60. Brent Lang, "Star Wars: Lucasfilm Chief Previews 'Rogue One' and Han Solo
Spinoff," *Variety*, November 22, 2016, http://variety.com/2016/film/features/star
-wars-rogue-one-lucasfilm-jj-abrams-kathleen-kennedy-1201923806/.

61. Scott Mendelson, "Female Directors Don't Need 'Experience'—They Just
Need to Get Hired," *Forbes*, November 28, 2016, https://www.forbes.com/sites
/scottmendelson/2016/11/28/female-directors-dont-need-experience-they-just-need
-to-get-hired/#562e191050e8.

62. Yohana Desta, "How Do So Many White, Male Indie Directors Leap to the Big
Blockbusters?" *Mashable*, June 29, 2015, http://mashable.com/2015/06/29/hollywood
-white-male-directors/#ensOumekjqqG.

63. Francke, *Script Girls*, 100.

64. Amy Larocca, "Interview: Nancy Meyers," *New York Magazine*, September 7, 2015, https://www.vulture.com/2015/09/nancy-meyers-amy-larocca-in-conversation.html.

65. Interview by author, Elizabeth Martin and Lauren Hynek, screenwriters, Skype, August 2017.

66. Peter Sciretta, "Carrie Fisher, Script Doctor," *Slash Film*, December 29, 2016, https://www.slashfilm.com/carrie-fisher-script-doctor/.

67. Geena Davis, *Fresh Air*, hosted by Terry Gross, National Public Radio, August 7, 2019, https://www.npr.org/2019/08/07/749067994/this-changes-everything-geena -davis-on-empowering-women-in-hollywood.

68. Tatiana Siegel, "Leslie Dixon Addresses WGA Standoff," *Hollywood Reporter*, June 21, 2019, https://www.hollywoodreporter.com/news/leslie-dixon-wga-standoff -why-money-will-never-be-same-writers-1220221.

69. Tatiana Siegel, "Top Scribes Reap Pic Rewrite Riches," *Hollywood Reporter*, April 24, 2010, https://variety.com/2010/film/features/top-scribes-reap-pic-rewrite-riches -1118018205/.

70. Robert Mitchell, "Phoebe Waller-Bridge to Polish 'Bond 25' Script," *Variety*, April 17, 2019, https://variety.com/2019/film/news/phoebe-waller-bridge-bond-25 -script-1203191429/; Antonia Blyth, "Phoebe Waller-Bridge on Bringing Bond into the Present," *Deadline*, June 5, 2019, https://deadline.com/2019/06/phoebe-waller -bridge-bond-25-eclipse-fleabag-killing-eve-emmys-1202626221/; Ryan Lattanzio, "Here's How Phoebe Waller-Bridge Polished the 'No Time to Die' Script," *IndieWire*, February 24, 2020, https://www.indiewire.com/2020/02/heres-how-phoebe-waller -bridge-polished-the-no-time-to-die-script-1202213218/.

71. Interview by author, screenwriter, phone, December 2020 and May 2022.

72. Brooks Barnes, "Marvel Studios Unveils Diverse Film Lineup at Comic-Con," *New York Times*, 20 July 2019, https://www.nytimes.com/2019/07/20/business /media/marvel-film-lineup-comic-con.html; Borys Kit, "Marvel Studios' The Eternals' Finds Its Director with Chloe Zhao," *Hollywood Reporter*, September 21, 2018, https://www.hollywoodreporter.com/movies/movie-features/chloe-zhao-direct -marvel-studios-eternals-1143547/; Chris Evangelista, "'Eternals' Director Chloé Zhao Also Wrote the Screenplay," */Film*, January 4, 2021, https://www.slashfilm .com/578651/eternals-screenplay/; Christi Carras, "How Director Chloé Zhao Made 'Eternals' Epic, Intimate and Unlike Anything Else in the MCU," *Los Angeles Times*, November 4, 2021, https://www.latimes.com/entertainment-arts/movies/story/2021 -11-04/eternals-director-chloe-zhao-marvel-mcu.

73. Interview by author, Allison Schroeder, screenwriter, phone, August 2017, January 2018, and May 2022; Borys Kit, "'Frozen 2' Co-Writer Allison Schroeder Tackling 'Minecraft' Movie," *Hollywood Reporter*, June 24, 2019, https://www .hollywoodreporter.com/heat-vision/frozen-2-writer-allison-schroeder-tackling -minecraft-movie-1220710.

74. Bernardi and Hoxter, *Off the Page*, 82–83.

75. Rebecca Ford, "Disney Developing Live-Action 'Mulan' (Exclusive)," *Hollywood Reporter*, March 30, 2015, https://www.hollywoodreporter.com/news/general-news /disney-developing-live-action-mulan-784892/.

76. Ciara Wardlow, "'Mulan' Director Niki Caro Talks Authenticity, Research, and Responsible Filmmaking," *Film School Rejects*, August 31, 2020, https:// filmschoolrejects.com/niki-caro-mulan-interview/.

77. Justin Chang, "'Mulan' Reboot Is Beautiful, but Fails to Breathe New Life into an Old Tale," *NPR Movie Reviews*, September 3, 2020, https://www.npr.org/2020/09 /04/908349501/mulan-reboot-is-beautiful-but-fails-to-breathe-new-life-into-an -old-tale; Trilby Beresford and Abbey White, "'Mulan': What the Critics Are Saying," *Hollywood Reporter*, September 3, 2020, https://www.hollywoodreporter.com/news /general-news/mulan-what-the-critics-are-saying-4054876/. In 2019, the film's lead, Liu Yifei, spoke out in support of the Hong Kong police despite their brutal response to pro-democracy political protests. The backlash ultimately led to a social media call to #BoycottMulan. After the August 2020 release, *Mulan* came under criticism again, which was widely covered in the press, for shooting locations in Xinjiang, the province of China where the government has forced the Uighur Muslim population into mass internment camps. Amy Qin and Edward Wong, "Why Calls to Boycott 'Mulan' over Concerns about China Are Growing," *New York Times*, September 8, 2020, https://www.nytimes.com/2020/09/08/world/asia/china-mulan-xinjiang.html.

78. Mia Galuppo and Pamela McClintock, "From 'Bond' to 'Mulan': All the Films Delayed Due to Coronavirus," *Hollywood Reporter*, March 17, 2020, https:// www.hollywoodreporter.com/heat-vision/bond-mulan-film-releases-delayed-due -coronavirus-1285087.

79. Adam B. Vary and Rebecca Rubin, "With 'Mulan,' Disney Tests Out Entirely New Early VOD Model," *Variety*, August 4, 2020, https://variety.com/2020/film/news /mulan-disney-plus-premiere-1234711185/; Kate Fortmueller, *Hollywood Shutdown: Production, Distribution, and Exhibition in the Time of Covid* (Austin: University of Texas Press, 2021).

80. Theresa Rebeck, "What Came Next," in *Double Bind: Women on Ambition*, ed. Robin Romm (New York: Liveright Publishing, 2017), 22.

81. Interview by author, screenwriter, Los Angeles, April 2017.

82. Interview by author, screenwriter, Skype, August 2018.

83. Interview by author, screenwriter, Zoom, November 2021.

84. Interview by author, screenwriter, Los Angeles, July 2018.

85. Henderson, "The Culture behind Closed Doors," 146–147.

86. Dowd, "Women of Hollywood."

87. Interview by author, Allison Schroeder, screenwriter, phone, August 2017 and January 2018.

88. Interview by author, Allison Schroeder, screenwriter, phone, August 2017.

89. Dana Harris-Bridson, "Taraji P. Henson and Octavia Spencer Tearful but Eloquent as 'Hidden Figures' Considers Its Oscars Options in Toronto," *IndieWire*, September 11, 2016, https://www.indiewire.com/2016/09/taraji-p-henson-octavia -spencer-are-tearful-hidden-figures-oscars-1201725687/.

90. "'Hidden Figures' Scribe Allison Schroeder Is Used to Being the Only Woman in the Room," *KPCC Arts & Entertainment*, hosted by John Horn and Elyssa Dud-ley, January 4, 2017, https://www.scpr.org/programs/the-frame/2017/01/04/54212 /hidden-figures-scribe-allison-schroeder-is-used-to/.

91. Tracy Oliver, "'Girls Trip' Writer: How My Pitches about Women of Color Are Becoming More Accepted," *Hollywood Reporter*, December 8, 2017, https://www .hollywoodreporter.com/news/girls-trip-writer-how-my-pitches-women-color-are -becoming-more-accepted-guest-column-1063559.

92. Interview by author, independent producer, phone, September 2017.

93. Interview by author, independent producer, phone, August 2018.

94. A. O. Scott, "Review: Hidden Figures," *New York Times*, December 22, 2016, https://www.nytimes.com/2016/12/22/movies/hidden-figures-review.html?referrer=google_kp.

95. Interview by author, Elizabeth Martin and Lauren Hynek, screenwriters, February 2018.

96. Clare O'Connor, "Google Sued for Gender Discrimination by Female Former Employees," *Forbes*, September 14, 2017, https://www.forbes.com/sites/clareoconnor/2017/09/14/google-sued-for-gender-discrimination-by-female-former-employees/#68f4ba7650c9.

97. Interview by author, Elizabeth Martin and Lauren Hynek, screenwriters, July 2018 and May 2022.

98. Mary McNamara, "'She Said' Is More Important than 'All the President's Men.' There, I Said It," *Los Angeles Times*, September 12, 2019, https://www.latimes.com/entertainment-arts/books/story/2019-09-11/she-said-is-more-important-that-all-the-presidents-men-there-i-said-it.

99. Interview by author, producer, phone, May 2018.

Chapter 3. Production Work and Gendered Cultures (Leadership Gap)

1. Interview by author, producer, phone, May 2018.

2. Vicki Mayer, *Below the Line: Producers and Production Studies in the New Television Economy* (Durham, NC: Duke University Press, 2011); Hill, *Never Done*; Erin Hill, "Recasting the Casting Director: Managed Change, Gendered Labor," in *Making Media Work: Cultures of Management in the Entertainment Industries*, ed. Derek Johnson, Derek Kompare, and Avi Santo (New York: New York University Press, 2014), 142–164; Miranda J. Banks, "Production Studies," *Feminist Media Histories* 4, no. 2 (2018): 157–161; Banks, "Gender below-the-Line," 87–98; O'Brien, *Women, Inequality and Media Work*; Liddy and O'Brien, *Media Work, Mothers and Motherhood*.

3. Mayer, *Below the Line*, 4.

4. Schuyler Moore, "Why Film Budgets Are Important, beyond the Cost of Production," *Forbes*, April 13, 2019, https://www.forbes.com/sites/schuylermoore/2019/04/13/the-importance-of-film-budgets/?sh=6b06a35b27f5.

5. Mayer, *Below the Line*, 4.

6. Banks, "Gender below-the-Line," 91.

7. Janet Staiger, "The Package-Unit System: Unit Management after 1955," in *The Classical Hollywood Cinema: Film Style & Mode of Production to 1960*, by David Bordwell, Janet Staiger, and Kristin Thompson (New York: Columbia University Press, 1985), 336.

8. Herbert, Lotz, and Punathambekar, *Media Industry Studies*, 35.

9. Cynthia Chris, "Authorship and Auteurism," in *The Craft of Criticism: Critical Media Studies in Practice*, ed. Michael Kackman and Mary Celeste Kearney (New York: Routledge, 2018), 109–121.

10. Smyth, *Nobody's Girl Friday*, 16.

11. Deborah Jermyn, *Nancy Meyers* (London: Bloomsbury, 2017), 125.

12. Hill, *Never Done*, 2016.

13. Amy Dawes, "Steven Spielberg: Icons of the Century," *Variety*, October 16, 2005, https://variety.com/2005/scene/vpage/steven-spielberg-1117930615/; Derek Elley, "Quentin Tarantino: Hollywood's Boy Wonder," *Variety*, October 30, 1994, https://variety.com/1994/tv/reviews/quentin-tarantino-hollywood-s-boy-wonder -1200438747/.

14. Dana Kennedy, "Film: An Impatient Sisterhood," *New York Times*, June 2, 2002, https://www.nytimes.com/2002/06/02/movies/film-an-impatient-sisterhood.html.

15. Anthony Kaufman, "Jason Reitman on Directing 'Up in the Air': Former Wunderkind Comes into His Own, Finds the Magic," *Variety*, December 1, 2009, https://variety.com/2009/film/awards/jason-reitman-on-directing-up-in-the-air -1118012007/; Joe Utichi, "Damien Chazelle Finds the 'Fertile Terrain' of an Industry in Upheaval—Deadline Disruptors," *Deadline Hollywood*, May 23, 2017, https:// deadline.com/2017/05/damien-chazelle-la-la-land-first-man-movie-interview -1202095257/.

16. Chevigny, "Can She Pull It Off?"

17. Maureen Dowd, "Women of Hollywood."

18. Veronique Hyland, "Gal Gadot Is Unafraid to Face Industry Injustice," *Elle*, October 18, 2021, https://www.elle.com/culture/celebrities/a37927840/gal-gadot -women-in-hollywood-2021/.

19. Kim Masters, "Ray Fisher Opens Up about 'Justice League,' Joss Whedon and Warners: 'I Don't Believe Some of These People Are Fit for Leadership,'" *Hollywood Reporter*, April 6, 2021, https://www.hollywoodreporter.com/movies/movie-news /ray-fisher-opens-up-about-justice-league-joss-whedon-and-warners-i-dont-believe -some-of-these-people-are-fit-for-leadership-4161658/.

20. Anthony Kaufman, "Where Are the Girl-Wonders? Everywhere—but Who Noticed?" *Filmmaker Magazine*, February 21, 2019, https://filmmakermagazine.com /107053-where-are-the-girl-wonders-everywhere-but-who-noticed/.

21. Kate Erbland, "Every Studio Film Directed by Female Filmmakers Coming Out in 2019 and 2020," *IndieWire*, January, 2, 2019, https://www.indiewire.com/2019/01 /studio-film-directed-by-female-filmmakers-2019-2020-1202030909/; Cara Buckley, "More Women than Ever Are Directing Major Films, Study Says," *New York Times*, January 2, 2020, https://www.nytimes.com/2020/01/02/movies/women-directors -hollywood.html; Benjamin Lee, "Will 2020 Be a Turning Point for Female Film-Makers?" *Guardian*, February 4, 2020, https://www.theguardian.com/film/2020/feb /04/2020-turning-point-female-film-makers-sundance-festival.

22. Kaufman, "Where Are the Girl-Wonders?"

23. "Greta Gerwig Explores Mother-Daughter Love (and Angst) in 'Lady Bird,'" *Fresh Air*, hosted by Terry Gross, National Public Radio, November 16, 2017, https:// www.npr.org/2017/11/16/564579012/greta-gerwig-explores-mother-daughter-love -and-angst-in-lady-bird.

24. As quoted in Wheeler Winston Dixon, "Ida Lupino," *Senses of Cinema*, April 2009, http://www.sensesofcinema.com/2009/great-directors/ida-lupino/#6.

25. Catalyst, "The Double-Bind Dilemma for Women in Leadership: Damned If You Do, Doomed If You Don't," July 15, 2007, https://www.catalyst.org/research/the -double-bind-dilemma-for-women-in-leadership-damned-if-you-do-doomed-if-you -dont/.

26. Chevigny, "Can She Pull It Off?"

27. Interview by author, director, phone, July 2018.

28. Pamela Romanowsky, "The Side of Hollywood You Never Hear About," *Refinery29*, August 29, 2016, https://www.refinery29.com/en-us/2016/08/121399 /hollywood-sexism-female-director-pamela-romanowsky.

29. Elizabeth Wagmeister, "'The Handmaid's Tale's' Reed Morano on 'Widening the Pool' of Female Directors," *Variety*, August 9, 2017, https://variety.com/2017/tv /awards/reed-morano-the-handmaids-tale-divorce-emmys-interview-1202514756/.

30. "Was Offered 'Black Widow' Film by Marvel Studios, Says Lucrecia Martel," *Pioneer*, October 30, 2018, https://www.dailypioneer.com/2018/entertainment/was -offered—black-widow—film-by-marvel-studios—says-lucrecia-martel.html.

31. Cath Clark, "'I Enjoy How Sexy She Is, as Long as She's in Control': Black Widow's Cate Shortland on Scarlett Johansson," *Guardian*, July 2, 2021, https:// www.theguardian.com/film/2021/jul/02/i-enjoy-how-sexy-she-is-as-long-as-shes-in -control-black-widows-cate-shortland-on-scarlett-johansson; Kelsea Stahler, "Never Forget, Marvel Owed Black Widow Her Solo Movie," *Refinery29*, July 8, 2021, https:// www.refinery29.com/en-us/2021/07/10557358/black-widow-sexism-in-mcu-movies -chronological-list.

32. Shawna Kidman, "The Disneyfication of Authorship: Above-the-Line Creative Labor in the Franchise Era," *Journal of Film and Video* 73, no. 3 (Fall 2021): 3–22.

33. Kate Erbland, "'Black Widow': Why Director Cate Shortland Knew 'Really Gritty' Violence Was Essential," *IndieWire*, July 8, 2021, https://www.indiewire.com /2021/07/black-widow-violence-fighting-1234645982/.

34. Adam B. Vary, "Cate Shortland Turned Down Directing 'Black Widow.' So Scarlett Johansson Called Her on Zoom," *Variety*, 2021, https://variety.com/2021/film /news/cate-shortland-black-widow-scarlett-johansson-1235008158/; Clark, "'I Enjoy How Sexy She Is, as Long as She's in Control.'"

35. "Gina Prince-Bythewood's 'The Old Guard'" *The Business*, podcast hosted by Kim Masters, July 27, 2020, https://www.kcrw.com/culture/shows/the-business/gina -prince-bythewood-old-guard.

36. Rebeck, "What Came Next," 28–29.

37. Interview by author, director, phone, June 2021.

38. Interview by author, director, Los Angeles, July 2018; interview by author, director, Los Angeles, April 2017.

39. Melena Ryzik, "What It's Really Like to Work in Hollywood (If You're Not a Straight White Man)," *New York Times*, February 24, 2016, https://www.nytimes.com /interactive/2016/02/24/arts/hollywood-diversity-inclusion.html.

40. Interview by author, Ry Russo-Young, Zoom, May 2021.

41. Mynette Louie, "A Female Producer Explains 4 Ways Women Get a Raw Deal in Hollywood," *Vulture*, July 7, 2015, https://www.vulture.com/2015/07/how-hollywood -discriminates-female-filmmakers.html.

42. Interview by author, director, phone, March 2018.

43. Timothy Havens and Amanda D. Lotz, *Understanding Media Industries*, 2nd ed. (Oxford: Oxford University Press, 2017).

44. Interview by author, director, Zoom, May 2021.

45. Interview by author, independent producer, phone, September 2017; Alejandro

Pardo, "The Film Producer as a Creative Force," *Wide Screen* 2, no. 2 (2010): 1; Andrew Spicer, A. T. McKenna, and Christopher Meir, eds., *Beyond the Bottom Line: The Producer in Film and Television Studies* (New York: Bloomsbury, 2016).

46. Banks, "Gender below-the-Line," 87.

47. Lauzen, "2019 Celluloid Ceiling."

48. Ben Schott, "Assembling the Billing Block," *New York Times*, February 23, 2013, https://archive.nytimes.com/www.nytimes.com/interactive/2013/02/24/opinion /sunday/ben-schott-movies-billing-blocks.html.

49. The Producer's Mark was introduced in 2013 to ensure that creative producers receive proper credit. Producers Guild of America, "Code of Credits: Theatrical Motion Pictures"; Producers Guild of America, "Rules and Procedures for Producers Mark Eligibility—Motion Pictures," available via PDF, March 2021; Producers Guild of America, "Producers Mark (p.g.a.)," https://producersguild.org/producers-mark/; Gregg Kilday, "PGA Awards: Producers' Mark Introduced to Help Keep Credits Honest," *Hollywood Reporter*, January 25, 2013, https://www.hollywoodreporter.com /movies/movie-news/pga-awards-producers-mark-introduced-414261/.

50. Interviews by author, 2017–2020.

51. Interview by author, Alix Madigan, producer, phone, August 9, 2018.

52. Interview by author, independent producer, phone, September 2017.

53. Interview by author, Alicia Van Couvering, producer, phone, June 9, 2021.

54. Interview by author, Van Couvering.

55. Sustainability and precarious labor are major issues for independent producers, many of whom have to take on additional nonproducing jobs to pay their bills. The 2021 "Producer Sustainability Survey Report," commissioned by Rebecca Green, who runs the industry platform Dear Producer, published the results of a survey of 550 producers: 41 percent stated they earned $25,000 or less from producing work in 2019, and 61 percent reported they cannot afford health care. https://dearproducer .com/wp-content/uploads/2021/02/REPORT-DearProducer-Sustainability-Survey -Jan2021-FINAL-1.pdf.

56. Siegel and Kit, "How Film Producers Became the New Expendables."

57. Kathleen E. Grogan, "How the Entire Scientific Community Can Confront Gender Bias in the Workplace," *Nature Ecology & Evolution* 33 (January 2019): 3–6.

58. David Hesmondhalgh and Sarah Baker, "Sex, Gender and Work Segregation in the Cultural Industries," *Sociological Review* 63, no. 1 (2015): 26.

59. David Cantor, "What's Keeping Girls from Translating 'Soft Skills' Superiority into STEM Field Success?" *Forbes*, February 15, 2019, https://www.forbes.com/sites /the74/2019/02/15/whats-keeping-girls-from-translating-soft-skills-superiority-into -stem-field-success/?sh=7f7785d9d67b; Renyi Hong, "Soft Skills and Hard Numbers: Gender Discourse in Human Resources," *Big Data & Society* (July–December 2016): 1–13.

60. Interview by author, producer, Los Angeles, July 2017.

61. Interview by author, producer, phone, September 2018.

62. O'Brien, *Women, Inequality and Media Work*, 39.

63. Arlie Hochschild, *The Managed Heart: Commercialization of Human Feeling* (Berkeley: University of California Press, 2012). The ways in which Erin Hill, Miranda J. Banks, Vicki Mayer, and Anne O'Brien use emotional labor as a way to

examine the layers of gendered media work have greatly influenced my own thinking throughout this book project. Mayer and Hill each have extensively explored how emotional labor is embedded in below-the-line work predominantly held by women, including the roles of casting directors and secretaries. See Mayer, *Below the Line*; Hill, *Never Done*.

64. Hochschild, *Managed Heart*, 7.

65. Amy S. Wharton, "The Sociology of Emotional Labor," *Annual Review of Sociology* 35 (2009): 150.

66. Interview by author, independent producer, phone, September 2017.

67. Hochschild, *Managed Heart*, 167.

68. Interview by author, producer, Los Angeles, July 26, 2017.

69. O'Brien, *Women, Inequality and Media Work,* 36.

70. O'Brien, *Women, Inequality and Media Work,* 40.

71. Interview by author, producer, phone, June 2021.

72. Interview by author, producer, Zoom, October 2020.

73. Warner, "Strategies for Success?" 173.

74. B. Ruby Rich, "What Is at Stake: Gender, Race, Media, or How to Brexit Hollywood," *Film Quarterly* 70, no. 1 (2016): 7; see also Christina N. Baker's discussion of Effie Brown and *Project Greenlight* in her book, *Contemporary Black Women Filmmakers*.

75. Effie Brown, "'People Didn't Want to Work with Me' after Calling Out Matt Damon on 'Project Greenlight' Diversity Issues," *Hollywood Reporter*, June 18, 2020, https://www.hollywoodreporter.com/news/general-news/producer-effie-brown -reflects-matt-damon-project-greenlight-1298785/.

76. Brown, "'People Didn't Want to Work with Me'"; Lorraine Wheat, "'Dear White People' Producer Effie T. Brown Named CEO at Gamechanger Films," *Variety*, January 7, 2020, https://variety.com/2020/film/news/gamechanger-films-effie-t-brown -ceo-1203460169/.

77. Interview by author, producer, Los Angeles, April 2017.

78. Peter Frost and Sandra Robinson, "The Toxic Handler: Organizational Hero— and Casualty," *Harvard Business Review* (July–August 1999): 98.

79. Frost and Robinson, "Toxic Handler," 98.

80. Frost and Robinson, "Toxic Handler," 99.

81. Interview by author, producer, phone, June 2021.

82. Dowd, "Women of Hollywood."

83. Interview by author, producer, Los Angeles, July 2018.

84. Interview by author, producer, phone, January 2018.

85. Interview by author, producer, Los Angeles, July 2017.

86. Interview by author, producer, November 2020.

87. Interview by author, producer, phone, June 2021.

88. Hochschild, *Managed Heart*, 173.

89. Interview by author, Amy Adrion, phone, August 2018.

90. O'Brien, *Women, Inequality and Media Work*, 29.

91. Leslie Felperin, "'Half the Picture': Film Review Sundance 2018," *Hollywood Reporter*, January 23, 2018, https://www.hollywoodreporter.com/movies/movie -reviews/picture-review-1077529/.

Chapter 4. Film Festivals and Markets (Programming Gap)

1. Dorota Ostrowska, "Making Film History at the Cannes Film Festival," in *Film Festivals: History, Theory, Method Practice*, ed. Marijke de Valck, Brendan Kredell, and Skadi Loist (London: Routledge, 2016), 29.

2. Christine Vachon, *A Killer Life: How an Independent Film Producer Survives Deals and Disasters in Hollywood and Beyond* (New York: Limelight Edition, 2007), 110.

3. The Cannes Film Festival originated in France due to the perceived snubbing of French film by the Mussolini-era Venice Film Festival. While originally set to launch in 1939, due to growing political instability across Europe, the first Cannes festival was not held until 1946. For more on the history of the film festival circuit, see Marijke de Valck, *Film Festivals: From European Geopolitics to Global Cinephilia* (Amsterdam: Amsterdam University Press, 2007); Cindy Hing-Yuk Wong, *Film Festivals: Culture, People, and Power on the Global Screen* (New Brunswick, NJ: Rutgers University Press, 2011).

4. Wong, *Film Festivals*, 129–158.

5. Dina Iordanova, "Film Festival as an Industry Node," *Media Industries Journal* 1, no. 3 (2015): 9, https://quod.lib.umich.edu/cgi/p/pod/dod-idx/film-festival-as-an -industry-node.pdf?c=mij;idno=15031809.0001.302;format=pdf.

6. For further film festival studies scholarship, see de Valck, *Film Festivals*; Wong, *Film Festivals*; Dina Iordanova, ed., *The Film Festival Reader* (St. Andrews: St. Andrews Film Studies, 2013); Marijke de Valck, Brendan Kredell, and Skadi Loist, eds., *Film Festivals: History, Theory, Method, Practice* (London: Routledge, 2016).

7. "Imagined Futures: Sundance 2020," Sundance Institute website, https://www .sundance.org/festivalhistory#2020.

8. "New Study Charts the 'Post-Festival Chasm' for Women Directors," *Women and Hollywood*, June 3, 2015, https://womenandhollywood.com/new-study-charts -the-post-festival-chasm-for-women-directors-219df79b77a9/; Christina Lane, "Just Another Girl outside the Neo-Indie," in *Contemporary American Independent Film: From the Margins to the Mainstream*, ed. Chris Holmlund and Justin Wyatt (New York: Routledge, 2004), 193–209.

9. "Sundance Timeline: 1985," Sundance Institute official website, https://www .sundance.org/timeline.

10. John Pierson, *Spike, Mike, Slackers, & Dykes: A Guided Tour across a Decade of American Independent Cinema* (New York: Hyperion, 1995); Peter Biskind, *Down and Dirty Pictures: Miramax, Sundance, and the Rise of Independent Film* (New York: Simon & Schuster, 2005); Alisa Perren, *Indie, Inc.: Miramax and the Transformation of Hollywood in the 1990s* (Austin: University of Texas Press, 2012).

11. Lane, "Susan Seidelman's Contemporary Films," 70–86.

12. For further work on the American independent film industry, see Geoff King, *Indiewood, USA: Where Hollywood Meets Independent Cinema* (London: I. B. Tauris, 2009); Michael Z. Newman, *Indie: An American Film Culture* (New York: Columbia University Press, 2011); Perren, *Indie, Inc.*; Geoff King, Claire Molloy, and Yannis Tzioumakis, eds., *American Independent Cinema: Indie, Indiewood and Beyond* (London: Routledge, 2012); Linda Badley, Claire Perkins, and Michele Schreiber, eds., *Indie Reframed: Women's Filmmaking and Contemporary American Independent Cinema* (Edinburgh: Edinburgh University Press, 2016); Yannis Tzioumakis, *American Independent Cinema*, 2nd ed. (Edinburgh: Edinburgh University Press, 2017).

13. Gabriella Paeilla, "*First Cow* Director Kelly Reichardt on Making Quiet Art and the Failure of American Individualism," *GQ*, July 21, 2020, https://www.gq.com/story /first-cow-kelly-reichardt-interview.

14. Lane, "Just Another Girl outside the Neo-Indie," 195.

15. Caryn James, "Critic's Notebook: For Sundance, Struggle to Survive Success," *New York Times*, January 25, 1994, https://www.nytimes.com/1994/01/25/movies /critic-s-notebook-for-sundance-struggle-to-survive-success.html; "Interview with Rose Troche," *Fresh Air*, hosted by Terry Gross, National Public Radio, June 6, 1994, https://www.npr.org/1994/06/06/1107716/independent-film-director-producer-and -writer-rose-troche-tro-shay.

16. Lane, "Just Another Girl outside the Neo-Indie," 193; Charles Lyons and Christian Moerk, "Screen Gems Punches Up 'Girlfight' Rights," *Variety*, January 25, 2020, https://variety.com/2000/film/news/screen-gems-punches-up-girlfight-rights -1117765697/.

17. Lorenza Munoz, "How 'Girlfight' Fell Flat on Its Face," *Los Angeles Times*, February 23, 2001, https://www.latimes.com/archives/la-xpm-2001-feb-23-ca-28975-story.html.

18. Rebecca Ford, "Sundance's Top Prize Doesn't Always Open Doors for Female Directors: 7 Winners Gather to Share Stories," *Hollywood Reporter*, January 25, 2019, https://www.hollywoodreporter.com/news/7-female-winners-sundances-top-prize -gather-share-stories-1178386.

19. Stacy L. Smith, Katherine Pieper, and Marc Choueiti, "Exploring the Careers of Female Directors: Phase III," Media, Diversity, & Social Change Initiative, April 21, 2015, https://www.womeninfilm.ca/_Library/Advocacy/Sundance_phase-III-female -filmmakers-initiative.pdf; Sundance Film Festival programs, 2010–2014.

20. Kenneth Turan, "Sundance Film Festival: 'Like Crazy' Director Drake Doremus Is a Romantic," *Los Angeles Times*, January 21, 2011, https://www.latimes.com /entertainment/la-xpm-2011-jan-21-la-et-sundance-doremus-20110121-story.html.

21. Eric Kohn, "Sundance Review: A Familiar Sundance Romance in 'Like Crazy,'" *IndieWire*, January 27, 2011, https://www.indiewire.com/2011/01/sundance-review -a-familiar-sundance-romance-in-like-crazy-54574/; Peter Travers, "Film Review: 'Like Crazy,'" *Rolling Stone*, October 27, 2011, https://www.rollingstone.com/movies /movie-reviews/like-crazy-109278/.

22. Kenneth Turan, "Movie Review: 'Winter's Bone,'" *Los Angeles Times*, June 11, 2010, https://www.latimes.com/archives/la-xpm-2010-jun-11-la-et-winters-20100611 -story.html.

23. Interview by author, director, Los Angeles, March 2016.

24. Sharon Waxman, "More Deals: Roadside Buys 'Winter's Bone,'" *The Wrap*, January 30, 2010, https://www.thewrap.com/more-deals-roadside-buys-winters-bone -13708/.

25. Smith, Pieper, and Choueiti, "Exploring the Careers of Female Directors."

26. Gregg Kilday, "Maya Entertainment Snags Worldwide Rights to 'All She Can,'" *Hollywood Reporter*, May 24, 2011, https://www.hollywoodreporter.com/movies /movie-news/maya-entertainment-snags-worldwide-rights-191615/.

27. Jay A. Fernandez, "Roadside Attractions to Distribute Sundance Audience Award Winner 'Circumstance,'" *Hollywood Reporter*, February 10, 2011, https:// www.hollywoodreporter.com/movies/movie-news/roadside-attractions-distribute -sundance-audience-98103/.

28. Dowd, "Women of Hollywood."

29. In an informal conversation, a former Sundance programmer recalled an effort to secure DuVernay's first feature, *I Will Follow*, as a selection for the 2010 lineup. Sundance passed, and the film premiered at the 2010 Urbanworld Film Festival in New York City.

30. Manohla Dargis, "The Director Gap: Making History," *New York Times*, December 3, 2014, https://www.nytimes.com/2014/12/07/movies/ava-duvernay-makes -a-mark-with-selma.html.

31. Leah Rose Chernikoff, "Why Ava DuVernay Hates the Word Diversity," *Elle*, October 21, 2015, https://www.elle.com/culture/movies-tv/a31310/ava-duvernay -diversity-and-self-care/. While Trevorrow was hired to direct *Star Wars: Episode IX* in 2015, he was replaced in 2017 by J. J. Abrams. Trevorrow still received story credit on the film.

32. Paeilla, "'First Cow' Director Kelly Reichardt."

33. Dowd, "Women of Hollywood"; Louie, "A Female Producer Explains."

34. Lesli Linka Glatter, "*Homeland* Director: "What Happens to All These Women after They Direct Their First Film?," *Hollywood Reporter*, December 15, 2014, https:// www.hollywoodreporter.com/news/homeland-director-what-happens-all-754654; Desta, "How Do So Many White, Male Indie Directors Leap to the Big Blockbusters?"

35. Quoted in Rodrigo Perez, "Colin Trevorrow Expands His Twitter Comments Regarding Gender Imbalance among Directors in Hollywood," *IndieWire*, August 22, 2015, http://www.indiewire.com/2015/08/colin-trevorrow-expands-his-twitter -comments-regarding-gender-imbalance-among-directors-in-hollywood-260580/.

36. Interview by author, producer, Los Angeles, July 2018.

37. Interview by author, producer, phone, June 2021.

38. Ragan Rhyne, "Film Festival Circuit and Stakeholders," in *The Film Festival Reader*, ed. Dina Iordanova (St. Andrews: St. Andrews Film Studies, 2013), 135–150; Wong, *Film Festivals*.

39. Wong, *Film Festivals*, 141.

40. Iordanova, "Film Festival as an Industry Node," 8; Mark Peranson, "First You Get the Money, Then You Get the Power," in *The Film Festival Reader (Films Need Festivals, Festivals Need Films)*, ed. Dina Iordanova (St. Andrews: St. Andrews Film Studies, 2015), 25–26. The majority of festivals around the world operate as audience festivals. From the experimental-focused Ann Arbor Film Festival to the women-centric Bentonville Film Festival, the audience model represents a diverse group of organizations that may focus on a mode of filmmaking, identity group, or community and make up the majority of festivals operating around the world. The Dallas–Fort Worth area, where I live in Texas, holds more than twenty small local festivals each year, including the Dallas International Film Festival, Denton Black Film Festival, Festival de Cine Latino Americano, and Oak Cliff Film Festival.

41. Jeffrey Ruoff, "Introduction: Programming Film Festivals," in *Coming Soon to a Festival near You: Programming Film Festivals*, ed. Jeffrey Ruoff (St. Andrews: St. Andrews Film Studies, 2012), 3.

42. Marijke de Valck and Mimi Soeteman, "'And the Winner Is . . .': What Happens behind the Scenes of Film Festival Competitions," *International Journal of Cultural Studies* 13, no. 3 (2010): 294. See also Liz Czach, "Affective Labor and the Work of Film Festival Programming," in *Film Festivals: History, Theory, Method, Practice,*

ed. Marijke de Valck, Brendan Kredell, and Skadi Loist (London: Routledge, 2016), 196–208; Thomas Elsaesser, "Film Festival Networks: The New Topographies of Cinema in Europe (2005)," in *The Film Festival Reader*, ed. Dina Iordanova (St. Andrews: St. Andrews Film Studies, 2013), 69–96.

43. Elsaesser, "Film Festival Networks," 85.

44. Joseph Turow, *Media Systems in Society: Understanding Industries, Strategies, and Power* (New York: Longman, 1992).

45. Tracy Brown, "Women and People of Color Are 'Vastly Underrepresented' at Film Fests, Says New Study," *Los Angeles Times*, January 25, 2020, https://www .latimes.com/entertainment-arts/movies/story/2020-01-25/women-of-color -underrepresented-film-festival-inclusion-study.

46. Scott Macaulay, "IFP Screen Forward: 5 Questions for SXSW Film Director Janet Pierson," *Filmmaker Magazine*, September 23, 2015, https://filmmakermagazine .com/95752-ifp-screen-forward-5-questions-for-sxsw-film-director-janet-pierson /#.YbjHQH3MLJw.

47. Neha Aziz, "25 Years of SXSW Film Festival—Lena Dunham," South by Southwest website, November 2, 2017, https://www.sxsw.com/film/2017/25-years-sxsw -film-festival-lena-dunham/.

48. Anne del Castillo, "An Interview with Janet Pierson of SXSW," POV's Documentary Blog, March 12, 2009, https://archive.pov.org/blog/news/2009/03/an _interview_with_janet_pierso/; Joanna Robinson, "We're Not Like Other Places": How Janet Pierson Transformed SXSW," *Vanity Fair*, March 16, 2018, https://www .vanityfair.com/hollywood/2018/03/janet-pierson-sxsw-profile.

49. From 2009 to 2019, the annual Cannes posters featured either a female star (seven times) or a female star in an on-screen heteronormative couple (two times).

50. Le Collectif 50/50, "Study: Cannes Film Festival (1946–2018)," https:// collectif5050.com/en/studies/cannes-film-festival.

51. Manohla Dargis, "Pointed Fanfare over the Year of la Femme at Cannes," *New York Times*, May 14, 2015, https://www.nytimes.com/2015/05/15/movies/the-year-of -la-femme-at-the-cannes-film-festival.html.

52. Jessica Phelan, "Cannes 2012: Film Festival Accused of Sexism for Lack of Female Directors," *The World*, May 16, 2012, https://www.pri.org/stories/2012-05 -16/cannes-2012-film-festival-accused-sexism-lack-female-directors; Tim Appelo, "Cannes 2012: 700 Protesters Sign Petition Demanding More Women Directors," *Hollywood Reporter*, May 17, 2012, https://www.hollywoodreporter.com/news/cannes -2012-female-directors-protesters-petition-325721; Fanny Cottençon, Virginie Despentes, and Coline Serreau, "A Cannes, les femmes montrent leurs bobines, les hommes, leurs films," *Le Monde*, March 7, 2014, https://www.lemonde.fr/idees /article/2012/05/11/a-cannes-les-femmes-montrent-leurs-bobines-les-hommes-leurs -films_1699989_3232.html; Nick Dawson, "La Barbe's Open Letter on Women & Cannes," *Filmmaker Magazine*, May 18, 2012, https://filmmakermagazine.com/45880 -la-barbes-open-letter-on-women-cannes/#.Xuoi_RNKjIE.

53. Kate Erbland, "Cannes 2019: One Year after Gender Parity Pledge, Female-Directed Competition Titles See Small Increase," *IndieWire*, April 18, 2019, https:// www.indiewire.com/2019/04/cannes-2019-female-directed-competition-films -1202059942/.

54. Iordanova, "Film Festival as an Industry Node," 9.

55. Dargis, "Pointed Fanfare over the Year of la Femme at Cannes"; Nick Vivarelli, "'Mad Max: Fury Road' Gives Cannes a Testosterone Jolt with a Feminist Twist," *Variety*, May 14, 2015, https://variety.com/2015/film/news/mad-max-fury-road-gives-cannes-a-testosterone-jolt-with-a-feminist-twist-1201496426/.

56. André Bazin, "The Festival Viewed as a Religious Order," in *Dekalog 03: On Film Festivals*, ed. Richard Porton (New York: Wallflower Press, 2009).

57. Alex Ritman, "Cannes: Festival Stumbles over 'Flatgate' Controversy," *Hollywood Reporter*, May 19, 2015, https://www.hollywoodreporter.com/news/cannes-2015-festival-stumbles-flatgate-796747.

58. Lauren Le Vine, "Julia Roberts Went Barefoot on the Cannes Red Carpet," *Vanity Fair*, May 12, 2016, https://www.vanityfair.com/style/2016/05/julia-roberts-barefoot-cannes-red-carpet.

59. Upon attending the in-person Cannes Film Festival in 2022, I can report a slightly more relaxed dress code for attending evening gala screenings. Female attendees now have the option to wear flats as well as dress pants in addition to the traditional cocktail or evening dresses with heels. However, this policy change feels motivated more by COVID-era flexibility and less by a directive toward inclusivity.

60. Ariston Anderson, "Venice: Festival Head Alberto Barbera Defends Lack of Women in Lineup (Again)," *Hollywood Reporter*, July 25, 2018, https://www.hollywoodreporter.com/amp/news/venice-film-festival-head-defends-lack-women-lineup-again-1129767?utm_source=Sailthru&utm_medium=email&utm_campaign=THR%20Breaking%20News_now_2018-07-25%2010%3A55%3A17_jkonerman&utm_term=hollywoodreporter_breakingnews&__twitter_impression=true; Steve Pond, "Cannes' Female Troubles: Women Directors Have Always Been Scarce," *The Wrap*, May 8, 2018, https://www.thewrap.com/cannes-female-troubles-women-directors-always-scarce/.

61. Melanie Goodfellow, "Cannes: Thierry Fremaux Interview," *Screen Daily*, April 15, 2016, https://www.screendaily.com/news/cannes-thierry-fremaux-interview/5102645.article.

62. Anderson, "Venice."

63. Anderson, "Venice."

64. Brent Lang, "Does Cannes Have a Woman Problem?" *Variety*, May 8, 2018, https://variety.com/2018/film/markets-festivals/cannes-film-festival-woman-female-filmmakers-problem-1202802561/.

65. Kate Erbland, "Cannes 2017: The Competition Has a Higher Percentage of Female Filmmakers, but It's Still Pretty Bad," *IndieWire*, May 12, 2017, https://www.indiewire.com/2017/05/cannes-2017-female-filmmakers-competition-1201815568/.

66. Interview by author, film festival director and programmer, Los Angeles, July 2018.

67. Erbland, "Cannes 2017."

68. Elsaesser, "Film Festival Networks," 84.

69. Nicolas Rapold, "Venice Film Festival Tends Its Prestige with Care," *New York Times*, August 29, 2017, https://www.nytimes.com/2017/08/29/movies/venice-film-festival-tends-its-prestige-with-care.html?action=click&module=RelatedCoverage&pgtype=Article&region=Footer.

70. De Valck and Soeteman, "'And the Winner Is . . . ,'" 293; Marijke de Valck, "Fostering Art, Adding Value, Cultivating Taste: Film Festivals as Sites of Cultural

Legitimization," in *Film Festivals: History, Theory, Method Practice*, ed. Marijke de Valck, Brendan Kredell, and Skadi Loist (London: Routledge, 2016), 105.

71. Le Collectif 50/50, "Study: Cannes Film Festival."

72. Eric Kohn, "As Sundance, Berlin, and Other Major Film Festivals Hire Top Positions, Women Are Ideal Candidates," *IndieWire*, February 14, 2018, https:// www.indiewire.com/2018/02/film-festivals-programmers-women-berlin-sundance -cannes-tiff-1201928032/.

73. Turow, *Media Systems in Society*, 21.

74. Glenn Whip, "38 Women Have Come Forward to Accuse Director James Toback of Sexual Harassment," *Los Angeles Times*, October 22, 2017, https://www .latimes.com/entertainment/la-et-mn-james-toback-sexual-harassment-allegations -20171018-story.html.

75. Interview by author, producer, phone, March 2018.

76. Marc Choueiti, Stacy L. Smith, and Katherine Pieper, "Critic's Choice 2: Gender and Race/Ethnicity of Film Reviewers across 300 Top Films from 2015–2017," Annenberg Inclusion Initiative, September 2018, http://assets.uscannenberg.org/docs /critics-choice-2.pdf.

77. Le Collectif 50/50, "Film Critics in Europe: 2018–2019," https://collectif5050 .com/en/film-critics-in-europe/.

78. Rebecca Sun, "How the Film Festival Media Diversity Push Could Actually Work," *Hollywood Reporter*, June 22, 2018, https://www.hollywoodreporter.com/news /how-film-festival-media-diversity-push-could-actually-work-1121525.

79. Karen K. Ho, "A Film Festival Increases Press Diversity, but Challenges Remain," *Columbia Journalism Review*, September 13, 2019, https://www.cjr.org /analysis/tiff-press-diversity.php.

80. Sun, "How the Film Festival Media Diversity Push Could Actually Work"; Nicole Sperling, "TIFF Organizers Hope Revamped Inclusion Efforts Pay Dividends," *Vanity Fair*, September 6, 2018, https://www.vanityfair.com/hollywood/2018/09 /tiff-organizers-push-for-more-diversity-among-critics-attending-the-film-festival; Matt Donnelly, "Despite Uptick, Female Film Critics Remain Outnumbered by Men," *Variety*, May 30, 2019, https://variety.com/2019/film/news/female-film-critics-study -2019-gender-parity-1203228844/.

81. Vachon, *Killer Life*, 110.

82. Interview by author, Mark Horowitz, former independent sales agent and producer, Cannes, France, May 2014.

83. As a scholar who studies film distribution, I find this to be one area of the market in which access is difficult to track and nearly impossible to gain an expansive view of due to the wide array of distributor acquisitions and sales companies operating in the United States and globally. Like the vast array of production companies in the contemporary Hollywood climate, all distributors are not the same. It is hard to compare a massive distribution arm of a major Hollywood studio like Sony Pictures or an Indiewood sibling boutique unit like Sony Pictures Classics with the scale of independent companies ranging across A24, Neon, and Magnolia. Distributors compile unique slates, relationships with filmmakers, and distribution plans based on the size of their pockets and their brand based on acquired films.

84. Interview by author, Mark Horowitz, former independent sales agent and producer, Los Angeles, July 2017 and July 2018.

85. Mike Fleming Jr., "Open Road Falls Hard for 'Before I Fall'; Commits To Wide Release for Awesomeness Pic as Good Universe Shops Intl: Cannes," *Deadline Hollywood*, May 13, 2016, https://deadline.com/2016/05/before-i-fall-open-road -cannes-wide-release-commitment-lauren-oliver-young-adult-novel-1201755928/.

86. Sundance Institute, "2021 Sundance Film Festival: Full Program Announced," December 15, 2020, https://www.sundance.org/blogs/news/2021-sundance-film -festival-full-program-announced/.

87. Kate Erbland, "One-Third of the Films at Sundance Were Directed by Women, but That Shouldn't Be Confused with the Real World," *IndieWire*, January 30, 2017, https://www.indiewire.com/2017/01/sundance-2017-female-filmmakers-inclusion -diversity-1201775242/.

88. Jeremy Kay, "Sundance: 'City of Ghosts,' 'Bushwick,' 'Beach Rats' Find Homes," *Screen Daily*, January 28, 2017, https://www.screendaily.com/sundance-news /sundance-city-of-ghosts-bushwick-beach-rats-find-homes/5114277.article.

89. De Valck and Soeteman "'And the Winner Is . . . ,'" 294.

90. Graham Winfrey, "Neon Acquires Teen Drama 'Beach Rats'—Sundance 2017," *IndieWire*, January 28, 2017, https://www.indiewire.com/2017/01/neon-beach-rats -sundance-film-acquisition-1201775165/.

91. Interview by author, Alix Madigan, producer, phone, August 9, 2018.

92. Interview by author, Charlotte Mickie, international sales agent and executive, Berlin, February 2017.

93. Havens, *Black Television Travels*; Yuen, *Reel Inequality*.

94. Motion Picture Association, "2019 Theme Report (Total Theatrical & Home/ Entertainment)," March 2020, 20, https://www.mpa-apac.org/research-docs/2019 -theme-report/.

95. Interview by author, producer, Los Angeles, August 2018.

96. Chris Gardner and Rhonda Richard, "Cannes: Cate Blanchett–Led Women's March Takes Center Stage on Red Carpet," *Hollywood Reporter*, May 12, 2018, https:// www.hollywoodreporter.com/amp/news/cannes-cate-blanchett-led-womens-march -takes-center-stage-red-carpet-1111329?__twitter_impression=true.

97. Interview by author, Anna Serner, CEO Swedish Film Institute, Stockholm, Sweden, August 22, 2017.

98. Ann Numhauser-Henning, "The Policy on Gender Equality in Sweden," Study for the FEMM Committee, European Parliament, 2015, https://www.europarl.europa .eu/RegData/etudes/STUD/2015/510011/IPOL_STU(2015)510011_EN.pdf.

99. Interview by author, Anna Serner, CEO Swedish Film Institute, Stockholm, Sweden, August 22, 2017.

100. Kate Erbland, "Cannes 2019 Announces Full Selection Committee, Including Four Prominent Women," *IndieWire*, January 15, 2019, https://www.indiewire.com /2019/01/cannes-2019-selection-committee-women-1202035328/.

101. Rebecca Davis and Brent Lang, "At Cannes, Female-Dominated Films Take Center Stage," *Variety*, May 16, 2019, https://variety.com/2019/film/markets -festivals/cannes-female-dominated-films-cliffhanger-1203217181/; Brent Lang, "Cannes Grows More Inclusive, Boosts Number of Female Filmmakers," *Variety*, April 18, 2019, https://variety.com/2019/film/news/cannes-more-inclusive-female -filmmakers-official-selection-1203192348/.

102. Erbland, "One-Third of the Films at Sundance Were Directed by Women";

Tatiana Siegel, "Sundance Unveils Female-Powered Lineup Featuring Taylor Swift, Gloria Steinem, Abortion Road Trip Drama," *Hollywood Reporter*, December 4, 2019, https://www.hollywoodreporter.com/news/sundance-2020-unveils-female-powered -lineup-taylor-swift-gloria-steinem-films-1259538.

103. Eric Kohn, "Sundance Names Kim Yutani as New Director of Programming," *IndieWire*, May 8, 2018, https://www.indiewire.com/2018/05/kim-yutani-sundance -film-festival-director-of-programming-1201961575/.

104. Share Her Journey, Toronto International Film Festival, https://www.tiff.net /shareherjourney.

105. Interview by author, former executive, Toronto International Film Festival, Toronto, Canada, March 2018.

106. Kate Erbland, "How TIFF Sets the Standard for Film Festivals to Build Filmmaker Gender Parity," *IndieWire*, April 18, 2019, https://www.indiewire.com /2018/09/tiff-2018-female-filmmakers-gender-parity-1202000255/amp/?__twitter _impression=true.

107. Brent Lang, "Toronto Film Festival Kicks Off $3 Million Campaign to Support Female Filmmakers," *Variety*, July 10, 2017, https://variety.com/2017/film/news /toronto-film-festival-female-directors-campaign-1202490942/amp/.

108. Erbland, "How TIFF Sets the Standard for Film Festivals."

109. Etan Vlessing, "TIFF Programmers on How Toronto Is Leading the Push for Gender Parity," *Hollywood Reporter*, September 7, 2018, https://www .hollywoodreporter.com/amp/news/tiff-programmers-how-toronto-is-leading-push -gender-parity-1140699?__twitter_impression=true.

110. Elsa Keslassy, "Cannes Rules Out Physical Edition for Now, Will Host Screen- ings at Fall Festivals," *Variety*, May 10, 2020, https://variety.com/2020/film/global /coronavirus-cannes-cancels-physical-edition-venice-official-selection-1234603004/; Eleanor Stanford, "Venice Film Festival to Return with Masks and without Block- busters," *New York Times*, July 28, 2020, https://www.nytimes.com/2020/07/28 /movies/venice-film-festival-2020-coronavirus.html.

111. Kate Erbland, "Sundance Layoffs: Institute Cuts 13 Percent of Staff, Reduces Budgets, and Will Consolidate Labs Programs," *IndieWire*, July 1, 2020, https:// www.indiewire.com/2020/07/sundance-layoffs-cut-staff-budgets-labs-1234570905/; Etan Vlessing, "Toronto Film Festival Implements Pandemic-Era Layoffs, Salary Cuts," *Hollywood Reporter*, June 23, 2020, https://www.hollywoodreporter.com/news /toronto-film-festival-launches-pandemic-era-layoffs-salary-cuts-1299964.

112. Guy Lodge, "At Venice Film Festival, New Talent and Female Directors Will Uplift a Testing Year (Column)," *Variety*, July 28, 2020, https://variety.com /2020/film/global/venice-2020-female-directors-susanna-nicchiarelli-chloe-zao -1234718210/; Brent Lang, "Toronto Film Festival Boasts Record Number of Women Directors, Nears Gender Parity," *Variety*, July 30, 2020, https://variety.com/2020 /film/news/toronto-film-festival-lineup-women-directors-mira-nair-regina-king -spike-lee-1234720788/; Elsa Keslassy, "Thierry Fremaux Says Cannes 2020 Selection Has Younger Directors, More International Films," *Variety*, June 2, 2020, https:// variety.com/2020/film/news/cannes-2020-thierry-fremaux-san-sebastian-festival -1234623147/; Kate Erbland, "Cannes 2020 Boasts 'Significant Increase' in Films from Women, but That's Only Part of the Story," *IndieWire*, June 3, 2020, https:// www.indiewire.com/2020/06/cannes-2020-female-filmmakers-1202235071/; Nick

Vivarelli, "Venice Film Festival Unveils Details of Slimmer Lineup Structure," *Variety*, July 7, 2020, https://variety.com/2020/film/global/venice-film-festival-coronavirus-lineup-structure-alberto-barbera-1234699752/?cx_testId=51&cx_testVariant=cx_2&cx_artPos=1#cxrecs_s.

113. Erbland, "Cannes 2020 Boasts 'Significant Increase.'"

114. Elizabeth Wagmeister, "Riley Keough on Carving Her Own Path in Hollywood and Her Directorial Debut 'War Pony' with Gina Gammell," *Variety*, May 20, 2022, https://variety.com/2022/film/news/riley-keough-gina-gammell-war-pony-cannes-1235273426/.

115. Ben Dalton, "Black Directors Make Just 1% of Competition Films at Major Festivals (exclusive)," *Screen Daily*, December 13, 2021, https://www.screendaily.com/news/black-directors-make-just-1-of-competition-films-at-major-festivals-exclusive/5165691.article?utm_medium=email&utm_campaign=UK%20%20Europe%20Daily%20Dec%2013&utm_content=UK%20%20Europe%20Daily%20Dec%2013+CID_94a3faee00c1116e5102242758d25acc&utm_source=Newsletter&utm_term=Black%20directors%20make%20just%201%20of%20competition%20films%20at%20major%20festivals%20exclusive.

Chapter 5. Distribution and Marketing (Bankability Gap)

1. As quoted by Julie Miller, "Meryl Streep Celebrates Women in Film, Ponders Hollywood's Fascination with 'Tent-Pole Failures,'" *Vanity Fair*, June 13, 2012, https://www.vanityfair.com/hollywood/2012/06/meryl-streep-women-in-film-crystal-lucy-awards-2012.

2. Manohla Dargis, "Women in the Seats but Not behind the Camera," *New York Times*, December 10, 2009, https://www.nytimes.com/2009/12/13/movies/13dargis.html.

3. In *Nobody's Girl Friday: The Women Who Ran Hollywood*, J. E. Smyth argues that "between 1924 and 1954, Hollywood was, more than any other American business enterprise, enriched by women: women's pictures, women audiences and fans, and women filmmakers" (239).

4. Smukler, *Liberating Hollywood*.

5. Jane Wilson, "Hollywood Flirts with the New Woman," *New York Times*, May 29, 1977, https://www.nytimes.com/1977/05/29/archives/hollywood-flirts-with-the-new-woman-after-a-decade-of-social-change.html.

6. Emma Green, "A Lot Has Changed in Congress since 1992, the 'Year of the Woman,'" *Atlantic*, September 26, 2013, https://www.theatlantic.com/politics/archive/2013/09/a-lot-has-changed-in-congress-since-1992-the-year-of-the-woman/280046/.

7. Richard Schickel, "Gender Bender over Thelma & Louise," *Time*, June 24, 1991, https://content.time.com/time/subscriber/article/0,33009,973234,00.html.

8. Caryn James, "Film View: The Year of the Woman? Not in Movies," *New York Times*, January 10, 1993, https://www.nytimes.com/1993/01/10/movies/film-view-the-year-of-the-woman-not-in-movies.html.

9. Mary Schmich, "Good Riddance to Year of the Woman; Better Luck to Next Year's 'Honoree,'" *Chicago Tribune*, December 28, 1992, https://www.sun-sentinel.com/news/fl-xpm-1992-12-29-9203090296-story.html.

10. Rebecca Ford and Mia Galuppo, "1993 Was Oscar's 'Year of the Woman,' Has

Anything Changed in 25 Years?," *Hollywood Reporter*, March 2, 2018, https://www
.hollywoodreporter.com/lists/1993-was-oscars-year-woman-has-anything-changed
-25-years-1089077.

11. Bernard Weinraub, "What Do Women Want? Movies," *New York Times*, February 10, 1997, https://www.nytimes.com/1997/02/10/movies/what-do-women-want
-movies.html.

12. Lane, "Just Another Girl outside the Neo-Indie," 193–209.

13. Anthony Kaufman, "Was 2018 the Year of the Woman at the Sundance Film
Festival?" *Filmmaker Magazine*, March 8, 2018, https://filmmakermagazine.com
/104910-was-2018-the-year-of-the-woman-at-the-sundance-film-festival/#.YA8A
-JNKhGM; Leonard Goi, "The Current Debate: Sundance 2020, the Year of Women,"
February 4, 2020, https://mubi.com/notebook/posts/the-current-debate-sundance
-2020-the-year-of-women; David Sims, "The Most Exciting Films at Sundance Were
Made by Women," *Atlantic*, January 28, 2020, https://www.theatlantic.com/culture
/archive/2020/01/standout-films-2020-sundance-festival/605626/.

14. Michael Cieply, "In Toronto, Directing Is Clearly Women's Work," *New York
Times*, September 10, 2009, https://www.nytimes.com/2009/09/11/movies/11women
.html; Kathleen Newman-Bremang, "It's the Year of the Woman at TIFF," *Refinery29*,
September 9, 2019, https://www.refinery29.com/en-us/2019/09/8371558/tiff-2019
-year-of-the-woman.

15. Obst is not the first to point out this trend, as a number of women I interviewed shared similar observations. Rebecca Traister, "Early Signs of a 'Bridesmaids'
Bump," *Salon*, September 27, 2011, https://www.salon.com/2011/09/27/lynda_obst
_interview/.

16. Balio, *Hollywood in the New Millennium*, 70.

17. Brent Lang, "Look Who's Winning the B.O. Battle of the Sexes," *The Wrap*,
December 8, 2009, https://www.thewrap.com/look-whos-winning-bo-battle-sexes
-11046/#.

18. Scott Mendelson, "The Grim Box Office Fate of 'Annihilation' Was an Inevitable
Tragedy," *Forbes*, February 26, 2018, https://www.forbes.com/sites/scottmendelson
/2018/02/26/annihilations-grim-box-office-fate-was-an-inevitable-tragedy/?sh=
7b01892a4ed9.

19. Eliana Dockterman, "8 Lessons from a Summer Where Women Ruled the Box
Office," *Time*, August 27, 2015, https://time.com/4010560/women-summer-box
-office/.

20. Amy Ryan, "Is Hollywood No Longer in the Leading-Lady Business?" *Entertainment Weekly*, August 4, 2020, https://ew.com/article/2007/10/10/women-in-movies/.

21. Irin Carmon, "'Fuck Them': *Times* Critic on Hollywood, Women, & Why Romantic Comedies Suck," *Jezebel*, December 14, 2009, https://jezebel.com/fuck-them
-times-critic-on-hollywood-women-why-ro-5426065.

22. Motion Picture Association, "2018 Theatrical Home Entertainment Market
Environment Report," March 21, 2019, https://www.motionpictures.org/research
-docs/2018-theatrical-home-entertainment-market-environment-theme-report/.

23. Pamela McClintock, "Femme-Driven Films Score at B.O.," *Variety*, November
7, 2008, https://variety.com/2008/film/features/femme-driven-films-score-at-b-o
-1117995510/.

24. McClintock, "Femme-Driven Films Score at B.O."; Nicole LaPorte and Gabriel

Snyder, "Auds Dance with 'The Devil,'" *Variety*, July 9, 2006, https://variety.com/2006/film/news/auds-dance-with-the-devil-1200340464/.

25. Anne Thompson, "Elizabeth Gabler Guides Fox 2000," *Variety*, January 8, 2009, https://variety.com/2009/film/columns/elizabeth-gabler-guides-fox-2000-1117998253/.

26. Bill Higgins, "My Week with Elizabeth Gabler," *Forbes*, September 19, 2008, https://www.forbes.com/2008/10/13/0929_FLEW080a.html?sh=11efd5901a44; Kim Masters, "Elizabeth Gabler Breaks Silence on Sony Move, Disney Exit, HarperCollins and Streaming Plans (Exclusive)," *Hollywood Reporter*, September 18, 2019, https://www.hollywoodreporter.com/news/elizabeth-gabler-talks-disney-exit-harpercollins-streaming-1240141.

27. LaPorte and Snyder, "Auds Dance with 'The Devil.'"

28. Brandon Gray, "Superman Returns Solid If Unspectacular," *Box Office Mojo*, July 5, 2006, https://www.boxofficemojo.com/article/ed3715630084/.

29. Breeanna Hare, "Yes, Hollywood, Women Do Go to Movies," *CNN*, December 4, 2009, http://edition.cnn.com/2009/SHOWBIZ/Movies/12/04/women.audience.box.office/; Nia Vardalos, "'Women Don't Go to Movies'—Huh?," *Huffington Post*, December 6, 2017, https://www.huffpost.com/entry/women-dont-go-to-the-movi_b_212888.

30. Diane Negra, "Quality Postfeminism? *Sex and the Single Girl* on HBO," *Genders* 1998–2013, April 1, 2004, https://www.colorado.edu/gendersarchive1998-2013/2004/04/01/quality-postfeminism-sex-and-single-girl-hbo; Kim Akass and Janet McCabe, eds. *Reading Sex and the City* (London: I. B. Tauris, 2004); Deborah Jermyn, *Sex and the City* (Detroit: Wayne State University Press, 2009).

31. Sharon Waxman, "For New Line, an Identity Crisis," *New York Times*, February 19, 2007, https://www.nytimes.com/2007/02/19/business/media/19new.html.

32. After cost-cutting efforts the following year, parent company Time Warner folded New Line into the Warner Bros. film division and downsized from six hundred to fifty employees. As a result, New Line Cinema ceased to operate as a full-service, stand-alone unit; marketing, publicity, and distribution teams are now coordinated closely with Warner Bros.

33. Stuart Elliott, "'Sex and the City' and Its Lasting Female Appeal," *New York Times*, March 17, 2008, https://www.nytimes.com/2008/03/17/business/media/17adco.html.

34. Elliott, "'Sex and the City'"; "'Sex and the City': A Product-Placement Roundup," *Vanity Fair*, May 30, 2008, https://www.vanityfair.com/news/2008/05/sex-and-the-cit.

35. Radner, *Neo-Feminist Cinema*, 196.

36. For further discussion, see Courtney Brannon Donoghue, "Shop, Makeover, Love: Female-Driven Franchises and Consumer Fandom in Conglomerate Hollywood," in *Point of Sale: Analyzing Media Retail*, ed. Daniel Herbert and Derek Johnson (New Brunswick, NJ: Rutgers University Press), 142–159.

37. Pamela McClintock, "'Sex' Drives Box Office," *Variety*, June 1, 2008, https://variety.com/2008/film/box-office/sex-drives-box-office-1117986698.

38. McClintock, "'Sex' Drives Box Office."

39. Anne Thompson, "'Twilight' Ready for Blockbuster B.O.," *Variety*, November

6, 2008, https://variety.com/2008/film/columns/twilight-ready-for-blockbuster-b-o
-1117995425/.

40. Nicole LaPorte, "Is the 'Twilight' Witch Hunt Over at Paramount?" *The Wrap*, January 27, 2009, https://www.thewrap.com/twilight-witch-hunt-over-paramount
-1009/.

41. David Carr, "The Vampire of the Mall," *New York Times*, November 16, 2008, https://www.nytimes.com/2008/11/17/movies/17twil.html.

42. Kirk Honeycutt, "'Twilight': Film Review," *Hollywood Reporter*, November 20, 2008, https://www.hollywoodreporter.com/review/film-review-twilight-125111.

43. Lisa Bode, "Transitional Tastes: Teen Girls and Genre in the Critical Reception of *Twilight*," *Continuum: Journal of Media & Cultural Studies* 24, no. 5 (October 2010): 707–719.

44. Brooks Barnes, "For Studio, Vampire Movie Is a Cinderella Story," *New York Times*, November 19, 2008, https://www.nytimes.com/2008/11/20/business/media
/20summit.html; Honeycutt, "'Twilight'"; LaPorte, "Is the 'Twilight' Witch Hunt Over at Paramount?"; David Edelstein, "The Gospel of Harvey Milk," *New York Magazine*, November 21, 2008, https://nymag.com/movies/reviews/52432/; Richard Verrier, "'Twilight' Leaves Its Box-Office Mark," *Los Angeles Times*, November 24, 2008, https://www.latimes.com/archives/la-xpm-2008-nov-24-fi-boxoffice24-story
.html.

45. Carr, "The Vampire of the Mall."

46. Verrier, "'Twilight' Leaves Its Box-Office Mark"; Brooks Barnes, "Box-Office Pulse: Blood Lust Runs Hot," *New York Times*, November 23, 2008, https://www
.nytimes.com/2008/11/24/movies/24box.html.

47. Verrier, "'Twilight' Leaves Its Box-Office Mark."

48. McClintock, "Femme-Driven Films Score at B.O."; Verrier, "'Twilight' Leaves Its Box-Office Mark."

49. Thompson, "'Twilight' Ready for Blockbuster B.O."

50. Mark Cina, "Catherine Hardwicke: 'Thank the Lord' I Walked Away from 'Twilight,'" *Hollywood Reporter*, March 3, 2011, https://www.hollywoodreporter.com
/news/catherine-hardwicke-thank-lord-i-163905; Nikki Finke, "Hardwicke Nixed for 'Twilight' Sequel; Summit Looks for 'New Moon' Director," *Deadline Hollywood*, December 7, 2008, https://deadline.com/2008/12/hardwicke-fired-from-twilight
-franchise-7696/.

51. Grace Orriss, "Why Does Hollywood Keep Handing Romance Franchises to Male Directors?" *PopSugar*, March 16, 2021, https://www.popsugar.com
/entertainment/why-arent-more-romance-movies-directed-by-women-48184379.

52. Julie Bosman, "Universal Acquires Movie Rights to Trilogy of Erotic Novels," *New York Times*, March 26, 2012, https://mediadecoder.blogs.nytimes.com/2012/03
/26/universal-acquires-movie-rights-to-trilogy-of-erotic-novels/.

53. Kim Masters, "'Fifty Shades' of Cray: The Inside Story of a Director, EL James and Their Squabbles," *Hollywood Reporter*, February 11, 2015, https://www
.hollywoodreporter.com/news/fifty-shades-cray-inside-story-772282.

54. Traister, "Early Signs of a 'Bridesmaids' Bump"; Meghan Daum, "Breaking Comedy's Raunch Barrier," *Los Angeles Times*, May 19, 2011, https://www.latimes
.com/archives/la-xpm-2011-may-19-la-oe-daum-bridesmaids-20110519-story.html.

55. Pamela McClintock, "'Bridesmaids' Rocks Weekend Box Office with $24.6 Million Opening," *Hollywood Reporter*, May 15, 2011, https://www.hollywoodreporter .com/news/general-news/bridesmaids-rocks-weekend-box-office-188509/.

56. *Bridesmaids* marketing poster, http://www.impawards.com/2011/bridesmaids _ver2_xlg.html.

57. Christopher Hitchens, "Why Women Aren't Funny," *Vanity Fair*, January 1, 2007, https://www.vanityfair.com/culture/2007/01/hitchens200701.

58. Helen Warner and Heather Savigny, "'Where Do You Go after *Bridesmaids*?' The Politics of Being a Woman in Hollywood," in *The Politics of Being a Woman: Feminism, Media and 21st Century Popular Culture*, ed. H. Savigny and H. Warner (London: Palgrave Macmillan UK, 2015), 114.

59. David T. Friendly, "'Bridesmaids' Effect: Why Female Comedies Are Making a Comeback," *Hollywood Reporter*, June 19, 2011, https://www.hollywoodreporter.com /news/bridesmaids-effect-why-female-comedies-203160.

60. Gabrielle Moss, "The 'Bridesmaids' Effect: How Did 'Bridesmaids' Change Hollywood?" *Bitch Media*, June 6, 2013, https://www.bitchmedia.org/post/the -bridesmaids-effect-what-impact-does-bridesmaids-have-on-women-in-hollywood.

61. Martha M. Lauzen, "Bridesmaids and Bigelow: Debunking Their 'Effects,'" *Media Report to Women* 40, no. 3 (Summer 2012): 22–23.

62. Interview by author, producer, phone, August 2019.

63. Friendly, "'Bridesmaids' Effect."

64. Emma Mustich, "'Bridesmaids' Saves the Chick Flick. Now What?" *Salon*, July 5, 2011, https://www.salon.com/2011/07/05/bridesmaids_success/.

65. Pamela McClintock, "'Bridesmaids' Rocks Weekend Box Office with $24.6 Million Opening," *Hollywood Reporter*, May 15, 2011, https://www.hollywoodreporter .com/news/bridesmaids-rocks-weekend-box-office-188509#:~:text='Bridesmaids' %20Rocks%20Weekend%20Box%20Office,%2424.6%20Million%20Opening%20%7C %20Hollywood%20Reporter.

66. Kristen J. Warner, "Value Added: Reconsidering Women-Centered Media and Viewership," *Communication Culture & Critique* 12 (2019): 168.

67. Dave McNary, "'Birds of Prey' Lays an Egg at the Box Office," *Variety*, February 8, 2020, https://variety.com/2020/film/news/box-office-birds-of-prey-1917-bad-boys -1203497399/; Pamela McClintock, "Box Office: 'Birds of Prey' Flies off Course with $13M Friday," *Hollywood Reporter*, February 8, 2020, https://www.hollywoodreporter .com/news/box-office-birds-prey-flies-course-13m-friday-1277445.

68. Anthony D'Alessandro, "Did the Title of 'Birds of Prey' Just Change to 'Harley Quinn: Birds of Prey'?" *Deadline Hollywood*, February 11, 2020, https://deadline.com /2020/02/birds-of-prey-title-change-harley-quinn-birds-of-prey-movie-theaters -1202857825/.

69. Rafael Motamayor, "'Birds of Prey' Director Cathy Yan Is Disappointed over Box Office Narratives," *The Playlist*, April 4, 2020, https://theplaylist.net/birds-of -prey-director-box-office-20200404/.

70. A. O. Scott, "Maybe 20 Years from Now, Tonto," *New York Times*, August 23, 2013, https://www.nytimes.com/2013/08/25/movies/reconsidering-box-office-bombs -years-after-the-fact.html?smid=tw-share.

71. David Blum, "The Road to Ishtar," *New York Magazine*, March 16, 1987, 34–43.

72. For a more detailed history of Elaine May's career, see Smukler, *Liberating Hollywood*, 78–93.

73. Scott Tobias, "Mimi Leder on the Struggles of Being a Female Director," *New York Times*, October 12, 2015, https://www.nytimes.com/2015/10/13/arts/television /mimi-leder-on-the-struggles-of-being-a-female-director.html?partner=rss&emc=rss &smid=tw-nytmovies&smtyp=cur&_r=0&referer=http://t.co/JM9Kya5H1j.

74. Matthew Hammett Knott, "Heroines of Cinema: Mimi Leder and the Impossible Standard for Women Directors in Hollywood," *IndieWire*, April 17, 2014, https:// www.indiewire.com/2014/04/heroines-of-cinema-mimi-leder-and-the-impossible -standard-for-women-directors-in-hollywood-27635/.

75. Adam B. Vary, "'I'm Not Going Away, People,'" *Buzzfeed News*, April 8, 2016, https://www.buzzfeed.com/adambvary/karyn-kusama-the-invitation-girlfight.

76. Knott, "Heroines of Cinema."

77. Lynda Obst, "Producer Lynda Obst's No-B.S. Advice for Fighting Hollywood Gender Inequality (Guest Column)," *Hollywood Reporter*, February 16, 2017, https:// www.hollywoodreporter.com/news/producer-lynda-obsts-no-bs-advice-fighting -hollywood-gender-inequality-guest-column-976220.

78. Tobias, "Mimi Leder on the Struggles of Being a Female Director."

79. Hoai-Tran Bui, "Patty Jenkins Is 'Grateful' for Her 'Thor 2' Experience, but Walked Away to Avoid Director's Jail," *Slashfilm*, January 1, 2021, https://www .slashfilm.com/patty-jenkins-thor-2-stories/.

80. Carmon, "'Fuck Them.'"

81. Tatiana Siegel, "Exclusive: Fake Accounts Fueled the 'Snyder Cut' Online Army," *Rolling Stone*, July 18, 2022, https://www.rollingstone.com/tv-movies/tv -movie-features/justice-league-the-snyder-cut-bots-fans-1384231/.

82. Scott Mendelson, "The Biggest Reason 'Justice League' Failed at the Box Office," *Forbes*, November 20, 2017, https://www.forbes.com/sites/scottmendelson /2017/11/20/a-justice-league-that-copied-the-avengers-was-doomed-to-fail/?sh= 1642323b9832.

83. Kyle Buchanan, "'Justice League,' Recut by Zack Snyder, Will Come to HBO Max," *New York Times*, May 20, 2020, https://www.nytimes.com/2020/05/20/movies /justice-league-snyder-cut-hbo-max.html; Umberto Gonzalez and Ross A. Lincoln, "'Justice League': Snyder Cut to Include Footage from a Week of Additional Shooting," *The Wrap*, September 23, 2020, https://www.thewrap.com/justice-league-snyder -additional-shooting/.

84. Siegel, "Exclusive: Fake Accounts Fueled the 'Snyder Cut' Online Army."

85. Brooks Barnes, "At the Box Office, It's No Longer a Man's World," March 22, 2015, https://www.nytimes.com/2015/03/23/business/media/at-the-box-office-its -no-longer-a-mans-world.html; Bob Mondello, "This Year, Women (and Girls) Rule the Big Screen," June 10, 2015, https://www.wgbh.org/news/post/year-women-and -girls-rule-big-screen; Thelma Adams, "Female-Driven Movies Make Money, So Why Aren't More Being Made?," *Variety*, October 6, 2015, https://variety.com/2015/film /news/female-driven-movies-box-office-women-1201610849/.

86. Robert Ebert, "Supergirl," *Chicago Sun-Times*, January 1, 1984, https://www .rogerebert.com/reviews/supergirl-1984; Scott Mendelson, "Famous Flops: 'Supergirl' Doomed Girl-Powered Comic Book Movies," *Forbes*, May 8, 2015, https://www

.forbes.com/sites/scottmendelson/2015/05/08/famous-flops-supergirl-doomed-girl
-powered-comic-book-movies/?sh=6f19271b6d4d.

87. This widely held gendered narrative about superhero films did not allow for the distinction between Marvel and DC properties and differing studio franchise management that frames so many discussions of Marvel as successful and DCEU as struggling.

88. "Marvel CEO Doesn't Believe in Female Superheroes," Women and Hollywood, May 4, 2015, https://womenandhollywood.com/marvel-ceo-doesnt-believe-in-female -superheroes-fcdbc3d80c50/.

89. Mark Hughes, "Warner Bros. Sets Sights on Female Directors for Wonder Woman," *Forbes,* October 24, 2014, https://www.forbes.com/sites/markhughes /2014/10/24/warner-bros-sets-sights-on-female-directors-for-wonder-woman /#7db7035c5187.

90. Matt Patches, "Hack Knowledge: A Brief History of Hollywood's 'Cleopatra' False Starts and Failures," *Grantland*, December 15, 2014, https://grantland.com /hollywood-prospectus/cleopatra-sony-hack-email-scott-rudin-amy-pascal-angelina -jolie-steven-soderbergh/.

91. Eric Alt, "Why Falling Down Stairs in Your Underwear Is Solid Prep for Being a Female Director," *Fast Company*, November 7, 2014, https://www.fastcompany.com/ 3038166/falling-down-stairs-in-underwear-is-solid-prep-for-being-a-female-director.

92. Angie Han, "Look Back at Wonder Woman's Long and Winding Journey to the Big Screen," *Mashable*, May 29, 2017, https://mashable.com/2017/05/29/wonder -woman-movie-history/#VINQULVB3kqp.

93. Tatiana Siegel, "The Complex Gender Politics of the Wonder Woman Movie," *Hollywood Reporter*, May 31, 2017, http://www.hollywoodreporter.com/features /complex-gender-politics-wonder-woman-movie-1008259.

94. Kevin Lincoln, "What DC, and Hollywood, Needs from *Wonder Woman*," *Vulture*, June 1, 2017, https://www.vulture.com/2017/06/wonder-woman-box-office -what-its-success-would-mean.html.

95. Interview by author, screenwriter, Los Angeles, April 2017.

96. Chris Thilk, "Why the Marketing of Wonder Woman at Warner Bros. Is Coming under Fire," *Ad Week*, May 17, 2017, http://www.adweek.com/creativity/why-the -marketing-of-wonder-woman-at-warner-bros-is-coming-under-fire/.

97. Shana O'Neil, "Where Is the Wonder Woman Movie Advertising?," *Syfy*, April 25, 2017, https://www.blastr.com/2017-4-25/wonder-woman-movie-advertising; Donna Dickens, "You Aren't Imagining It, 'Wonder Woman' Really Isn't Being Well Promoted," *Uproxx*, April 27, 2017, http://uproxx.com/hitfix/wonder-woman-no -promotion/; Thilk, "Why the Marketing of Wonder Woman at Warner Bros. Is Com- ing under Fire"; Warner Bros., YouTube Channel, https://www.youtube.com/user /WarnerBrosPictures/videos.

98. Seth Kelley, "Can 'Wonder Woman' Save the Summer Box Office?" *Variety*, May 31, 2017, https://variety.com/2017/film/news/wonder-woman-box-office-save -summer-1202449235/; Brooks Barnes, "'Wonder Woman' Deflects Doubt to Win Bat- tle at the Box Office," *New York Times*, June 4, 2017, https://www.nytimes.com/2017 /06/04/movies/wonder-woman-deflects-doubt-to-win-battle-at-the-box-office.html.

99. Steven Zeitchik, "Analysis: Hollywood's Box-Office Woes: Is the Industry Aim- ing Too Narrowly at Men?" *Los Angeles Times*, July 18, 2017, https://www.latimes.com

/entertainment/movies/la-et-mn-box-office-women-20170718-story.html; Pamela McClintock, "Box Office: 'Wonder Woman' Holding Better than Any Superhero Movie in 15 Years," *Hollywood Reporter*, July 13, 2017, https://www.hollywoodreporter.com/heat-vision/wonder-woman-box-office-superhero-movies-1020621.

100. Ryan Faughnder, "Hollywood's Summer Has Flopped So Far. Here Comes Wonder Woman to the Rescue," *Los Angeles Times*, May 30, 2017, http://www.latimes.com/business/hollywood/la-fi-ct-movie-projector-wonder-woman-20170530-htmlstory.html.

101. Michael Cavna, "How 'Wonder Woman' Director Patty Jenkins Cracked the Superhero-Movie Glass Ceiling," *Washington Post*, May 31, 2017, https://www.washingtonpost.com/news/comic-riffs/wp/2017/05/31/how-wonder-woman-director-patty-jenkins-cracked-the-superhero-movie-glass-ceiling/?utm_term=.ef25289fbaf9.

102. Jim Rutenberg, "'Wonder Woman' Could Be the Superhero Women in Hollywood Need," *New York Times*, June 4, 2017, https://www.nytimes.com/2017/06/04/business/media/mediator-wonder-woman-movie-hollywood.html?_r=0; Gregg Kilday, "What 'Wonder Woman' Really Means for Female Directors," *Hollywood Reporter*, June 14, 2017, http://www.hollywoodreporter.com/heat-vision/what-wonder-woman-means-female-directors-1013265; Seth Kelley, "'Wonder Woman': How Patty Jenkins Saved the DC Extended Universe," *Variety*, June 4, 2017, http://variety.com/2017/film/news/wonder-woman-box-office-analysis-patty-jenkins-warner-bros-1202453504/.

103. Chris Evangelista, "Warner Bros. Decides the Best Business Plan for DC's Future Is to Make Good Movies," *IndieWire*, June 18, 2018, https://www.slashfilm.com/future-dceu-films/.

104. Borys Kit, "'Wonder Woman' Sequel: Patty Jenkins Officially Set to Return as Director," *Hollywood Reporter*, September 11, 2017, https://www.hollywoodreporter.com/amp/heat-vision/wonder-woman-sequel-patty-jenkins-officially-set-return-as-director-1031052; Justin Kroll, "Patty Jenkins Closes Deal to Direct 'Wonder Woman' Sequel (EXCLUSIVE)," *Variety*, September 11, 2017, https://variety.com/2017/film/news/patty-jenkins-wonder-woman-sequel-director-1202548413/.

105. Aaron Couch and Ela Bittencourt, "First 'Wonder Woman 1984' Trailer Brings Back Gal Gadot's Warrior," *Hollywood Reporter*, December 8, 2019, https://www.hollywoodreporter.com/heat-vision/wonder-woman-1984-trailer-brings-back-gal-gadots-warrior-1260653.

106. Seth Kelley, "'Wonder Woman': How Patty Jenkins Saved the DC Extended Universe," *Variety*, June 4, 2017, http://variety.com/2017/film/news/wonder-woman-box-office-analysis-patty-jenkins-warner-bros-1202453504/; Dave McNary, "Ava DuVernay to Direct DC's Superhero Epic 'New Gods,'" *Variety*, March 15, 2018, http://variety.com/2018/film/news/ava-duvernay-superhero-movie-new-gods-dc-1202725043/; Anthony D'Alessandro, "How Cathy Yan Landed the 'Birds of Prey' Directing Gig: U.S.-China Entertainment Summit," *Deadline Hollywood*, October 30, 2018, https://deadline.com/2018/10/margot-robbie-birds-of-prey-cathy-yan-directing-warner-bros-1202492504/.

107. Matt Donnelly, "Marvel Phase 4 Plan Revealed, but Comic-Con's Big Winner Is Disney Plus," *Variety*, July 20, 2019, https://variety.com/2019/film/news/marvel-phase-4-plan-revealed-but-comic-cons-big-winner-is-disney-plus-1203274765/; Walt

Disney Company, "Marvel Studios Reveals Plans for Phase Four at San Diego-Comic-Con," July 20, 2019, https://thewaltdisneycompany.com/marvel-studios-reveals-plans-for-phase-four-at-san-diego-comic-con/.

108. Rebecca Rubin, "'Wonder Woman 1984' to Debut Both on HBO Max and in Theaters," *Variety*, November 18, 2020, https://variety.com/2020/film/news/wonder-woman-1984-hbo-max-release-1234804411/.

109. Anthony D'Alessandro, "Warner Bros Sets Entire 2021 Movie Slate to Debut on HBO Max along with Cinemas in Seismic Windows Model Shakeup," *Deadline*, December 3, 2020, https://deadline.com/2020/12/warner-bros-2021-movie-slate-hbo-max-matrix-4-dune-in-the-heights-1234649760/; Rebecca Rubin and Matt Donnelly, "Warner Bros. to Debut Entire 2021 Film Slate, Including 'Dune' and 'Matrix 4,' Both on HBO Max and in Theaters," *Variety*, December 3, 2020, https://variety.com/2020/film/news/warner-bros-hbo-max-theaters-dune-matrix-4-1234845342/.

110. Kim Masters, "A Different Kind of Sundance, and WWE Goes to Peacock," *The Business*, January 31, 2021, https://www.kcrw.com/culture/shows/the-business/time-documentary/banter-sundance-wwe-peacock; Jennifer Maas, "HBO Max and HBO Lose 1.8 Million U.S. Subscribers after Exit from Amazon Channels," *The Wrap*, October 21, 2021, https://www.thewrap.com/hbo-max-subscribers-down-45-million-amazon-global-subs-rise/.

111. Rebecca Keegan, Natalie Jarvey, and Pamela McClintock, "2020's Big Plot Twist: How 'Wonder Woman 1984' Came to Upend Hollywood's Future," *Hollywood Reporter*, December 16, 2020, https://www.hollywoodreporter.com/features/2020s-big-plot-twist-how-wonder-woman-1984-came-to-upend-hollywoods-future.

112. "After the Glass Ceiling, a Glass Cliff," *Freakonomics*, podcast hosted by Stephen Dubner, February 14, 2018, http://freakonomics.com/podcast/glass-cliff/.

113. Ryan Faughnder, "Scarlett Johansson Sues Disney over 'Black Widow' Release. Will More Suits Follow?" *Los Angeles Times*, July 29, 2021, https://www.latimes.com/entertainment-arts/business/story/2021-07-29/scarlett-johansson-sues-disney-over-black-widow-release-strategy.

114. Chris Gardner, "Women in Film, ReFrame and Time's Up Accuse Disney of 'Gendered Character Attack' on Scarlett Johansson," *Hollywood Reporter*, July 30, 2021, https://www.hollywoodreporter.com/movies/movie-news/scarlett-johansson-lawsuit-times-up-1234991071/.

115. "Debating 'Wonder Woman' and Summer Jams," *Still Processing*, podcast hosted by Wesley Morris and Jenna Wortham, June 8, 2017, https://www.nytimes.com/2017/06/08/podcasts/debating-wonder-woman-and-summer-jams.html.

116. Justin Kroll, "'Star Wars': Patty Jenkins Tapped to Direct New Movie 'Rogue Squadron' for Disney and Lucasfilm," *Deadline Hollywood*, December 10, 2020, https://deadline.com/2020/12/star-wars-patty-jenkins-1234654018/; Brent Lang, "'Star Wars' Spinoff 'Rogue Squadron' Delayed due to Patty Jenkins' Scheduling Conflict," *Variety*, November 8, 2021, https://variety.com/2021/film/news/star-wars-rogue-squadron-delayed-patty-jenkins-1235107457/; Ryan Lattanzio, "Warner Bros. Drops Ava DuVernay's DC Film 'New Gods' and Won't Revive It without Her," *IndieWire*, April 1, 2021, https://www.indiewire.com/2021/04/ava-duvernay-new-gods-warner-bros-dc-slate-1234627540/.

Conclusion. Gendered Value in a Changing Media Marketplace

1. Erbland, "Every Studio Film Directed by Female Filmmakers."

2. Stacy L. Smith, Katherine Pieper, and Al-Baab Khan, "Inclusion in the Director's Chair: Analysis of Director Gender & Race/Ethnicity across 1,500 Top Films from 2007 to 2021," February 2022, https://assets.uscannenberg.org/docs/aii-inclusion -directors-chair-2022.pdf.

3. Wreford and Cobb, "Data and Responsibility."

4. Brian Welk, "Women and POC Filmmakers See Sustained Growth as Directors of Top Films Despite Pandemic," *The Wrap*, February 9, 2022, https://www.thewrap .com/women-poc-directors-usc-annenberg-inclusion-study-filmmakers/; Chris Lindahl, "Streamers More Likely to Hire Female Directors, While Women of Color See Little Growth at Studios: Study," *IndieWire*, February 9, 2022, https://www .indiewire.com/2022/02/inclusion-in-the-directors-chair-study-2021-1234697640/.

5. Lindahl, "Streamers More Likely to Hire Female Directors."

6. "2021," Box Office Mojo.

7. Caldwell, *Production Culture*.

8. Caldwell, *Production Culture*, 34.

9. For a thorough examination of changing Hollywood business models and studio practices in the first year of the pandemic, see Fortmueller, *Hollywood Shutdown*.

10. Ryan Faughnder, "Disney to Furlough Employees amid Coronavirus Crisis," *Los Angeles Times*, April 2, 2020, https://www.latimes.com/entertainment-arts/business /story/2020-04-02/disney-to-furlough-employees-amid-coronavirus-crisis.

11. Danielle Kurtzleben, "Women Bear the Brunt of Coronavirus Job Losses," *All Things Considered*, May 9, 2020, https://www.npr.org/2020/05/09/853073274/women -bear-the-brunt-of-coronavirus-job-losses; Alisha Haridasani Gupta, "Why Some Women Call This Recession a 'Shecession,'" *New York Times*, May 9, 2020, https:// www.nytimes.com/2020/05/09/us/unemployment-coronavirus-women.html; Ellen McCarthy, Caitlin Gibson, Helena Andrews-Dyer, and Amy Joyce, "A Working Mom's Quarantine Life," *Washington Post*, May 6, 2020, https://www.washingtonpost .com/lifestyle/2020/05/06/coronavirus-pandemic-working-moms-quarantine-life /?arc404=true; Courtney Connley, "Women's Labor Force Participation Rate Hit a 33-Year Low in January, According to New Analysis," *CNBC*, February 8, 2021, https://www.cnbc.com/2021/02/08/womens-labor-force-participation-rate-hit-33 -year-low-in-january-2021.html.

12. Anne Cohen, "How Women in Hollywood Are Dealing with Their Sets Being Shut Down," *Refinery29*, April 14, 2020, https://www.refinery29.com/en-us/2020/03 /9585542/hollywood-women-coronavirus-stories.

13. Aric Jenkins, "Disney Makes $5 Million Pledge to Social Justice Organizations," *Fortune*, June 4, 2020, https://fortune.com/2020/06/04/disney-pledge-social-justice -organizations-george-floyd/; Meg James and Greg Braxton, "These Entertainment Companies Are Donating to Antiracist Causes. Here's How Much," *Los Angeles Times*, June 12, 2020, https://www.latimes.com/entertainment-arts/business/story/2020 -06-12/entertainment-companies-anti-racism-social-justice-funds.

14. Julia Boorstin, "Netflix Will Spend $100 million to Improve Diversity on Film Following Equity Study," *CNBC*, February 26, 2021, https://www.cnbc.com/2021/02

/26/netflix-will-spend-100-million-to-improve-diversity-on-film-following-equity
-study.html.

15. Anousha Sakoui and Ryan Faughnder, "Solidarity, or Joining the 'Bandwagon'? Some Corporate Activism Backfires amid Protests," *Los Angeles Times*, June 1, 2020, https://www.latimes.com/entertainment-arts/business/story/2020-06-01/solidarity -joining-bandwagon-some-corporate-activism-backfires-amid-protests.

16. Richard Rushfield, "Class Photos," *The Ankler*, June 13, 2020, https://theankler .com/p/class-photos; Ryan Faughnder and Meg James, "Hollywood's C-suites Are Overwhelmingly White. What Are Studios Doing about It?" *Los Angeles Times*, July 1, 2020, https://www.latimes.com/entertainment-arts/business/story/2020-07-01 /hollywood-diversity-corner-offices-black-executives-black-lives-matter.

17. "Why Hollywood Is *Still* So White, and Why Responding to the Protests Isn't Enough," *Vanity Fair*, June 4, 2020, https://www.vanityfair.com/hollywood/2020/06 /little-gold-men-podcast-franklin-leonard-tananarive-due; Jake Coyle, "Hollywood Says Black Lives Matter, but More Diversity Needed," *ABC News*, June 18, 2020, https://abcnews.go.com/Entertainment/wireStory/hollywood-black-lives-matter -diversity-needed-71324118.

18. Tambay Obenson, "In 2020, Hollywood Reckoned with Its Past—and Present— When It Came to Diversity, *Variety*, December 29, 2020," https://www.indiewire .com/2020/12/2020-diversity-in-film-tv-1234606659/; Jay Tucker, "Hollywood Shells Out for Diversity, but It Costs Much More than Money," *Variety*, August 6, 2020, https://variety.com/vip/hollywood-social-justice-diversity-costs-more-than-money -1234725607/; Greg Braxton and Ryan Faughnder, "Hollywood Says Its Antiracism Push Is Not a 'Fad.' Is the Industry Keeping Its Promises?" *Los Angeles Times*, September 13, 2021, https://www.latimes.com/entertainment-arts/story/2021-09 -13/hollywood-george-floyd-amazon-netflix-disney-warner-sony-universal; Steve Chiotakis, "Retired Hollywood Workers: Industry Isn't Diversifying as Fast as It Should Be over Past 50 Years," *KCRW Greater LA*, April 22, 2021, https://www.kcrw .com/news/shows/greater-la/hollywood-earth-day/below-the-line-film-tv-workers -diversity-poc.

19. Tucker, "Hollywood Shells Out for Diversity."

20. Justin Chang, "Why Chloé Zhao's Historic Best Director Oscar Win Matters," *Los Angeles Times*, April 25, 2021, https://www.latimes.com/entertainment-arts /movies/story/2021-04-25/oscars-2021-chloe-zhao-best-director-nomadland; Sandra Gonzalez, "Chloé Zhao Has Made Oscar History," *CNN* Entertainment, April 25, 2021, https://www.cnn.com/2021/04/25/entertainment/chloe-zhao-oscar-win/index.html.

21. Kit, "Marvel Studios' 'The Eternals' Finds Its Director with Chloe Zhao."

22. Joey Nolfi, "Chloé Zhao Shatters Oscars Tradition as First Woman of Color to Win Best Director," *Entertainment Weekly*, April 25, 2021, https://ew.com/awards /oscars/chloe-zhao-wins-best-director-oscars/.

23. Hill, *Never Done*; Warner, "Strategies for Success?"

24. "Total Theatrical & Home/Entertainment," in *Motion Picture Association 2020 Theme Report*, https://www.motionpictures.org/wp-content/uploads/2021/03/MPA -2020-THEME-Report.pdf. The MPA credits this data as coming from FX Networks Research. While the scripted category does not include children's programming, daytime serial dramas, or unscripted programming like reality series, it is unclear

whether this includes only English-language programming and how it accounts for streamers like Netflix aggressively investing in non-English-language original programming available to US subscribers. It is important to note the drop from 532 series in 2019 to 493 series in 2020 is undoubtedly a result of Covid production delays and restrictions.

25. Meredith Blake, "Ava DuVernay Doubles Down on Women Directors for 'Queen Sugar': Meet the New Crew," *Los Angeles Times*, June 20, 2017, https://www.latimes.com/entertainment/tv/la-et-st-queen-sugar-female-directors-season-2-20170620-htmlstory.html.

26. Elisabeth Subrin, "'Changing the Industry Game': *Queen Sugar* Showrunner and Directors Talk Career Advancement at IFP Week," *Filmmaker Magazine*, September 19, 2018, https://filmmakermagazine.com/106012-changing-the-industry-game-queen-sugar-showrunner-and-directors-talk-career-advancement-at-ifp-week/#.YcDfs33MLJx.

27. Blake, "Ava DuVernay Doubles Down on Women Directors."

28. Lacey Rose, "How Reese Witherspoon Took Charge of Her Career and Changed Hollywood," *Hollywood Reporter*, December 11, 2019, https://www.hollywoodreporter.com/movies/movie-features/how-reese-witherspoon-took-charge-her-career-changed-hollywood-1260203/.

29. John Koblin, "Reese Witherspoon's Second Act: Big-Time Producer," *New York Times*, January 27, 2018, https://www.nytimes.com/2018/01/27/business/media/reese-witherspoon-producer.html; Rose, "How Reese Witherspoon Took Charge."

30. Chris O'Falt, "'Big Little Lies' Season 2 Turmoil: Inside Andrea Arnold's Loss of Creative Control," *IndieWire*, July 12, 2019, https://www.indiewire.com/2019/07/big-little-lies-season-2-andrea-arnold-lost-creative-control-jean-marc-vallee-1202156884/.

31. Jackie Strause, "HBO Stands by 'Big Little Lies' Director amid Report of Behind-the-Scenes Drama," *Hollywood Reporter*, July 12, 2019, https://www.hollywoodreporter.com/tv/tv-news/big-little-lies-director-drama-hbo-responds-season-2-report-1224152/; Melissa Silverstein, "Why 'Big Little Lies' Fucking Over Andrea Arnold Feels Especially Frustrating," *Women and Hollywood*, July 15, 2019, https://womenandhollywood.com/why-big-little-lies-fucking-over-andrea-arnold-feels-especially-frustrating/.

32. Danny Leigh, "Does Andrea Arnold's Experience on *Big Little Lies* Suggest That Auteurs Are Doomed?" *Guardian*, July 18, 2019, https://www.theguardian.com/film/2019/jul/18/does-andrea-arnolds-experience-on-big-little-lies-suggest-that-auteurs-are-doomed?CMP=Share_AndroidApp_Tweet.

33. David Sims, "The End of an Era for HBO—and for Television," *Atlantic*, March 1, 2019, https://www.theatlantic.com/entertainment/archive/2019/03/hbo-ceo-richard-plepler-steps-down-att/583894/.

34. Lang and Rubin, "Reese Witherspoon's Hello Sunshine Sold for $900 Million."

35. Koblin, "Reese Witherspoon's Second Act."

36. Joshua Glick, "Studio Branding in the Streaming Wars," *Los Angeles Review of Books*, June 24, 2021, https://lareviewofbooks.org/article/studio-branding-in-the-streaming-wars/.

37. Mikey Glazer, "Netflix Ratings Leak: 200,000 Start 'Grey's Anatomy' from

Episode One Each Month, Says ABC Chief," *The Wrap*, October 22, 2017, https://www .thewrap.com/netflix-ratings-leak-200000-start-greys-anatomy-episode-one-month -says-abc-chief/.

38. Wendy Lee, "Netflix Releases Weekly List of Top Shows by Viewing Hours," *Los Angeles Times*, November 16, 2021, https://www.latimes.com/entertainment-arts /business/story/2021-11-16/netflix-releases-weekly-list-of-top-shows-by-viewing -hours.

39. Mikey O'Connell, "Courtney A. Kemp Is Trading 'Power' for Scale at Netflix: 'I Want to Challenge My Audience,'" *Hollywood Reporter*, October 7, 2021, https://www .hollywoodreporter.com/tv/tv-features/courtney-kemp-power-netflix-1235026060/.

40. Christopher Harris, "'Power' Is Ending. Here's How Starz's Most-Watched Series Began," *Washington Post*, January 31, 2020, https://www.washingtonpost.com /lifestyle/style/power-is-ending-heres-how-starzs-most-watched-series-began/.

41. Nicole LaPorte, "These Female Showrunners Reveal the Truth about Holly- wood Diversity," *Fast Company*, September 28, 2021, https://www.fastcompany.com /90679638/these-women-tell-you-what-diversity-in-hollywood-really-means.

42. Michal Lev-Ram, "Once upon a Time at Netflix," *Fortune*, October 2019, 74–82.

43. Kristen J. Warner, "Blue Skies Again: Streamers and the Impossible Promise of Diversity," *Los Angeles Review of Books*, June 24, 2021, https://lareviewofbooks.org /article/blue-skies-again-streamers-and-the-impossible-promise-of-diversity/.

44. Warner, "Blue Skies Again."

45. Wendy Lee and Melissa Hernandez, "After Layoffs at Netflix, Questions Mount over Diversity Efforts," *Los Angeles Times*, May 24, 2022, https://www.latimes .com/entertainment-arts/business/story/2022-05-24/lat-et-ct-netflix-lay-offs-poc -diversity.

46. "Netflix Promised Good Jobs at Tudum. Now, One of Its Teams Has Been Laid Off," NPR's *All Things Considered*, April 29, 2022, https://www.npr.org/2022/04/29 /1095642535/netflix-promised-secure-jobs-at-tudum-now-one-of-its-teams-has-been -laid-off#:~:text=Netflix%20has%20laid%20off%20some,and%20films%20streamed %20on%20Netflix.

47. Jodi Kantor, Arya Sundaram, and Melena Ryzik, "Time's Up C.E.O. Resigns amid Crisis over Cuomo Ties," *New York Times*, August 26, 2021, https://www .nytimes.com/2021/08/26/business/times-up-tina-tchen.html; Caroline Framke, "Time's Up Is Losing Itself to Conflicts of Interest," *Variety*, August 27, 2021, https://variety.com/2021/voices/opinion/times-up-tina-tchen-out-cuomo-sexual -harassment-1235050754/; Lili Loofbourow, "How Did Time's Up Go So Wrong?" *Slate*, September 23, 2021, https://slate.com/news-and-politics/2021/09/how-times -up-imploded-workplace.html.

48. Time's Up organization website, https://timesupnow.org/.

49. Interview by author, creative producer, Zoom, January 2021.

50. Interview by author, screenwriter, Zoom, November 2021.

51. Kristen J. Warner, *The Cultural Politics of Colorblind TV Casting* (New York: Routledge, 2015); Alfred L. Martin Jr., *The Generic Closet: Black Gayness and the Black- Cast Sitcom* (Bloomington: Indiana University Press, 2021).

52. Interview by author, writer-producer, phone, December 2021.

53. Interview by author, screenwriters, Zoom, May 2022.

Index

Note: Page numbers in italic type indicate information contained in images or image captions.

business-oriented film festivals. *See* festival marketplaces

Butch Cassidy and the Sundance Kid, 71

Buzzfeed News, 218–219

Byrne, Rose, 210

Cahiers du Cinéma, 112

Caldwell, John, 80, 236

California Department of Fair Employment and Housing, 44

California employment laws and gender pay gap, 84

Campion, Jane, 73, 173, 225

Candler, Kat, 245

Candyman, 236

Cannes Film Festival: activism for gender parity, 168–169; COVID impact on, 190–192; gender inequity red carpet protest 2018, 182–184; leadership roles and structure, 166; Marché du Film (market), 78, 177, 178, 180–181, 190; marginalization of female-directed films, 167–170; origin of, 290n3; overview, 149; Palme d'Or prize, 165, 168, 169, 172, 173, 191–192; parity progress profile late 2000s, 191–192; platform overview, 165

Can You Ever Forgive Me?, 74

Captain America, 14, 121

Captain Marvel, 40, 62, 122, 224, 229

Cardoso, Patricia, 245

Carlisle, Chris, 204

Carman, Emily, 31–32, 77

Caro, Niki, 62, 92–93

Catalyst (global nonprofit), 118, 120

Cattrall, Kim, 204

Catwoman, 224

Cavill, Henry, 222

"Celluloid Ceiling, The" (Lauzen) (employment report), 5, 39, 40–41, 66, 235–236

Center for the Study of Women in Television and Film (San Diego State University), 39

Chang, Justin, 93

Chapek, Bob, 233

Chaplin, Charlie, 29

Chapman, Rebecca, 47

Charlie's Angels, 75, 208

Chastain, Jessica, 77–79, 84

Chazelle, Damien, 99, 114

Cheese Stands Alone, The, 71

Chevigny, Katy, 114, 118–119

Chiarelli, Peter, 85–86

Chicago Tribune, 199

"chick flicks," 12

China Beach, 217

Choueiti, Marc, 41, 158

Chris, Cynthia, 113

Christopher Robin, 91

Chu, Jon M., 86

Cinderella (2015 live-action version), 92, 223, 224

CinemaCon 2015, 223

"circumscribed agency," 128

Circumstance, 159

Citizen Kane, 113

Clark, Hannah, 41

Cleopatra project, 225

Clerks, 154

Clinton, Hillary, 57

Clueless, 37

CNN, 242

Cobb, Shelley, 20, 40–41, 48, 49, 50

Cody, Diablo, 219, 220

Coiro, Kat, 235

Colbert, Claudette, 77

Comcast, 3, 42, 72, 241, 244

comedy: and "*Bridesmaids* Effect," 210–215; romantic comedies (rom-coms), 11–15, 74–75, 90; and "women aren't funny" narrative, 211

"comps" and risk assessment, 10

conglomeration/consolidation of industry, effects of: corporate culture and gender disparity, 21–22, 29–30, 63–64, 258, 274n53; distillation of themes/offerings, 9–11, 33, 71–75; and increase in opportunities for women, 238

consumer culture and product placement, 204–205

continuity work, 30–31

Coogler, Ryan, 122

"Cool Girl" persona, 59
Coolidge, Martha, 73, 74
Cooper, Bradley, 189, 210
Cooper, John, 187
Coppola, Sofia, 37, 171
coproducer role, 130
Corinealdi, Emayatzy, 160
Corsini, Catherine, 191
Costner, Kevin, 103
costume design, 110
Cotillard, Marion, 78
COVID-19, impact of, 3, 38, 94, 190,
    229–230, 239–241
Cox DiGiovanni, Fanshen, 47
Craddock, Kerri, 189–190
Crazy Rich Asians, 85–86
Creative Nonfiction, 167
creative producer, roles of, 68, 130–134
Cretton, Destin Daniel, 122
critics (film), gender disparity in,
    175–177, 207
Cruz, Penélope, 78
Cuomo, Andrew, 254
cycle of forgetting, 196, 197–201

DaCosta, Nia, 91, 122, 229, 236
Daisy Jones & The Six, 78, 246
Damon, Matt, 139–141
Dargis, Manohla, 160, 168, 196, 202,
    221–222
Darjeeling Limited, The, 222
Das, Nandita, 189
Dash, Julie, 37, 245
"data shaming," 48–49
Da Vinci Code, The, 165
Davis, Geena, 28, 39, 189, 198–199. *See
    also* Geena Davis Institute on Gender
    in Media
Davis, Kristin, 204
Davis, Viola, 43–44, 102
Davis Institute. *See* Geena Davis Insti-
    tute on Gender in Media
day-and-date release strategy, 230–231,
    232–233
DC Extended Universe (DCEU): *Birds
    of Prey and the Fantabulous Emanci-
    pation of One Harley Quinn*, 215–216,
224, 229; box-office failures for
    male vs. female directors, 215–216,
    222–223; focus on female-driven
    superhero projects, 229–230; and
    industry focus on IP, 72; *Justice
    League*, 115, 222–223, 227. *See also*
    Batman franchise; Wonder Woman
    franchise
Deadline Hollywood, 209, 230
Deep Impact, 217
de Havilland, Olivia, 32
del Río, Dolores, 32
Dempsey, Rachel, 60
Denis, Claire, 189, 192
Dern, Laura, 247
Desilu Productions, 33
Desperately Seeking Susan, 73
Destroyer, 220
de Valck, Marijke, 165, 172–173, 180
development process: elements of and
    roles in, 67–70; experience para-
    dox, 86–89; female-led projects
    and characters, example, 97–104;
    first-look deals ("pacts"), decline of,
    75–79; gendered culture of, 65–67;
    midbudget film production decline,
    72–75; negotiating pay, 83–86; during
    pandemic, 240; pitching process
    and power dynamic, 79–83, 95–97;
    rewrites as experience path, 89–94;
    script notes, 94–95; "spec" market
    decline, 70–72
Devil Wears Prada, The, 74, 195, 202–203
"D" girls, 34–35
Di Novi, Denise, 53, 77
Diop, Mati, 186
Directing Workshop for Women (Ameri-
    can Film Institute), 35
director-as-author ideology, 112,
    113–114. *See also* auteurist ideologies
director positions, quantitative analysis,
    41. *See also* above-the-line (ATL)
    positions
Directors Guild of America (DGA),
    35–36, 39, 246
Discovery and Masters sections of TIFF,
    189–190

Disney and film divisions: acquisitions/ expansions and gender disparity, 61–64, 74–76; contributions to social justice, 241; focus on franchise development, 9–10, 122; increased opportunities for writers, 91–92; live-action remakes, 92, 223, 224; Miramax division, 5, 153; missteps with *Mulan*, 93–94. *See also* Disney+ streaming service; Marvel Cinematic Universe (MCU)

Disneyfication, 93

Disney+ streaming service, 3, 94, 244, 249

distribution and marketing: day-and-date release strategy, 230–231, 232; gender disparity in deals, 157–158; gendered expectations and "overperforming" discourse, 196, 202–205, 208–210, 228; international festival market deals, 177–182; value of film festivals to, 174–175. *See also* bankability gap; "*Bridesmaids* Effect"; "movie jail"; post-festival chasm and examples

Divergent franchise, 208, 223

diversity, racial. *See under* racial equity and inclusion issues

Divide, The, 191

Dixon, Aimee, 30

Dixon, Leslie, 89–90

Doremus, Drake, 155, 157

Dornan, Jamie, 209

double bind of gendered expectations: adjusted communication skills, 123–126; excessive oversight and limited creative autonomy, 126–128; experience paradox, 86–89, 140–141, 161–163, 246; leadership behavior strategies, 117–121, 125; misconceptions around female-led action films, 121–123; power dynamic stereotypes and "likability," 51–58; and rationalization of male on-set toxic behavior, 115

Double Bind: Women on Ambition (Rebeck), 94–95, 123–124

Dowd, Maureen, 4–5

Downey, Robert, Jr., 77

Downey, Susan, 77

dress/clothing and stereotyping, 56–57, 169–170

Dry White Season, A, 36

Ducournau, Julia, 173, 191–192

Dunaway, Faye, 224

Dungey, Channing, 252

Dunham, Lena, 132, 146, 167

Dunye, Cheryl, 37, 245

Duplass, Mark, 160

Durra, Zeina, 159

Duvall, Shelley, 198

DuVernay, Ava, 109–110, 145, 159–161, 182, 229, 234, 244–246

Ebert, Roger, 224

economic value and gendered industry lore. *See* bankability gap

Education, An, 200

education, postsecondary or industry specific, 37, 129

Edwards, Gareth, 88

Ehrin, Kerry, 248

Eight Mountains, The/Le otto montagne, 192

Elektra, 224

Elevation Pictures, 179

Elsaesser, Thomas, 165, 172

Emmerich, Toby, 228–229

Emmy Awards, 43

emotional labor of production work, 134–141

employment gap, gendered: "Cool Girl" trap, 58–59; discursive strategies and follow-up, 19, 48–50, 235–236; emotional self-protection, 59–60; employment data studies, 38–42; investigations into hiring practices, 44–45; overview, 27–29; power dynamic stereotypes and "likability," 51–58; twentieth-century reflections, 29–37; twenty-first-century overview, 37–38. *See also* activism and legal actions; pay/salary inequities (gender and race)

on marginalization of women in film industry, 27–28; on precarious path for producers, 133–134; Rebecca Sun on experience/pay paradox, 86; Reese Witherspoon on gender bias, 246; and Reece Witherspoon's bias-busting initiatives, 246–247; on risks of *Wonder Woman* film, 226–227; on Roy Price sexual harassment accusations, 5; Stacy Smith on inclusion riders, 47; on success of *Wonder Woman*, 228; Tracy Oliver on pitching Black female characters, 86; on Warner Bros.' day-and-date distribution strategy, 230–231; on "year of the woman" posturing, 199

homogenization of ideas, 96–97

Hopper, Grace, 103–104

Horowitz, Mark, 178

Hot Flashes, The, 74

Hot Topic stores, 208

House of Cards, 249

Howard Hughes Medical Institute, 104

Howard the Duck, 216

How Stella Got Her Groove Back, 13

How to Get Away With Murder, 250, 251

How to Lose a Guy in 10 Days, 12

Hoxter, Julian, 92

Hudson, Jennifer, 204

Hudson, Kate, 12

Hulu platform, 78, 246, 248–249, 251

Hunger Games franchise, 158, 208

Hunt, Helen, 217

Hurston, Zora Neale, 30

Hurt Locker, The, 212

Hustlers, 40, 200, 235

hybrid release model, 230–231, 232

Hynek, Lauren, 88–89, 92, 103–104

Ice Age franchise, 202

IDC Films, 179

Igbokwe, Pearlena, 252

Iger, Bob, 62

Illich, Ivan, 137

"Inclusion in the Director's Chair" (employment report), 41, 235, 235–236

inclusion riders, 45, 46–47

independent films: distribution process overview, 180–181; and film festival participation, 73, 152, 158, 162–163; international market in, 181; production process overview, 132–133

IndieWire: on 2021 female-directed films, 235; Cate Shortland on directing action blockbuster, 122–123; on diversity initiatives, 242; on Drake Doremus, 157; on employment gender gap, 42; on female-directed films, 115; on gender parity in 2020s, 236; Mimi Leder on "movie jail," 218

Indiewood divisions of studios, 153

industry lore, gendered/racialized: around international marketability, 69, 181; around target audiences, 180–182, 201–205; denial of industry structural inequities, 170–171; experience paradox and gender bias, 87–89, 140–141, 161–163, 246; and masculine-imposed stereotypes, 52, 60, 95; overviews, 19, 66, 68–70; perceptions of risk vs. value, 236, 258; and "women aren't funny" narrative, 211; women cannot helm action/blockbuster films, 19, 120–123, 162

"in-group bias," 51

Institute on Gender in Media, 28

Insurgent, 223

intellectual property-driven productions: corporate auteurism and branding, 122; franchise-building strategies, 9–11, 14, 201–202, 228–232; and increasing industry consolidation, 21–22, 72

Intern, The, 88

International Federation of Film Producers Associations (FIAPF), 150

International Film Festival Rotterdam (IFFR), 179

Invisible Woman, The, 75

Invitation, The, 220

Iordanova, Dina, 151, 169

IP (intellectual property). *See* intellectual property-driven productions

Iron Lady, The, 195